ARIZONA FIRESTORM

ARIZONA FIRESTORM
Global Immigration Realities, National Media, and Provincial Politics

Edited by
Otto Santa Ana and Celeste González de Bustamante

ROWMAN & LITTLEFIELD PUBLISHERS, INC.
Lanham • Boulder • New York • Toronto • Plymouth, UK

Published by Rowman & Littlefield Publishers, Inc.
A wholly owned subsidary of The Rowman & Littlefield Publishing Group, Inc.
4501 Forbes Boulevard, Suite 200, Lanham, Maryland 20706
http://www.rowmanlittlefield.com

10 Thornbury Road, Plymouth PL6 7PP, United Kingdom

British Library Cataloguing in Publication Information Available

Library of Congress Cataloging-in-Publication Data

Arizona firestorm : global immigration realities, national media, and provincial politics / [edited by] Otto Santa Ana and Celeste Gonzalez de Bustamante.
    p. cm.
    Includes index.
    ISBN 978-1-4422-1415-6 (cloth : alk. paper) — ISBN 978-1-4422-1417-0 (ebook)
    1. Arizona--Emigration and immigration—Government policy. 2. Immigrants—Government policy—Arizona. 3. Arizona—Politics and government—1951–
4. Emigration and immigration—Press coverage—Arizona. 5. Emigration and immigration—Press coverage—United States. I. Santa Ana, Otto, 1954– II. Gonzalez de Bustamante, Celeste, 1965–
    JV6912.A85 2012
    325.791—dc23
                                                                    2012003174

To the memory of Otto G. Santa Anna, whose civic life
was devoted to making Arizona a better place for all its people.

To Héctor and Claire for keeping matters calm
in the midst of the firestorm.

Contents

List of Tables and Figures

Tables

Figures

Preface

Juan González

THE RAGING PUBLIC DEBATE over immigration in the United States has generated too much heat and too little light in recent years. Politicians, journalists—even some academics—have invariably gravitated to sensational sound bites or simplistic framing of the issue. Such facile approaches typically ignore the long and tortuous history of U.S. immigration policy. They neglect to acknowledge how that policy is deeply influenced by the needs of transnational markets, by foreign policy goals of our leaders in Washington, by the rise and fall of colonial empires and despotic governments in other parts of the world.

That is why *Arizona Firestorm* is so timely and remarkable. This collection of essays begins by documenting how the controversial "show me your papers" law approved in 2010—one that provoked an international outcry—was part of a series of measures adopted by the state's conservative white leaders, following the 2008 economic crisis, to scapegoat Arizona's growing Mexican-American and Mexican immigrant population.

The examination doesn't stop with contemporary Arizona, however. They delve into the contentious history between Anglos and Mexicans in Arizona and throughout the Southwest. They place the migrant flows between Mexico and the United States in the context of the spread of global capital.

Our country, of course, is hardly unique in its growing unease over immigration. Since World War II, the shrinking of the modern world through air travel and mass communications and the widening chasm between the developed countries on the one hand, and the poorest areas of Asia, Africa, and Latin America on the other, has fueled unprecedented immigration to the West. Invariably, those Third World immigrants gravitated to the metropolises of their former colonial masters: Algerians and Tunisians to France; Indians, Pakistanis, and Jamaicans to England; Turks to Germany; and Latin Americans to the United States. Such vast demographic changes have understandably led to deep insecurity among the older inhabitants of those countries, and the less accurate the information those inhabitants receive about how and why the new immigrants have settled in their midst, the easier it is for demagogues to arouse anti-immigrant fervor.

Thus, *Arizona Firestorm*'s most important contribution could well be its examination of how news media narratives, both Spanish and English language, in both the U.S. and Mexico, have failed to provide ordinary Americans and Mexicans adequate facts and context to understand this enormous movement of peoples between the two countries.

We are both Americans of the New World, after all, and our most dangerous enemies are not each other, but the great wall of ignorance between us. This book pokes a huge hole through that wall.

Acknowledgments

Our concern for the people of Arizona, Otto's home state and Celeste's adopted one, grew in the days after Governor Jan Brewer signed SB 1070. In the midst of the worst recession in memory, its residents would now experience entirely gratuitous pain. We both knew a sizable proportion of Arizonans did not share the governor's views. Many Arizonans might feel immediate relief but would endure significant economic losses as a result of this legislation. We were most distressed that Arizona's youth would suffer the long-term consequences of the shortsighted policies of their elders. Our gloom deepened with the knowledge that the unfolding media blitz would contribute to the success elsewhere in the country of demagogues like Russell Pearce and political opportunists like Tom Horne.

A few days after SB 1070 was signed, Celeste contacted Otto to find out what research he was conducting on SB 1070 and the media. Her idea was to coauthor an article, and he responded with the idea of putting together a book! We collaboratively designed *Arizona Firestorm* to deepen the nation's understanding of the globalization processes and unintended consequences of reactionary immigration policy and to fill in the gaps left by the news media. We hope it might help avert other political conflagrations prompted by emotion and incomprehension. It is our sincere hope it contributes to deeper understanding and tolerance.

We want to thank the scholars who gave generously of their valuable time to produce a tightly controlled chapter on an exceedingly short timeline. All of our contributors quickly said *Yes!* Patricia Gándara responded within an hour! We were encouraged by their authoritative responses to ignorance and reasoned opposition to wrath. Their commitment to a better-informed citizenry shines through each chapter. We especially want to thank the following contributors who produced a chapter in less than three months when sickness or overcommitment forced others to step away from our project. *Arizona Firestorm* is a testament to the outstanding dedication of Jack Chin, Judith Gans, Carissa Hessick, Lilliam Martínez-Bustos, Marc Miller, Anna Ochoa O'Leary, Andrea Romero, and Mercedes Vigón.

Two UCLA people were instrumental in making possible Otto's work on *Arizona Firestorm*. Chicana/o Studies Department Chair Abel Valenzuela and Arts and Science Dean Alessandro Duranti facilitated his UCLA leave during the academic year when the book was put together. He also wants to thank University of District of Columbia Trustee Fernando Barrueta, Provost Graeme Baxter and Dean Rachel Petty, who materially supported his scholarship during his leave. He also counted on the support and friendship of Rodolfo Acuña, Frederick Aldama, Katherine Archuleta, Michael Camuñez, Cecilia Castillo Ayometzi, Katherine Benton-Cohen, Ronaldo Cruz, Jesse De Anda, Gabrielle Foreman, Edmundo Gonzales, Jane Hill, Tsianina Lomawaima, Roberto Lovato, Reynaldo Macías, Christine Marín, Lauren Mason Carris, Steven Means, Alfonso Morales, Teresa Niño, Juan Muñoz, Roberto Reveles, Roberto Rodríguez, Ron Schmidt, Juan Sepúlveda, Guy Shroyer, Ricardo Stanton-Salazar, Federico Subervi, and Ana Celia Zentella.

Celeste acknowledges and thanks her base at the University of Arizona's School of Journalism, including her former director Jacqueline Sharkey, Jeannine Relly, Maggy Zanger, Linda Lumsden, Rogelio Garcia, and Dave Cuillier. From the Center for Latin American Studies, she is thankful for the support she has received from Scott Whiteford, Julieta Goméz González, Raúl Saba, and Colin Deeds.

From outside the firestorm state Celeste received encouragement from many friends, including Sallie Hughes, Petra Guerra, Elena Sabogal, Lucila Vargas, Federico Subervi, Manuel Chavez, Maritza De la Trinidad, and Tracy Goode. She also extends a big thanks to her friends and colleagues who are part of the Border Journalism Network.

We benefited from Amelia Tseng's thoughtful editing, Delvan Hayward's timely support, as well as our editors, Jon Sisk and Darcy Evans.

We want to express our deep appreciation to Diane Grajeda, who created the powerful and memorable anti-SB 1070 poster that is reproduced as part of our book cover.

Otto would not be able to achieve much of anything without the love and support of his bride of eighteen years, Thelma Meléndez. ¡Gracias, Corazón!

Otto dedicates this book to the memory of his father, Otto G. Santa Anna, who contested the racism he experienced in the state he loved, as a union leader who fought to eliminate dual-tier treatment of Mexican miners, as a councilman working for broader electoral representation in municipal government in his hometown of Miami, Arizona, and as a leader in many Arizona civic organizations. He taught his children by example to always strive to contribute to the greater good.

Celeste extends *mil gracias* to her two pillars of strength in the midst of what seemed like chaos (finishing two books at the same time): Héctor and Claire. It is to her understanding and wonderful husband and daughter that she dedicates this book.

Part I

BACKGROUND

1

Arizona's Provincial Responses to its Global Immigration Challenges

Introduction to Arizona Firestorm

Otto Santa Ana

IN THE SPRING OF 2010, the state of Arizona experienced a firestorm of national and international outrage and scrutiny over its legislative responses to unauthorized immigration. The outcry began when Governor Janice Brewer signed Senate Bill (SB) 1070. This law expressly created state-level immigration policy, apparently contravening the constitutional principle that federal law takes precedence over conflicting state law. SB 1070 established stringent racial laws[1] designed to end undocumented immigration to the state. Among its controversial provisions, each Arizona law enforcement officer would require a detained person to prove his immigrant status with documentation above and beyond a driver's license, if "reasonable suspicion" existed that he or she was unauthorized to be in the country. This raised the specter of racial profiling. After a U.S. Department of Justice challenge, a federal judge enjoined parts of this law. Still, other contentious provisions that the judge left standing will continue to provoke litigation in the coming years.

SB 1070 prompted weeks of intense news reporting. National and international correspondents reported on every move and statement of Governor Brewer. Likewise, the news media followed the opinions of other Arizona officials, including State Senator Russell Pearce, the main sponsor of SB 1070 and dozens of other anti-immigrant measures. They were interviewed, as were many legislators from across the country, who proclaimed their intent to follow Arizona's lead. In response, Latino activists marched in the withering Arizona summer heat and made searing public statements about the authors and supporters of SB 1070. Latino organizations called for what became an effective national boycott of Arizona conventions and other business activities. As expected, a flurry of commentators of all political stripes stated their opinions. All of these were covered by the media.

Although SB 1070 was the most widely covered Arizona news item in 2010, it was not the only issue that directly impacted the state's Latino population. That same year state officials advanced several other problematic measures and decisions, some of which were purportedly not generated by recent immigration concerns. However, they arguably were designed to reduce the political and cultural ascendancy of the state's growing Latino population. National news media did not dwell on these other decisions and decrees, although they also have far-reaching consequences for Arizona, and our country.

During the SB 1070 media blitzkrieg, the reporting mostly focused on political conflict. Little airtime was dedicated to why immigration has become a feature of life in Arizona, around the country and globe. After the saturation reporting, typical news consumers were likely to recall the personality quirks of the antagonists, but were unlikely to be able to comment beyond the simple "they're invading our country," or "they're looking for a better life," let alone on the geoeconomic reasons for mass movements of people across national borders. Insofar as our citizens remain uninformed, the nation's news media failed in its responsibility to help its citizenry become knowledgeable on crucial policy matters.[2] U.S. journalists for more than one hundred years have expressly proclaimed the importance of the Fourth Estate role of an independent press to strengthen our nation's democracy. As the result of the media's inability to fulfill its duty, the electorate, which continues to depend on good journalism to form its views, remains unequipped to democratically address the immigration issue.

The outrage that was unleashed in Arizona in 2010 was not an exceptional event. Unauthorized immigration is a prominent feature of twenty-first century life, creating anguish and anger across the world. Nor is the United States alone in its inability to respond nationally to immigration. Most countries of the world, including the most advanced industrialized countries, generally do not handle migration well.[3] These nations are unable to manage migration because their electorates fear rather than comprehend it. Sadly, the lopsided news coverage of Arizona in 2010 was also not exceptional. In other immigration crises in cities like Hazelton, Pennsylvania,[4] states such as Georgia or Alabama,[5] and countries like Spain,[6] we witness the same saturation coverage of the political conflicts, with relatively few elucidating reports. When journalists and news commentators cover immigration crises, they generally fail to report on the forces that compel people to leave their homes. This reporting generates dismay and anxiety among readers and viewers, not deeper understanding.

In lieu of responsible journalistic coverage, *Arizona Firestorm* offers succinct, readable, and authoritative descriptions of the background leading up to Arizona's measures and actions, as well as a set of studies on the quality of news programming about the Arizona controversies of 2010.

As long as America has a growing economy, it will be unable to prohibit immigration without inflicting even greater economic self-destruction. No country can. Each year thousands of Dominicans living on less than two dollars a day[7] eagerly board homemade *yolas*, unseaworthy fishing boats, to brave the sixty-mile stretch of shark-infested open ocean called the Mona Passage, trying to make it to Puerto Rico. Without navigation or communication systems or means of self-propulsion, they can end up lost or adrift. And when typical five- to fifteen-foot ocean waves catch them, these yolas with three-foot sides regularly flounder.[8] And if by some miracle they survive a mid-ocean sinking, the economic refugees will board another yola to try again. Asian workers pay up to ten thousands of dollars for illegal intercontinental transport in cargo bays, knowing full well they will become indentured servants for years. Mexicans brave a merciless desert that kills healthy young men, women, and children in a single day. If they survive but are caught by border authorities, they will turn around to try once again.[9] A wall—no matter how long, tall, or sophisticated—will not stop immigration. Regardless of thousands of deaths, they don't stop. It makes no sense to ask how to stop them. The correct question is: What drives their desperation?

Across the planet an estimated 214 million people are on the move, principally for better economic opportunities.[10] Only ten years ago, the figure was 150 million. The forces driving this movement, what we call *globalization*, are benignly understood as the processes that are making the world smaller. These processes can cause havoc. These forces bring everyone closer together by integrating economic and social relations, making distance irrelevant across the globe with cheap transportation and more efficient communication.[11] These technologies influence business as well. Corporations now must become multinationals, conducting business across the globe, seeking out and exploiting distant markets, and optimizing their operations with no regard for national borders. They lobby for legislation to remain competitive, and congresses and parliaments across the world now work to expand transnational commerce, to bring down national trade barriers, and to establish regional common markets. The 2008 worldwide recession is evidence of an increasingly interconnected global economy.

Globalization reduces a nation's ability to control its economy and manage its borders. It increases corporate need for cheaper labor. And for people, globalization does not only mean that they can now support their families from a continent away, but that they must.

Given our ever-shrinking world, the appropriate place to address the immigration policy is at the international level. Local and state legislation can only treat the symptoms. Even federal actions that don't address the global character of immigration will only marginally manage the effects of these global processes, and ultimately will fall short.

Although the engine of immigration is global, its impact is local. The reduction of state and national economic autonomy puts unrelenting stress on weaker economies, making the people who are comprised of them more vulnerable to market swings and to corporate and national economic policy decisions. Millions of people's livelihoods have become imperiled, or simply lost. Immigration to the cities, and then to other countries, becomes a necessity. Greater tension is felt when the impoverished immigrants move to areas that have relatively weak economies, as is the case in Arizona. Here the receiving communities are less able to absorb the influx, because they too are subject to larger market forces.

The effect of globalization is not limited to economics. There is a cultural dimension. In Arizona, as in other settings across the world, cultural anguish grows when the immigrants are viewed as different than the people of the recipient community. In Arizona, the immigrants are primarily Mexicans. This is ironic since Mexicans have been a significant part of Arizona's cultural mix since the early eighteenth century. However, after the end of the U.S.-Mexican War in 1848, and the California gold rush of 1849, fifty thousand mostly Anglo migrants poured into Arizona. (*Anglo* is the southwestern term for white.[12]) Subsequently, Arizona's Mexican population was comparatively small. By the 1970s it constituted only about 16 percent of the population. Anglo Arizonans made up nearly 80 percent of the state.

However, Latinos now make up nearly 30 percent of the state's 6.4 million residents. Anglo Arizonans now sense a demographic shift that is eroding their hegemony, because the Anglo population is older than the growing Latino population. After a century-long position of relative privilege, many Anglo Arizonans tend to assume that they have greater claim to the way of life of Arizona than Mexican Arizonans do; that the Latino newcomer should urgently acculturate to Anglo values; and all Latinos should continue to accede to Anglo control. The nativist complaint is more blunt: a Mexican "invasion" is "destroying" or "ruining" Arizona. Such demagogic statements transform anxiety into fear. One of the many ironies at this historical juncture is that great numbers of Anglo Arizonans cannot count more than a generation of state residence—they too are immigrants[13]—while both U.S. born and recently immigrated Mexican Arizonans enjoy a culture and history of longer standing in the state.

Thus Arizona's current immigrant antipathy is a combination of economic vulnerability, anxiety over demographic and hegemonic shifts, and cultural conflict. But twenty years ago, things were different. In the early 1990s few immigrants made their way north via sparsely inhabited parts of Arizona. Instead, unauthorized immigrants chose to cross at U.S. urban centers near the U.S.-Mexican border in California and Texas, where they could swiftly and safely melt into urban communities. This was a time of sustained economic growth, so border control was lax. However, the 1989 end of the Cold War led to the first post–World War II recession in California, and subsequent anti-immigrant resentment led President Clinton in 1994 to authorize Operation Gatekeeper, to restrict immigration around San Diego, then the nation's busiest border.[14]

Although hailed as a success, such policing measures never address the immigrants' need for work and employers' desire for cheap labor. As a result, desperate immigrants crossed elsewhere, ultimately through 70 to 180 miles of the fragile and perilous ecology of the Sonoran Desert, to Tucson and Phoenix. Temperatures that regularly reach 105–109°F have killed five thousand migrants trying to find work crossing the U.S.-Mexican border in the last fifteen years; about one person a day.[15]

Arizonans were not merely innocent bystanders to this humanitarian crisis. The state's economy has long been heavily based on tourism and construction, hence on cheap immigrant labor. According to the Census Bureau, Arizona's Maricopa County built more housing units than any other county in the country. In fiscal 2005 alone, it added 52,000 new homes.[16] When growth peaked in 2006, about 30 percent of the Phoenix area's economic output was tied to real estate and construction.[17] Consequently, when the subprime mortgage crisis initiated the 2008 global financial collapse, Phoenix experienced one of the nation's most dramatic real estate crashes, devastating a city that depended on the construction sector. In 2008–2009, Phoenix alone lost 41,000 construction jobs and 136,000 overall, accounting for 7 percent of its workforce.[18] Arizona now counts an estimated 460,000 unauthorized immigrants,[19] a figure that has increased fivefold since 1990.[20]

As the anxiety over immigration increased in the past decade so did the number of bills that sought to limit unauthorized workers. Democrat Governor Janet Napolitano vetoed a series of measures that she viewed as excessive attacks on immigrants that were sponsored by angry state legislators. When the global economic collapse of 2008 struck, it hurt everyone, but smaller, less diversified economies like that of Arizona were wounded much more deeply. With the state in financial turmoil, President Barack Obama tapped Governor Napolitano in 2009 to become U.S. Secretary of Homeland Security. She was replaced by Brewer, who sympathized with anti-immigrant legislators. In the midst of an election campaign that centered on immigration, Governor Brewer signed SB 1070 in April and set off the firestorm.

Arizona Firestorm is designed to offer authoritative and accessible essays on Arizona's official responses to the global phenomenon of immigration, as well as the media's role in this circumstance. Although composed by many authors (who certainly do not agree on every point), the book has two overarching theses. Parts 1 and 2 address the first: All the political actions enacted in Arizona were parochial and will prove ineffective in the face of the global challenge. Moreover, events like Arizona 2010 will recur elsewhere in the nation and across the world, unless international statesmanship addresses immigration globally through the implementation of transnational economic policies that take into consideration the human impacts of globalization.

Part 1 of *Arizona Firestorm* offers both a contextualizing history and a description of the contemporary economic circumstances of Arizona. Celeste González de Bustamante in chapter 2 describes the "moral geography" of Arizona, a one-hundred-year history of the sociopolitical relations of Arizona's Mexican Americans with the dominant Anglo majority. In brief, she documents how the Anglo majority undertook strategies and actions over the past one hundred years to exclude Mexican Arizonans from economic and political power. In chapter 3, she offers an annotated timeline of the acts and decisions that have contributed to Arizona's current moral landscape. In chapter 4, Judith Gans complements González de Bustamante's longitudinal studies with a scrupulously politically neutral analysis of Arizona's economy. Gans first documents the demographic growth of the last ten years, then carefully explains her sophisticated economic modeling of a single year in Arizona. She answers the crucial question: Do immigrants contribute to or deplete Arizona's coffers? Gans's bottom line: immigrants provide a net *positive* result to the state's economy.

With a better sense of the economic and sociopolitical context of Arizona, in part 2 we turn to the specific legislative measures and other official mandates. Anglo Arizonans previously maintained a significant economic and political advantage over Mexican Arizonans. And as Gans demonstrates, even recent immigrants have contributed positively to the state's economic strength. However, conservative state leaders did not dispassionately recognize the positive contribution that Mexican Arizonans (native and immigrant) make to the state, instead they used emotional nativist rhetoric to galvanize support for anti-Latino and anti-immigrant legislation. They vented their frustrations, rather than addressing the fundamental sources of change or seeking to reduce social tensions. Angry Anglo Arizonans lashed out at the immigrants, who are the true pawns in the ongoing global economic realignment.

Gabriel Chin, Carissa Byrne Hessick, and Marc Miller open part 2 with a clear assessment of the law created by SB 1070. In chapter 5 these prominent legal scholars discuss its controversies, including the racial profiling provisions. They note that Governor Brewer was wrong to say that SB 1070 would not lead to racial profiling. The professors will surprise many readers when they point out that racial profiling is already the law of the land. Indeed Eric Holder, the first African American U.S. Attorney General, currently allows his staff to argue in court citing laws that employ racial (specifically Latino), physical, and cultural criteria. The professors also discuss other contentious SB 1070 provisions. In sum, they state that good law mediates conflict and constrains abuses of power, but this law exacerbates social tensions. They conclude that SB 1070 is another stain on Arizona's moral landscape.

Anglo Arizonans have maintained cultural and demographic dominance since statehood in 1912. But this hegemonic ascendancy has eroded, and Mexican Arizonans are in line to become an electoral majority. However, they are a young and less educated population. Consequently, legislative and state-level actions that do not nurture Arizona's youth can be viewed as efforts to resist the political consequences of demographic change by further disenfranchising young Mexican Arizonans. Sadly, these are not forward thinking actions; the resultant weakened state economy and leadership of the next decade will leave Arizona even less able to compete in the global marketplace.

We turn next to legislation which is not designed to eliminate immigration, but to respond to its attendant political power shift. In chapter 6, Anna Ochoa O'Leary, Andrea Romero, Nolan Cabrera, and Michelle Rascón provide the history of Arizona House Bill (HB) 2281, which in 2010 authorized the Arizona Superintendent of Public Instruction to punish school districts that conduct classes promoting the overthrow of the U.S. government, creating race resentment, and advocating ethnic solidarity over individualism. It targeted one high school Mexican American studies program. Had that program actually been seditious, this reaction might be understood. However, Ochoa O'Leary, Romero, Cabrera, and Rascón reveal that the vague provisions of HB 2281 were written to eliminate a program that was open to *all* students and taught them their civil rights as it introduced them to the histories of the civil rights movement and of Mexican Americans among other peoples in Arizona. It used a proven student-centered pedagogy to help develop critical thinking skills among students of all ethnicities. The program was so relevant to their lives that it engaged them academically, and they did much better during the rest of their school day.

Quite appropriately, the State Superintendent of Public Instruction John Huppenthal ordered an independent audit of the program before passing judgment. But when the auditors surprised him and reported that they found "no observable evidence" that the program violated HB 2281, Huppenthal disregarded the audit findings and unilaterally ruled that the school district had violated the law. Ochoa and her coauthors argue that HB 2281 is ideologically slanted legislation that led, ironically, to students applying their purportedly "unpatriotic" lessons not to plot the overthrow of the state, but to peacefully demonstrate for a better education for themselves and others.

In chapter 7 Patricia Gándara continues the theme of Arizona's dismal public education of young Latinos, this time of English language learners (ELLs). Her chapter addresses litigation and K–12 educational policy. She provides a lucid description of the legal rights of ELLs, and the pedagogical issues underlying their education, as she chronicles the remarkable efforts of Latino parents to compel Arizona, by litigation, to provide a better public education for its ELL children. She also documents the state's concerted efforts to oppose change to the abysmal status quo. This twenty-year-old Arizona court case, *Horne v. Flores*, reached the Supreme Court in 2009 and was remanded to federal court in Arizona, where a ruling is expected any day. Meanwhile, Gándara describes the recent moves of former State Superintendent of Public Instruction, Tom Horne, to restrict the educational options of ELLs. In 2008, Horne mandated a statewide ELL program that educational experts widely reject as an ineffective and counterproductive pedagogy. Gándara reproaches Horne for recreating the racially segregated "Mexican classrooms" that the 1954 Supreme Court *Brown* ruling once outlawed. Thus, Gándara warns that the pending court decisions in *Horne v. Flores* have implications for the education of ELLs, that is to say immigrant children, across the country. Moreover, the decisions of the most recent two top state education officials seemed determined, not to advance, but to prevent the educational success of the poorest and most disenfranchised of Arizona's youth.

Jennifer Leeman in chapter 8 presents another of Horne's 2010 edicts that made headlines: Arizona schools must certify that their teachers do not speak English "with an accent." Although Arizona education officials portrayed the policy as consistent with the goal of providing ELLs with qualified instructors and high-quality instruction, in the context of SB 1070 and HB 2281, opponents saw the directive as further evidence of antipathy toward Mexican Arizonans. These opponents include professional educational and linguistic associations across the country, which also condemned Horne's policy. Leeman explains the fundamental issue: this is one more expression of America's language ideology that presupposes that speaking any language other than English is un-American. In our inexorably shrinking world, Leeman demonstrates that Horne's edict cannot be viewed simply as a symbolic call for ELL children to become fully integrated into U.S. society. Rather it is an attack on Mexican Arizonans that further racializes them, immigrants and speakers of Spanish. For Leeman and the vast majority of education scholars and professionals, Horne's edict advances an arrogant and self-defeating agenda for all Arizonans and Americans.

The final high-profile reaction to Mexican Arizonan political ascendance, under the guise of immigration policy, are proposals floating throughout the country to modify the Fourteenth Amendment of the U.S. Constitution, which grants citizenship to all children born on U.S. soil.[21] Russell Pearce, sponsor of SB 1070, in early 2011 proposed a pair of bills that would "clarify" U.S. citizenship and authorize a distinct Arizona birth certificate for children born to unauthorized immigrants.[22] Pearce claimed to seek to return the amendment to its original intent and to eliminate the incentive of immigrants to bear their "anchor babies" on American soil because they make deportation difficult. "They use it as a wedge," he said. "This is an orchestrated effort by them to . . . gain access to the great welfare state we've created."[23] To address such state-level proposals, former U.S. Attorney General Alberto Gonzales writes in chapter 9 about the history, logic, and implications of the Fourteenth Amendment.

While Judge Gonzales's conservative views on militarizing border enforcement might raise eyebrows, he is adamant that "clarifying" the U.S. Constitution is misguided and the wrong strategy to address increased immigration. Gonzales's description of the 1898 Supreme Court interpretation of the Fourteenth Amendment in a case of a child born to Chinese immigrant parents remains pertinent one hundred years later. At the time, Chinese immigrants were demonized as "utterly unfit" to be citizens. In 2011 Pearce stated: "Anchor babies are an unconstitutional declaration of citizenship to those born of non-Americans. It's wrong, and it's immoral."[24] Efforts to delimit the Fourteenth Amendment focus on removing a purported incentive for immigrants, but Gonzales points out these "will do little to discourage illegal migration." Gonzales ends his chapter with an urgent call for Congress to take up comprehensive immigration policy reform.

Part 3 explores the role of national and international news reporting about immigration issues in Arizona in 2010. The second thesis we argue in *Arizona Firestorm*: while journalists play an integral role to shape public opinion, the media covered the responses of Arizona politicians as ends in themselves, rather than anything more substantive. News professionals certainly recognize the nativist nature of legislation such as SB 1070 and HB 2281, but they failed to edify the public on more than a superficial level. And when the media do not set local responses into an international context, they contribute to the nation's myopia.

The three chapters on the news media, as part of their investigations, use one form or another of "frame analysis." Although the notion of the frame constitutes an approach rather than a single theory or method in communication studies, I can venture a simplifying example. The facts of any given story, say of a fatal car crash, are merely a set of points, the framing of these mere facts situates them into different kinds of stories. Different narrative framing of these mere facts creates different stories, such as a personal tragedy or an account of a government agency. Different thematic frames of the very same set of facts can create a crime story or a mystery. Although the authors use different framing analyses, the goal of each chapter was to characterize the ideas that news consumers take away, and the quality of the journalistic coverage about the events surrounding SB 1070.

In chapter 10, Manuel Chavez and Jennifer Hoewe characterize the topical frames of three influential U.S. newspapers which set the agenda of events surrounding SB 1070 for other national and regional papers. Among their important findings, they explain that the framing was primarily in terms of "public protests" and "legislation," and minimally about economics. They also note that these "elite" newspapers expressed public distaste for SB 1070 and sympathy for the immigrants, when national polls indicated widespread support for the measure.

Mercedes Vigón, Lilliam Martínez-Bustos, and Celeste González de Bustamante in chapter 11 report on Spanish-language television news on the SB 1070 events. The audience and the medium are different, but in a rich analysis that resists summary, they also note that 93 percent of the thematic framings are about "conflict," while less than 4 percent (4/117) employ economic frames. Their analysis further reveals that the largest and most profitable Spanish-language networks, Univision and Telemundo, have assumed a social advocacy role, with new reports that regularly add for news viewers more information on the implications of the political events and the steps that viewers can take to help shape the political debate. The authors found both good and bad journalistic practices in the networks' efforts to promulgate a new assertive identity among their viewers.

Chapter 12 gives an account of Mexican news reporting on migration topics during 2010, including the events surrounding SB 1070. Like the three U.S. newspapers discussed in chapter 10, Manuel Guerrero and María Eugenia Campo undertake a systematic narrative frame analysis of three Mexican national newspapers that set the tone for other news media in Mexico. They find two complementary narrative frames of the migrant. One is as heroes who successfully overcome adversity to make their way to work and settle in the United States. The second is as victims of a system that marginalizes them. The authors note that this pair of narratives places the conflict and its resolution squarely in the United States and diverts Mexican audiences from considering the fundamental structural reasons for emigration from Mexico. Most strikingly, Guerrero and Campo determine that there is one major source of information for these reports: Mexican federal government officials, rather than multiple independent sources. Thus these agenda-setting newspapers are not immune to the charge that they serve as the Mexican government's mouthpiece. Guerrero and Campo test this hypothesis with the reporting on a Mexican domestic news story, a drug cartel massacre of seventy-two Central and South American migrants who were in transit through the country. The kind and amount of news reporting of this tragedy reveals challenging issues for migration reporting in Mexico.

The major finding in part 3 confirms the second thesis we propose: the news media—in the United States and Mexico, whether in Spanish or English—offer abundant superficial reporting on the conflicts surrounding the topic of immigration, but little enlightening reporting. News consumers on both sides of the U.S.-Mexico border, namely the electorate, are left uninformed about the fundamentals of immigration, making them subject to manipulation by nativists and demagogues. The media are not promoting the spread of reason and reflection across the country, but anxiety and fear. Just in the first half of 2011, 246 bills and resolutions on immigration have been enacted by state legislatures, excluding 10 that awaited a governor's signature. In the same time period Alabama, Georgia, Indiana, South Carolina, and Utah passed bills similar to or more harsh than SB 1070, many of which have already been challenged in court.[25] Moreover, when the 2012 presidential contenders talk about immigration, they make no reference to global processes or international collaboration. Thus, journalists should reconsider their very active roles in the spread of fear and loathing toward immigrants, and the tenor of political discourse in our country.

Finally, in part 4 we offer two chapters on future prospects. In chapter 13 Marcelo Suárez-Orozco and Carola Suárez-Orozco offer an eloquent and erudite perspective on immigration in the United States, as well as a close-up look at the faces of immigrants. They offer a set of consistent principles, based on a realistic understanding of global migration, to move us toward a humane and sensible national immigration policy for the second decade of the twenty-first century.

The volume closes with a brief chapter by Otto Santa Ana and Celeste González de Bustamante who ask how Americans can be coaxed toward thinking about immigration as a global issue, as well as a national and local issue, and if our new twenty-first-century technologies can equip the nation's citizenry to re-conceptualize themselves as global citizens, because all the major social issues of the twenty-first century will not be effectively addressed in traditional local or federal ways.

The economic and political pressures of globalization will not wane, so other immigration firestorms will certainly flare up in the United States and elsewhere. The goal of *Arizona Firestorm* is to offer readers sufficient context to re-imagine immigration to Arizona (and elsewhere) as a symptom of increasing global pressures, and to give them the frames of reference to demand that their media and politicians speak to the American electorate about unauthorized immigration in global, not parochial, terms.

Notes

1. SB 1070 is racial law. In the context of immigration enforcement in the United States, race remains a valid legal criterion. In chapter 5 of this text, Chin and his co-authors observe that standing interpretations of the U.S. and Arizona Constitutions allow for the use of race in such circumstances. Thus simply looking like a Latino gives law enforcement officers grounds to detain an individual.

2. Knott, 2005.

3. From the International Organization for Migration, a 132-nation organization based in Geneva. Its report can be retrieved at http://publications.iom.int/bookstore/free/WMR_2010_ENGLISH.pdf.

4. In 2006 Hazelton, Pennsylvania, officials passed a law that allowed the city to revoke business licenses for those companies that employed illegal immigrants, and fine landlords who knowingly rented to them. A federal appeals court struck it down as in violation of the Supremacy clause of the U.S. Constitution which makes federal law supreme and preempts state and local laws that contradict federal law.

5. Altschuler, 2011.

6. In 2009 Spain forcibly rejects Moroccan and North African immigrants seeking work.

7. Cabasso and Shaughnessey, 2009.

8. Just two 2004 reports: NBC *Nightly News* reported the Coast Guard seized a forty-foot yola that was heartbreakingly overloaded with 245 people seated inches from the water in calm seas. Later that year NBC offered a news brief entitled "Coast Guard rescues Dominicans." Here a homemade boat carrying ninety-four people from the Dominican Republic capsized in a rough ocean. The Coast Guard tried to rescue the refugees, losing three people. ABC also ran stories on their predicament. (See Santa Ana, 2012, chapter 4.)

9. Cave, 2011.

10. United Nations' Trends in Total Migrant Stock: The 2008 Revision, http://esa.un.org/migration. Drawn from The International Organization for Migration, (http://www.iom.int/jahia/Jahia/about-migration/facts-and-figures/lang/en).

11. Robertson, 1992; Castells, 1999.

12. The terms *Latino, Hispanic, Mexican American,* and *Chicano* have been a source of confusion and misuse among the news media, and hence the public. Nationally, the term *Hispanic* is the federal government's umbrella term for Latin Americans and their U.S.-born descendants, variably including and excluding Spaniards and Brazilians. The U.S. Census originally designated Hispanics as nonblacks, and later allowed individuals to self-designate their race. Many U.S. Latinos consider themselves white. However, race is a social construction, not a hereditary attribute. Because Latinos are under assault in the public sphere, Mexican Arizonans are more likely to feel "racialized," namely not as white as Anglos, particularly if they have a Native American phenotype. (See Chin, Hessick, and Miller, and Leeman, this volume.) The preferred national term today is *Latino*, which includes U.S.-born Latinos of Mexican, Central American, Latin American, and Spanish-speaking Caribbean ancestry. This at times can include the corresponding non-U.S.-born immigrants. In Arizona, the term *Anglo* developed in the early twentieth century when whites reserved the term *American* for themselves, using the word *Mexican* with derision to refer to both Mexican nationals and U.S.-born Americans of Mexican descent. In the southwest, the term Mexican remains a term of certain discomfort. During the twentieth century, Mexican Americans have variably self-identified as Mexican, Mexican American, Chicano, or Spanish, to avoid the often scorned term, *Mexican*. The coeditors of *Arizona Firestorm* recommend that the news media use the term *U.S. Latino* (not *Hispanic*) and use a modifying term for an ethnic group, such as *Mexican American*. Our contributors use distinct terms to suit their needs and perspectives.

13. Rex, 2002.

14. By 1997, the INS budget had doubled to 800 million dollars, with more than twice the number of U.S. Border Patrol agents, doubling the fencing as well as other barriers. Although this reduced immigrant crossings through the San Diego corridor, it only diverted them to more dangerous routes.

15. Jiménez, 2009.

16. Arizona home construction boom, 2007.

17. Rudolf, 2010.

18. Riccardi, 2009.

19. Cooper and Davenport, 2010.

20. Passel, 2004.

21. In January 2011, Alabama, Delaware, Idaho, Indiana, Michigan, Mississippi, Montana, Nebraska, New Hampshire, Oklahoma, Pennsylvania, Texas, and Utah indicated interest in similar legislation (Bentley, 2011).

22. In February 2011, the Arizona Senate bills in question were tabled for lack of sufficient sponsorship, but not before the news media reported on this and other state-level efforts across the country.

23. http://www.youtube.com/watch?v=cP5V84RJ5JE, retrieved 11 August 2011.

24. Nowiski, 2010.

25. "State Laws Related to Immigration and Immigrants" (9 August 2011). The National Conference of State Legislatures. Retrieved on 15 September 2011 from www.ncsl.org/default.aspx?tabid=19897. For a summary see Baksh, 2011.

References

Altschuler, D. (2011, June 24). The Georgia and Alabama anti-immigration laws. *Americas Quarterly.* Retrieved 22 September 2011 from http://www.americas quarterly.org/node/2611.

Arizona home construction boom. (2007, January 16). Retrieved 2 September 2011 from http://www.housingbubblebust.com/ConstructionBoom/Arizona.html.

Baksh, S. (2011, August 22). *How states broke the record on immigration bills in 2011.* Retrieved 22 September 2011 from http://colorlines.com/archives/2011/08/more_state_legislatures_tackling_immigration_laws.html.

Bentley, L. (2011, January 5). Sen. Russell Pearce to introduce 14th Amendment bill. *Sonoran News (The Conservative Voice of Arizona).* Retrieved 1 August 2011 from www.sonorannews.com/archives/2011/110105/frontpage-Pearce.html.

Cabasso, A., & Shaughnessy, D. (2009). *Poverty alleviation in the Dominican Republic.* Retrieved 2 September 2011 from http://www.microfinancegateway.org/gm/document-1.9.37388/Poverty%20Alleviation%20in%20the%20Dominican%20Republic.pdf.

Castells, M. (1999). *Information technology and social development.* UNRISD Discussion Paper No. 114, pp. 1–23. New York: United Nations Research Institute for Social Development.

Cave, D. (2011, October 3). Crossing over, and over. Mexican immigrants repeatedly brave risks to resume lives in U.S. *New York Times,* pp. A1, A6.

Cooper, J. J., & Davenport, P. (2010, April 25). Immigration advocacy groups to challenge Arizona law. *Washington Post.* Retrieved 2 September 2011 from http://www.washingtonpost.com/wp-dyn/content/article/2010/04/24/AR2010042402200.html.

Jiménez, M. (2009, October 1). *Humanitarian crisis: Migrant deaths at the U.S-Mexican border.* Report of the ACLU of San Diego and Imperial Counties (California) and La Comisión Nacional de Derechos Humanos de México (Mexico's National Commission of Human Rights). Retrieved 1 August 2011 from http://www.scribd.com/doc/62552799/Migrant-Deaths-at-the-US-Mexico-Border.

Knott, A. (2005, April 8). The "fourth branch" of government. *AlterNet.* Retrieved 8 August 2008.

Nowiski, D. (2010, June 19). Ariz. plan for "anchor babies" is a D.C. topic. *Arizona Republic,* p. A6.

Passel, J. (2004). *Mexican immigration to the U.S.: The latest estimates.* Washington, DC: Migration Information Source. Retrieved 22 September 2011 from http://www.migrationinformation.org/usfocus/display.cfm?ID=208.

Rex, T. (2002). *Arizona statewide economic study 2002: Retirement migration in Arizona.* Seidman Business Research Institute, College of Business, Arizona State University. Retrieved 2 September 2011 from http://www.innovationarizona.com/doclib/prop/sesreports/Retirement.pdf.

Riccardi, N. (2009, May 18). Phoenix's housing bust goes boom. *Los Angeles Times.* Retrieved 2 September 2011 from http://articles.latimes.com/2009/may/18/nation/na-phoenix18.

Robertson, R. (1992). *Globalization: Social theory and global culture.* London: Sage.

Rudolf, J. C. (2010, March 16). Phoenix meets the wrong end of the boom cycle. *New York Times.* Retrieved 2 September 2011 from http://www.nytimes.com/2010/03/17/realestate/commercial/17phoenix.html.

Santa Ana, O. (in press). *Juan in a Hundred: The Representation of Latinos on Network News.* Austin: University of Texas Press.

2

Arizona and the Making of a State of Exclusion, 1912–2012

Celeste González de Bustamante

THE ARIZONA-SONORA BORDERLANDS have a long history of ecological and human contestation. Much of the land is *chaparral* (high desert): geography defined by extreme temperatures and limited natural resources, barring the exception of an abundant supply of mostly untapped solar energy. Scarce arable land and water are just two of the environmental factors that make life difficult for those who have chosen to call this region home. Extreme social, political, economic, and cultural tensions also have contributed to the region's *moral geography*. Using the concept of moral geography and through the lens and advantage of history, this chapter explains how in 2010 Arizona became known as the "Show Me Your Papers State"—that is in reference to Senate Bill (SB) 1070 signed into law by Arizona Governor Janice Brewer on April 23, which, before it was tied up in the courts, would have required local police to demand proof of a person's legal status if the officer had "reasonable suspicion" to believe that the person was in the country "without papers." That law led many reporters to ask Governor Brewer, "What does an illegal look like?" The governor responded that she didn't know what an "illegal" looked like, and she added that she was certain that there would be no racial profiling as a result of the law. As some legal scholars have noted, the law in some cases might actually *require* racial profiling. (For more on SB 1070 and racial profiling, see Chin et al., this volume, and Chin et al., 2010).

In the present chapter I make two fundamental arguments: First, the white hegemony that emerged in Arizona created and implemented strategies to exclude certain ethnic groups (including Mexicans and well as indigenous Arizonans) from social, political, economic, and cultural power from before statehood to the present day. Although all people of color have suffered as a result of these strategies, I concentrate in this chapter on the largest ethnic minority in present-day Arizona, Latinos, who make up one-third of the state's population. At the end of the first decade of the twenty-first century, Latinos were mostly Mexican, with nine out of ten Latinos in Arizona being either Mexican born or Mexican American.[1] This ethnic group appeared to be the target of the latest round of exclusionary policies supported by a majority of conservative whites in state elected office. Second, news media in Arizona, perhaps to a greater extent than in other states, from nineteenth century newspapers to twenty-first century bloggers, have played an important role in fomenting the efforts of those who have wielded political and economic power.[2]

Policies over the past century have been reported in the news media, first newspapers, and other "legacy media" such as radio and television, and now online. These media have played a role not just in reflecting society, but also in shaping public opinion and attitudes, and in doing so, news organizations and their staffs have been complicit in creating and perpetuating negative images of Latinos in Arizona and the United States, contributing to an environment in which legislation such as SB 1070 gained popular and political support.

The Importance of History and Moral Geography

On February 14, 2012, the state of Arizona celebrated its centennial as the forty-eighth state of the United States of America. What happened over the past century that contributed to the current state of *this* state? The politics of exclusion and the general (mainstream) media's complicity in these politics have been influenced by three recurring themes or phenomena. These phenomena are directly connected to the state's immigration history: (1) Restrictive labor practices, especially in the areas of mining and agriculture; (2) Economic weakness and vulnerability, which made the state less able to respond to cyclical boons and busts; (3) External political and economic influence. Because the state shares a 362-mile international border with Mexico, events and developments must be put into a transnational context. What happened south of the border affected events in Arizona and vice versa. Arizona and Sonora, for better and for worse, have been more interdependent than some politicians would care to admit.[3]

Most of the U.S.-Mexico border was delineated after a two-year war between the neighboring countries and the signing of the Treaty of Guadalupe Hidalgo in 1848. As a result, Mexico, a country less than thirty years old, lost half of its land, including California, the New Mexico Territory which included present-day Arizona, Nevada, Utah, Texas, and parts of Colorado and Wyoming (Figure 2.1). Still suffering from the economic and social effects of two decades of independence wars with Spain, Mexico had few resources to fight a U.S. invasion and was forced to hand over an enormous quantity of land for a price of $15 million. It would become "the most monumental land grab in North American history."[4] Even after the land grab, Anglo American filibusters continued into Sonora and other northern Mexican states.[5]

Arizona, north of the Gila River (see Figure 2.1), was included in the Treaty of Guadalupe Hidalgo, but the southern part of Arizona, which included Tucson, Nogales, Sásabe, or everything south of the Gila River, had to wait until 1853 and the signing of the Gadsden Purchase to become part of U.S. terrain. Both Washington and Mexico City considered Arizona and New Mexico to be on the fringes of their respective domains. As a result, the residents were not a priority for the administrators of the Spanish Colonial Empire, Mexico, or the United States. Aside from a physical divide, the Gila River would come to represent an ethnic as well as political-economic division between the whiter and more prosperous area north of the river, and the browner, less prosperous region south of the demarcation. Why were Anglo Americans committed to laying claim to the land? It was obvious to *New York Daily Times* writers that the United States sought to acquire "El Paso and the country through which the Gila runs, that we may have a better Southern route to the Pacific than

FIGURE 2.1
Map of the United States and Mexico, with land from the Treaty of Guadalupe Hidalgo and Gadsden Purchase. Courtesy of Nicholas Kay from www.brown.edu/aravaipa.

we now possess."[6] A little over three decades after the signing of the Gadsden Purchase, workers finished the Southern Pacific Railroad that ran through El Paso and Tucson, linking the Atlantic and Pacific coasts.

From members of the Tohono O'Odham Indian Nation, whose tribal lands are roughly the size of the state of Connecticut and whose nation was sliced in half by the creation of the international boundary, to those who fought against forces in Washington, D.C., in favor of Arizona statehood, to current politicians who say they are angry over the federal government's "failure to seal the border," to the growing number of disenfranchised Latinos who feel they are being targeted by politicians, Arizona has been and continues to be contested terrain. Because of this historical tension among various social and ethnic groups, it is useful to conceptualize the struggle over what to do about immigrants and immigration (in this case mainly undocumented migrants and migration) as a debate over Arizona's *moral geography.*

Moral geography can be described as a contested space where ethical choices are made about "a particular people and place, and . . . also an 'internal logic' that belongs to a particular people and place."[7] Bluntly put, Arizona residents had distinct visions about what was right and good, and what was wrong and bad for the region. During the course of the twentieth century, the first century of mass media, newspapers, film, radio, and television played an important role in shaping and reflecting conflicting moral geographies that were debated. The moral geography of the Arizona-Sonora region of the U.S.-Mexico borderlands has been fraught with a series of ideological fault lines; with one of the most prominent fractures at the international boundary. Another schism is marked by the Gila River, which became a locus of political divisions between the more populated and Anglo Maricopa County and home of the state capital of Phoenix, and Southern Arizona, the state's second most populated area, and whose population historically has had a higher percentage of Mexican origin residents. Fault lines can be thought of as physical as well as ideological lines that shift during "hot moments."[8] The major "events" that jolted the region's inhabitants that this chapter discusses include: the Great Depression of the 1930s and subsequent "repatriation" of Mexican origin residents; the U.S. Border Patrol's mass deportation effort of 1954, "Operation Wetback," and the resurgence of nativism in the 1970s and 1980s in the midst of economic downturn. A more recent "hot moment" includes the 2010 signing of Arizona's SB 1070. Thus, as the means through which we communicate on a mass scale, mainstream media of the twentieth century and mediated communications of the twenty-first century have both shaped and reflected conflicting moral geographies that continue to be debated. In other words, it is through media content, whether on screen or in print, where moral geographies appear as representations of reality and the very *ideological soul* of a community.

Historical Antecedents: The Making of a State of Exclusion

In Arizona—as in other contested lands—the dominant moral geography was defined by people who held economic and political power. These power brokers, some of them politicians as well as owners of media outlets, worked to become the arbiters of social and cultural attitudes and behaviors. Prior to Spanish contact, indigenous peoples including Apaches, Opata, Tohono O'Odham, and Pima battled over control of the terrain. When the Spanish arrived in Tucson in the late eighteenth century they established a *presidio*, which became the Empire's northernmost garrison. Through missionary projects and presidios, the Spanish crown attempted to control the Native American groups that had occupied the region long before European contact. Then, by the mid-nineteenth century, driven by similar desires of the Spaniards before them, and spurred by the California gold rush, outsiders from the West and East drifted into the Sonoran Desert. The possibility of "striking it rich" was no secret in the Arizona-Sonora region, which had a long-established mining tradition. By the late seventeenth century income from Sonoran mines accounted for as much as a third of the silver mined in all of Nueva Vizcaya, the Spanish colonial province that included much of present-day U.S. Southwest and northern Mexico.[9]

Frontiersmen set up mining operations in Tubac (south of Tucson) and in the Prescott area (north of Phoenix). The California gold rush of 1849 brought some 50,000 people across southern Arizona including Tucson on their way west.[10] Those who passed through had disdain for the former Mexican pueblo. Travelers, including newspaper writers such as John E. Durivage of the *New Orleans Daily Picayune* were some of the first Anglos to describe Tucson as a "miserable old place garrisoned by about one hundred men."[11]

Those types of comments did not dissuade all would-be settlers. Samuel Heintzelman, a German entrepreneur, and Charles Debrille Poston established the Sonora Mining and Exploring Company to mine for gold in southern Arizona. The two used the abandoned presidio of Tubac as their company headquarters. Anglo companies were dependent on Mexican labor, and this began a long-standing practice of discrimination against Mexican workers. Anglo workers were paid thirty to seventy dollars a month, while Mexican laborers garnered twelve to fifteen dollars a month.[12] Mexican and Native American workers were also forced to live in substandard sections of the company towns. Mining barons claimed that Mexican laborers were "less capable due to less nourishing food," and that "they would be demoralized by a higher wage scale."[13]

Settlers found pockets of gold in northern Arizona as well which paved the way for increased development and the shifting of power from Tucson to above the Gila River. By 1863 Congress passed the Arizona Organic Act, making Fort Whipple the first capital of the Arizona Territory. Power and control over the territory ensued as the capital was moved to Prescott, then to Tucson, and then back to Prescott.[14] Anglos north of the Gila River avoided setting up the territorial seat in Tucson—which had been the historical political center of the region—because of their concerns over warring Apaches and Mexican power holders.

As in other parts of the West and Southwest, the arrival of Anglo newspapers coincided with mining interests. Barbara Cloud argues that these early newspapers acted as "boosters" for emerging Western and mining towns—and that they helped to "legitimize" the affairs of local business people.[15] These booster efforts provided written justification for the Manifest Destiny attitudes and behaviors of "pioneers." After all, it was a journalist who coined the term *Manifest Destiny* in the mid-nineteenth century. In his magazine *United States Magazine and Democratic Review*, John L. O'Sullivan wrote in 1839:

> The expansive future is our arena, and for our country. . . . The far-reaching, the boundless future will be the era of American greatness. In its magnificent domain of space and time, the nation of many nations is destined to manifest to mankind the excellence of divine principles, to establish on earth the noblest temple ever dedicated to the worship of the Most High—the Sacred and the True.[16]

In 1845, O'Sullivan used the term overtly when he praised the annexation of Texas claiming the "fulfillment of our *manifest destiny* to overspread the continent allotted by the Providence for the free development of our yearly multiplying millions."[17]

In the U.S. West and Southwest, "free development" meant capitalist development, and that included the freedom of newspaper owners to set up shop. The capitalist desires of newspaper editors and the political pleasures of frontier residents often blurred, and it appears Arizona was a "special case." The first Secretary of the Arizona Territory Richard McCormick, who hailed from New York, quickly tapped into his East Coast journalism experience by setting up the *Miner* in Prescott. In 1867, three years after he was appointed Territorial Secretary, McCormick became the Territorial Governor, when he moved south to the new, but brief capital in Tucson. Before moving, he sold his paper to mining prospector John Marion, who commented that the *Miner* would be an "organ of the White People of Arizona," illuminating an overt strategy to cater to a certain readership.[18]

To say that once Anglo settlers arrived in Arizona they immediately usurped power overnight from the region's Mexican elite would both understate the importance of Mexican-origin power brokers in towns like Tucson, as well as oversimplify the process of cultural contestation and collaboration. The demographics of migration helped transfer power from the state's Mexican elite to a white dominant power. By and large most of the Anglo settlers were men. An 1860 federal census showed that out of 168 Anglos living in Tucson, 160 were men.[19] These men frequently married into Mexican families, which is how many managed to move into elite circles. Despite the growing presence of Anglo-owned storefronts, Tucson retained a bicultural atmosphere, making it distinct from other communities in the Southwest. As Sheridan states about communities like Tucson, Florence, and Yuma, "Mexicans assimilated Anglos rather than the other way around."[20] By statehood though, it was clear that the lion's share of economic and political power had shifted into Anglo hands.

Labor practices and processes helped move power from one ethnic group to another. With the building of the Southern Pacific Railroad, West and East Coast entrepreneurs needed another steady supply of labor. This time Chinese workers provided most of the cheap labor, as they were paid one dollar a day, fifty cents less than Anglo workers. That Chinese workers dominated the railroad construction jobs heightened racial tensions between Mexicans and Chinese. Even after the railroad had been inaugurated the Spanish-language newspaper *El Fronterizo* reported, "The Chinaman is a fungus that lives in isolation, sucking the sap of other plants."[21] On March 20, 1880, with dignitaries from San Francisco aboard, the Southern Pacific Railroad officially chugged into Tucson.[22]

The arrival of the railroad drastically changed the political economies of towns such as Tucson which had historically been interdependent with cities south of the border. When the trains arrived, they brought with them economic interests based on East-West trade, and this forced many Mexican owned companies out of business. Along with the loss of their businesses, entrepreneurs such as the Tully and Ochoa families began to lose political power. The Tully and Ochoa trucking company represented one of the few successful Anglo Mexican business enterprises. Estevan Ochoa, an exception to the circumstances and experience of most Mexican-origin people in Arizona of the time, managed to serve several terms on the Arizona Territorial legislature, and in 1875 was elected mayor of Tucson.[23]

By the early part of the twentieth century, with the railroads built and the country in an economic recession, Congress passed the Chinese Exclusion Act of 1882. This law aimed to severely restrict Asian immigration and prohibited Chinese from becoming naturalized citizens. As a result, the demand for Mexican labor increased once the economy picked up again. During the latter part of the nineteenth century numerical restrictions on

Mexican immigration had not yet been implemented, and Mexican nationals were not barred from citizenship. Indeed, the Treaty of Guadalupe Hidalgo, signed in 1848, stipulated that all Mexican citizens living in the new U.S. Southwest would be granted automatic citizenship.

As Anglo migration to the Arizona Territory increased and as the territory became more interconnected with transcontinental business enterprises, many residents clamored for statehood, though Washington was not sure that Arizona was ready to stand alone. The battle over statehood illuminated the desires and discriminatory attitudes of some of Arizona's and the country's Anglo politicians. Many Democrats in Congress argued against statehood claiming that neither Arizona nor New Mexico were economically sufficient enough to sustain themselves, and that "neither the desert sands of Arizona" nor the "humble Spanish-speaking people of New Mexico" were prepared for admission into the union.[24] Indiana Republican Alfred Beveridge came up with what he thought was an ideal plan—combine the two territories into one and make Arizona and New Mexico one state. New Mexicans voted in favor of the proposal, while Arizonans voted against it. One of the reasons Arizonans shied away from joint statehood with New Mexico related to the racist and discriminatory attitudes of the number of Anglos in high-ranking political positions, that New Mexico had too many Mexicans. This prompted one South Carolina senator to claim that Arizona's opposition to joint statehood was "a cry of a pure blooded white community against the domination of a mixed breed aggregation of citizens of New Mexico, who are Spaniards, Indians, Greasers, Mexicans and everything else."[25] These sorts of sentiments often were printed without question or critical analysis in local and national newspapers.

Newspapers also printed pejorative statements about Mexican miners who organized to protest the mining industry's two-tier wage practice and systemic discrimination.[26] Reports often portrayed Mexican workers involved in labor movements as "bandits" who were "easily swayed by agitators," who had the potential for carrying out a "race war."[27] By the early part of the twentieth century, negative stereotypes about Mexicans and immigrants were well entrenched in the public and political discourse, which worked to strengthen a dominant moral geography of Arizona.[28] Images of Mexicans as "bandits" gained more traction with the Mexican Revolution (1910–1920), especially after Pancho Villa's infamous raid on Columbus, New Mexico, on March 8, 1916. Although Villa had signed a contract with a Hollywood film studio and garnered some favorable news coverage, by and large national newspapers such as those owned by the Hearst family often portrayed him and other revolutionaries as "comic-opera bandits, ruthless, uncouth, and uncivilized."[29] In 1914, two years prior to Villa's raid, *The World Herald* printed these words about the revolutionary:

Everything that has been told of Villa shows him as a monster of brutality and cruelty. His entire history is that of a robber and assassin, lifted now, by the fortunes of war, into a conspicuous position which he has filled with such signal military ability as to give him a coating of semi-respectability.[30]

Undoubtedly, these depictions of Villa and other revolutionaries had real on the ground consequences for Mexicans who headed north trying to escape the violence in their country. On the Mexican side of the border, Villa and other revolutionaries such as Emiliano Zapata were hailed as national heroes.

U.S. Immigration Policy, 1921–1965

While Mexico struggled through more than a decade of civil war, the United States went to war in Europe. Both conflicts had consequences for immigration and border policy and what Ngai calls a "new global age."[31] In Mexico, as many as two million people died in the Revolution—a number that totaled more than one-fifth of the country's population.[32] Thousands survived by migrating north into the United States. At the same time, back from involvement in World War I, U.S. officials, who had grown increasingly concerned about its nation's borders, sought to stop the number of refugees heading north from Mexico and south from Canada by passing new security and legal measures. The importance of the nation-state and territoriality led to the creation of the U.S. Border Patrol at this time and also gave life to a new social category and enduring concept—"illegal alien."[33]

In 1924, Congress passed the Immigration Act, which continued to exclude the Chinese, as well as the "mentally retarded" and the "insane" from the country. The act established quotas for the first time, placing limits on the number of immigrants who could legally enter the country to 150,000 per year. That figure represented less than 15 percent of the immigration rate prior to World War I, when approximately one million people a year entered the country. The law created procedures for the deportation of unauthorized immigrants. The 1924 Immigration Act had several important consequences. Perhaps the most insidious was that it created a new class of people, "illegal immigrants." The term *illegal immigrant* had class and racial dimensions. Ngai sums up the public and legal discourse about the distinctions among European and Canadian and Latino immigrants:

Europeans and Canadians tended to be disassociated from the real and imagined category of illegal alien, which facilitated their national and racial assimilation as white Americans. In contrast, Mexicans emerged as the iconic illegal aliens. Illegal status became constitutive of a racialized Mexican identity and of Mexicans' exclusion from the national community and polity.[34]

That Mexicans became the "iconic illegal aliens" was no accident. During the century prior, white America constructed a pejorative image of Mexican-origin people through media, travel accounts, and political discourse.[35] These images went part and parcel with embedded notions of racial superiority among the white hegemony in the Southwest as well as in Washington, D.C.

By 1930, with a quota system based on country of origin in place and the beginning of a depression, the U.S. government had the tools necessary to deport almost 39,000 persons.[36] In regards to the Mexican-origin peoples who were mostly living in states such as California, Texas, New Mexico, and Arizona, the U.S. government implemented a "repatriation" program, which led to the deportation of as many as one million Mexicans and Mexican Americans, many of whom were citizens. Deportees were rounded up in mining towns like Miami and Globe, Arizona (Figure 2.2).

Sending workers to their home country during times of economic downturn had begun prior to the Great Depression. In the 1910s and 1920s, U.S. authorities had initiated the process of putting miners and field hands on boxcar trains and sending them south.[37] Not surprisingly, it became commonplace on playgrounds[38] and in work environments for whites to make

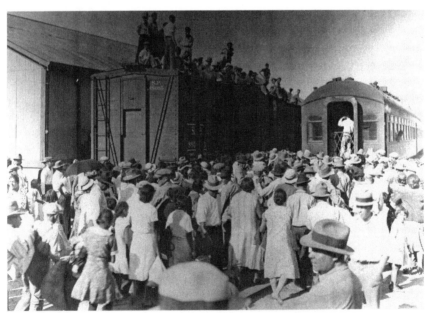

FIGURE 2.2
Photo of "repatriation" in Miami, Arizona, 1930s. Courtesy of Arizona State University Libraries.

comments suggesting that Mexicans and other people of color, whether U.S. born or not, should "go back home," meaning to their home countries.

Despite obvious connections between the economy and immigration, public policy began to move away from recognizing economic realities to emphasizing the importance of national boundaries when it came to justifying deportation.[39] Authorities increasingly stressed the difference between those who crossed national borders legally and those who entered "illegally." A *Los Angeles Times* newspaper article published on January 26, 1931, reported that C. P. Visel, coordinator for the citizens' committee on relief of unemployment in Los Angeles, claimed that the elimination of Mexican immigrants, "will give many jobs they are occupying to natives of this country and aliens who have made legal entry."[40]

World War II and the need for the country to produce materials for the war effort brought the country out of recession and increased demands for labor. By 1942, U.S. and Mexican officials had crafted a temporary guest worker system known as the *Bracero* (Spanish for "one who works with his arms") program, which sought to bring in cheap labor primarily from Mexico, but also from the Bahamas, Barbados, as well as Canada, although 70 percent of the workers came from Mexico.[41] This demonstrated that in Arizona and in other parts of the country in boom times, Mexicans were welcomed as workers, but they were shunned during economic downturns. If they did not leave voluntarily, the U.S. government established programs to deport them, such as "Operation Wetback," a mass deportation program, in 1954.[42] Three years prior to the official implementation of "Operation Wetback," *Los Angeles Times* reporter Bill Dredge's front-page article stated that: "In March, a total of 16,000 flowed across the international boundary as wetbacks and were returned, along the 275 miles of mountainous, desert border from Arizona to the Pacific."[43]

Not all white Americans supported the effort to deport. The same article included interviews with farmers who complained about the sudden departure of their labor pool, claiming that Americans were not equipped to compete with their Mexican counterparts because Americans "won't do this kind of work. They can't. It gets too hot to kneel out here and tie carrots—too hot for everybody but these Mexican *braceros*." On June 10, 1954, it was clear that the farmers' arguments and complaints had not persuaded U.S. immigration restrictionists to change their strategy. U.S. Border Patrol officials geared up for the deportation operation, and the *Los Angeles Times* ran a story with the headline, "Government Maps War on Wetbacks." The report read that:

> A major war on wetbacks, employing a reinforcement of 491 immigration officers recruited from all parts of the country will be launched along the California-Mexico border next Thursday to send tens of thousands of illegally entered Mexican aliens back into Mexico.[44]

Once they were apprehended they were to be taken to a "collection station" in Nogales, Arizona, where they were to be released into Mexico.

The *Los Angeles Times* reporter's use of the discourse of war to refer to a group of people from a country with whom the United States was at peace illustrates the level of tension between Anglos and Mexicans in California and the Southwest at the time. It also brings into sharp relief notions about acceptable terms to use in public. The uncritical use of the term *wetbacks* in reference to unauthorized Mexicans was commonplace in newspapers throughout this period. Undocumented immigrants who crossed the northern border via Canada were not referred to in this way in the news media or in public discourse, providing evidence of the ethnic and class dimensions to labor and immigration policies.

Discriminatory practices in Arizona went beyond new male migrants. Female citizens of Mexican origin were excluded from certain economic opportunities. Companies such as Mountain Telephone and Telegraph purposely excluded Mexican American women (who undoubtedly were native speakers of American English) from clerical positions such as operators because company executives assumed they had "language difficulties."[45] (See Leeman, this volume, for Arizona's contemporary linguistic prejudices.) Ethnic and racial segregation extended to the educational system, where Mexican-origin students were either sent to separate and inferior schools or a "Mexican Room."[46] (See Gándara, this volume, for details about ethnic segregation in Arizona schoolrooms.)

Although the 1924 Immigration Act remained in effect for more than four decades, it was fraught with problems and challenges, and as a result Congress amended the law thirty-two times between 1953 and 1964.[47] By 1965, the political and economic winds had changed, which enabled federal lawmakers to pass the "most open and egalitarian immigration law in the twentieth century."[48] Low levels of immigration and a booming economy created a political environment that allowed Congress to pass the 1965 Immigration Act. The law, signed by President Lyndon B. Johnson, eliminated racially motivated national origin quotas and repealed policies that had their roots in the Chinese Exclusion Act, which severely restricted immigration from Asian-Pacific nations. Instead of national quotas, preference was to be given to individuals with special education and skills. The law also placed a priority on family unification. Although the law did away with quotas based on nation of origin, for the first time it capped the number of immigrants from the Western Hemisphere, including individuals from Canada and Mexico, to a total of 120,000 annually. Many supporters of the act, including President Johnson, did not foresee how much influence it would have on the face of America. In fact, President Johnson stated the law would not "reshape the structure of our daily lives or add importantly to either our wealth or our power."[49] The law reflected the country's sentiments at the height of the civil rights movement. Before the U.S. House and Senate passage of the law, in a letter to the editor of *The New York Times*, Edward Corsi, Chairman of the Board of the American Council for Nationalities Service, opined, "Let us wholeheartedly support the bills, which would remove ancient and outmoded discrimination in our immigration law and which would advance our own national welfare."[50]

Back in Arizona, the state's two largest cities benefited from post–World War II economic development, and city leaders in Phoenix and Tucson looked for ways to modernize their growing urban centers. In Tucson, city officials sought to change the urban geography by razing the downtown area known as *La Calle* (literally, "the street"). After decades of neglect and as land values began to soar, city leaders created a plan to "clean up" the area by demolishing homes and neighborhoods, paving the way for the Tucson Community Center. It was no accident that this part of Tucson was home to the city's largest Mexican and black communities. News media and publicity campaigns painted those who promoted the urban development plan as "unselfish negotiators working for the betterment of the city and all Tucsonans."[51] In reality, the plan reflected notions of a moral geography that dismissed the aspirations of lower income Mexicans and blacks, further excluding the political participation of working class people of color, while prioritizing the interests and desires of the city's mostly white elite. City leaders inaugurated the new Tucson Community Center in 1971.

Post–Civil Rights Era and New Age of Migration

By the 1970s, with the civil rights era nearing an end, and the country again in the midst of a recession prompted by the nation's dependency on foreign oil, nativists returned to a familiar historical pattern and blamed immigrants for the country's economic problems. In 1976, the issue of undocumented migration took on special significance in states such as Arizona where residents *perceived* to a greater extent than other people around the country that the number of undocumented people was increasing.[52] By 1977, undocumented migrants became scapegoats for the country's economic woes.[53] The same year, President Jimmy Carter asked Congress to devise an immigration reform plan to include: (1) sanctions on employers who hired undocumented workers; (2) an increase in U.S. Border Patrol resources; and (3) an amnesty plan for undocumented immigrants already in the country.[54] By 1980, in a Roper Organization public opinion poll, 91 percent of those surveyed thought the government should make an "all out effort" to stem the "tide of illegal immigrants."[55] In March 1981, the Carter Commission on Immigration and

Refugee Policy issued its final report, which included the three major elements that Carter had recommended.

Televised news reports during the 1970s allowed a complex picture about the Arizona-Sonora borderlands and its moral geographies to come into focus. News media portrayals about undocumented immigrants illuminated conflicting ideas about how the region should be defined, and who was allowed to define it. On October 29, 1977, Ku Klux Klan Grand Wizard David Duke paid a visit to Tucson, Arizona. In an interview televised on the local CBS affiliate KOLD-TV, Duke announced the Klan's plans to patrol the American side of the U.S.-Mexico border. Lee Joslyn reported that Klansmen:

> Intend to detain the illegal aliens until authorities can be notified to their whereabouts. It is believed that at least three or maybe even four dozen members will be concentrating on the state's southeastern border. And word is Douglas, Arizona is where they plan to start.[56]

A year later, on the same television station, community activist Margo Cowan refuted claims that undocumented workers were taking jobs away from Americans, stating:

> I would challenge you to find young American Blacks, young Chicanos and heads of households that would work in laundries, work in fields, work in hotels, work in hospitals for a buck ninety-five an hour, or fifty or sixty hours a week.[57]

Because of its ability to reach thousands of viewers at a time, local and national television programs became the principle vehicle through which the moral geographies could be constructed as well as articulated. From U.S. Border Patrol agents and anti-immigrant groups to Chicano activists, all shared their views of the immigration debate and the borderlands on television. In so doing, they contributed to the construction of moral geographies that would be reinforced as well as contested on the air.

By 1986, the U.S. Congress passed the Immigration Reform and Control Act (IRCA). This was the last major reform to U.S. immigration policy. The law allowed to individuals who had entered the United States without authorization prior to 1982 and who had been living continuously in the United States to file for legal residency—what some would call amnesty. The law also included penalties for employers who knowingly hired undocumented workers.

Changing Arizona and U.S.-Mexico Border, 1994–2000

By 1990, Arizona's population and economy boomed as it became one of the fastest-growing states in the nation. Between 1990 and 2000, the population soared by 40 percent.[58] New residents came from within the United States, as well as from outside of the country. Yet, what seemed to worry the state's conservative political wing was the fact that growth among Latinos outpaced their white counterparts. The surge in Latino residents was in large part driven by economic forces. The housing market soared like never before. News reports during the 1990s used the phrase "an acre an hour," in reference to how much of the Arizona desert was being razed for housing development. In other words, the construction industry wanted cheap labor to keep up with market demands, and Mexico provided it, as it had done in the past. The 1994 North American Free Trade Agreement (NAFTA), which supporters claimed would reduce immigration, actually became another "pull factor" for Mexican workers. The undoing of trade barriers allowed foreign companies to move into Mexican agricultural markets, including the important area of corn production. U.S. corn producers ended up undercutting small farmers in southern Mexico, especially in the states of Chiapas and Oaxaca. Unable to compete on the world market, Oaxacan and other farmers in southern Mexico were forced north to the United States and Canada to look for another way to earn a living. For the first time Oaxaca and Chiapas became two of the largest "sending" states in the 1990s and first decade of 2000.

Federal limits on the number of individuals allowed to enter the country from Mexico and other countries did not coincide with the U.S. demand for cheap labor, especially in states like Arizona. Public frustrations over an apparent increase in undocumented migration, mainly across the southern border, prompted authorities to implement a new strategy of immigration enforcement. The strategy involved three basic elements: (1) Dramatic escalation in the number of U.S. Border Patrol agents along the entire U.S.-Mexico border; (2) The use of high technology to "secure the border"; and (3) Physical buildup of the border, through walls and the expansion of ports of entry. This strategy aimed to deter migrants away from urban areas, thereby forcing them to traverse more "hostile terrain," and signaled a clear departure from the agency's previous approach of waiting to apprehend migrants after they crossed the border.[59] The strategy of deterrence began in El Paso in 1993 when the U.S. Border Patrol implemented "Operation Blockade," better known by its subsequent title "Operation Hold-the-Line." The following year, the agency implemented "Operation Gatekeeper" in San Diego, with local support from conservatives such as gubernatorial incumbent Republican Pete Wilson, who won reelection by scapegoating immigrants for the state's economic woes.[60] With a crackdown in place in San Diego and El Paso, the Arizona desert was transformed into a deadly crossing for migrants. The border patrol implemented a similar approach to discourage unauthorized entry at urban centers at the Arizona-Sonora border near Nogales. As expected, migrants were not deterred from crossing; they only shifted their crossing points away from urban ports of entry to some of the most inhospitable parts of the country. By mid-2011, the death toll of unauthorized crossers reported along the U.S.-Mexico border had reached more than 5,000, with most migrants having perished in the Sonoran Desert.[61] All of this led to what scholars call a "thickening" of the border region,[62] or what human rights activists call a militarized zone.

The militarization of the border could only happen with approval from federal lawmakers and support from a vocal public. Signed in 1996 by then-President Bill Clinton, the Illegal Immigration Reform and Individual Responsibility Act (IIRIRA) enabled the U.S. Border Patrol to expand its efforts. The law funded one thousand additional border patrol agents per year over five years. Stiffer sanctions against employers who knowingly hired undocumented workers also became part of the legislation, as well as employee verification pilot programs; precursors to what would become E-verify.[63] On the state level, Arizona politicians clamored for even greater enforcement, and conservatives began to draft a new host of anti-immigrant measures that would attack the growing number of Latinos, primarily Mexicans, residing in the state. As this chapter has revealed, this was not the first time this ethnic group was targeted.

As the border thickened, national media seemed to march in unison with militarization efforts. Between the 1970s and 1990s, graphic and textual representations of the U.S.-Mexico border changed in tandem with the increase in immigration enforcement. In the 1970s, television news reports about Mexican immigration had depicted the U.S.-Mexico border as a "thin line." By the 1990s, in both graphics and photographs, the border frequently became a thicker and often darker "red line."[64] Stories about Mexican immigration moved away from nonborder cities in the United States and Mexico to the border itself. One study of network news reports about Mexican immigration aired between 1971 and 2000 showed a dramatic increase in connecting immigration with the border. In the decade of the 1970s, just over 20 percent had a dateline at the U.S.-Mexico border. During the 1990s, Mexican immigration reports with a dateline at the border represented 61 percent of stories.[65]

Arizona's Perceived "Triple Threat"

Over the past century, Arizona has gone from one of the least populated states to the nation's fourteenth most populous state by 2008.[66] The increase in population involved a shift in the state's demographics: by 2010, Latinos made up one-third of the state's population. At this historical juncture, in the midst of the worst global recession in fifty years, a conservative governor in place, and almost nine years after the September 11 attacks on the World Trade Center and Pentagon, Arizona politicians took aim at a perceived triple threat: (1) the U.S.-Mexico border—a place where presumably terrorists from any country could enter, and drug violence could "spill over" into the United States; (2) a vulnerable economy—a system that remained overly dependent on the volatile construction and tourism sectors, which in the Great Recession of 2008 has not ended in Arizona. (See Gans, this volume, for a balanced economic analysis that belies this one-dimensional view.) At the writing of this chapter, the Phoenix metro area had the second highest foreclosure rate in the country;[67] and (3) changing demographics—conservative politicians feared an increase in Latinos in the state would alter the culture and politics of a state that had been dominated by white hegemony for more than one hundred years.

Despite these perceived threats, studies showed that since 2007, undocumented migration was at a thirty-year low. Part of the reason was economic: with fewer jobs in Arizona, less migrants headed into the state. Douglas Massey's research showed that other factors influencing Mexicans' decisions to head north were at play, including rising educational levels and a reduction in the Mexican birth rate, along with violence along Mexico's northern border.[68] Further, contrary to the heated political rhetoric of 2010, crime had dropped in all states with the highest numbers of undocumented residents. Across the border from Ciudad Juárez, Chihuahua, the city of El Paso ranked as *the* safest city in the United States, according to CQ Press's ranking of cities with a population of more than 500,000. San Diego came in at number five.[69] Although drug violence was a real problem on the Mexican side of the border, in contrast to what some Arizona politicians and border and nonborder sheriffs had stated during the election season, border communities in the United States were relatively safe, and according to public opinion polls, residents who lived in border areas felt safe.[70] Nevertheless, 2010 was an election year, and candidates who clamored to "secure the border" and "clamp down on illegal immigration" got votes, especially in Arizona. Republican Governor Janice Brewer saw her numbers jump almost immediately after she signed SB 1070. Governor Brewer first moved into the state's chief executive office in 2008, after President Barack Obama appointed then Democratic Governor Janet Napolitano to head the Department of Homeland Security. Brewer was elected in November 2010, much like her California counterpart, Governor Pete Wilson in 1994, after he called for the passage the anti-immigrant referendum, Proposition 187. Brewer's signing of SB 1070 on April 23, 2010, codified another chapter of exclusion in Arizona's history. The measure's passage ignited widespread protests among activists and ordinary citizens who demanded just and humane immigration reform. News coverage of the movement against SB 1070 signaled the existence of another vision and moral geography for Arizona's future: one that emphasized what immigrant activists as well as those who understood the global realities of immigration deemed was right for authorized and unauthorized borderlanders.

Over the past one hundred years, Arizonans and especially Latinos have endured a legacy of discriminatory patterns and practices that once again resurfaced in 2010. Even before the arrival of the first Anglo settlers, the region had been a conflict zone, where inhabitants struggled to survive in a place of extremely limited natural and economic resources. White hegemony added new and long-standing ethnic and class dimensions to the practice of defining power, and to the struggle over the moral geography of the region. News content printed and aired through media outlets owned primarily by white businessmen served to reinforce the ideas and attitudes of the dominant group.

Although white elected officials have retained a majority at the state level for the past century, Arizona's history has been marked by deep political and regional divisions. A political grand canyon has deepened over the past two decades between the more populated and conservative county of Maricopa (essentially the Phoenix metropolitan area) and southern Arizona, mainly less conservative Pima County (essentially the Tucson metropolitan area). Because state politics and money have been controlled in the state capital of Phoenix, no matter what their ethnic backgrounds, many Tucsonans and southern Arizonans frequently have spoken of feeling alienated from state-level decision making. By 2010, some felt so disenfranchised they initiated a campaign to create a new state, Baja Arizona, with the capital being seated in Tucson. Ironically, the boundaries of the new state (if it would ever come to be) would basically comprise the area south of the Gila River, roughly the area of the state that was included in the Gadsden Purchase.

An iconic part of Tucson's landscape, Tumamoc Hill remains a popular place for area hikers and naturalists. Those who frequent the hill cannot help notice its geography, as well as the view at the top, which offers an expansive perspective of Arizona's second largest city. Just a few miles from the city's downtown, giant saguaro cacti distinguish the hill and surrounding area as unequivocally part of the Sonoran Desert. More than 2,500 years ago indigenous peoples inhabited the top of the hill, and later the Tohono O'Odham maintained spiritual ties to the area. The view from atop Tumamoc calls to mind the history of fast-paced development characteristic of many Southwest cities. Observant walkers notice the concave shape at its base, evidence of nineteenth century quarrying by laborers (more than likely of Mexican descent) who hauled volcanic rock to various parts of the city for construction of area buildings, including the University of Arizona. Evidence and memories of development efforts can be spotted easily, such as the late 1960s urban renewal project that led to the destruction of historically Mexican and black neighborhoods. Occasionally, the peaceful sounds of nature are interrupted by whistles from the nearby Southern Pacific Railroad trains, or by U.S. Border Patrol helicopters flying by. At the same time, Tumamoc stands as an island of diversity in Arizona. The hill beckons to people of all "walks of life," who are up for the challenge of climbing the 700-foot incline, including news photographers who use the spot to take majestic and wide-angle shots of the sprawling Tucson valley. Certainly, the Arizona-Sonora border region has been defined by contestation, but on any given sweltering Saturday morning, Native Americans, Asians, Anglos, African Americans, and Latinos of all ages, walk individually, and in groups, all with the same goal: to reach the summit.

Notes

1. "Demographic Profile of Hispanics in Arizona," Pew Hispanic Center, 2008. Retrieved 14 February 2011 from http://pewhispanic.org/states/?stateid=AZ.
2. Chomsky, 1988.
3. Lujan Cadava, 2008; Chavez, 2004; Wong González, 2004.
4. Sheridan, 1995, p. 51.
5. Rippy, 1922.
6. "The Mexican Boundary," *New York Daily Times*, August 4, 1853, p. 4.
7. Opie, 1998; Taylor, 2007, and in press.
8. González de Bustamante, 2011; Lévi-Strauss, 1966, p. 259; Schwartz, 1982.
9. Radding, 1997, p. 36.
10. Sheridan, 1995, p. 53.
11. Sheridan, 1995, p. 65.
12. Sheridan, 1995, p. 65.
13. Pierce Williams to Harry Hopkins, Federal Emergency Relief Administration (FERA), October 7, 1933, FERA Records, NARA, cited in Ríos Bustamante, 1998.
14. Sheridan, 1995, p. 70. Phoenix became Arizona's territorial capital in 1889.
15. Cloud, 2008, p. 67.
16. Cloud, 2008, pp. 205–206; cf. O'Sullivan, 1839.
17. Cloud, 2008, p. 206; cf. O'Sullivan, 1839.
18. Cloud, 2008, p. 120.
19. Sheridan, 1995, p. 109. See also Benton-Cohen, 2009.
20. Sheridan, 1995, p. 110.
21. *El Fronterizo*, August 4, 1894, cited in Sheridan, 1992, p. 84.
22. Sheridan, 1992, p. 55.
23. Martinez, 2001, p. 25.
24. Sheridan, 1995, p. 174.
25. Sheridan, 1995, p. 174. Also see Nieto-Phillips, 2004, pp. 90–91.

26. Benton-Cohen, 2009, pp. 80–119, 198–238. "In August 1914, [Arizona] Governor Hunt . . . visited Ray [Arizona] and called conditions for the Mexican miners there 'feudalism'" (p. 204).

27. Meeks, 2001.

28. Martinez, 2001, p. 56.

29. Katz, 1998, p. 323.

30. Katz, 1998, p. 323.

31. Ngai, 2003, pp. 69–107.

32. Buchenau, 2008, p. 90.

33. Ngai, 2003, pp. 69–107.

34. Ngai, 2003, p. 72.

35. Nieto-Phillips, 2004, pp. 69–73, 90–94; Benton-Cohen, 2009, pp. 86–104, 184–185, 235–242, 256.

36. Ngai, 2003, pp. 69–107.

37. *Mohave County Miner and Our Mineral Wealth*, May 5, 1922, p. 8. See also, Benton-Cohen, 2009, and Sheridan, 1995, p. 216.

38. In 1920, in a strange act reminiscent of the 1917 Bisbee deportation of over one thousand striking miners (many of whom were Mexican or Mexican American), 400 Mexican American children were ritually marched out of an integrated school and through downtown Bisbee, Arizona, to a segregated school (Benton-Cohen, 2009, p. 231).

39. Ngai, 2003, pp. 69–107.

40. "Unified Effort to Oust Aliens Being Evolved," *Los Angeles Times*, January 26, 1931, p. A1.

41. Reimers, 1992, p. 41.

42. Even the official language of U.S. institutions demonstrates Anglo American racial disdain. The Border Patrol's program employed an extremely derogatory term for Mexican immigrant.

43. Dredge, 1950, p. 1.

44. "Government Maps War on Wetbacks: 491 Additional Immigration Men to Join in Mass Roundup of Aliens," *Los Angeles Times*, June 10, 1954, p. A13.

45. Flores, 1951/1973, pp. 16–31.

46. De la Trinidad, 2008.

47. Gimpel and Edwards, 1999, p. 99.

48. Gimpel and Edwards, 1999, p. 100.

49. Ludden, 2006.

50. Corsi, 1965, p. 38.

51. Otero, 2011, p. 91.

52. Fernández and Pedroza, 1981.

53. Leach and Zamora, 2006.

54. Griswold del Castillo, 1992/1993.

55. Lee, 1998, p. 28; Santa Ana, 2002.

56. Lee Joslyn, "KKK/Border Patrol," *KOLD-TV News*, October 29, 1977. The KOLD-TV videotapes analyzed for this period are housed at the Arizona Historical Society (Tucson, AZ), hereon after AHS.

57. Margo Cowan, "Alien Hearing," *KOLD-TV News*, September 1, 1978, AHS.
58. http://www.azcommerce.com/EconInfo/Demographics/
59. "Border Patrol Strategic Plan 1994 and Beyond: National Strategy," U.S. Border Patrol, 1994, p. 7, cited in Timothy Dunn, *Blockading the Border and Human Rights: The El Paso Operation That Remade Immigration Enforcement* (Austin: University of Texas Press, 2009), p. 2.
60. Santa Ana, 2002, chapter 3.
61. Derechos Humanos/Human Rights Organization. Retrieved 7 July 2011 from http://derechoshumanosaz.net/projects/arizona-recovered-bodies-project/.
62. Andreas, 2003.
63. Gimpel and Edwards, 1999, p. 293.
64. Johnson, 2003.
65. Johnson, 2003.
66. R. Saenz, *Latinos, Whites, and the Shifting Demography of Arizona*, Population Reference Bureau. Retrieved 22 February 2011 from http://www.prb.org/Articles/2010/usarizonalatinos.aspx.
67. "Phoenix No. 2 in foreclosures; Tucson is 19th highest in US." *Arizona Daily Star*, July 29, 2011, p. A14.
68. Massey and Sánchez, 2010. For a news report on Massey and Sánchez' findings, see D. Cave, "Better Lives for Mexicans Cut Allure of Going North." (July 6, 2011). *The New York Times*, July 6, 2011. Retrieved 6 July 2011 from http://www.nytimes.com/interactive/2011/07/06/world/americas/immigration.html?emc=eta1.
69. CQ Press City Crime Rankings 2010–2011. Retrieved 7 July 2011 from http://os.cqpress.com/citycrime/2010/City_Crime_Rankings_bypop_2011-2011.pdf.
70. "Border Community Security Poll," Border Network for Human Rights Report, August 2010. Retrieved 22 February 2010 from https://org2.democracyinaction.org/o/5681/images/BorderPollREPORT.pdf.

References

Andreas, P. (2003). Redrawing the line: Borders and security in the twenty-first century. *International Security, 28*(2), 78–111.

Benton-Cohen, K. (2009). *Borderline Americans: Racial division and labor war in the Arizona borderlands*. Cambridge, MA: Harvard University Press.

Border Community Security Poll. Border Network for Human Rights Report, August 2010. Retrieved 22 February 2010 from https://org2.democracyinaction.org/o/5681/images/BorderPollREPORT.pdf.

Buchenau, J. (2008). *Mexican mosaic: A brief history of Mexico*. Wheeling, IL: Harlan Davidson.

Chavez, M. (2004). The North American border cooperation model: Local challenges for a security agenda. *Journal of Borderlands Studies, 19*(1), 143–161.

Chin, G., Hessick, C. B., Massaro, T., & Miller, M. (2010, August). A legal labyrinth: Issues raised by Arizona Senate Bill SB 1070. *Arizona Legal Studies* Discussion Paper No. 10-24, pp. 1–39.

Chomsky, N. (1988). *Manufacturing consent: The political economy of the mass media.* New York: Pantheon Books.

Cloud, B. (2008). *The coming of the frontier press: How the West was really won.* Evanston, IL: Northwestern University Press.

Corsi, E. (1965, March 6). Our immigration law. *New York Times,* p. 38.

Cowan, M. (1978, September 1). Alien hearing, *KOLD-TV News.*

CQ Press City Crime Rankings 2010–2011. Retrieved 7 July 2011 from http://os.cqpress.com/citycrime/2010/City_Crime_Rankings_bypop_2011-2011.pdf.

De la Trinidad, M. (2008). *Collective outrage: Mexican American activism and the quest for educational equality and reform.* Unpublished doctoral dissertation, University of Arizona: Tucson.

Derechos Humanos/Human Rights organization. Retrieved 7 July 2011 from http://derechoshumanosaz.net/projects/arizona-recovered-bodies-project/.

Dredge, B. (1950, May 2). Thousands of Mexicans illegally cross U.S. border each month. *Los Angeles Times,* p. 1.

Dunn, T. (2009). *Blockading the border and human rights: The El Paso operation that remade immigration enforcement.* Austin: University of Texas Press.

El Fronterizo. (1894, August 4), cited in Sheridan, *Los Tucsonenses,* 84.

Fernández, C., & Pedroza, L. (1981). The Border Patrol and the news media coverage of undocumented Mexican immigration during the 1970s: A quantitative analysis in the sociology of knowledge. *California Sociologist 5*(2), 1–26.

Flores, R. (1951/1973). *The socio-economic status trends of the Mexican people residing in Arizona.* Unpublished master's thesis, Arizona State University. R and E Research Associates, San Francisco.

Gimpel, J., & Edwards, J., Jr. (1999). *The Congressional politics of immigration reform.* Needham Heights, MA: Allyn and Bacon.

González de Bustamante, C. (2011, April). Hot moments, cool media: The struggle over the moral geography of the U.S-Mexico borderlands. Paper presented at the Rocky Mountain Council for Latin American Studies, annual meeting, Santa Fe, New Mexico.

Government maps war on wetbacks: 491 additional immigration men to join in mass roundup of aliens. (1954, June 10). *Los Angeles Times,* p. A13.

Griswold del Castillo, R. (1992/1993). Latinos and the new immigration: Mainstreaming and polarization. *Renato Rosaldo Lecture Series Monograph, 10,* 1–36.

Johnson, M. (2003). Network immigrant images: U.S. network news coverage of Mexican immigration, 1971–2000. Paper presented at the International Communication Association annual meeting, San Diego, CA.

Joslyn, L. (1977, 29 October). KKK/Border Patrol, *KOLD-TV News.* http://www.azcommerce.com/EconInfo/Demographics/

Katz, F. (1998). *The life and times of Pancho Villa.* Stanford, CA: Stanford University Press.

Leach, M., & Zamora, A. (2006). Illegals/*Ilegales*: Comparing anti-immigrant/anti-refugee discourses in Spain and Australia. *Journal of Iberian and Latin American Studies, 12*(1), 51–64.

Lee, K. (1998). *Huddled masses, muddled laws: Why contemporary immigration policy fails to reflect public opinion*. Westport, CN: Praeger.

Lévi-Strauss, C. (1966). *The savage mind*. Chicago: University of Chicago Press.

Ludden, J. (2006). The 1965 immigration law changed the face of America. *National Public Radio*, May 9. Retrieved 7 July 2011 from http://www.npr.org/templates/story/story.php?storyId=5391395.

Lujan Cadava, G. (2008). *Corridor of exchange: Culture and ethnicity in Tucson's modern Borderlands*. Unpublished doctoral dissertation, Yale University, New Haven, Connecticut.

Martinez, O. (2001). *Mexican-origin people in the United States: A topical history*. Tucson: University of Arizona Press.

Massey, D., & Sánchez, M. (2010). *Brokered boundaries: Creating immigrant identity in anti-immigrant times*. New York: Russell Sage Foundation. Retrieved 8 July 2011 from http://www.nytimes.com/interactive/2011/07/06/world/americas/immigration.html?emc=eta1.

Meeks, E. (2001). *Border citizens: Race, labor and identity in south-central Arizona, 1910–1965*. Unpublished doctoral dissertation, University of Texas, Austin.

The Mexican boundary. (1853, August 4). *New York Daily Times*, p. 4.

Mohave County Miner and Our Mineral Wealth (a Kingman, Arizona weekly newspaper). (1922, May 5), p. 8.

Ngai, M. (2003). The strange career of the illegal alien: Immigration restriction and deportation policy in the United States, 1921–1965. *Law and History Review, 21*(1), 69–107.

Nieto-Phillips, J. (2004). *The language of blood: The making of Spanish-American identity in New Mexico, 1880–1930s*. Albuquerque: University of New Mexico Press.

Opie, J. (1998). Moral geography in High Plains history. *Geographical Review, 88*(2), 241–258.

O'Sullivan, J. (1839). The great nation of futurity. *The United States Magazine and Democratic Review, 6*(23).

Otero, L. (2011). *La Calle: Spatial conflicts and urban renewal in a southwest city*. Tucson: University of Arizona Press.

Pavlakovich-Kochi, Morehouse, B., & Wastl-Water, D. (Eds.). *Challenged borderlands: Transcending political and cultural boundaries* (pp. 123–152). Hantz, England: Ashgate.

Pew Hispanic Center. (2008). Demographic profile of Hispanics in Arizona. Retrieved 14 February 2011 from http://pewhispanic.org/states/?stateid=AZ.

Phoenix No. 2 in foreclosures; Tucson is 19th highest in US. (2011, July 29). *Arizona Daily Star*, A14.

Radding, C. (1997). *Wandering peoples: Colonialism, ethnic spaces, and ecological frontiers in northwestern Mexico, 1700–1850*. Durham, NC: Duke University Press.

Reimers, D. (1992). *Still the golden door: The third world comes to America* (2nd ed.). New York: Columbia University Press.

Ríos Bustamante, A. (1998). As guilty as hell: Mexican copper miners and their communities in Arizona, 1920–1950. In J. Hart (Ed.), *Border crossings: Mexican and Mexican-American workers* (pp. 163–183). Wilmington, DE: Scholarly Resources.

Rippy, J. F. (1922). Anglo-American filibusters and the Gadsden Treaty. *Hispanic American Historical Review, 5*(2), 155–180.

Saenz, R. (2010). *Latinos, whites, and the shifting demography of Arizona.* Population Reference Bureau. Retrieved 22 February 2011 from http://www.prb.org/Articles/2010/usarizonalatinos.aspx.

Santa Ana, O. (2002). *Brown tide rising: Metaphors of Latinos in contemporary American public discourse.* Austin: University of Texas.

Schwartz, B. (1982). The social context of commemoration: A study in collective memory. *Social Forces, 61*(2), 374–402.

Sheridan, T. (1992). *Los Tucsonenses: The Mexican community in Tucson, 1854–1941.* Tucson: University of Arizona Press.

Sheridan, T. (1995). *Arizona: A history* (p. 216). Tucson: University of Arizona Press.

Taylor, L. (2007). Centre and edge: Pilgrimage and the moral geography of the US/Mexico border. *Mobilities, 2*(3), 383–393.

Taylor, L. (in press). Moral entrepreneurs and moral geographies on the US/Mexico border. *Social and Legal Studies.*

Unified Effort to Oust Aliens Being Evolved. (1931, January 26). *Los Angeles Times,* p. A1.

Wong González, P. (2004). Conflict and accommodation in the Arizona Sonora region. In V. Pavlakovich-Kochi, B. J. Morehouse, & D. Wastl-Walte (Eds.), *Challenged borderlands: Transcending political and cultural boundaries* (pp. 123–152). Surrey, UK: Ashgate.

3

A Chronology of Exclusion in Arizona and the United States, 1880–2011

Celeste González de Bustamante

T HE FOLLOWING CHRONOLOGY outlines the avenues through which federal and state-elected officials and government authorities have attempted to reduce the ethnic minority participation in society in Arizona and the United States. The chronology will give readers a quick guide and reference to the number of and distinct ways (legal, educational, political, and cultural) that measures of exclusion have been implemented. It will also demonstrate that local, state, and federal authorities in many ways have not changed their strategies for handling new immigrants and the country's changing demographics over the past one hundred years.

The reader will notice that immigration policies for more than a century have been promulgated by and large from a unilateral perspective, without consideration of the global political, economic, social, and environmental factors that have driven immigration to the United States. The following chronology describes briefly many of the major pieces of legislation and measures that are mentioned in the chapters throughout *Arizona Firestorm*, but is not intended to be a comprehensive list of all measures and laws of exclusion.

1882—U.S. Chinese Exclusion Act. This federal law placed a moratorium on immigrants from China and excluded individuals based on race. In 1952, the federal laws excluding Asian immigrants were repealed through the McCarran-Warren Act, though the number of immigrants allowed to enter the country from Asian countries remained low.

1910s—Arizona's new state-elected officials (statehood in 1912) passed numerous Jim Crow laws including: (1) Prohibiting intermarriage among whites and "tabooed groups," Asians, African Americans, and Native Americans; (2) Educational segregation between whites, Mexicans, Native Americans, and African Americans; (3) Restricting job opportunities for nonwhites and noncitizens; and (4) Prohibiting Asians from purchasing land. (See chapters 2 and 4 in this volume.)

1924—Congress passed the Asian Exclusion and National Origins Act: This placed numerical quotas on those allowed to enter the country, and expanded the Chinese Exclusion Act to include immigrants from all of the countries within the "Asian Pacific Triangle," such as the Philippines, Japan, Laos, Siam (Thailand), Cambodia, Singapore (then a British colony), Korea, Vietnam, Indonesia, Burma (Myanmar), India, Ceylon (Sri Lanka), and Malaysia.

1930s—Even before the Great Depression, during economic downturns, the practice of deportation began. In the 1930s, state authorities used the U.S. Border Patrol and federal troops to "repatriate" as many as one million Mexican-origin workers and residents in Arizona and throughout the Southwest, many of whom were U.S. citizens.

1954—In response to the recession of 1953 and an overabundant supply of labor, which was spurred in part by the Bracero Program (1945–1964 guest worker program), the U.S. Border Patrol initiated "Operation Wetback": a mass deportation effort throughout the Southwest.

1960s—*De facto* segregation of Mexican students in Arizona continued, even after the 1954 U.S. Supreme Court decision *Brown v. Board of Education* (see Leeman; Gándara; and O'Leary et al., all three of this volume).

1971—Twenty-three years before California's Proposition 187 which denied state funded services to undocumented immigrants, Arizona's (and Pennsylvania's) legislatures passed laws denying state benefits to noncitizens. The U.S. Supreme Court repealed the law with its 1971 *Graham v. Richardson* ruling.

1975—*United States v. Brignoni-Ponce.* This U.S. Supreme Court decision allowed race to be considered in immigration enforcement of Mexicans in which "the likelihood that any given person of Mexican ancestry is an alien is high enough to make Mexican appearance a relevant factor." (See Chin et al., this volume.)

1986—Congress passed the Immigration Reform and Control Act (IRCA). The law granted amnesty for long-time unauthorized residents, created employer sanctions for companies that hired undocumented workers, and increased border enforcement.

1988—Arizona voters passed Proposition 106, making English the state's "official language." In 1998, the Arizona Supreme Court ruled that the law violated the First Amendment Rights of non-English-speaking citizens.

1992—Nogales, Arizona, parent, Miriam Flores filed a lawsuit against the state of Arizona, arguing that the state is not providing an adequate education for English language learner (ELL) students. The case became known as *Horne v. Flores,* went to the U.S. Supreme Court, and in 2011 was still tied up in U.S. District Court (see Gándara, this volume).

1994—Operation Gatekeeper signaled the first major shift of the twentieth century regarding border and immigration enforcement. The enhanced border enforcement program instituted under President Bill Clinton redirected migrants away from urban California and Texas, toward less populated areas such as the desert in Arizona.

1994—Following Operation Gatekeeper, the U.S. Border Patrol implemented Operation Safeguard along the Arizona-Sonora border, which resulted in heightened enforcement through an increase in border patrol agents and advanced technology. This was part of the agency's change in overall strategy of apprehending undocumented immigrants after they crossed the border to a "strategy of deterrence." The approach created a deadly corridor for immigrants attempting to cross through the Arizona desert.

1996—President Bill Clinton signed the Illegal Immigration Reform and Individual Responsibility Act (IIRIRA), which apportioned greater funding so the U.S. Border Patrol could implement its "strategy of deterrence."

1996—The Arizona Supreme Court ruled in *Arizona v. González-Gutierrez* that "enforcement of immigration laws often involves a relevant consideration of ethnic factors." The court reaffirmed that law enforcement could use race to determine reasonable suspicion regarding Mexicans, stating that "Mexican ancestry alone, that is, Latino appearance, is not enough to establish reasonable cause, but if the occupants' dress or hair style are associated with people currently living in Mexico, such characteristics may be sufficient" (see Chin et al., this volume).

2000—Arizona voters passed Proposition 203, which banned bilingual education for ELLs.

2005—Congress passed the Border Protection, Antiterrorism, and Illegal Immigration Control Act of 2005, which increased criminalization of undocumented people by making it a crime to be unauthorized in the United States. Previously, "unlawful presence" in the country was a civil, not criminal, violation of immigration law.

2006—Arizona voters passed Proposition 300 which prohibits students who cannot prove legal residency from paying in-state tuition, or from receiving state financial aid (see O'Leary et al., this volume).

2010—The Arizona state legislature passed and Governor Janice Brewer signed a number of stringent anti-Latino and anti-immigrant laws:

- SB 1070, the "Show me your papers law." This law was an overt strategy by state level politicians to supersede federal immigration law and raised the specter of racial profiling (see Chin et al. in this volume).

- HB 2281. This law targeted Tucson Unified School District, the city's largest. It financially punishes school districts that conduct classes that "promote the overthrow of the government," create race resentment, and advocate for ethnic solidarity over individualism (see Ochoa O'Leary et al., in this volume).
- State Superintendent of Public Instruction Tom Horne launched an audit of Arizona teachers in an attempt to exclude teachers who speak English with accents (see Leeman, this volume).
- Voters approved Proposition 107 and Governor Janice Brewer signed this law that bans state government units including colleges and universities from using race, ethnicity, or gender in decisions regarding hiring or acceptance.

2011—Some Arizona legislators and a few conservative federal lawmakers proposed "clarifications" of the Fourteenth Amendment to deny birthright citizenship to the children of undocumented immigrants (see Gonzales, this volume). These measures failed.

- Led by Arizona Senate President Russell Pearce, state lawmakers attempted to pass an omnibus bill that would have barred undocumented children from attending school, prohibited unauthorized immigrants from driving or purchasing a vehicle, and would have denied the ability of undocumented immigrants to obtain a marriage license in the state. The bill died in the legislature after pressure from the state's business industry.

4

The Economic Impact of Immigrants in Arizona[1]

Judith Gans

Introduction

A RIZONA'S 362-MILE BORDER with Mexico is integral to its history. It shapes immigration's impact on the state and colors the ways Arizona grapples with myriad elements of immigration debates: numbers and types of immigrants, the extent of unauthorized immigration, and the impact of immigrants on the state's fiscal and economic health. This study is intended to provide data and analysis that deepens our understanding of the economic consequences of immigration in Arizona. To this end, I analyze the role immigrants play, both as consumers and as workers, and examine their fiscal impact on the state's budget. The availability of data dictated that this analysis is done for calendar year 2004.[2]

A few definitions of terms are in order. The terms *immigrant* and *foreign born* are used interchangeably. These terms, in turn, divide into two subcategories: naturalized citizens and noncitizens. As in the U.S. Census, immigrants or foreign born are defined as the *sum* of naturalized citizens plus noncitizens.

Arizona's foreign-born population increased dramatically between 1990 and 2004 by more than 300 percent. Most immigrants are of working age and have come to the United States seeking employment. This is a central determinant of their economic impact in Arizona.

The likelihood that many of Arizona's noncitizens are unauthorized immigrants has made public discussion of immigration politically contentious. In Arizona and elsewhere, public discourse equates *immigration* and *"illegal immigration."* This narrow focus risks overlooking the broader economic dimensions of immigration. This study cannot address the myriad issues surrounding unauthorized immigration. Its objective is to suspend, for the moment, the narrow discussion of this topic, and instead to offer an examination of immigrants' full impact on Arizona's economic and fiscal health. In this way, the public can gain a more thorough understanding of the economic costs, benefits, and tradeoffs involved in immigration.

Demographic Characteristics

Arizona's total population in 2004 was 57 percent larger than it was in 1990. Its native-born population grew by 32 percent between 1990 and 2000, and another 10 percent by 2004 to a total of 4,912,979. Arizona's foreign-born population also grew significantly after 1990. By the year 2000, the number of immigrants had grown by 143 percent from 268,729 to 652,220 and by 2004 it had grown to 830,855 people, an increase of over 300 percent from 1990. The largest increases occurred among noncitizens, whose numbers rose from 163,321 to about 619,818, an increase of almost 180 percent. These data are reported in Table 4.1.

We do not know how much of this population growth in Arizona was due to unauthorized immigration. The U.S. Census does not ascertain individuals' legal status in the United States when conducting its surveys and the noncitizen category includes both legal and unauthorized immigrants. There are, however, statistically derived estimates that in 2002 there were between 250,000 and 350,000 unauthorized immigrants in Arizona, most of whom came from Mexico, and that by 2005 their numbers had increased to as many as 500,000.[3]

TABLE 4.1
Growth in Arizona's Population

	1990	2000	1990–2000 Change	2004
Native-born U.S. Citizens*	3,396,610	4,478,413	32%	4,912,979
Foreign-born Persons	268,729	652,220	143%	830,855
Naturalized Citizens	105,408	194,878	85%	211,037
Noncitizens	163,321	457,342	180%	619,818
Total	3,934,068	5,782,853	43%	6,574,689

Source: 1990 & 2000 U.S. Census and 2005 American Community Survey (ACS).

*The native-born and foreign-born shares of total population for 2004 are assumed to be the same as reported in the 2005 American Community Survey.

These immigrants live in urban, rather than rural, Arizona. More than two out of three immigrants in Arizona live in Maricopa County; the second largest concentration, at 14 percent, is in Pima County, followed by Yuma County at 7 percent. This concentration reflects the reality that a large share of Arizona's economic activity, especially in manufacturing, is centered in Maricopa County. This means that the economic benefits and costs of immigration occur disproportionately in Arizona's urban counties, and urban settings more generally.

Arizona's immigrants are primarily of working age. Children born in the United States to immigrant parents are native-born citizens and therefore counted as such (see Gonzales, this volume). Of 1,365,000 native-born children eighteen and under, 263,000 have at least one foreign-born parent. The growth in Arizona's immigrant population has been concentrated among people of working age while the native-born population has seen greater growth among people under twenty-five and over thirty-five years old. The number of native-born women in Arizona between the ages of twenty-five and thirty-four actually declined during the period and the number of native-born men increased only slightly.[4] This means that immigrants have been critical to the growth in Arizona's labor force between the ages of twenty and thirty-five.

In economic analyses, educational attainment is a commonly used proxy for skill and provides an indication of the extent to which immigrants compete for employment with native-born workers. The extent of workforce competition between immigrants and native-born persons depends directly on how similar the skills of these two groups are. When immigrants' skills are very similar to native-born workers, the two groups are more likely to compete with each other in the workplace. This competition leads to lower wages and higher profits, and investment in existing industries tends to increase. On the other hand, when immigrants' skills are very different from those of native-born workers, as we will see is the case in Arizona, the two groups are more likely to play complementary roles in the workplace. In this case, the types of production possibilities expand and wages of complementary workers tend to rise. Expanded production possibilities mean increased investment in new industries, as well as in existing industries that rely on immigrants' skills. (It should be noted that educational attainment as a measure of workplace competition is most valid in those occupations where knowing English is not important.)

Immigrants differ, on average, from native-born Arizonans in their levels of education. Among immigrants, naturalized citizens also differ from noncitizens. Table 4.2 shows educational attainment for Arizona adults twenty-five

TABLE 4.2
Educational Attainment by Citizenship Status

Number	Native Born 2,781,531	Foreign Born 469,433		Naturalized Citizens 175,003		Noncitizens 294,430
Up to 9th grade	4%	32%	=	22%	+	38%
Some high school	10%	19%		15%		21%
High school graduate	26%	18%		21%		17%
Some college	35%	17%		24%		12%
College graduate	16%	8%		11%		7%
Master's degree	6%	4%		5%		3%
Professional degree	2%	2%		2%		1%
Ph.D.	1%	1%		1%		1%

Source: 2000 U.S. Census, Numbers of People 25 Years of Age and Older.

and older. Note that relatively few native-born Arizonans are low skilled—over 86 percent of native born have at least a high school education. Among naturalized citizens, 64 percent are high school graduates while only 41 percent of noncitizens have graduated high school.

Examining immigrants' share of a given educational attainment category sheds further light on the role of immigrant and native-born workers in various skill segments of Arizona's labor force. Over half (60 percent) of all Arizonans with less than a ninth-grade education are foreign born. Native-born citizens are the majority of all other education categories with the largest concentrations occurring among those with a master's degree or less. Immigrant shares of those with professional degrees and doctorates are higher than other categories beyond high school.

These data indicate that low-skilled immigrants are likely to be working in jobs that are less well-suited for most native-born workers, with their higher levels of education; and high-skilled immigrants are also filling specific niches in Arizona's labor markets. According to the U.S. Census, 38 percent of all medical scientists in Arizona are foreign born, as are 35 percent of astronomers and physicists, 17 percent of chemists and materials scientists, 17 percent of electrical and electronics engineers, and 16 percent of computer hardware engineers. Thus, Arizona's immigrants are concentrated at the two ends of the skill spectrum: those with less than a high school education and to a lesser extent those with graduate degrees. This illustrates the economic incentives that fill gaps in the native-born labor force with immigrants. They make up 14 percent of Arizona's labor force. However, they constitute a higher percentage of workers in specific sectors such as agriculture, construction, and manufacturing. Some service industries, such as the leisure and hospitality sectors, are particularly reliant on noncitizen labor.

Finally, Table 4.3 details immigrants' importance to certain Arizonan economic sectors: manufacturing, services to buildings, landscaping, and so forth. Immigrants are also vital to specific occupations within these and other industries. Every industry requires a range of skills in its workforce. In construction, for example, completing a building requires filling an array of occupations including construction managers, framers, electricians, brick masons, stonemasons, drywallers, roofers, and so forth. If one or more of those occupations is heavily reliant on immigrant labor, then the entire enterprise, in a real sense, also depends on immigrant labor. This is the essence of what is meant by "complementary skills."

TABLE 4.3
Sectors with High Foreign-born
Employment by Percent

Industries	Foreign Born	=	Naturalized Citizen	+	Noncitizen
Manufacturing:					
Food	35		10		25
Textile	46		15		31
Metal	22		7		15
Building Service	34		6		28
Landscaping	51		7		44
Traveler Lodging	26		7		19
Restaurant	23		5		18
Private Household	33		8		25
Occupations					
Construction	27		5		22
Farm	59		11		48
Production	28		8		20
Building Maintenance	38		8		30
Food	22		5		17
High Skill					
Medical Scientists	38		14		24
Physicians	19		12		7
Physicists	36		12		24
Computer Engineers	16		9		7
Electrical Engineers	17		9		8
Computer Engineers	18		6		12
Economists	15		5		10

Fiscal Analysis

In addition to measuring immigrants' contributions to Arizona's economy, this report examines the *fiscal costs* of immigration, namely the costs to Arizona's government generated by immigrants, as well as the taxes generated by immigrants' roles in Arizona's economy. Fiscal costs accrue when the state provides public services such as education and health care to immigrants. On the other side, the positive financial contributions of immigrants to Arizona's economy come about from their roles as consumers and as workers along with the sales and income taxes they pay. Thus I will analyze the four positive and negative aspects of the immigrants' role in Arizona's economy:

- The costs of immigrants to state government in the areas of education, law enforcement, and health care.
- The consequences for output, job growth, and incomes of immigrants as consumers.
- Immigrant workers' contributions as producers in Arizona's economy.
- Tax receipts generated by immigrant spending and productive contributions to the economy.

While the calculations involved in an input-output model are not simple, the overall approach is straightforward, as illustrated in the following schematic:

- **+ Productive Contributions** of immigrants as workers.
- **+ Direct and Indirect Impacts** of immigrants as consumers.[5]
- **+ Fiscal Gains** from state taxes paid by immigrants directly and generated indirectly.
- **– Fiscal Costs** to taxpayers to educate, provide health care, and enforce the law.
- **= Net Economic Impact of Immigrants in Arizona.**

Input-output models are designed to analyze the economic and fiscal consequences for a region's economy of specific circumstances, which for the purposes of this analysis are called "events." I examine two "events" with regard to immigrants in Arizona: (1) the economic stimulus resulting from immigrant spending in the economy (immigrants as consumers); and (2) the productive capacity and consequent output of immigrants in the workforce (immigrants as workers). By looking at the economic consequences of these two aspects of immigrants' roles in the economy we can disentangle the various economic benefits and costs of immigrants in Arizona.

For a number of reasons, I distinguish naturalized citizens from noncitizens in this analysis. Naturalized citizens, by and large, came to the United States through legal channels that favor people with high skills. Naturalized citizens, on average, have been in the country long enough to learn English and achieve the degree of social and economic integration required for naturalization. This means that naturalized citizens are generally older and better educated than noncitizens and their demographic and education profiles more closely resemble those of native-born citizens than noncitizens. Average incomes of naturalized citizens are higher than those of noncitizens and, because household spending patterns differ by income level, their spending has a different type of impact than does that of noncitizens. Separating naturalized citizens and noncitizens thus allows us to isolate significant differences between the two groups and their impacts on Arizona's economic and fiscal health.

Costs to State Government and Arizona Taxpayers

I examined the major types of costs to state government, known as fiscal costs, associated with immigrants in Arizona. These include immigrant use of the education system, health care, and some aspects of law enforcement. Data availability determined the approach used to estimate each of these costs and some estimates are more precise than others.

In the specific area examined, we are able to provide measures of the fiscal costs associated with immigrants. I do not, however, claim to have captured *all* fiscal costs associated with immigrants. The categories examined are those where costs are attributable directly to individuals. As such, an increase or decrease in the numbers of immigrants is directly correlated with increases or decreases in these costs. There are other public expenditures (such as road maintenance and fire protection) which are fiscal costs of community infrastructure. While immigrants certainly add to these costs, the figures do not exist that allow us to discern the extent to which they do. Further, it is unlikely that there is a one-to-one relationship between decreases in the number of immigrants and decreases in these costs. Having addressed these caveats, we begin our fiscal analysis with the first large state expenditure for immigrants: public education.

Education

Data obtained from the Arizona Department of Education (ADE) provides an accounting of 2004 funds, by district and by county, spent to educate immigrant children. These figures were calculated by ADE staff using the funding formulas followed in allocating funds to schools.

English language learner (ELL) enrollment was used as a measure of the number of immigrant children in Arizona schools. The total number of students classified as ELL in 2004 was 160,666. Most of these children were foreign-born or native-born children of an immigrant parent living in non-English-speaking households. We consider ELL enrollment costs to be a reasonable proxy for the impact of immigrants in Arizona's public schools. However, I lowered the ELL numbers to exclude estimates of Native American ELL students.[6] The adjusted cost of educating ELL students in 2004 was about $544.1 million. The majority (65 percent) of these costs were incurred in Maricopa County. Pima County had the next highest ELL costs at 14 percent of the total. See Table 4.4. (For more on ELL education, see Gándara, this volume.)

TABLE 4.4
Arizona's 2004 Public Education Costs of English Language Learner (ELL) Students

County	ELL Enrollment	Weighted Count*	ELL Costs[†]
Apache and Navajo[‡]	11,341	18,026	$51,519,036
Mohave and La Paz	1,689	2,332	$6,664,931
Gila and Pinal	3,344	4,487	$12,823,897
CGGS§	9,552	12,638	$36,120,776
Pima	20,271	26,187	$74,842,453
Maricopa	95,248	123,217	$352,156,920
Coconino[‡]	4,032	5,540	$15,834,157
Yavapai	1,690	2,369	$6,769,352
Yuma	13,499	16,516	$47,204,446
Subtotal	160,666	211,312	$603,935,968
Native American Adjustment			(59,826,166)
Non-Native American ELL Costs			**$544,109,802**

Note: $2,848.02 was the 2004 ADE's per-pupil financial allocation (Base Support Level) before adjusting for a district's Teacher Experience Index (TEI). (See Gándara, this volume, for discussion of the controversy over state support of ELL education.) The TEI is a factor by which a district's funding is further increased to reflect the seniority of its teachers. Because the presence of immigrant children does not influence this index, it was not included in the per-pupil cost of immigrant children.

*In calculating funding levels, the number of ELL children in a district is further weighted (increased) by other support-level weights such as the child's grade level.
†Total cost = Base Support Level × Weighted ELL Count.
‡ELL enrollment in these counties is greater than the foreign-born share of the population would indicate. Of Arizona's immigrant population, 0.6 percent lives in Apache and Navajo Counties and 0.9 percent lives in Coconino County. Because of the large numbers of Native American children in these counties, I presume that the majority of ELL students in these counties are Native American. I assume that 10 percent of the ELL children in Apache and Navajo Counties and 15 percent of the children in Coconino County are immigrants, and calculated the adjustment as follows: $59,826,166 = (−.9 × $51,519,036) + (−.85 × $15,834,157).
§CGGS refers to Cochise, Graham, Greenlee, and Santa Cruz counties as aggregated by the U.S. Census Bureau in its data collection.

Health Care

Arizona incurs another major fiscal cost when it provides health care to immigrants. Measuring immigrants' impacts on health care costs requires examining two areas: uncompensated care costs incurred by hospitals, and immigrant reliance on the public health care system. We get the latter figures from the Arizona Health Care Cost Containment System (AHCCCS), which is Arizona's Medicaid administration agency.

Hospitals and community health clinics do not consistently collect information on patients' nativity and citizenship status. As a result, I relied on a combination of information sources to estimate these costs. Data on insurance rates for native-born, naturalized citizens, and noncitizens in Arizona from the U.S. Census Bureau's American Community Survey (ACS) was used to calculate the percentages and numbers of people in each nativity category who have private insurance, rely on public insurance, or are uninsured. These data were then used to estimate immigrant impacts on health care costs.

This approach relies on a central assumption: immigrants use the health care system at the same rates as native-born people. To the extent that immigrants use health care more than native-born people, this approach underestimates their impacts on health care costs. To the extent that immigrants use health care less than native-born people, this approach overstates their impacts on heath care costs. Numerous national studies have indicated that immigrants use health care at lower rates than do native-born people.[7] This suggests that the estimated health care costs in this report may be overstated. By having assumed similar use of health care by immigrants and native born in our calculations, I am confident that these costs are not *under*estimated.

The American Community Survey (ACS) provides data on insurance coverage by nativity and by type of insurance. The Arizona Department of Health Services publishes annual reports for all hospitals in the state and these reports include data on bad debt, which I will use as a proxy for uncompensated care costs. Working the ACS data and the Arizona Department of Health Services data, I was able to estimate the uncompensated care costs in Arizona incurred by immigrants. Table 4.5 offers a summary of the results of this analysis, presented by nativity to illustrate naturalized citizens' and noncitizens' impacts on uncompensated care costs relative to those of native-born persons.

While not shown in Table 4.5, the majority of uncompensated care costs are incurred in the Phoenix metropolitan area of Maricopa County.[8] Native-born people have a larger impact on uncompensated care costs ($270.3 million) than do immigrants ($149.3 million). Noncitizens have a much larger impact ($135.4 million) than do naturalized citizens ($13.9 million), reflect-

TABLE 4.5
2004 Costs to Arizona for Uncompensated Hospital Care by Nativity

Naturalized Citizen	$13,874,157	3.3%
+ Noncitizen	$135,375,845	32.3%
(subtotal) Foreign Born	$149,250,003	35.6%
Native Born	$270,349,207	64.4%
Total	**$419,599,210**	**100.0%**

Source: Hospital bad debt as reported by the Arizona Department of Health Services.

ing the fact that a greater proportion of noncitizens than naturalized citizens lack health insurance.

Again, using the ACS data, the number and percent of native-born, naturalized citizens, and noncitizens who rely on public insurance was calculated. These percentages were then used to allocate total 2004 AHCCCS expenditures to native-born, naturalized citizens and noncitizens as a way of estimating each cohort's share of these costs. The results of this analysis are depicted in Table 4.6. As with uncompensated care costs, the majority of AHCCCS costs are attributable to native-born citizens living in Maricopa County. The next largest share is incurred by native-born citizens living in Pima County. Immigrant use of AHCCCS is approximately $642 million out of $4.26 *billion* in total expenditures. Again, the majority—$477.4 million—of immigrant AHCCCS costs are attributable to noncitizens.

Law Enforcement and Other Fiscal Costs

The final major fiscal expenditure attributable to immigrants that we examine is Arizona's law enforcement costs. There are two elements of law enforcement costs: those incurred by local police and sheriff's departments in the normal

TABLE 4.6
2004 Arizona Costs due to Immigrant Reliance on Public Health Care by Nativity

Naturalized Citizen	$164,569,930	3.9%
+ Noncitizen	$477,365,976	11.2%
(subtotal) Foreign Born	$641,935,906	15.1%
Native Born	$3,615,920,537	84.9%
Total	**$4,257,856,443**	**100.0%**

Source: Costs as calendar year expenditures, calculated from fiscal year data, as reported to the Arizona State Legislature in the AHCCCS Appropriations Status Reports.

course of providing for public safety and those incurred through the Arizona Department of Corrections to incarcerate immigrants convicted of crimes. Regrettably, records kept by local and county public safety departments do not allow systematic identification of costs that result from the presence of immigrants in Arizona. While anecdotal reports are made regarding specific costs, there is no systematic, comprehensive way to allocate these costs by nativity.

On the other hand, the Arizona Department of Corrections provide incarceration costs of immigrants, as shown in Table 4.7. The vast majority of incarceration costs are for noncitizens. The total cost to Arizona for calendar year 2004 was $90.95 million, of which $89.1 million was for noncitizens. And, again, the vast majority of these cases were in relatively urban counties.

It should be noted that Arizona receives some federal funding to offset these law enforcement costs. In 2004, Arizona received $12,139,971 as a State Criminal Alien Assistance Program (SCAAP) grant. These monies can vary widely from year to year.

Communities along the U.S.-Mexico border bear additional costs associated with unauthorized entry to the United States from Mexico. One such cost is for cleaning up the trash left behind by migrants. Authorities estimate that each border crosser leaves behind about eight pounds of trash and abandoned belongings. In 2002, the United States estimated that the cost of removing the trash in just a portion of Southeastern Arizona would be about $4.5 million. Arizona taxpayers do not bear all of the costs incurred in Arizona's border communities because since 2002 the U.S. Congress has appropriated some $3.4 million for environmental remediation in Southern Arizona. From 2006 to 2011, Congress is expected to spend on the order of $62.9 million for environmental remediation in Southern Arizona.[9]

TABLE 4.7
Arizona's 2004 Costs for Immigrant Inmates*

FY2004 Actual Operating Budget	$643,963,000	100.0%
Naturalized Citizens		
Number of Inmates	129	
Average Days Incarcerated	260	
Subtotal	$1,886,635	0.3%
Noncitizens		
Number of Inmates	6,367	
Average Days Incarcerated	249	
Subtotal	$89,067,162	13.8%
Total Cost of Immigrant Inmates[†]	**$90,953,798**	14.1%

*Fully allocated costs: Arizona Department of Corrections data.

†Average cost of incarceration per day: $56.19.

While I am confident of these estimates for the three large categories of fiscal costs associated with immigrants, I recognize that I have not gathered together all of the costs associated with immigration, especially unauthorized immigration. Nonetheless, in this chapter I have attempted to measure, when possible, the most significant costs to Arizona's taxpayers of immigrants (authorized or unauthorized) in Arizona.

Economic Contributions of Immigrants

Having estimated the three major fiscal costs associated with immigrants, we will now turn to immigrants' contributions to Arizona's economy as consumers and as workers. I examine naturalized citizens and noncitizens separately.

As Consumers

Measuring the impacts of immigrant consumers' spending requires estimating the after-tax disposable income available to immigrant households—referred to as *buying power*—for spending on goods and services. This spending has direct as well as indirect consequences for output, employment, incomes, and tax revenues. Input-output economic models allow us to trace the way that consumer spending drives economic activity and generates tax revenues. I used the IMPLAN statistical model for the calculations presented in this chapter.[10]

The Census Bureau's American Community Survey (ACS) estimates that in 2004 there were 2,156,000 households in Arizona. An estimated 5.6 percent or 120,720 were headed by naturalized citizens and 6.9 percent or 148,700 were headed by noncitizens. ACS estimates an average 2004 income for $71,700 for naturalized citizen households, and an average $42,300 for noncitizen households. (Note: The income for noncitizen households may seem high but household incomes are higher than individual incomes because households often have multiple wage earners.) I then adjusted these income figures downward to account for savings, tax payments, and remittances sent to countries of origin to arrive at estimates of *disposable income* for each category of household. Total buying power was calculated for each group by multiplying the number of households by average disposable income. To summarize, I estimate that the buying power of Arizona naturalized citizen households in 2004 to be $6.06 billion, and $4.41 billion for noncitizen households.

Consequently immigrant buying power in 2004 made significant contributions to Arizona's economy. Table 4.8 describes the direct impacts that include private-sector output of approximately $10.2 billion dollars, an increase

TABLE 4.8
Arizona's 2004 Immigrant Consumer Spending

	Estimated Contribution to Economic Activity			
	Output*	Employment[†]	Labor Income	Other Income[‡]
Naturalized				
Citizens	$5,937,000,000	38,500	$1,230,000,000	$903,000,000
Noncitizens	$4,310,000,000	27,960	$926,000,000	$563,000,000
Total Contribution	$10,247,000,000	66,460	$2,156,000,000	**$1,466,000,000**

	Estimated Contribution to Taxes[§]			
	Personal Taxes**	Business Taxes[††]	Sales Taxes	Total
Naturalized				
Citizens	$49,000,000	$194,000,000	$214,000,000	$457,000,000
Noncitizens	$36,000,000	$134,000,000	$148,000,000	$319,000,000
Total Fiscal Impact	$85,000,000	$328,000,000	$362,000,000	**$776,000,000**

*Labor income and other income are subcategories of Output.
†Employment in IMPLAN is measured in full-time equivalent jobs and thus appears lower than estimates from other sources.
‡Other income includes payments to individuals for rents, royalties, dividends, and corporate profits.
§The IMPLAN model calculates total tax impacts by category of taxes. The direct share of business tax impacts was estimated to be in proportion to direct-to-total output impacts. The direct share of sales and personal taxes were estimated to be in proportion to direct-to-total labor income impacts.
**Personal taxes include income, personal motor vehicle and property taxes, and fines and fees.
††Business taxes include taxes on corporate profits and dividends, business motor vehicle, business property, and severance taxes, as well as other state/local business nontax fees.

in employment of an estimated 66,500 full-time equivalent jobs. The output attributed to immigrants included increased labor income of about $2.2 billion and increased other income of approximately $1.5 billion. The share of these impacts attributable to naturalized and noncitizens is also shown.

Because of the economic activity it generated, immigrant consumer spending also had significant direct impact on tax revenues in Arizona. The tax consequences of immigrant consumer spending include incremental personal taxes estimated at $85 million, business taxes by $328 million, and sales taxes by $362 million (see Table 4.8).

Questions are often raised about the extent to which unauthorized immigrants pay income taxes. This depends on two factors: the proportion of unauthorized immigrants working with forged documents; and the number of exemptions claimed for withholding purposes by those using such forged documents. People who use forged documents have taxes withheld from their paychecks, but anecdotal evidence suggests that unauthorized immigrants often minimize the amounts withheld by claiming large numbers of exemptions on W-2 Forms. Because the noncitizen category includes a significant number of unauthorized immigrants, the estimated personal tax impacts of $36.5 million may be overstated. However, personal taxes of noncitizens only make up 11 percent of the estimated direct tax impacts of noncitizens and 5 percent of the total estimated direct tax increases resulting from consumer spending by immigrants.

As Workers

As detailed earlier in this report, immigrants constitute 14 percent of the workforce in Arizona and a much larger share of the workforce in specific sectors of the economy such as agriculture, manufacturing, construction, hotels, restaurants, and certain service sectors. But naturalized citizen and noncitizen immigrants work in and therefore contribute to virtually every sector of Arizona's economy. Measuring immigrants' contributions as workers in Arizona's economy requires examining their participation across the economy as a whole, not just in those sectors that employ large numbers of immigrants.

Our purpose in this immigrants-as-workers section is to estimate their economic and fiscal contributions. We will examine two broad areas. First we will look at immigrants as workers across *all* sectors of Arizona's economy to measure the portion of output, employment, labor, and other income, and state tax revenues that can be attributed to immigrants. Naturalized citizens and noncitizens are analyzed separately because they tend to work in different areas of the economy. Second, we statistically simulate what would occur if specific industries—agriculture, construction, manufacturing, and certain service sectors—were to magically lose a large share of their noncitizen workers.

Contributions to All Sectors

Immigrants work in most sectors of Arizona's economy. The foreign-born share of each sector's workforce was calculated using data from the U.S. Census Bureau, which indicates the number and share of native-born, naturalized citizen, and noncitizen workers in each industry sector in Arizona.[11] These share-of-workforce calculations provide the estimates of the number of naturalized citizen and noncitizen workers in 495 different industry sectors for Arizona, as provided in the IMPLAN model. Using the census employment data, I ran simulations to calculate the proportion of output, employment, labor, and other income, and tax revenues that can be attributed to these immigrant workers.

TABLE 4.9
2004 Direct Impact of Immigrants in the Workforce

	Output*	Employment†
AZ Baseline Totals	$351,625,000,000	3,058,002
	Direct Immigrant Contributions	
Naturalized Citizens	$14,804,000,000	121,378
Baseline Percentage	4.2	4.0
Noncitizens	$28,965,234,345	278,085
Baseline Percentage	8.2	9.1
Total Economic Impacts	$43,768,740,885	399,463
Baseline Percentage	12.4	13.1

*Output is a combination of labor income and other income. Other income includes payments to individuals for rents, royalties, dividends, and corporate profits. See Gans, 2008 for details.
†Employment is measured in full-time equivalent jobs.

Approximately 121,380 full-time equivalent jobs in 2004 could be attributed to naturalized-citizen workers, along with output of $14.8 *billion*. Approximately 278,000 full-time equivalent jobs can be attributed to noncitizen workers, along with an estimated $29 *billion* in output. These estimates are described in Table 4.9.

As can be seen in Table 4.10, the IMPLAN model estimates that the economic activity generated by naturalized citizens resulted in approximately $862.1 million in taxes, of which 44 percent were business-related taxes and 41 percent were sales taxes. Economic activity generated by noncitizens resulted in fiscal contributions in the form of tax revenues to the state of approximately $1.5 *billion*, of which 39 percent were business-related taxes and 45 percent were sales taxes. Total tax revenues were $2.36 *billion* of which 41 percent were business-related taxes and 43 percent were sales taxes.

TABLE 4.10
Direct Immigrant Contributions to Arizona Taxes in 2004*

	Personal Taxes†	Business Taxes‡	Sales Taxes	Total
Naturalized Citizens	$132,650,000	$376,720,000	$352,720,000	$862,090,000
Noncitizens	$234,100,000	$590,070,000	$669,340,000	$1,493,510,000
Total Tax Revenue	$366,750,000	$966,790,000	$1,022,060,000	**$2,355,600,000**

*The IMPLAN model calculates total tax impacts by category of taxes. The direct share of business tax impacts was estimated to be in proportion to direct-to-total output impacts. The direct share of sales and personal taxes were estimated to be in proportion to direct-to-total labor income impacts.
†Personal taxes include income, personal motor vehicle, and property taxes, and fines and fees.
‡Business taxes include taxes on corporate profits and dividends, business vehicles, business properties and severances, and other state/local business nontax fees.

TABLE 4.11
Direct Output Generated by Naturalized Citizens
(Dollar Amount and Rank by Top 20 Industry Sectors)

Rank	*Sector*	*Direct Contribution*	*Rank*	*Sector*	*Direct Contribution*
1	Real estate	$1,131,000,000	11	Search instruments	$237,000,000
2	New nonfarm housing	$909,000,000	12	Telecommunications	$215,000,000
3	Wholesale trade	$884,000,000	13	Space vehicle manufacturing	$204,000,000
4	Semiconductors manufacturing	$783,000,000	14	Other ambulatory health care services	$179,000,000
5	Health offices	$344,000,000	15	Auto maintenance (not car washes)	$178,000,000
6	Hospitals	$321,000,000	16	Motor vehicle and parts	$173,000,000
7	Food services	$307,000,000	17	Insurance carriers	$165,000,000
8	Management	$287,000,000	18	Architectural and engineering services	$156,000,000
9	Certain credit intermediation	$279,000,000	19	Miscellaneous retailers	$151,000,000
10	Commercial buildings	$274,000,000	20	Hotels and motels	$149,000,000
				Total	**$7,326,000,000**

In addition to examining sectors where immigrants are a large share of the workforce, we also look at sectors where immigrants, first in this naturalized citizens case, generate large dollar impacts as a small share of the workforce because the sectors themselves are large. Table 4.11 lists in rank order the top twenty sectors where the size of the output contributed by naturalized citizens is largest. The table reveals the cumulative economic contributions of naturalized citizens in Arizona. Here almost 50 percent (49.5 percent)[12] of the total output occurs in these twenty economic sectors. The remaining 50 percent of output generated by naturalized citizens in Arizona is spread across the other 475 sectors of the economy.

Table 4.12 presents those sectors, in rank order, where noncitizens made the largest dollar contributions to Arizona's economy.[13] The specific sectors and rankings differ from those for naturalized citizens, reflecting the fact that these two categories of immigrants tend to have different levels of education and skills. The cumulative contributions indicate that about 13 percent of the output generated by noncitizens occurs in one sector—new residential construction—and that 55.7 percent of the total output generated by noncitizens occurs in these twenty sectors.[14] The remaining 44 percent of output generated by noncitizens is spread across the other 475 sectors of the economy.

TABLE 4.12
Direct Output Generated by Arizona Noncitizens
(Dollar Amount and Rank by Top 20 Industrial Sectors)

Rank	Sector	Direct Impact	Rank	Sector	Direct Impact
1	New nonfarm housing	$3,637,000,000	11	Hotels and motels	$419,000,000
2	Wholesale trade	$1,938,000,000	12	Motor vehicle and parts	$410,000,000
3	Food services and drinking places	$1,715,000,000	13	Employment services	$384,000,000
4	Real estate	$1,337,000,000	14	Ranching and farming	$351,000,000
5	Commercial buildings	$1,095,000,000	15	Telecommunications	$334,000,000
6	Semiconductors manufacturing	$862,000,000	16	Other professional services	$322,000,000
7	Services to buildings	$633,000,000	17	Hospitals	$321,000,000
8	Vegetable and melon farming	$547,000,000	18	Health profession offices	$313,000,000
9	Auto maintenance (not car washes)	$524,000,000	19	Other new construction	$277,000,000
10	New residential alterations	$481,000,000	20	Some credit intermediation	$246,000,000
					Total $16,146,000,000

Contributions to Specific Industries

To measure the contribution of immigrants to specific sectors of the economy, I used IMPLAN to simulate what would occur if certain industries were to lose their immigrant workers. I focused on agriculture, construction, manufacturing, and certain service sectors because they employ large numbers of low-skilled, noncitizen workers, many of whom are likely undocumented. I simulated losing immigrant workers in these sectors to quantify the economic loss of their output, employment, labor incomes, and tax revenues to the state in the event of a significant reduction in the undocumented immigrant population in Arizona.

To prepare for the simulation, Table 4.13 provides the base levels of output, employment, labor, and other income in each of the four key industrial sectors that will be analyzed. These baselines will be used to calculate the subsequent percent changes in each measure of economic activity that would occur with workforce reductions.

The 2000 U.S. Census identifies those industries in Arizona whose workforce is significantly made up of noncitizen immigrants. We focused on

TABLE 4.13
Base (Pre-Simulation) Levels of Immigrant Workforce Output

Sectors	Employment	Industry Output
Agriculture	22,033	$3,775,000,000
Construction	290,363	$34,054,000,000
Manufacturing	125,999	$38,220,000,000
Service Sectors	332,582	$16,147,000,000

Output is combination of labor income and other income. See Gans, 2008.

noncitizen workers because they are the most recent additions to Arizona's workforce, a significant number are low skilled, and a significant number are unauthorized. From census figures, I adjusted the number of employees downward for the selected industries in the IMPLAN model. This was done to allow for some replacement of immigrant workers by native-born workers. I then used the IMPLAN model to calculate the consequences of an immigrant workforce reduction for Arizona employment, output, incomes, and tax revenues. These simulations should be understood as a series of "what ifs" that quantify the *magnitude* of the reductions in output, employment, income, and taxes consequent upon a specific reduction in employment. The reductions in employment and output including labor and other income that resulted from these workforce reductions are presented in Table 4.14.

TABLE 4.14
Direct Industry Cost of Workforce Reductions

Sector	Industry Output*	Employment†
Agriculture	−601,000,000	−3,294.80
Reduction:	−15.9%	−15%
Construction	−6,564,000,000	−55,721
Reduction:	−19.3%	−19.2%
Manufacturing	−3,771,000,000	−12,286
Reduction:	−9.9%	−9.8%
Service Sectors	−2,475,000,000	−53,960
Reduction:	−15.3%	−16.2%

*Output is a combination of labor income and other income. See Gans, 2008 for details.
†Employment is full-time equivalent jobs.

The details of the drop in Arizona tax revenues that resulted from these workforce reductions can be seen in Table 4.15.

To summarize the results of these simulations:

- For agriculture, a 15 percent workforce reduction would result in losses to Arizona of $600.9 million in output, and the loss of 3,300 jobs (full-time equivalents), labor income of $198.6 million, and other income of

$116.1 million. The reduction of state tax revenue would amount to approximately $24.8 million.

- In construction, a 19 percent workforce reduction would result in losses to Arizona of $6.56 *billion* in output, 55,721 full-time equivalent jobs, labor income of $2.59 *billion* and $450.5 million in other income. The lost tax revenue to the state for this sector alone would be approximately $269.2 million.
- A 10 percent reduction in the manufacturing workforce would result in losses of $3.77 *billion* in output, 12,286 full-time equivalent Arizona jobs, labor income of $740.8 million, and other income of $286.1 million. The lost tax revenue to the state would be approximately $104.4 million.
- In the service sectors analyzed, a 16 percent reduction in the labor force would translate to losses in output of $2.48 *billion,* the loss of 53,960 full-time equivalent jobs, reduced labor income of $901.3 million, and reductions in other income of $273.0 million. The lost tax revenue to the state would be approximately $156.9 million.

TABLE 4.15
Summary of Direct Tax Losses due to Workforce Reduction

Sector	Corporate Taxes	Sales Taxes	Personal Taxes	Industry Totals
Agriculture	−11,000,000	−11,000,000	−5,000,000	−25,000,000
Construction	−99,000,000	−109,000,000	−61,000,000	−269,000,000
Manufacturing	−48,000,000	−39,000,000	−17,000,000	−104,000,000
Services	−61,000,000	−75,000,000	−21,000,000	−157,000,000
Totals	−219,000,000	−234,000,000	−104,000,000	**−555,000,000**

With these simulations, we go beyond a simple understanding that immigrant workers are important to sectors such as construction and agriculture by quantifying the magnitude of contribution of immigrant workers. This analysis provides an estimate of the dollar amounts that can be attributed to these workers and, of equal importance, of the tax consequences of their work for the state of Arizona.

When considering the fiscal impacts of immigrants, public attention is generally focused on direct taxes paid, particularly in the form of income taxes, relative to services used. However, the ancillary tax consequences of the immigrants' role as workers are rarely considered, in part because this revenue is difficult to measure. The present analysis provides insight into the magnitude of these fiscal impacts.

I focused on the direct impacts of workforce reductions on the major industries. A 15 percent reduction in employment in construction resulted in about a 19 percent reduction in output in construction. Recall that there are also indirect consequences that ripple through the economy. The magnitude of these indirect impacts, however, is quite small. The indirect impact of the 15 percent reduction in construction employment was an additional 1.6 percent reduction in output and 2 percent reduction in employment in Arizona. For this reason, we focus on the direct consequences for the construction industry and on the direct fiscal impacts for Arizona.

Net Impact of Immigrants

Having examined the fiscal costs of immigrants and measured their aggregate contributions to Arizona's economy, we can now estimate their *net* impact on Arizona's fiscal health. People often limit their thinking about the fiscal impacts of immigrants to the costs of services used by immigrants compared to the taxes paid directly by immigrants. However, there are also *ancillary* tax consequences of immigrants as workers and as consumers. Because immigrants are an integral part of Arizona labor markets, they are making possible economic activity that would not otherwise occur. This economic activity also generates tax revenues in the form of business, sales, and personal taxes that should also be considered when evaluating the net fiscal impacts of immigrants. While these direct fiscal impacts are part of the story, they are not the whole story. There are very real *ancillary* fiscal consequences resulting from the economic activity that immigrants make possible as consumers and as workers.

Table 4.16 recaps the fiscal costs of immigrants in each of the major public service categories for Arizona. We see that the total fiscal cost of all immigrants (naturalized citizens plus noncitizens) was approximately $1.4 *billion* in 2004.

Table 4.17 summarizes the Arizona tax revenues that accrued as a result of immigrants in Arizona's workforce. The economic output that these workers

TABLE 4.16
Arizona's 2004 Fiscal Costs Attributable to Immigrants

Foreign-Born ELL Costs	$544,109,802
Uncompensated Care Costs	$149,250,003
AHCCCS Costs	$641,935,906
Law Enforcement	$90,953,798
Subtotal	$1,426,249,509
Less Federal SCAAP Reimbursement	($12,139,971)
Total	**$1,414,109,538**

SCAAP: State Criminal Alien Assistance Program.

TABLE 4.17
Net Impact of Immigrants in Arizona in Terms of 2004 Fiscal Costs and Tax Revenues*

	Personal Taxes[†]	Business Taxes[‡]	Sales Taxes	Total
Naturalized Citizens	$132,650,000	$376,720,000	$352,720,000	$862,090,000
Noncitizens	$234,100,000	$590,070,000	$669,340,000	$1,493,510,000
			Subtotal	$2,355,600,000
	Total Estimated Fiscal Costs (Table 4.16)			(1,414,110,000)
			Net Fiscal Impact	**$941,490,000**

*The IMPLAN model calculates total tax impacts by category of taxes. The direct share of business tax impacts was estimated to be in proportion to direct-to-total output impacts. The direct share of sales and personal taxes were estimated to be in proportion to direct-to-total labor income impacts.
†Personal taxes include income taxes, personal motor vehicle taxes, property taxes, fines, and fees.
‡Business taxes include taxes on corporate profits and dividends, business motor vehicle taxes, business property taxes, severance taxes, and other state/local business nontax fees.

generate in turn generates tax revenues that would not accrue if there were no immigrant workers. In sum: approximately $2.36 *billion* in tax revenues are attributable to immigrants as workers.

Balanced against the $1.4 *billion* in estimated fiscal costs, the single major finding of this study is that immigrants have a positive fiscal impact on the state of Arizona. They contribute approximately $941.5 million net, most of which is in the form of sales and business taxes.

Summary and Conclusions

Arizona's foreign-born population grew by more than 300 percent between 1990 and 2004, to a total of 830,860 persons. Most of this growth occurred among noncitizens, with between 450,000 and 500,000 of these unauthorized immigrants. Immigrants in Arizona are primarily of working age and accounted for 52 percent of the increase in the number of twenty- to forty-five-year-olds in Arizona between 1990 and 2000. They comprise over half of those lacking a high school education and are an important source of low-skilled workers. These workers are employed primarily in construction, agriculture, manufacturing, leisure, and service industries. Among high-skilled workers, immigrants constitute 15 percent of those with professional degrees and 17 percent of those with Ph.D.s. Sixty-eight percent of Arizona's foreign born are from Mexico and most live in Maricopa County.

The IMPLAN input-output modeling software was used to examine the economic contributions of immigrants as consumers and as workers, and to estimate the fiscal gains resulting from these economic contributions in 2004. I also estimated fiscal costs of immigrants, naturalized citizens, and noncitizens, in the areas of education, law enforcement, and health care.

The fiscal costs of immigrants largely fall into these three categories and totaled $1.41 billion in 2004. Discussions of the fiscal impacts of immigrants are generally limited to a simple comparison of the costs of state services used by immigrants versus the direct personal and sales taxes that they pay. However, there are also ancillary tax consequences of immigrants as workers because immigrants are filling gaps in Arizona's labor force; they make possible economic activity that would not otherwise occur. This economic activity generates tax revenues in the form of business, sales, and personal taxes that should also be considered when evaluating the immigrants' net fiscal impact. Immigrants as workers contributed approximately $2.36 billion, thus providing the state with a net fiscal gain of $941.5 million.

Immigrants make up 14 percent of the workforce in Arizona. The portion of Arizona's economic activity attributable to naturalized citizens includes 121,380 full-time equivalent jobs and $14.8 billion in total output. The share of Arizona's economic activity that can be attributed to noncitizens is 278,000 full-time equivalent jobs and $29 billion in total output. As consumers, immigrants also possess significant spending power. The 2004 spending power of naturalized citizens was approximately $6.06 billion and of noncitizens was approximately $4.41 billion. The economic activity that can be attributed to this spending power includes 66,400 full-time equivalent jobs and $10.2 billion in output. Approximately $776 million state tax revenues can be attributed to this spending power.

Simulations were run to determine the economic and fiscal consequences of eliminating a significant share of Arizona's low-skilled workers. This quantified the negative impact of such scenarios for three industry sectors. In agriculture, a 15 percent workforce reduction cut its output by $600 million, with approximately $25 million in lost tax revenue. In construction, a 15 percent workforce reduction diminished construction output by $6.6 billion, and eliminated approximately $269 million in tax revenues. A 10 percent manufacturing workforce reduction slashed the sector's output by $38 billion with attendant losses of tax revenues totaling approximately $104 million. Finally a 16 percent reduction in the immigrant workforce in the service sectors analyzed resulted in $2.5 billion in lost output and reduced Arizona's tax revenues by $157 million.

Immigration is a global phenomenon. The rapid growth of Arizona's immigrant population, and the number of unauthorized immigrants in the United States has made immigration a controversial issue in Arizona. The present study offers a deeper understanding of the costs and contributions that immigrants make to Arizona. In sum, immigrants make significant net contributions to Arizona's economy and play an important role in the state's fiscal health.

Notes

1. Abridged from Gans, 2008.

2. In this chapter the economic role of immigrants in Arizona was analyzed using 2004 data. The economic circumstances have changed dramatically since then, as a result of the global economic recession. However, the basic framework for understanding the role of immigrants in the economy has not changed. In 2004 major sectors of Arizona's economy relied significantly on immigrant workers; in the present they continue to rely on these workers. Immigrants continue to be a crucial source of workers for specific sectors of the labor force, making possible economic activity that would not otherwise occur.

3. Passel, Capps, and Fix, 2004; Passel, 2005.

4. Details on gender data can be found in Gans, 2008.

5. "Direct Impacts" include estimates of demand for all the inputs to, for example, the housing sector, such as plywood, appliances, and so forth. "Indirect Impacts" estimate new economic activity that results from the increased demand for plywood, appliances, and so forth. The source of the direct impacts calculation is the IMPLAN analysis, fully reported in Gans, 2008.

6. Apache and Navajo Counties had a combined enrollment of almost 9 percent of the ELL students in Arizona in 2004, yet as of the 2000 Census just 0.6 percent of the foreign-born population lived in these two counties. I assume that 90 percent of the ELL students in these counties were Native American children, not immigrants. Similarly, 2004 ELL enrollment in Coconino County was 3 percent of ELL students in Arizona, yet as of the 2000 Census just 0.9 percent of foreign born lived in Coconino County. I assumed that 85 percent of the ELL students in Coconino County in 2004 were Native American rather than immigrants. I want to thank the research staff at the ADE for these data.

7. See "Fact Sheet on Immigrants and Health Care."

8. Consult Gans, 2008, for these details.

9. Davis, 2006.

10. IMPLAN is proprietary software, an input-output system for regional economic accounting. It quantifies the structural relationships among sectors of the economy, tracing flows between producers, intermediate users, and final consumers. It calculates the consequences of these flows for incomes, output, employment, and taxes. It is widely used to estimate the impacts of specific "events" on a region's economy.

Final demand (purchases by consumers) drives the IMPLAN model. To meet final demand, industries produce goods and services for use by consumers, which, in turn, requires the purchase goods and services from other producers. Other producers, in turn, purchase goods and services, and so on. These subsequent purchases create *multiplier effects* beyond the initial purchases by consumers.

The IMPLAN model mathematically describes the buying and selling of goods and services throughout a region's economy and estimates a set of multipliers that quantify the change in output for *all* industries caused by a one-dollar change in final demand for *any given* industry. These multipliers measure the consequences for a region's economy of specific "events" such as an increase in final demand or an increase in the labor supply, and calculates the tax consequences of the event under consideration. When these multipliers result in economic activity that otherwise would not have happened, they represent net additions to a region's economy.

Regarding multipliers: It is difficult to determine how much of the spinoff, or multiplier, effects result in net additions to the economy and how much are a reallocation of activity that would have occurred anyway. While direct impacts are accurate measures of the economic costs and benefits of an event, indirect, or spinoff, effects can be understood as additional *possible* impacts. Some portion of these indirect impacts are net additions to the economy; however, counting 100 percent of them risks overstating the benefits (or costs) of an event. For this reason, the direct impact and spinoff impact are listed separately in this report.

11. Please refer to *Employment by Industry and Occupation* for data on the share of foreign-born workers by industry sector and occupation at: http://udallcenter.arizona.edu/programs/immigration/immigrants_in_arizona.html.

12. For details, see Gans, 2008.

13. For details, refer to Gans, 2008.

14. For details, consult Gans, 2008.

References

Davis, T. (2006, July 30). Crossers burying border in garbage. *Arizona Daily Star*. Retrieved on 20 February 2012 from http://azstarnet.com/news/local/border/article_0890669e-3556-57d5-9ad4-71287fee1a1c.html.

Employment by Industry and Occupation. Retrieved from http://udallcenter.arizona.edu/programs/immigration/immigrants_in_arizona.html.

Fact Sheet on Immigrants and Health Care. Retrieved from http://udallcenter.arizona.edu/programs/immigration/publications/fact_sheet_no_2_health_care_costs.pdf.

Gans, J. (2008). *Immigrants in Arizona: Fiscal and Economic Impacts*. Tucson, AZ: The Udall Center for Studies in Public Policy, University of Arizona.

IMPLAN [Computer software]. (1993). Hudson, WI: MIG, Inc.

Passel, J. (2005). *Unauthorized migrants: Numbers and characteristics*. Washington, DC: Pew Hispanic Center.

Passel, J., Capps, R., & Fix, M. (2004). Undocumented immigrants: Facts and figures. Washington, DC: Urban Institute Immigration Studies Program.

Part II

FIRESTORM

5

Arizona Senate Bill 1070

Politics through Immigration Law

Gabriel J. Chin, Carissa Byrne Hessick, and Marc L. Miller

IN 2010, ARIZONA IGNITED a national controversy over state regulation of immigration. It did so by enacting Senate Bill (SB) 1070, a statute through which Arizona tried to establish its own immigration policy. That Arizona, of all states, became the center of controversy over immigration policy was hardly surprising. The debate about SB 1070 is only the latest of many occasions in which Arizona's legal policies on race and immigration drew national attention.

This chapter addresses the background, substance, and consequences of SB 1070. It briefly sketches some of the important events in race and law in Arizona, the development and passage of SB 1070, and explores the terms and provisions of SB 1070.[1] It also touches on the influence of SB 1070 in other states, and the existing and potential consequences of such reforms.

The Legal, Political, and Historical Background of the Firestorm

For much of the past two decades, the national image of Arizona has not been shaped primarily by images of race. There were legislative and political battles in Arizona in this period framed in racial terms, and the origins of SB 1070 can be seen in earlier proposals and in state-level political battles. But in spite of the occasional national news story about citizen efforts at border enforcement, the dominant national image of Arizona focused on its astounding population growth, often leading all states in the nation.

Arizona's Racial Past

There is a longer history in the state, however, that is not so sunny. Arizona's history is marked by episodes of racial oppression and discrimination. There was slavery in the territory when it was acquired by the United States as part of the Gadsden Purchase in 1853. During the Civil War, large parts of the state voted to secede, and the Arizona Territory (including southern New Mexico) was admitted to the Confederate States of America.

Arizona became a state in 1912. Its law embraced many of the traditional forms of Jim Crow racial segregation. For example, Caucasians were prohibited from marrying those with "tabooed blood,"[2] namely African Americans, Asian Americans, and Indians. African Americans could not attend public school with whites.[3] And Arizona denied Indians the right to vote, even those who paid state taxes and lived and worked off the reservation.[4]

Perhaps the most persistent and distinctive discriminatory Arizona law targeted immigrants. Only two years after statehood, Arizona's voters passed a law in 1914 designed to protect the "native born" from competition with other workers. By initiative, Arizona voters enacted a statute restricting the employment of noncitizens and naturalized U.S. citizens. Businesses with at least five workers had to reserve 80 percent of their jobs for voters or native-born U.S. citizens. The U.S. Supreme Court held this statute unconstitutional in 1915, explaining that if the state could prevent those whom the federal government had admitted into the United States from working, for practical purposes, they would have to leave the state.[5] Later Arizona passed a law designed to prevent Asians from owning land;[6] in 1934, the law generated an international incident as the U.S. Secretary of State intervened after Japanese and Indian farmers were threatened by "Aryans."[7]

In the 1960s Arizona was one of the states leading efforts to deny public benefits to lawfully resident noncitizens. In 1971, the Supreme Court unanimously invalidated an Arizona statute denying welfare benefits to noncitizens, stating this was a decision for the federal government to make.[8]

Finally, in the 1990s, the United States faced a wave of legislation designed to require the use of the English language only. Arizona voters enacted a constitutional amendment requiring state government officers to "act" only in English. The Arizona Supreme Court unanimously held this initiative unconstitutional for several reasons, one of which is that it denied the constitutional rights of those who did not speak English.[9]

To be sure, Arizona has had liberal and progressive initiatives and leaders on issues of race and law as well. Mexican-born Raul Hector Castro was elected Arizona's governor in 1974. Progressive Democrats, including the DeConcinis and Udalls, have been prominent in Arizona and national politics. Women have been allowed to vote in Arizona since statehood, several years before the policy was adopted nationwide. This chapter is not an exhaustive review of race and law in Arizona; our point is that in spite of the ways in which Arizona has been liberal and progressive in matters of civil rights, anxiety about race and immigration are a persistent part of Arizona culture and politics.

Arizona Demographics

Arizona, of course, was once part of Mexico. Not surprisingly, much of the population is of Latino ancestry; in 2000, Latinos represented just over 25 percent of Arizona's population; by 2010, Latinos were almost 30 percent.[10] One might think that a group representing nearly a third of the population would wield substantial political power. However, Latinos have far less influence in Arizona than their numbers would suggest. Only U.S. citizens can vote. Accordingly, undocumented noncitizens and lawfully admitted immigrants who have not naturalized cannot vote. Thus, as of 2008, Latinos represent only 11 percent of voters in Arizona.[11] However, under the Fourteenth Amendment, those born in the United States are citizens. (For more on the Fourteenth Amendment, see Gonzales, this volume.) Accordingly, all Latino children, like all other children, born in Arizona are U.S. citizens. Therefore, if the Latino population keeps growing in absolute and relative terms, Latinos eventually will obtain substantial political power in the state.

If one has a benign view of immigration—that is, that the United States, to its benefit, is a nation of immigrants—then the influx of our neighbors from the south is not alarming. Rather it is part of a historical pattern of growth and development. Some take a different view; they fear that Mexican immigration is part of a metaphorical (or, perhaps, actual) war of reconquest by Mexico, seeking to regain its former territory.[12] On this view, Arizona is near a dangerous tipping point, where there is little time left to prevent political and cultural domination of the state by non-Americans, along with a potentially permanent and negative change to Arizona society. There are equally complex positions that do not fit this easily into a pro-immigrant or anti-immigrant perspective at either a policy or a collective psychological level. For example, *The New York Times* reported that Arizona is a very hospitable state for refugees.[13]

Arizona Legislation in the Decade before SB 1070

In the decade before SB 1070, Arizonans passed many laws dealing with immigration.[14] Perhaps the two most important leaders in this area, but on opposite sides, were Senator Russell Pearce and Governor Janet Napolitano.

Republican Senator Pearce, a self-described Tea Party member, was a Deputy Sheriff in Maricopa County, and he eventually became the Chief Deputy under Sheriff Joe Arpaio.[15] Pearce also served in other government posts before being elected to the legislature representing Mesa in 2000. His son, also a Deputy Sheriff, was shot and critically wounded by an undocumented noncitizen, but even before that incident Pearce made undocumented immigration his signature legislative issue.[16]

Democrat Janet Napolitano had been U.S. Attorney for the District of Arizona and served as the elected Attorney General of Arizona before being elected governor in 2002, and reelected in 2006. During her term as governor, she was the anti-Pearce: Although Napolitano possessed sterling law enforcement credentials and was no fan of undocumented immigration, she believed immigration was largely the responsibility of the federal government. Accordingly, she vetoed many bills passed by the Republican-controlled legislature that she believed went too far.

Still, Senator Pearce had many legislative successes. In 2004, the voters passed an initiative he sponsored, Proposition 200, which required proof of citizenship for public benefits and for voter registration.[17] The bill passed even though many leaders on both sides of the aisle opposed the measure, including then-Governor Janet Napolitano and the Arizona Chamber of Commerce. In 2006, the voters passed Proposition 100, denying bail to undocumented noncitizens accused of serious crimes.[18] He was also the sponsor of an employer sanctions law that was upheld by the U.S. Supreme Court in 2011.[19]

However, Governor Napolitano prevented a number of other measures from becoming law. She vetoed a 2005 law allowing local officers to make arrests for federal immigration violations.[20] She vetoed two 2006 laws making it an Arizona crime to be in the United States in violation of federal law,[21] as well as a 2008 law encouraging local agencies to cooperate with federal authorities.[22] However, in December 2008, Governor Napolitano was nominated by President Obama to serve as Secretary of Homeland Security. When she went to Washington, Republican Secretary of State Jan Brewer became governor. With Napolitano in Washington, Governor Brewer signed SB 1070 and has been a central figure in the SB 1070 debate.

Senate Bill 1070

In his immigration work, Senator Pearce worked closely with Kris Kobach, a former Justice Department lawyer who became a professor at the University of Missouri, Kansas City, and was elected Secretary of State of Kansas in 2010. Professor Kobach was a leader of the immigration restriction movement, writing several articles outlining legal strategies for states to intervene in immigration policy. Professor Kobach was one of the principal authors of SB 1070, and Senator Pearce was a principal sponsor. SB 1070 included many of the ideas identified in Professor Kobach's writing and several provisions inform previous bills, successful and unsuccessful.

SB 1070 is an extraordinary law[23] that has provoked intense reactions—in support, and opposition—from political leaders, commentators, and the public. The bill raises critical issues of race, security, sovereignty, civil rights, state power, and foreign relations. When the U.S. government filed a court challenge to SB 1070, the media coverage of the legislation intensified. (For more on this media coverage, see the separate chapters in this volume by Chavez and Hoewe, by Guerrero and Campo, and by Vigón, Martínez-Bustos, and González de Bustamante.)

Despite the intense media coverage of SB 1070, the public was often unclear about the content of the legislation and the nature of the federal government's challenge. Indeed, at times, the legislation and the court battle symbolized the fierce debate over immigration, and parties to that debate focused more on the social and political effect of those symbols, at times mischaracterizing the content of SB 1070 or the federal government's legal arguments in the court challenge.

The content of SB 1070 and the nature of the legal arguments in the court challenge are far from simple. The bill creates many new crimes and duties, some unprecedented in Arizona, federal, or state law. The court challenge raises complicated questions about constitutional and immigration law, some of which have not been addressed by the U.S. Supreme Court for decades, if at all. And, the Arizona law itself is subject to a number of different interpretations.

What SB 1070 means, including ultimate judgments about its constitutionality, will in the end depend on a number of ensuing decisions by federal judges and state officials who will enforce those portions of SB 1070 that remain in effect. U.S. District Judge Susan Bolton has preliminarily enjoined parts of the law and left others in force,[24] and her decision was upheld by a panel of the U.S. Court of Appeals for the Ninth Circuit.[25] The U.S. Supreme Court has decided to review the case. At the time this volume went to press, the Court had not yet issued a decision.

This chapter does not pretend to give easy answers to the difficult questions raised by SB 1070. Instead it offers a brief overview of the content of the bill and it situates the bill and the court challenge in the context of the social and political context of 2010.[26] Although additional time and distance from the events of 2010 will undoubtedly provide more insight into both its impetus and consequences, some tentative conclusions can already be drawn.

SB 1070 was not the first piece of state legislation to claim state control over immigration, but it is a watershed moment for state involvement in immigration law and policy. The public attention that SB 1070 received acted as a catalyst for other states to try their own hands at similar legislation, with some states, including Alabama, adopting measures which if enforced would be even more aggressive than SB 1070.[27] The state-level developments have focused new attention on federal immigration policies, and the Obama administration feels the rising political pressure. What this will mean in terms of actual federal-level reform, however, remains to be seen. Depending on how the U.S. Supreme Court ultimately decides the SB 1070 case, we may gain some answers in the ongoing constitutional uncertainty surrounding state and federal power over immigration law and policy.

The Content of SB 1070

SB 1070 creates several new state crimes related to immigration, and it also implements new immigration-related police powers and responsibilities. As section 1 of the bill explains, these new crimes and police powers and responsibilities are "intended to work together to discourage and deter the unlawful entry and presence of aliens and economic activity by persons unlawfully present in the United States."

The legislature further clarified in section 1 of the bill: "The legislature declares that the intent of this act is to make attrition through enforcement the public policy of all state and local government agencies in Arizona." Put simply, the legislature explicitly designed the various sections of SB 1070 to keep undocumented immigrants out of Arizona.

New State Immigration Crimes

SB 1070 drew heavily on federal immigration law to create new Arizona crimes that are analogous to federal crimes. SB 1070 also created a set of its own novel crimes. Each new crime will be briefly described and discussed in this section.

Willful Failure to Complete or Carry an Alien Registration Document

SB 1070 creates a new state crime of "willful failure to complete or carry an alien registration document."[28] This section has been preliminarily enjoined in the U.S. government's lawsuit. To be convicted under the new state statute a person must *not* be authorized by the federal government to be in the United States. It does not apply to people who have valid visas or other legal grounds to remain in the United States.[29] The defendant's status may be determined by "a law enforcement officer who is authorized by the federal government to verify or ascertain an alien's immigration status."[30]

Although the new state crime is triggered by a violation of federal law, the federal penalties for violation of the federal provisions are different than the state penalties. This portion of SB 1070 has extremely limited application, although the Arizona legislature likely did not intend this outcome, since this provision is tied to federal statutes that are difficult to violate. The statute is not violated simply because the defendant is undocumented or otherwise subject to deportation. The defendant also must be "in violation" of one of two specific federal statutes. While conviction under this section of SB 1070 may be difficult, it nonetheless may be a rich source of police power to arrest. Courts have previously held that evidence of foreign birth coupled with a lack of immigration documentation amounts to probable cause, which is sufficient grounds for law officers to arrest an individual.[31]

Crimes Associated with Employment

Section 5 of the Arizona Revised Statutes creates three crimes associated with a person unlawfully in the United States who tries to work: the crime of impeding traffic if being hired to work; the crime of applying for work, of soliciting work in a public place, or of actually performing work; and the crime of impeding traffic to hire such an individual for work. The federal judge enjoined only the prohibition on unauthorized noncitizens applying, soliciting, or performing work. The other two crimes went into effect.

Transporting Aliens While Committing Another Crime

Borrowing from federal law, section 5 creates an Arizona crime against human trafficking. It has several distinct requirements. First, the law applies when a person "is in violation of a criminal offense,"[32] that is, the person must be committing some other crime. Second, the person must be transporting, moving, harboring, or concealing noncitizens, or encouraging their entry into Arizona. Third, the defendant must know that the noncitizens have come to or remained in the United States in violation of the law. Finally, at least for the transportation offense, the defendant must act "in furtherance of the illegal presence" of the noncitizen.

The core misconduct of these statutes is human trafficking: transporting noncitizens in the interior of the United States, hiding them along the way, and helping them evade law enforcement (or, perhaps, concealing them from law enforcement officers who would free them from compelled labor). The "in violation of a criminal offense" section of the statute apparently contemplates that the smuggling will be discovered while enforcing some other provision of law, such as a traffic crime. Although the federal government specifically sought to enjoin this section of SB 1070, the federal courts permitted this section to go into effect.

Although the core purpose is clear, several interpretive puzzles remain regarding the full contours of when a person "is in violation of a criminal offense." This phrase is not used in any other state or federal statute now in force, so its meaning is a matter of speculation. It seems to apply to a person who, at the time of transporting, harboring, or encouraging an undocumented immigrant, is also committing a crime, for example, a person transporting undocumented people across the border while going twenty miles an hour or more over the speed limit. However, a person transporting undocumented noncitizens who violated a mere civil traffic rule[33] would not seem to be "in violation of a criminal offense" and therefore would not be liable under the statute.

However, it would also be possible to argue that someone who violated a criminal statute, for example, recently failing to file an income tax return, is "in violation" of a criminal offense. Of course, this would make liability very broad. The statute also does not say whether commission of an Arizona crime is required, or if a federal violation would be sufficient. If a federal violation is enough, then if unlawful entry to the United States is deemed a continuing offense, perhaps most undocumented people could be liable.

Another difficulty with this section is the precise relationship of the Arizona enactments to federal law. Like the section that creates a new state crime of failure to complete or carry an alien registration document, this section draws from several federal statutes. Still, this section does not simply cite the relevant federal statutes; it restates them with slightly different wording. Therefore, violation of Arizona law does not require a violation of federal law. It is unclear whether the legislature intended to create new Arizona human trafficking crimes with distinct meanings or intended to adopt the federal laws and their associated federal judicial interpretations.

Arizona's law is one of several in the United States criminalizing the transportation of "illegal aliens," including Colorado, Florida, Missouri, Oklahoma, South Carolina, Utah, and an earlier version in Arizona itself.[34] None is identical in their coverage, the exceptions they provide, or the penalties they established. Accordingly, these laws mark the beginning of a network of customized local regulation of the same area of law across the nation. These statutes are among the murkiest and most unsettled in the U.S. Code, since different circuits' courts follow different tests.[35] Other wrinkles come from the legislature's explicit exceptions, such as child protective services officers or ambulance drivers transporting unauthorized noncitizens. By implication if these service employees were not covered by an exception, they would become liable to the statute, which suggests that the statute's scope may be quite broad.

New Police Powers and Responsibilities

SB 1070 also imposes new duties and creates new powers for Arizona police in all phases of immigration enforcement. It gives them a greater role in investigating immigration status, reporting of immigration status to federal authorities, arresting deportable noncitizens, and assisting in their removal by delivering them to federal authorities.

Warrantless Arrests

Section 6 of SB 1070 adds to Arizona's warrantless arrest statute. It allows peace officers to arrest someone without a warrant, based on probable cause, if the individual "has committed any public offense that makes the person removable from the United States."[36]

Because Arizona law already grants law enforcement officers broad authority to make warrantless arrests, the U.S. District Judge who ruled on the legal challenge to SB 1070 interpreted this section as granting peace officers the power to arrest individuals on the basis of civil deportability.[37] For example, a warrantless arrest would be permitted of noncitizens who have been convicted of crimes in another state. As the judge noted, this would require officers to determine whether that out-of-state conviction would have made such a person removable. Because such determinations would require officers to have knowledge of out-of-state statutes, as well as the complicated federal scheme governing removability, the court ruled that it was likely that errors would be made, given the complexity of civil deportation.[38]

Racial Profiling and the Duty to Investigate and Verify Immigration Status

Section 2 is perhaps the most controversial provision in SB 1070. It has been preliminarily enjoined in the U.S. government's lawsuit. This section requires law enforcement to take reasonable steps to investigate immigration status, when a person has been lawfully stopped, detained, or arrested, and there is reasonable suspicion that the individual is an undocumented noncitizen, unless it is impracticable. The section also requires that law enforcement officers verify, by checking federal government databases, the immigration status of every arrested person. However, in this case a driver's license or other similar document is not enough. This provision is potentially significant because Arizona law defines an "arrest" as including a stop and issuance of a citation.[39] Accordingly, many people charged with low-level offenses who ordinarily would be released could be jailed pending federal verification.

The most contentious aspect of the controversial section 2 has been whether it authorizes racial profiling. Racial profiling has been defined as "the reliance on race, skin color and/or ethnicity as an indication of criminality, reasonable suspicion, or probable cause, except when part of a description of a suspect, and said description is timely, reliable, and geographically relevant."[40] Arizona Governor Jan Brewer has stated that it is "crystal clear and undeniable that racial profiling is illegal, and will not be tolerated in Arizona."[41] The sponsor of SB 1070, Arizona State Senator Russell Pearce, has written that SB 1070 "explicitly prohibits racial profiling."[42] On the other hand, opponents of SB 1070 have claimed that the bill "gives racial profiling the green light"[43] or "amounts to state sanctioned racial profiling."[44] Neither side is precisely correct. SB 1070 says:

> A law enforcement official or agency of this state or a county, city, town or other political subdivision of this state *may not consider race*, color or national origin in implementing the requirements of this subsection except to the extent permitted by the United States or Arizona Constitution.[45]

At first blush it might seem this wording prohibits racial profiling entirely. But that is not the case. The phrase "except to the extent permitted" means that racial profiling is allowed to the extent permitted by the U.S. and state constitutions.

As a general matter, the U.S. Constitution "prohibits selective enforcement of the law based on considerations such as race."[46] However, in the context of immigration enforcement, both the U.S. and Arizona constitutions have been interpreted to permit law enforcement to consider an individual's race when determining whether to stop or investigate that individual. According to the 1975 U.S. Supreme Court decision *United States v. Brignoni-Ponce*, the U.S. Constitution allows race to be considered in immigration enforcement: "*The likelihood that any given person of Mexican ancestry is an alien is high enough to make Mexican appearance a relevant factor.*"[47]

The Arizona Supreme Court agrees that "*enforcement of immigration laws often involves a relevant consideration of ethnic factors.*"[48] In 1996, this court reaffirmed the relevance of race in determinations of reasonable suspicion:

> Mexican ancestry alone, that is, Latino appearance, is not enough to establish reasonable cause, but if the occupants' dress or hair style are associated with people currently living in Mexico, such characteristics may be sufficient.[49]

Because both the U.S. and Arizona constitutions permit the consideration of race in immigration enforcement, proponents of SB 1070 are incorrect when they claim that the legislation prohibits racial profiling. Preexisting interpretations of the U.S. and Arizona constitutions already permit racial profiling. SB 1070 means the same thing as if it said "racial profiling is permitted to the maximum extent allowed by the U.S. and Arizona Constitution."

However, even if section 2 was read to bar racial profiling, the day-to-day application of SB 1070 might ultimately result in increased use of race by law enforcement. Whether SB 1070 will result, in practice, in increased racial profiling will depend on administrative policy, law enforcement training, and a number of other factors. What is more, additional provisions require law enforcement officers to enforce immigration laws to the full extent permitted by federal law, which might also affect the extent to which Arizona law enforcement considers an individual's race in the context of immigration enforcement.

Because federal law permits race to be a "relevant factor" in determining reasonable suspicion for stops and inquiries, the combined effect of this section with other provisions aimed at full enforcement of SB 1070 may *require* state officers to use race to the full extent permitted by federal law. One such provision, the citizen suit statute, arguably allows a citizen to sue a local police or prosecutorial agency, if as a matter of policy that agency is not considering race as a factor, as will be discussed in more detail next.

The authors of this chapter believe that *Brignoni-Ponce* and its state analogues in Arizona and elsewhere should no longer be regarded as good law. The idea of using race or ethnicity—and particularly having a Latino appearance—in a legal statute as in the phrase "race can be a relevant factor," is now unacceptable. While the U.S. Supreme Court and state high courts have yet to explicitly disavow their earlier cases, such as *Brignoni-Ponce*, many legislators, executive branch officials, and a large portion of the public would now renounce such a racial criterion. However, both Department of Justice and courts of the United States continue to cite *Brignoni-Ponce* to press their positions,[50] and the courts regularly accept it.[51] We would welcome a change in federal policy with regard to the use of race in immigration enforcement. We would also welcome a similar statement of policy by Arizona executive branch officials. But even then it would be hard for Arizona to plausibly interpret the phrase "*to the extent permitted by the United States or Arizona Constitution*" to limit the use of race, since it is the current constitutional doctrine.

In addition to the racial profiling issue, section 2 (below) has also created controversy regarding whether SB 1070 creates a general duty on the part of all citizens and residents to carry specific forms of identification:

> A person is presumed to not be an alien who is unlawfully present in the United States if the person provides to the law enforcement officer or agency any of the following: 1. A valid Arizona driver license. 2. A valid Arizona non-operating identification license. 3. A valid tribal enrollment card or other form of tribal

identification. 4. If the entity requires proof of legal presence in the United States before issuance, any valid United States federal, state or local government issued identification.[52]

This section does not require Arizona residents to carry evidence of citizenship. Indeed, another portion of SB 1070 is directly contrary to such an interpretation.[53] However, its real world impact may be considerably different. The presumption of legal presence created by the listed documents makes it prudent for citizens or residents—especially those more likely to be subject to police inquiries—to carry appropriate identification. In this way, their citizenship status can be verified on the street, rather than as they wait in jail while the records are checked.

Provisions Aimed at Full Immigration Enforcement

To ensure full enforcement of immigration laws in the state of Arizona, SB 1070 includes two striking provisions previously unknown in U.S. law. The first is section 2(A), which provides: "No official or agency of this state or a county, city, town or other political subdivision of this state may limit or restrict the enforcement of federal immigration laws to less than the full extent permitted by federal law." The second is the citizen suit provision in section 2(G), which provides:

> A person who is a legal resident of this state may bring an action in superior court to challenge any official or agency of this state . . . that adopts or implements a policy that limits or restricts the enforcement of federal immigration laws . . . to less than the full extent permitted by federal law.

The federal judge did not enjoin these provisions. The meaning of "the full extent permitted by federal law" is unclear, other than that it increases the discretion of individual officers and decreases the authority of police supervisors to set the workload of line officers.[54] One literal but highly implausible reading is that state officials must allow officers in the field to enforce federal immigration laws, if they choose, in preference to any other assignments they might be given. If so, the provision is extremely broad.

On the other hand, the provision might be read simply to prohibit agency heads from issuing policies directing line staff to not enforce federal immigration laws. Perhaps law enforcement managers can set priorities. Patrol officers could be told, for example, to investigate immigration offenses whenever not protecting life and property, such as responding to 911 calls, or investigating unsolved rapes, burglaries, or murders. If such a policy is permitted, the provision has little substance, since it only bans general prohibitions against enforcing federal immigration law, such as declaring a municipality a "sanctuary city" which will refuse to cooperate with federal immigration authorities. However, if the provision is read broadly, field officers who would prefer to investigate immigration offenses must be allowed to decline to respond to serious crimes. This would radically alter normal police management authority. Intermediate interpretations are not obvious from the provision's wording, although it seems clear that policies against investigating the immigration status of crime victims or witnesses to crimes would be impermissible.[55]

We believe the citizen suit and "full extent" provisions are unwise policies from the standpoint of public safety. They might tie up courts and law enforcement agencies defending policies that we believe the courts will likely uphold. We believe state courts will work hard within the law to avoid readings that would lead courts to regulate the day-to-day workings of local police departments. In our view, the legislature should eliminate the citizen suit provisions. In any event, these provisions are so unfamiliar that the "full extent" and citizen suit provisions may raise additional legal issues.[56]

Implications: Immigration Policy and "Our Federalism"

SB 1070 has implications for the development of law, but also more generally for Arizona and for the nation. Within the legal realm, our interest is in its potential to influence state power generally, and to affect both state and national politics and culture. The federal government's lawsuit regarding SB 1070 turns on complicated questions of constitutional law, namely whether federal law preempts state laws such as SB 1070. Although "preemption" is an interesting legal question, public discussion about SB 1070 has rarely focused on the extent of "Our Federalism."[57] While some SB 1070 supporters essentially admit the law is preempted, many comments in the public discussion have betrayed misunderstanding about the concept.[58]

The Supremacy Clause makes clear that valid federal law is the supreme law of the land. This constitutional principle lets federal laws "preempt," or take precedence over, any conflicting state law. There are three doctrinal variations on preemption. First, Congress can preempt state legislation by statute. Second, under the "field preemption" doctrine, if extensive federal action indicates that the federal government occupies a legal domain, those actions imply that state laws are preempted. If neither foregoing doctrine applies, a third doctrine may: a state law is preempted if it is impossible to comply with both state and federal law, or state law will conflict with the achievement of congressional goals. The second and third types of preemption may be at issue here because the states have some authority over immigrants, and the United States has no statute entirely banning the states from regulating noncitizens.

Arizona legislators effectively concede part of the preemption question by declaring that they acted because the executive branch was not fully enforcing federal immigration statutes.[59] If the states believed they had power to act, their legislators presumably would not feel compelled to justify their actions in terms of federal inaction. Instead, proponents of SB 1070 (and other measures) make clear that they are stepping into a perceived void where Congress is expected to act first and foremost, if not exclusively. Although they also assert that preemption power is weakest where it butts up against "traditional" state powers, they do not rely exclusively on "states rights" arguments.[60] That is, they do not insist that Congress has no legitimate power or overstepped its authority in this arena.

In addition, it has become common to intone these days that "all states are border states." As such, a national solution to the border issue seems imperative, lest interstate dynamics thwart our ability to forge sensible policy in this arena. The stunning proliferation of new state laws that attempt to grapple with the consequences of immigration[61] compounds the need for a coherent solution. Copycat bills with the broad scope of SB 1070 have passed in Utah (March 2011), Georgia (May 2011), and Alabama (June 2011). Bills patterned after SB 1070 also have been introduced in Florida, Arkansas, Minnesota, and Rhode Island. Similar though more limited laws are already on the books in Colorado, Florida, Oklahoma, Missouri, South Carolina, and Utah. If a comparably Byzantine patchwork of laws were to emerge regarding interstate highway safety or aspects of homeland security, the need for a federal trumping solution would be obvious and incontrovertible.

Arizona's legislative action amounts to a demand that the federal government step up to the regulatory plate and "do something."[62] Indeed, a number of commentators have complained that the federal government sued to prevent Arizona from tackling immigration problems, while itself failing to provide such solutions.[63] However, the Obama administration's successful efforts to become the most aggressive enforcer of federal criminal and civil immigration laws in history has not muted its critics' claims. Critics fails to understand the difference between laws designed to stamp out conduct entirely, like laws against rape, robbery, and murder, and laws designed to regulate an area that is generally desirable, like traffic laws, banking laws, or immigration laws. The latter form of regulation, by its nature, is designed to keep a lid on extreme forms of wrongdoing, while tolerating minor violations. That is, the United States has neither the money nor the will to ensure that most speeders or pot smokers or other minor law violators are caught and prosecuted.

Nevertheless, SB 1070 and copycat legislation may ultimately force or encourage congressional action. It put immigration at the top of the policy agenda.

For its part, Arizona could have claimed political credit for enacting SB 1070, and then attempted to partner with a willing federal law enforcement apparatus and a willing Congress to develop more workable immigration laws. But this has not been the approach of Arizona legislative leaders. The passage of SB 1070 contributed to a quick set of state electoral victories, which led to further legislative efforts to restricting immigration in the fall of 2010 and spring of 2011. But these lawmakers have since faced criticism for pressing for more immigration legislation, rather than tackling difficult budget issues.[64] In November 2011 Arizona Senator Russell Pearce lost a recall election, presumably on account of his authorship of SB 1070 and other conservative legislation he sponsored.[65] Moreover, business and law enforcement groups have also criticized these legislative proposals in Georgia and Alabama, as well as Arizona. These extreme state immigration laws might produce a backlash from otherwise improbable coalitions of people, "bootleggers and Baptists," who hold contradictory political and cultural views.[66]

In a longer timeframe, SB 1070 and copycat legislation may signal a shift in American politics. We can imagine American politics moving farther to the right or the left, or toward ever more polarized voting blocs. While law should mediate conflict and constrain abuses of power, SB 1070 did neither. SB 1070 may ultimately prove to be little more than a sideshow, but its passage signals major clashes of American norms and values. The electorate, by way of its representatives and the mass media, must reconsider the state of our nation's culture, values, and politics that led to this legislative circus, and respond more rationally.

Notes

1. For a thorough legal analysis of SB 1070, see Chin, Hessick, Massaro, and Miller (2010), A Legal Labyrinth: Issues Raised by Arizona Senate Bill 1070. *Georgetown Immigration Law Journal, 25,* 47–92. The present chapter draws on that article, but offers only a portion of its coverage.

2. *State v. Pass,* 121 P.2d 882, 884 (Ariz. 1942).

3. *Dameron v. Bayless,* 126 P. 273 (Ariz. 1912). Also see a May 1912 letter to the editor of an Arizona newspaper written by "colored citizens of the United States and taxpayers of Tucson" in "vehement protest against the bill recently passed by the House segregating colored and white children in the public schools," http://azstar net.com/special-section/az-at-100/100-years-ago/article_003f72c9-56b9-534d-b9b8 -13a7bc677c3a.html, retrieved 16 August 2011.

4. *Porter v. Hall*, 271 P. 411 (Ariz. 1928), *overruled, Harrison v. Laveen*, 196 P.2d 456 (Ariz. 1948). The current chapter focuses on discrimination toward Arizona residents and citizens from other countries. The history of discrimination against Native Americans in Arizona is a critical but separate subject.

5. *Truax v. Raich*, 239 U.S. 33 (1915).

6. *Takiguchi v. State*, 55 P.2d 802 (Ariz. 1936).

7. Races: Two Suns on Arizona. (1934, September 3). *Time.*

8. *Graham v. Richardson*, 403 U.S. 365 (1971).

9. *Ruiz v. Hull*, 957 P.2d 984 (Ariz. 1998).

10. http://www.census.gov/prod/cen2010/briefs/c2010br-04.pdf

11. http://www.immigrationpolicy.org/just-facts/new-americans-grand-canyon-state

12. http://finance.townhall.com/columnists/phyllisschlafly/2001/11/28/is_it_assimilation_or_invasion/print

13. DeParle (2010, October 8). Arizona Is Haven for Refugees. *New York Times.*

14. Reich and Barth (2011). *Explaining State Activism on Immigration Policy: Restrictive vs. Accommodating Policies in Four States.* Paper presented at the 2011 meeting of the Midwest Political Science Association in Chicago.

15. Since 1992, the elected sheriff of Arizona's Maricopa County, Arpaio promotes himself as "America's Toughest Sheriff," focusing his harshness on unauthorized immigrants. Arpaio infamously set up a Tent City as an extension of the Maricopa County Jail, calling it a "concentration camp." On July 2011, when Phoenix temperature topped out at 118°F, Arpaio noted the temperature inside Tent City at 145°F. Inmates complained that their shoes were melting from the heat. Amnesty International published a report which found that Arpaio's Tent City was not an "adequate or humane alternative to housing inmates in suitable . . . jail facilities."

16. Outraged Defender of Border Pearce's Belief in "The Rule of Law" Drove Him to Become Co-Author of Proposition 200. (2005, July 10). *Arizona Republic*, p. A17.

17. See www.azsos.gov/election/2004/info/PubPamphlet/english/prop200.htm. Some parts of the initiative were found to be unconstitutional.

18. http://www.azsos.gov/election/2006/info/PubPamphlet/Sun_Sounds/english/prop100.htm

19. *Chamber of Commerce v. Whiting*, 131 S. Ct. 1968 (2011).

20. SB 1306, 47th Leg., 1st Reg. Sess. (Ariz. 2005).

21. HB 2577, 47th Leg., 2nd Reg. Sess. (Ariz. 2006), SB 1157, 47th Leg., 2nd Reg. Sess. (Ariz. 2006).

22. HB 2807, 48th Leg., 2nd Reg. Sess. (Ariz. 2008).

23. The document at issue is SB 1070, 49th Leg., 2d Sess., Ariz. Sess. Laws ch. 113 (2010), *as amended by* HB 2162, 49th Leg., 2d Sess., Ariz. Sess. Laws ch. 211 (2010).

24. *United States v. Arizona*, 703 F. Supp. 2d 980 (D. Ariz. 2010) (order on motion for preliminary injunction).

25. *United States v. Arizona*, 641 F.3d 339 (9th Cir. 2011), aff'g 703 F. Supp. 2d 980 (D. Ariz. 2010). Judge Bea offered a partial dissent.

26. See Chin et al. (*supra* note).

27. Friends and Foes Call Alabama's Immigration Law the Nation's Toughest. (2011, June 10). [Radio broadcast]. National Public Radio. www.npr.org/blogs/thetwo -way/2011/06/10/137107117/friends-and-foes-call-alabamas-immigration-law-the -nations-toughes; but see M. Harrison (2011, June 29). Sheriff, Police Call Costly Alabama Immigration Law Wrong. *DeKalb County Times Journal.*

28. SB 1070 § 3, Ariz. Rev. Stat. Ann. § 13-1509 (2010).

29. Ariz. Rev. Stat. Ann. § 13-1509(F) (2010).

30. Ariz. Rev. Stat. Ann. § 13-1509(B)(1) (2010).

31. Accordingly, a person who casually admits that she was born in Mexico and has no immigration documents can be lawfully arrested, even if, for example, the person has been naturalized or was born a citizen because she had U.S. citizen parents. See Chin, Hessick, Massaro, and Miller (2010, *supra* note).

32. Ariz. Rev. Stat. Ann. § 13-2929(A) (2010).

33. Ariz. Rev. Stat. Ann. § 28-1521 (1956), which states "A person who violates a provision of chapter 3 of this title or this chapter is subject to a civil penalty unless the statute defining the offense provides for a criminal classification."

34. Respectively: Colo. Rev. Stats. Ann. § 18-13-128; Fla. Stats. Ann. § 787.07; Mo. Stats. Ann. § 577.675; Okla. Stat. Ann. tit. 21, § 446 (West Supp. 2010); S.C. Code Ann. § 16-9-460 (Supp. 2009); Utah Code Ann. § 76-10-2901 (West 1953); Ariz. Rev. Stats. 13-2319.

35. See E. Jain (2010). Immigration Enforcement and Harboring Doctrine. *George-town Immigration Law Journal, 24,* 147–188.

36. Ariz. Rev. Stat. Ann. § 13-3883(A)(5) (2010).

37. Entering the country without documents is generally a federal misdemeanor, with a maximum penalty of six months in prison. When someone simply lacks legal resident status, "unlawful presence," such as by overstaying a visa, that person has not committed a criminal offense, only a civil violation.

38. *United States v. Arizona,* 703 F. Supp.2d 980, 1006-07 (D. Ariz. 2010) (order granting preliminary injunction in part).

39. Ariz. Rev. Stat. Ann. § 13-3883(A)(4) (2010) (citing Ariz. Rev. Stat. Ann. § 13-3903 (2010)).

40. See J. McMahon et al. (2002). *How to Correctly Collect and Analyze Racial Profiling Data: Your Reputation Depends on It!,* 97, defined "bias-based policing" as "the act (intentional or unintentional) of applying or incorporating personal, societal, or organizational biases and/or stereotypes as the basis, or factors considered, in decision-making, police actions, or the administration of justice." And see W. Moffitt (2000–2001), Race and the Criminal Justice System, *Gonzaga Law Revised, 36,* 305, 308, who comments: "We talk about things like racial profiling. What does that mean? The use of race as a presumption of guilt without evidence of criminal conduct."

41. Arizona Governor Jan Brewer, Statement of Signing of HB 2162 (April 30, 2010) *available at* http://janbrewer.com/article/statement-by-governor-jan-brewer -signing-of-hb-2162.

42. R. Pearce (2010, May 12). Arizona or San Francisco: Which Path Will America Take on Immigration? Townhall.com. Retrieved from http://townhall.com/columnists/RussellPearce/2010/05/12/arizona_or_san_francisco_which_path_will_america_take_on_immigration.

43. A writer with the byline "Let's Breakthrough" wrote: "The law [. . .] is the subject of national controversy coming under fire from civil rights advocates for giving racial profiling the green light." See in Breaking News—Justice Department Files Lawsuit Against Arizona, Daily Kos, July 6, 2010, http://www.dailykos.com/storyonly/2010/7/6/882163/-Breaking-newsDepartment-of-Justice-files-lawsuit-against-Arizona-law.

44. Chung-Wha Hong, in a letter to the editor of the *New York Times*, on May 1, 2010, wrote: "It's a shame that Gov. Jan Brewer didn't consider the downside to S.B. 1070, Arizona's new immigration law: It amounts to state-sanctioned racial profiling, usurps federal authority and feeds into a volatile dialogue on immigration in Arizona, which correlates with a rise in hate crimes."

45. HB 2162, 49th Leg., 2d Sess., Ariz. Sess. Laws ch. 211, § 3(2010) (emphasis added), codified at Ariz. Rev. Stat. §11-1051(B).

46. *Whren v. United States*, 517 U.S. 806, 813 (1996).

47. *United States v. Brignoni-Ponce*, 422 U.S. 873, 886-887 (1975) (emphasis added). See generally Gabriel J. Chin and Kevin R. Johnson (2010, July 13) Profiling's Enabler: High Court Ruling Underpins Arizona Immigration Law, *Washington Post*, July 13, 2010.

48. *State v. Graciano*, 653 P.2d 683, 687 n.7 (Ariz. 1982) (citing *State v. Becerra*, 534 P.2d 743 (Ariz. 1975)) (emphasis added).

49. *State v. Gonzalez-Gutierrez*, 927 P.2d 776, 780 (Ariz. 1996).

50. See, among others, for example, United States' Response in Opposition to Defendant's Motion to Suppress and Memorandum of Law, *United States v. Gustavo Telles-Montenegro*, 2009 WL 6478237, *7 (M.D. Fl. Dec. 21, 2009), which states that reasonable suspicion supported by "the apparent Mexican ancestry of the occupants of the vehicle", *defendant's motion denied, United States v. Telles-Montenegro*, 2010 WL 737640, *7 (M.D. Fl. Feb. 4, 2010), from which "Agent Fiorita testified that, in his experience, Hispanic males are typically the drivers of alien smuggling vehicles. Therefore, this is also a relevant consideration."

51. For example, *United States v. Bautista-Silva*, 567 F.3d 1266, 1270 (11th Cir. 2009), reversing suppression of evidence; reasonable suspicion existed based on seven factors, including that "the driver and all five passengers were Hispanic adult males."

52. Ariz. Rev. Stat. Ann. §11-1051 (2010).

53. The REAL ID Act, Pub. L. No. 109-13, 119 Stat. 302 (May 11, 2005) established national security standards for driver's licenses issued by states, but has proved deeply unpopular. See National Conference of State Legislators, Countdown to REAL ID, http://www.ncsl.org/default.aspx?tabid=13577.

54. See R. Su (2010). Commentary, The Overlooked Significance of Arizona's New Immigration Law, *108 Mich. L. Rev. First Impressions 76.*

55. Conceivably, the section prohibits police agencies' policies from refusing to enter into 287(g) agreements with federal authorities, for any agency deliberately

choosing not to enter into a 287(g) agreement would have a policy that "limit[ed] or restrict[ed] the enforcement of federal immigration laws to less than the full extent permitted by federal law." Arizona Revised Statute Ann. § 11-1051(A) (2010).

56. The allocation of power between state and local entities is a question of state and local law. It is a false analogy to federalism principles to claim that the state cannot co-opt and direct local law enforcement. States are not creatures of county and local government in the way that the federal Constitution and the federal government are a product of agreement among the states. For example, *Waller v. Florida*, 397 U.S. 387 (1970) which states that while state and federal governments are separate sovereigns for double jeopardy purposes, state and localities within that state are not.

57. In our constitutional structure, power and authority is parceled out in a hierarchy, with the federal government at the top. But states also have independent authority in their realm. This is the nature of federalism, a basic structural element of American government. But the term "Our Federalism" has also taken on political connotations.

58. While preemption is a one-way street (federal law can preempt state law, but state law cannot "preempt" federal law) a number of commentators framed the issue as a question whether the Arizona law "preempted" federal authority. See, for example, Arizona Goes Loco: Anti-immigrant Law Is Completely Over the Top. (2010, April 29). [Editorial]. *New York Daily News,* "The bottom line is that Arizona's law is counterproductive in the extreme. On the bright side, federal courts may well throw it out as an unconstitutional attempt by a state to preempt federal jurisdiction"; B. York. (2010, April 30). How Obama Could Lose Arizona Immigration Battle, *Washington Examiner,* noting "the claim . . . the Arizona measure pre-empts federal law." Also see B. O'Reilly (2010, July 7). [Television broadcast]. The O'Reilly Factor Flash, *Factor Mail,* http://www.billoreilly.com/show?action=viewTVShowandshowID=2640#7; and *Countdown With Keith Olbermann.* (2010, April 28). [Television broadcast]. MSNBC, transcript available at http://www.msnbc.msn.com/id/36846955/.

59. Arizona Senator Russell Pearce said: "We think [SB 1070] may interfere with the priorities of the Obama . . . administration's policy [of] non-enforcement. Of course, it's going to be in conflict with that!" *On the Record with Greta Van Susteren.* (2010, July 29). [Television broadcast]. FOX News, transcript available at http://www .foxnews.com/on-air/on-the-record/transcript/sb-1070-co-author-judge039s-ruling -039this-huge-victory-arizona039.

60. The absence of such states rights arguments here is telling, at an moment when states are defying the federal government in other arenas, especially health care.

61. A. Gorman, (2010, July 16). Arizona's Immigration Law Isn't the Only One. *L.A. Times.*

62. This is the intent of Arizona or other states that have introduced or passed bills dealing with unauthorized immigration. As Professor Kobach asserts: "It is undeniable that the urge to reduce illegal immigration has become a powerful force in state legislatures across the country." See Kobach, *supra* note, 459.

63. See, for example, *Suing Arizona Isn't Enough.* (2010, July 7). [Editorial]. *Washington Post,* which states: "It's easy to understand the frustration of people in Arizona who decided to take matters into their own legislative hands. Congress for years has ignored practical realities and succumbed to xenophobia and fear-mongering to derail

efforts to craft sensible immigration reforms. It's fine to claim a right to 'preempt' state law, but that right comes with a responsibility to do the job." Also see J. Myers, (2010, August 20). Flawed Analysis Blocks Part of 2010 Arizona Immigration Law. http://www.lexisnexis.com/Community/emergingissues/blogs/focusonimmigration/ archive/2010/08/20/julie-myers-wood-flawed-analysis-blocks-parts-of-2010-arizona-immigration-law-s-b-1070.aspx.

64. A. Cherny (2011, May 15). GOP-led Legislature Focused on "Sideshows," Not Mainstream Agenda. [Opinion]. *Arizona Capitol Times.*

65. "Pearce is perhaps best known for sponsoring the state's controversial [SB 1070]. But he's also pushed legislation to let the state nullify federal laws at will, and takes credit for . . . the idea to detain illegal immigrants in tent cities, used infamously by Sheriff Joe Arpaio, and once joked that "the best thing about [the immigration law] is that Obama may not be visiting Arizona because we actually require papers now." See http://tpm muckraker.talkingpointsmemo.com/2011/06/author_of_az_immigration_law_is_one_ step_closer_to.php, accessed 16 August 2011.

66. B. Yandle. (1983). Bootleggers and Baptists: The Education of a Regulatory Economist. *Regulation Magazine, 7*(3), 12.

References

Arizona Revised Statute Ann. section 11-1051(2010).
Arizona Revised Statute Ann. section 11-1051(A) (2010).
Arizona Revised Statute Ann. section 11-1051(B) (2010).
Arizona Revised Statute Ann. section 13-1509(B)(1) (2010).
Arizona Revised Statute Ann. section 13-1509(F) (2010).
Arizona Revised Statutes section 13-2319 (2009).
Arizona Revised Statute Ann. section 13-2929(A) (2010).
Arizona Revised Statute Ann. section 13-3883(A)(5) (2010).
Arizona Revised Statute Ann. section 13-3883(A)(4) (2010).
Arizona Revised Statute Ann. section 13-3903 (2010).
Arizona Revised Statute Ann. section 28-1521 (1956).
Arizona goes loco: Anti-immigrant law is completely over the top. (2010, April 29). *New York Daily News.*
Arizona Secretary of State. (2006). Ballot Proposition Guide. Phoenix, Arizona: Office of the Secretary of State. Retrieved 18 February 2012 from www.azsos.gov/election/2006/info/PubPamphlet/Sun_Sounds/english/prop100.htm
Breaking News—Justice Department Files Lawsuit Against Arizona. Daily Kos (July 6, 2010, 3:22:55 PM), accessible at http://www.dailykos.com/storyonly/2010/7/6/ 882163/-Breaking-newsDepartment-of-Justice-files-lawsuit-against-Arizona-law.
Brewer, J. (2010, April 30). Statement of Signing of HB 2162. http://janbrewer.com/ article/statement-by-governor-jan-brewer-signing-of-hb-2162.
Chamber of Commerce v. Whiting, 131 S. Ct. 1968 (2011).
Cherny, A. (2011, May 15). GOP-led legislature focused on "sideshows," not mainstream agenda. *Arizona Capitol Times.*

Chin, G., Hessick, C. B., Massaro, T., & Miller, M. (2010). A legal labyrinth: Issues raised by Arizona Senate Bill 1070. *25 Georgetown Immigration Law Journal,* 47–92.

Chin, J., & Johnson, K. (2010, July 13). Profiling's enabler: High court ruling underpins Arizona immigration law. *Washington Post.*

Colorado Revised Statutes Ann. § 18-13-128.

Countdown with Keith Olbermann, MSNBC television broadcast April 28, 2010, transcript available at http://www.msnbc.msn.com/id/36846955/.

Dameron v. Bayless, 126 P. 273 (Arizona 1912).

DeParle, J. (2010, October 8). Arizona is haven for refugees. *New York Times.*

Florida Statutes. Ann. § 787.07.

Friends and foes call Alabama's immigration law the nation's toughest. (2011, June 10). [Radio broadcast]. National Public Radio. Retrieved from www.npr.org/blogs/thetwo-way/2011/06/10/137107117/friends-and-foes-call-alabamas-immigration-law-the-nations-toughes).

Gorman, A. (2010, July 16). Arizona's immigration law isn't the only one. *L.A. Times.*

Graham v. Richardson, 403 U.S. 365 (1971).

Harrison v. Laveen, 196 P.2d 456 (Arizona 1948).

Harrison, M. (2011, June 29). Sheriff, police call costly Alabama immigration law wrong. *Dekalb County Times Journal.*

HB 2162, 49th Leg., 2d Session, Arizona Session Laws ch. 211, § 3(2010).

HB 2577, 47th Leg., 2nd Regular Session (Arizona 2006), SB 1157, 47th Leg., 2nd Regular Session (Arizona 2006).

HB 2807, 48th Leg., 2nd Regular Session (Arizona 2008).

Hong, C. (2010, May 1). Letter to the Editor. *New York Times.*

Immigration Policy Center. (2012, February 16). Just the Facts. Washington, DC: American Immigration Council. Retrieved 18 February 2012 from www.immigrationpolicy.org/just-facts/new-americans-grand-canyon-state.

Jain, E. (2010). Immigration enforcement and harboring doctrine. *Georgetown Immigration Law Journal, 24,* 147–188.

Kobach, K. (2008). Reinforcing the rule of law: What states can and should do to reduce illegal immigration. *Georgetown Immigration Law Journal, 22,* 459–484.

McMahon, J., Garner, J., Davis, R., & Kraus, A. (2002). *How to correctly collect and analyze racial profiling data: Your reputation depends on it!* Washington, D.C. & Alexandria, VA: U.S. Department of Justice, Office of Community Oriented Policing Services, & CNA Corporation.

Missouri Statutes. Ann. section 577.675.

Moffitt, W. (2000). Race and the criminal justice system. *Gonzaga Law Revised, 36,* 305, 308 (2000–2001).

Myers, J. (2010, August 20). *Flawed analysis blocks part of 2010 Arizona immigration law.* http://www.lexisnexis.com/Community/emergingissues/blogs/focusonimmigration/archive/2010/08/20/julie-myers-wood-flawed-analysis-blocks-parts-of-2010-arizona-immigration-law-s-b-1070.aspx.

National Conference of State Legislators. Countdown to REAL ID. http://www.ncsl.org/default.aspx?tabid=13577.

National Council of La Raza v. Gonzales, 468 F. Supp. 2d 429, 445 (E.D.N.Y. 2007), *aff'd*, 283 F. App'x 848 (2d Cir. 2008).

Non-Preemption of the Authority of State and Local Law Enforcement Officials to Arrest Aliens for Immigration Violations, Op. O.L.C. (2002), available at http://www.aclu.org/files/FilesPDFs/ACF27DA.pdf.

Oklahoma Statute Ann. tit. 21, section 446 (West Supp. 2010).

On the Record with Greta Van Susteren. (2010, July 29). [Television broadcast]. FOX News. Transcript available at http://www.foxnews.com/on-air/on-the-record/transcript/sb-1070-co-author-judge039s-ruling-039this-huge-victory-arizona039.

O'Reilly, B. (2010, July 7). [Television broadcast]. The O'Reilly Factor Flash, *Factor Mail.* http://www.billoreilly.com/show?action=viewTVShow&showID=2640#7.

Outraged defender of border Pearce's belief in "the rule of law" drove him to become co-author of Proposition 200. (2005, July 10). *The Arizona Republic*, p. A17.

Pearce, R. (2010, May 12). *Arizona or San Francisco: Which path will America take on immigration?* http://townhall.com/columnists/RussellPearce/2010/05/12/arizona_or_san_francisco_which_path_will_america_take_on_immigration.

Porter v. Hall, 271 P. 411 (Arizona 1928).

Races: Two suns on Arizona. (1934, September 3). *Time.*

REAL ID Act, Pub. L. No. 109-13, 119 Statute 302 (May 11, 2005).

Reich, G., & Barth, J. (2011). *Explaining state activism on immigration policy: Restrictive vs. accommodating policies in four states.* Paper presented at the 2011 meeting of the Midwest Political Science Association in Chicago.

Ruiz v. Hull, 957 P.2d 984 (Arizona 1998).

SB 1070, 49th Leg., 2d Sess., Arizona Session Laws ch. 113 (2010), *as amended by* HB 2162, 49th Leg., 2d Sess., Arizona Session Laws ch. 211 (2010).

SB 1070 section 3, Arizona Revised Statute Ann. section 13-1509 (2010).

SB 1306, 47th Leg., 1st Regular Session (Arizona 2005).

Schlafly, P. (2001). Is it assimilation or invasion? Retrieved 18 February 2012 from http://finance.townhall.com/columnists/phyllisschlafly/2001/11/28/is_it_assimilation_or_invasion/print.

Segregation of public schools was fought. (1912, May 5). *Arizona Daily Star.* http://az-starnet.com/special-section/az-at-100/100-years-ago/article_003f72c9-56b9-534d-b9b8-13a7bc677c3a.html, retrieved 16 Aug 2011.

South Carolina Code Ann. section 16-9-460 (Supp. 2009).

State v. Gonzalez-Gutierrez, 927 P.2d 776, 780 (Arizona 1996).

State v. Graciano, 653 P.2d 683, 687 n.7 (Arizona 1982), citing *State v. Becerra*, 534 P.2d 743 (Arizona 1975).

State v. Pass, 121 P.2d 882, 884 (Arizona 1942).

Su, R. (2010). The overlooked significance of Arizona's new immigration law. *108 Michigan Law Revised First Impressions 76.*

Suing Arizona isn't enough. (2010, July 7). *Washington Post.*

Takiguchi v. State, 55 P.2d 802 (Arizona 1936).

Truax v. Raich, 239 U.S. 33 (1915).

United States v. Arizona, 641 F.3d 339 (9th Cir. 2011), aff'g 703 F. Supp. 2d 980 (D. Ariz. 2010).

United States' Response in Opposition to Defendant's Motion to Suppress and Memorandum of Law, *United States v. Arizona*, 703 F. Supp.2d 980, 1006-07 (D. Arizona 2010).

United States v. Bautista-Silva, 567 F.3d 1266, 1270 (11th Cir. 2009).

United States v. Brignoni-Ponce, 422 U.S. 873, 886-887 (1975)

United States v. Gustavo Telles-Montenegro, 2009 WL 6478237, *7 (M.D. Fl. Dec. 21, 2009).

United States v. Telles-Montenegro, 2010 WL 737640, *7 (M.D. Fl. Feb. 4, 2010).

U.S. Census. (May 2011). The Hispanic Population: 2010 Census Briefs. Retrieved 18 February 2012 from www.census.gov/prod/cen2010/briefs/c2010br-04.pdf.

Utah Code Ann. section 76-10-2901 (West 1953).

Waller v. Florida, 397 U.S. 387 (1970).

Whren v. United States, 517 U.S. 806, 813 (1996).

Yandle, B. (1983). Bootleggers and baptists: The education of a regulatory economist. *Regulation Magazine, 7*(3), 12.

York, B. (2010, April 30). How Obama could lose Arizona immigration battle. *Washington Examiner.* http://www.azsos.gov/election/2004/info/PubPamphlet/english/prop200.htm.

6

Assault on Ethnic Studies

Anna Ochoa O'Leary, Andrea J. Romero,
Nolan L. Cabrera, and Michelle Rascón

Introduction

RACE AND CLASS HAVE ALWAYS BEEN at the crux of tension in the United States, from the initial oppression of Native American tribes, to the suppression of voting for blacks and Latinos.[1] Yet, perhaps it has been the nation's increasing ethnic diversity, much of which is a result of growing Latino populations,[2] that has contributed to recent cynicism, fear, distrust, and scapegoating of foreigners and immigrants.[3] In the aftermath of the terrorist attacks of 9/11, politicians, the media, and nativists clamored for increased border security and immigration enforcement.[4] Fanning the flames of the nation's growing anxiety over immigration were the media, whose gaze increasingly turned toward its border with Mexico (see the chapters by González de Bustamante, and by Vigón et al., this volume). Arizona's border, in particular, garnered national attention partly because of its consistent portrayal as lawless and rampant with violence, drug running, and welfare-benefits-seeking migrants.[5] Subsequently, the U.S. House of Representatives passed HB 4437, Border Protection, Antiterrorism, and Illegal Immigration Control Act of 2005. This landmark bill mandated, in exchange for greater restriction in the path to citizenship for nearly 12 million undocumented immigrants, increased criminalization[6] of undocumented people and heightened border security infrastructure that included stepped up Border Patrol recruitment efforts and surveillance technologies.[7] Although the 2005 bill failed to make it through the U.S. Senate, millions of immigrants and their allies responded politically in mass rallies in hundreds of cities across the country during 2006 in what is considered to be the largest civic mobilization since the civil rights era of the 1960s.[8] Noteworthy was the participation of youth in this mobilization,[9] and later, in the 2008 presidential elections.[10] Since, then, however, a repressive political and social backlash has followed.[11]

Arizona provides a case study for understanding how highly charged debates about immigration permeate almost every aspect of the state's political and social life.[12] In Tucson, Arizona, shortly after one of the community's largest public demonstrations against proposed immigration reform in April 2006, Dolores Huerta, cofounder with César Chávez of the United Farm Workers, was invited to speak at a special assembly at Tucson High Magnet School.[13] Student participation in Tucson's mobilization for immigration reform was not atypical, but in fact, it reflected the high involvement rate of students seen across the nation in this movement.[14] During her speech, Huerta remarked that "Republicans hate Latinos." Later Huerta explained that her comment was based on the extraordinary number of anti-immigration bills sponsored by Republicans. The incident came to the attention of then State Superintendent of Public Instruction Tom Horne who proceeded to reprimand the school for allowing a partisan speech to take place. Horne insisted that equal time be given to the State Deputy Superintendent, Margaret Garcia Dugan, a Latina and Republican, to rebut Huerta's comments. Prior to the event, school officials informed the students that Dugan would not take any questions. In response, students taped their mouths shut with duct tape, and turned their backs to the State Deputy Superintendent. Outraged, Horne publicly blamed Tucson High Magnet School's Mexican American studies curriculum and its teachers for these events, and made it his mission to dismantle ethnic studies in general, and in particular Mexican American studies in the Tucson Unified School District (TUSD) as evidenced in a 2007 letter he wrote calling on the citizens of Tucson to pressure the school district to eliminate ethnic studies.[15] Having failed in this, Horne helped craft a legislative measure in 2008 that sought to abolish ethnic studies programs. It was proposed as an amendment to a Homeland Security Bill in 2008 as Arizona Senate Bill 1108 (sponsored by Jack W. Harper, Republican District 4) and in this way it was strategically linked to anti-immigrant sentiment. This "anti-ethnic studies" bill sought to establish that "a primary purpose of public education is to inculcate values of American citizenship" by proposing to eliminate the state's ethnic studies programs and ethnic-based organizations characterized as "un-American." It would prohibit public tax dollars used in public schools that "denigrate American values and the teachings of western civilization," and prohibit organizations to operate in or around a school campus if its organization was based in any way on race. Although this bill failed to pass, a similar bill was proposed a year later as SB 1069.[16] This latter bill (sponsored by Jonathan Paton, Republican, District 30) proposed to grant more enforcement power to the State Superintendent of Schools, allowing this elected official to threaten school districts and charter schools with a loss of 10 percent of their funding if ethnic studies programs were found to be in violation of the law. However, with state budgetary issues pressing the Legislature in 2009, the proposal did not make it to the floor for a vote before the session adjourned on July 1. Finally, in May 2010, a third ethnic studies ban bill managed to pass through the State House and Senate, and Republican Governor Janice Brewer signed Arizona House Bill 2281 into law.

Similar to other education-related laws adopted throughout the history of public schools in the United States, the series of proposals designed to "delegitimize"[17] ethnic studies programs and scholarship in Arizona was rooted in larger political struggles over immigration, language and cultural rights, and racial-educational equity,[18] as well as issues relating to national security.[19] Reallocating scant public educational resources inequitably has long been a political exercise.[20] Mexican Americans are unavoidably linked to today's hotly contested issue of immigration. Because of early settlement and economic patterns, the conquest by the United States of the Mexico's northern territories, adaptive cross-border family ties, and daily economic exchanges with recent immigrants—as employees, employers, neighbors, or family—people interact across the border.[21] All defy contemporary efforts to categorize populations along simplistic dichotomies based on immigrant or nonimmigrant status and heighten anxieties. Arjun Appadurai conveys this eloquently:

> [T]hese various forms of uncertainty create intolerable anxiety about the relationship of many individuals to state provided goods—ranging from housing and health to safety and sanitation—since these entitlements are frequently directly tied to who "you" are and thus to who "they" are . . . especially when the forces of social uncertainty are allied to other fears about . . . loss of national sovereignty, or threats to local security and livelihood.[22]

In this way, the proposals in Arizona capitalized upon and raised questions about entitlement, belonging, and whether public resources were being used to support noncitizens.[23] Light and von Scheven point out that the dramatic increase in immigrant populations throughout the nation has contributed to "shock"[24] among residents in destination sites, typified by reactive intolerance toward Mexican immigrants who are more likely to be younger than Anglo populations, more likely to live in poverty, have young children, and therefore more likely to be consumers of publicly funded education resources (see Gans, this volume).[25] Maricopa County, where Phoenix and the state capitol are located, was ranked as the county with the second highest gain in Latino residents between the years 2000–2006.[26] It follows, then, that Arizona's legislative actions are responses to the recent growth of immigrant populations in the state and greater nativist anxiety about the new demographic reality. Moreover, Anglo Arizonan elite have restricted educational funding for Mexican-Arizonan schoolchildren, in so much as a poor education reliably limits political participation.[27] The larger story of HB 2281 and Arizona's assault on ethnic studies is thus set within both the state and the nation's immigration policy debate. As such, the contemporary analysis of the struggle for greater democracy and social justice in the United States necessitates the inclusion of immigration alongside ethnicity and class.

With the official implementation of HB 2281, alongside the passage of SB 1070, Arizonans arrived at a historical tipping point, brought about by multiple forces, including political parties and groups that increasingly rely on a racialized national ideology to undermine a historically subordinated group's claims of belonging by making them the object of fear and rage.[28] In this chapter, after providing a brief historical context of ethnic studies and the current Arizona political context, we will analyze HB 2281, Arizona's Anti-Ethnic Studies law, and discuss its implications for education, health, and the broader trend to exclude minority communities from greater democratic participation.

Ethnic Studies in Historical Context

During the late 1960s and early 1970s, Chicano and Chicana students,[29] along with their teachers, families, and other allies organized to protest, among other things, the structured inequality of the U.S. educational system.[30] Largely influenced by the momentum of the civil rights period (1955–1968), their actions helped ignite *El Movimiento,* "The Movement," a national movement that sought political empowerment and inclusion for Mexican Americans and Chicanos and Chicanas.[31] El Movimiento was particularly strong among Chicano and Chicana students at the college level, where there was a large concentration of student activists who formed organizations and advocated for educational reforms and Chicano Studies curricula. As political change swept throughout the country, institutions of higher education increasingly began to accommodate the demands made by historically marginalized groups to establish more meaningful curricula.[32] The history of the El Movimiento offers an important civics lesson. Civic engagement advances participatory democracy and can lead to policy remedies, in this case for long-standing educational inequities for minority students.[33] A testament to the movement's success is the growth of post-secondary Latino student participation in higher education and the establishment of nearly 400 ethnic studies programs, departments, programs, centers, and institutes in schools, colleges, and universities throughout the nation that are dedicated in whole or in part to the formal academic study of Chicanos and Chicanas, Mexican Americans, Raza, or U.S. Latinos/as.[34]

Over the past forty years, Chicano/a studies programs have become increasingly sophisticated at the university level, with scientific peer review articles and books, and professors with tenure. However, there are relatively few ethnic studies programs in K–12 public education, and even today few students entering post-secondary education institutions are exposed to the history and culture of those of Mexican descent.[35] Ideas about how marginalized populations become transformed through more awareness and increased knowledge about their history are part of the broad curricula of ethnic studies (e.g., Chicano/a studies).[36] Here TUSD was at the forefront. In fact, this high-school program, as with higher education ethnic studies programs, was rooted in multicultural education based on history and traditions of the socially transformative civil rights movement. One goal of ethnic studies classes is to raise awareness about the structural and historical roots of inequality, for it is through this awareness that greater tolerance for diversity and social justice may be achieved. Perhaps most important, such programs provide both teachers and students the academic infrastructure and scholarly communities for understanding and improving academic performance among students who already face mounting social and institutional obstacles to educational success. In many ways ethnic studies is consistent with an important tenet of multicultural education: to make education more relevant to racialized, ethnic, and linguistic minority students.[37] Some of the lessons we can learn from the emergence of ethnic studies during the Civil Rights Movement are (a) the importance of creating a positive ethnic identity as a source of civic and educational empowerment; (b) the importance of the elimination of "Americanization" programs and their goals to develop a positive ethnic identity; and (c) the ability of youth to change social inequalities through academic engagement and civic engagement.[38] Therefore, the law will have far-reaching implications for how public education programs—especially for ill-served impoverished student populations—that have demonstrated success using multicultural approaches to close the achievement gap for students of all ethnic backgrounds.

Legislative Trends in Arizona

Horne's reaction to Dolores Huerta's speech and HB 2281 are part of an onslaught of anti-immigrant measures that have emerged from Arizona's

Republican dominated state legislature that gained force as early as 2004. The onslaught began with Arizona Proposition 200, a voter initiative with financial backing from a national right-wing group called Protect Arizona Now (PAN).[39] This law imposed new identification requirements to vote and made state employees responsible—under penalty of law—for verifying the citizenship of those applying for local public benefits. Subsequent laws passed in Arizona would follow similar immigration enforcement type provisions.[40]

In the absence of any evidence that noncitizens were voting, critics of more restrictive voter identification laws argue that these laws only serve to create suspicion and distrust, place greater burdens on the poor and elderly, and sharpen distinctions between social categories based on perceptions of who are entitled (citizens) and those who are not.[41] Although the Voting Rights Act of 1965 was, for the most part, a response to the race-based obstacles to voting that African Americans faced, in the context of more recent immigration debates, recent voter restrictions have concentrated on Latino communities.[42] Consequently, such attitudes foster distrust of immigrants, their descendants, and those who support them, and contribute to the suppression of Latino civic and political participation that can ultimately threaten their political voice, and potentially the livelihoods and well-being of all Latino communities, regardless of citizenship status.[43] Arizona is one of more than twenty U.S. states that have since 2004 passed more restrictive voter-identification laws.

To date, there is no evidence that Prop 200 resulted in less voter fraud at the polls or savings among the "affected" public-benefit programs.[44] However, Michelson argues that notable political events that shift public attention to immigration issues succeed in altering in a negative way the "national mood" toward immigrants. Latinos, who are more often than not native-born or naturalized citizens, sense this mood and perceive greater discrimination.[45] When all Latinos are considered, 75 percent are native-born or naturalized citizens, according to the 2006 U.S. Census. In other words, citizenship status offers Latinos little protection from discrimination because they share many of the phenotypic, linguistic, and cultural traits with Latin American immigrants.[46] As such, they are susceptable to public humiliation and degrading treatment by officials[47] and racial profiling.[48] Thus, the openly inflammatory anti-immigrant rhetoric unleashed by Prop 200 aggravated social divisions and rekindled fears that have always "haunted" the U.S. imaginary:[49] Latinos are foreigners;[50] disaffected Americans who do not belong to U.S. society.[51] More to the point, generalized anxiety about non-"Americans" has the potential to spread to the broader Latino community, many of whom are U.S. citizens.[52] In this way, anti-immigrant measures are also anti-Latino.[53]

In 2005, during Arizona's 46th legislative session, lawmakers introduced close to thirty anti-immigrant bills making clear that a nativist agenda dominated the legislature that sought to exclude certain immigrants, regardless of the effects these punitive measures would have on broader social contexts: for example, entire families of immigrants that include U.S.-born children,[54] work environments, education, and civic and political life.[55] Lawmakers who insisted on such measures commonly reintroduced failed or vetoed bills in subsequent legislative sessions or put these measures before voters. For example, SB 1167 (English as the Official Language) was vetoed by then Governor Janet Napolitano in May 2005, but voters passed an initiative in 2006 declaring English as the state's official language. Another example is Prop 300, which when finally enacted in 2006 placed new restrictions on adult education programs (restricted to U.S. citizens and legal residents) and undocumented immigrant students' access to institutions of higher learning (requiring proof of legal residency to qualify for in-state tuition and state-funded financial aid). Prop 300 also prohibits adults who are not lawfully present from receiving childcare assistance from the Arizona Department of Economic Security.[56] Adult education was targeted because it appeared that Spanish-speaking undocumented immigrants comprised the bulk of those who took English classes. Thus, just when English became the state's official language, the state legislature placed additional obstacles to learning English.

Additional punitive laws would come, such as an employer-sanctions law that calls for the suspension and revocation of business licenses for employers who intentionally or knowingly hire unauthorized immigrant workers,[57] and perhaps most notoriously, Arizona SB 1070, which was signed into law in April 2010. A month later, HB 2281 was approved. We now turn to an analysis of the four provisions of HB 2281.

Demystifying the HB 2281 Provisions

Salvadoran immigrant and House Republican Steve Montenegro sponsored Arizona HB 2281, which Governor Jan Brewer signed into law on May 11, 2010. While HB 2281 is enshrined as part of "schools, prohibited curriculum, and discipline" under Arizona Revised Statues 15-112(A), we will continue to refer to HB 2281. It specifically targets the ethnic studies classes and programs in TUSD.[58]

The preface of the bill states that "the legislature finds and declares that public school pupils should be taught to treat and value each other as individuals and not be taught to resent or hate other races or classes of people."

The penalties are steep: Schools may lose up to 10 percent of their state funding if the classes or courses are found to do any of four things:

1. promote the overthrow of the government
2. promote resentment toward a race or class or people
3. are designed primarily for pupils of a particular ethnic group
4. advocate ethnic solidarity instead of the treatment of pupils as individuals

We will take up each of these four provisions individually. The law is decidedly authoritarian in that it assumes local school districts are not capable of oversight and implementation of local programs, and thus require direct supervision by state officials. Furthermore, the bill sets a dangerous precedent by shifting curricular and pedagogical decisions from local districts to the state. Ultimately, the State Superintendent of Public Instruction can decide to financially penalize the school, if this one person determines that an educational program violates one of the four elements of HB 2281. As we will show, TUSD finds itself in the crosshairs of HB 2281. Its school board had to choose either to fight for a very effective educational program at the threat of financial cuts, or to eliminate the program.[59]

Tom Horne's effort to ban the TUSD's Mexican American Studies (MAS) program continued after he was succeeded by John Huppenthal, the new State Superintendent of Public Instruction. Huppenthal immediately initiated enforcement action against TUSD. He commissioned an independent audit of the district's ethnic studies courses and curricula.[60] Cambium Learning, Inc. was reportedly paid $110,000[61] to conduct a twofold audit: (1) Determine if TUSD's MAS programs were designed to improve student achievement as claimed by the school district administrators, and if statistically valid measures indicated that student achievement occurred; and (2) Determine if the department was in compliance with the new Arizona statutes. Cambium Learning reported that it found "no observable evidence" to conclude the district's program violated the law.[62]

However, Superintendent Huppenthal chose to ignore the findings of the independent audit and ruled unilaterally that TUSD was still in violation. Consequently, the American Civil Liberties Union (ACLU) requested to examine the documents related to the ethnic studies audit of TUSD on June 16, 2011, to review how HB 2281 would be implemented. In the following four sections, we review the bill's four provisions in the light of the audit's findings and our own analysis.

"Promoting the Overthrow of the U.S. Government"

HB 2281 is legislation that grows out Arizona's political tensions and the divisive rhetoric that alleges that immigrants subvert the state's ability to regulate the distribution of resources and electoral processes.[63] HB 2281 is a particularly anti-Latino and anti-Mexican measure. However, it is also poorly written legislation. It is unclear how the first provision of HB 2281 could be objectively enforced, because it does not clearly define how a course of study "promotes" the overthrow of government. The assumption appears to be that ethnic studies encourages students to be unpatriotic and disloyal to the United States.[64] However, this provision is broad enough to encompass the basic democratic processes, such as voting and public discussion and critique that are essential to a functioning democracy, as well as necessary to challenge the dominant ways of knowing that might lead to institutional change.[65] This provision could limit democratic discourse in the classroom, which includes an accurate teaching of the history of racial minority groups and social movements. The complaint is that critiquing U.S. government policies represents disloyalty to the nation; especially when Latinos lodge the critique.[66] The language of the law implies that there is reason to distrust students who express their civil rights to agitate for a brighter educational future by conducting peaceful civil protests. This adult fear of activist high schoolers has been documented in the past.[67] In this case, a TUSD high school student group, United Non-Discriminatory Individuals Demanding Our Studies (UNIDOS), conducted a series of peaceful civil disobedience actions in April and May 2011. The news media portrayed the students as "radicals" who created "mayhem" and "chaos."[68] UNIDOS's later actions at public forums prompted adults to overreact by confronting the high school students with large numbers of police in riot gear.[69]

Language that equates brownness with criminality, anti-Americanism, and treason is not new,[70] but in the context of HB 2281, the actions of adults became state-sponsored oppression of student ethnic groups. The adults were denying *educational opportunities* to those students historically and currently ill-served by the educational system and yet it was these students who are actively engaging politically to change this.

"Promoting Resentment Toward a Race or Class of People"

Similar to the first provision, this one is also vague. The meaning of "resentment" promises to defy objective evaluation. It assumes that teaching the history of race and class in the United States to students will only make them believe they are oppressed victims, and consequently make them resentful. In other words, this history makes students feel bad. But as Cacho points out, to claim that a body of knowledge is the reason students feel bad is an attempt to render it as illegitimate.[71] Over the years ethnic studies scholars have developed sophisticated explanations of a wide range of topics about Mexican Americans' experience within the nation's history and development.[72] To diminish them because they provoke anxiety threatens to suppress any teaching of struggle against injustice.

It bears repeating that multicultural education resulted from a socially transformative civil rights movement that ultimately helped our society recognize unresolved racism and bigotry. Moreover, with increased understanding of cultures, we as a nation can enjoy a more learned, diverse, and tolerant democratic society.[73] Indeed, at least one study has found that individuals who know more about their ethnic heritage are more likely to have positive attitudes toward other ethnic groups.[74] A goal of multicultural education is to reach *all* students from *all* backgrounds, races, and classes and work with them as individuals through critical inquiry; rather than to assume that all students are the same and that the exact same pedagogy is effective with everyone in a diverse educational setting.[75] As a result, educators began to rethink conventional teaching methods. In the light of the criticism of renowned Brazilian educator Paulo Freire, teachers reevaluated their approaches, rejecting passive models and adopting socially interactive methods.[76] Models of instruction premised on the value of collaborative learning, social justice learning, or cooperative learning techniques provide viable alternatives that made education more meaningful by their connection to a supportive community.[77] Additionally, these innovative methods are more likely to be based on critical thinking that teach students to pose questions and evaluate multiple perspectives. They also provide an intellectual foundation for student-centered approaches to learning. The collaborative approach between students and the wider community builds bonds of mutual trust between individuals who make classroom exchange humanistic, relational, and appreciative of individual contributions to the broader social whole.[78] In summary, the provision that focuses on "promoting resentment toward a race or class of people" appears to demonize collective action, and attempts to thwart teaching about the nation's history of collective struggle and resistance.[79] The law seeks to replace social interactive approaches of learning with atomistic approaches, which will weaken social support mechanisms that have been shown to advance the educational attainment of Mexican-heritage populations.[80]

"Programs Designed Primarily for Pupils of a Particular Ethnic Group"

The audit that Huppenthal commissioned found no evidence that MAS courses were "designed primarily for pupils of a particular race." The audit stated, "A majority of evidence demonstrates that the Mexican American Studies Department's instruction is NOT designed primarily for pupils of a particular ethnic group."[81] Students from all racial and ethnic backgrounds could and did take these courses. While a higher proportion of Latino students took MAS classes, in TUSD these classes were only offered in majority-Latino high schools. Approximately 20 percent of students taking MAS classes were not Latino. Moreover, students of all racial and ethnic groups tended to improve their academic standing after taking MAS courses.[82]

We undertook our own analysis of the last four years of TUSD data, using the state's standardized test battery, the Arizona Instrument to Measure Standards (AIMS).[83] Our analysis corroborated the findings of the Huppenthal-commissioned audit: MAS courses were academically effective for all students, not just those of Latino heritage. Moreover, we found MAS to be particularly good at addressing the educational needs of low-income TUSD students, who have the lowest district rates of high school completion. Students who took the MAS courses, a largely low-income Latina/o population, passed the AIMS tests at rates equal to or higher than the non-MAS student population. These MAS students also graduated from high school at rates equal to or greater than those who did not take MAS courses:[84]

- Reading: 1 percentage point difference
- Writing: 1 percentage point difference
- Math: 1 percentage point difference[85]

After taking MAS classes, all students regardless of racial and ethnic background eliminate their achievement gap. Moreover, we made an unexpected finding. Students who took MAS courses (literature, history, American government, and art) made gains not only reading and writing, but also in math, despite the fact that there are no MAS math courses. This would indicate that taking an MAS course not only develops skills, but can also change a student's attitude toward school that can translate into academic success in other areas of study.

The other indicator, graduation rates for the 2010 cohort, again demonstrated near elimination of the achievement gap: MAS students had a graduation rate of 82.6 percent compared to 82.5 percent for non-MAS students.[86] Most strikingly, MAS graduation rates were substantially higher for districts defined "low income" and "very low income" students:

- Low income: 7.8 percentage point difference (74.9 percent of non-MAS students graduate; 82.7 percent of MAS students graduate)
- Very low income: 14.7 percentage point difference (64.3 percent of non-MAS students graduate; 78.9 percent of MAS students graduate).[87]

These are correlational statistics, not causal relations. However, they strongly indicated that MAS was effective for all students. This debunks the contention that the program was designed primarily for students of a specific ethnic group. Frequently, MAS students began their high school careers substantially behind their non-MAS peers academically. By their senior year, these differences disappeared for MAS students. They closed the achievement gaps for all intents and purposes. Indeed, there was evidence that *low* and *very low income* MAS students substantially outperformed their non-MAS counterparts.

MAS classes were open to all students and were effective at educating economically disadvantaged students of all ethnic backgrounds. Thus, the value of this ethnic studies program was not solely based on abstract notions of identity, solidarity and oppression, but was grounded instead on harsh material realities to which all economically disadvantaged students can relate.[88] Further, non-Mexican heritage students might come to appreciate how other groups struggle for equality and learn how to work for social justice. The Cambium audit offered evidence that MAS students narrowed the achievement gap. Thus it is logical to surmise that eliminating the MAS curricula reintroduced an academic barrier for these students.

"Curricula That Advocates Ethnic Solidarity Instead of the Treatment of Pupils as Individuals"

Again the final provision of HB 2281 is problematic because there is no clear definition of "ethnic solidarity." Moreover, as written "ethnic solidarity" is an undesirable outcome. The law inaccurately implies that with ethnic solidarity comes reverse discrimination. Because "ethnic solidarity" precludes clear definition and measurement, this provision ultimately allows the Arizona State Superintendent of Public Instruction to arbitrarily decide whether or not an ethnic studies program violates the law.

We will undertake a critique of the assumption underlying the provision. An ethnic group can be defined as a group of people who share a common heritage, language, culture, religion, values, or norms.[89] Scholars often use the term "ethnic identity" as a theme of study for all ethnic groups, including whites. Although there are many definitions of ethnic identity, no definition requires the mistreatment of other people. In fact, in most social science disciplines, ethnic identity is referred to positively as an individual's sense of belonging, affirmation, or pride in one's ethnic background.[90] For Mexican Americans, ethnic grouping has also been legally recognized for purposes of achieving educational equity.[91] Indeed, social science over the past forty years repeatedly has demonstrated that ethnic identity is strongly associated with a sense of well-being,[92] improved mental health, and educational outcomes.[93] Additionally, at the end of the process of ethnic identity development, young people obtain a more mature sense of belonging to their ethnic group based on knowledge of their history and traditions. These young people are more likely to be accepting of other ethnic groups than young people who don't have that kind of exposure.[94] However, given the wording of the bill and rhetoric associated with this and previous anti-ethnic studies bills, the overall viewpoint conveyed is that ethnic groupings should be suppressed, despite the fact that researchers have documented that over several generations all immigrant groups in the United States, including European Americans from the early 1900s, have maintained high levels of ethnic identity even after adopting U.S. cultural values and norms. So, without knowing exactly what legislators had in mind when they wrote this provision, the benefits of ethnic grouping and solidarity for students are ignored and disparaged, while the value of unaffiliated individualism is encouraged.

Ethnic solidarity emerges from culturally-mediated behaviors and expectations among people who share similar experiences.[95] Often, shared material hardships promote empathy and a charitable disposition toward those less fortunate, and a desire to help them achieve material gains. These social values promote reciprocity, mutual aid, and group identity, which are more likely to prioritize group harmony and well being for all.[96]

In contrast, individualism prioritizes the self above all other people. It is an ethos of domination and subordination that is suspicious of coalitions and disparages cooperation and empathy for the downtrodden. Furthermore, given Arizona's political climate, some teachers fear that teaching students to develop a stronger sense of ethnic identity is beyond the scope of appropriate educational practices.[97] For social conservatives, democracy itself can present a problem. Ethnic solidarity among Latinos and other people of color (i.e., coalition building) might legitimate a group sufficiently well organized to rationally and peacefully advocate for political change,[98] and that the continued existence of group-conscious minorities demonstrates our nation's failure to achieve a "purity of the national whole."[99]

The psychological cost of excessive individualism for racialized and marginalized adolescents is tangible. Students frequently describe how "ethnic studies saved them," that they previously felt atomized to the verge of nihilism, that U.S. society (including public schooling) had erased their sense of self. Perhaps this is why the discussion of personal identity among marginalized (particularly ethnic) high school students is often necessary to promote their academic advancement. To deny or scorn solidarity or otherwise to make the child to feel that he or she is wrong to need this kind of belonging is another way to delegitimize the child. Such attitudes also dismiss hard-won Civil Rights Movement accomplishments,[100] and falsely characterize cultural minorities as disloyal citizens who impede national unity.[101] Ethnic studies, by contrast, offers all students a broader perspective on our nation's history and literature, using both a racialized/ethnic/immigrant lens and the customary high school curricular lens.

To deny that ethnicity and ethnic identity or solidarity exists or to demonize it also negates two hundred years of social science research. Admittedly, this research flies in the face of the individualistic "pull yourself up by your bootstraps" mentality—an approach has been exhaustively researched and found to be a fallacy, unless you were raised in a privileged or white middle class setting.[102] Furthermore, within an educational context, to ignore ethnic/racial/immigrant disparities in educational attainment and to reject the utility of critical thinking about those disparities may only serve to keep students in the shadows and to prohibit innovative solutions to close the nation's educational achievement gaps. By turning a blind eye to collective disparities, we let minority students believe that the only reason they do not succeed is because they do not merit success, because they do not work hard enough. Part of ethnic studies teaching introduces students to the long-standing structural problems that create obstacles for marginalized students, which white middle class and upper middle class students do not encounter.

Conclusion

Discriminatory and exclusionary behavior—real or perceived—has always complicated school settings and encumbered the coping capacity of young adults. In the landmark U.S. Supreme Court case *Brown v. Board of Education*, Chief Justice Earl Warren wrote, "Feelings of inferiority based one's racial background may affect the minds and hearts of children in a way that may not be undone."[103] In one of two empirical social psychological studies, the two principal authors found that discriminatory legislation may contribute to students' perceptions that their ethnic or racial group is treated differentially and is perceived as inferior, with long-term implications for their overall sense of self-worth and their mental health.[104] In our second analysis with students from all ethnic backgrounds, we similarly found that all students report stress due to anti-ethnic studies proposed legislation.[105]

On the other hand, Latino students who report more knowledge of their ethnic history, traditions, and culture (exactly what ethnic studies courses offer them) reported significantly less depression and higher self-esteem. Moreover, we found that students who were actively engaged in talking, learning, praying, and activism against the Arizona Senate version of HB 2281 were more likely to retain a high self-esteem even at high levels of stress. In sum, our social psychological research confirmed students' ability to remain resilient, as well as illustrated the health benefits of remaining democratically engaged in talking and learning more about social policies affecting their education and lives, and as American citizens raising their voices to contribute to the public discourse about proposed legislation.

The logic underlying HB 2281 presumes that ethnic studies courses further marginalize students by fomenting distrust, hopelessness, and lack of faith in the institution of public education, leading to even greater political disenfranchisement. Although not well researched,[106] students' political activity has frequently been grounds for discipline and has been used historically to discourage Latino students from speaking out about inequitable conditions, more so than Anglo students.[107] Discipline often takes the form of expulsion and suspension from school, contributing to higher dropout rates for Latinos when compared to Anglos. A punitive law such as HB 2281 empowers state officials to discipline teachers, administrators, and students and potentially shut down educational programs that have proven to close achievement gaps. It also denigrates Mexican American culture, and has the potential to undermine Mexican American political and civic engagement. Without civic engagement that seeks greater representation in the classroom, board room, and local government, the subordinate status of Mexican Americans may continue.[108] However, the freedom that minority groups have to express dissenting opinions has always been seen—post hoc—as a positive value in Western democratic thought. It is only when minority dissent is accepted as part of the broader civic engagement process that the group will be recognized as bearers of real rights, as Appadurai argues:

> It has to do with the valuation of a rational debate, of the right to dissent, of the value of dissent as a sign of the larger value of free speech and opinion, and of the freedom to express dissenting opinions on matters of public moment without fear of retribution.[109]

To be sure, the political actions taken by MAS students to protest HB 2281 and the elimination of MAS represent vigorous engagement in our hallowed American democratic processes. Their commitment and engagement to their own education has deepened. These students and community members are more aware of the stakes involved in legislative activity, and have found a reason to express their civil rights in support for one of the few educational programs that they believed truly helped them succeed. They believe that HB 2281 is designed to thwart an education that gives them a better chance of educational success as it bolsters democratic activism.

We argue that legislative policies such as HB 2281—not the MAS courses—create racial division and feelings of resentment in Arizona.[110] HB 2281 is ideologically motivated legislation designed to keep Mexican-heritage students and other people of color from recognizing their commonalities, developing coalitions, and creating stronger democracy in Arizona. One tragic outcome of this law is that it eliminated a program that dramatically reduced the achievement gap among all low-income students.

Moreover, the implications of this bill reach beyond Mexican American studies and people of Mexican descent. The bill establishes a precedent that is likely to affect other ethnic studies departments, other school districts, programs other than ethnic studies, and eventually higher education. At stake in the public schools is the right of local communities to control public education.[111] The bill severely limits academic freedom; it limits teacher opportunities to help students develop their own critical thinking skills, so they can ask crucial questions about their world and to learn how to begin to answer these questions, thus to give them the keys to deepen their own understanding of their world. At its heart, the political fight over HB 2281 has been a struggle over the extent to which Arizona's students will engage in the American democratic process, and a struggle over how to prepare the next generation of Arizona's citizens and leaders.

Notes

1. West, 2004.
2. According to a Pew Report issued on July 14, 2011, the largest of all Latino groups, Mexican Americans grew by 7.2 million in the last decade (2000–2010), contributing to the rapid growth in the total number of Latinos in the United States. The report also shows that births among Mexican Americans have surpassed immigration as the main driver of the dynamic growth in the U.S. Latino population (Pew Research, 2011).
3. See, for example, Huntington, 2004.
4. Kilty and Vidal de Haymes, 2000; Short and Magaña, 2002.
5. Inda, 2006.
6. The bill proposed to changed the crime of being unlawfully present in the United States from a misdemeanor to an aggravated felony, which would have automatically made undocumented people "felons" and therefore permanently ineligible for any path toward legal residence.
7. For the text of this bill, go to www.govtrack.us/congress/bill.xpd?bill=h109-4437.
8. Fraga et al., 2010.
9. Bloemraad and Trost, 2008.
10. Passel and Taylor, 2010.
11. Cohen-Marks et al., 2009.
12. O'Leary, 2009.
13. See *Tucson Citizen* reporting about the event at: http://tucsoncitizen.com/morgue/2006/04/21/10060-tusd-chastised-for-huerta-speech/
14. Bloemraad and Trost, 2008.
15. Horne, 2007.
16. Arizona Legislature, 2009.
17. Cacho, 2010, 4.
18. Meier and Stewart, 1991.

19. Olsen, 2009.

20. Meier and Stewart, 1991, p. 5.

21. Sheridan, 1992; Heyman, 1991.

22. Appadurai, 2006, pp. 6–7.

23. Cacho, 2010, p. 29.

24. Light and von Scheven, 2008, p. 705.

25. Meier and Stewart, 1991.

26. U.S. Census, 2006.

27. Meier and Stewart, 1991, p. 61.

28. Appadurai, 2006.

29. Contemporary society has progressively grown sensitive to Spanish language conventions that systematically privilege the masculine subject (e.g., "Chicano") forms over the feminine (e.g., "Chicana'). Therefore, where possible and unless the particular author cited uses only the older conventions, we will include both masculine and feminine subjects, and be mindful that "Chicana Studies" curricula (mentioned next) may constitute a distinct discipline altogether from "Chicana Studies" curricula that evolved years afterward.

30. Rhoads and Martínez, 1988.

31. Gómez-Quiñones, 1994; Rosen, 1973.

32. Reuben, 1998.

33. Rhoads and Martínez, 1988.

34. This figure comes from The National Association of Chicano/Chicana Studies, an academic organization established in 1972 to promote communication and exchange of ideas among Chicana and Chicano scholars across all geographical and disciplinary boundaries (see www.naccs.org.)

35. O'Leary, 2005, 2007.

36. Hurtado, 2005; Pizarro, 1998.

37. Tanemura Morelli and Spencer, 2000.

38. Gonzalez, 2001; Muñoz, 1989; Pizarro, 1998.

39. Mazón and Weinberg, 2005.

40. O'Leary, 2009.

41. Levitts, 2007.

42. Although there are legal differences that determine legal and citizenship rights, the ability of the public and the media to make these distinctions among Latinos is questionable, which make Latinos in general more susceptible to prejudice and discrimination because they share many phenotypic and cultural traits with immigrants and noncitizens (Romero, 2008; Short and Magaña, 2002, 709; Plascencia, 2009).

43. O'Leary, 2009.

44. Crawford, 2008.

45. Michelson, 2001.

46. Short and Magaña, 2002.

47. Romero, 2008.

48. Goldsmith, Romero, Goldsmith, Escobedo, and Khoury, 2009.

49. Cacho, 2010, p. 29.

50. Even a cursory examination of the history of Mexican Americans in the United States will reveal that the questioning of the Latino place in U.S. society is not new.

51. Cohen-Marks et al., 2009; Kilty and Vidal de Haymes, 2000; Short and Magaña, 2002.

52. Fix and Zimmermann, 2001, 413; O'Leary and Sanchez, 2011; Pew Research, 2011; Romero, 2008.

53. O'Leary and Sanchez, 2011.

54. Fix and Zimmermann, 2001; O'Leary and Sanchez, 2011; Romero, 2008.

55. O'Leary, 2009.

56. A particularly insidious stipulation of Prop 300, a third component that received little attention during the election of November 2006, was that in addition to addressing eligibility requirement for education, the proposition also restricts eligibility for child care assistance to parents, guardians, and caregivers.

57. Although this law was later challenged alleging that it preempted U.S. exclusive jurisdiction over immigration regulation, on May 26, 2011, the U.S. Supreme Court ruled in a 5–3 vote to uphold the Arizona law.

58. On May 25, 2011, eleven TUSD teachers sued the state of Arizona. They alleged that the HB 2281 statutes were designed to unfairly limit freedom of expression. They claimed that when the school district was prohibited from using certain educational materials, the teachers' freedom to teach and students' freedom to learn were restricted. Their attorneys also claimed that four subsections of the statute lacked the "specificity and clarity" to stipulate what particular speech should be prohibited, and consequently the statute would be enforced arbitrarily. Their attorneys argued that this ambiguity threatened the teachers' rights to due process, because they could not anticipate what would be prohibited. The attorneys requested a summary judgment to invalidate the vague provisions of the law. On December 27, Administrative Law Judge Lewis Kowal rejected these claims and upheld State Superintendent Huppenthal's finding that TUSD was in violation of A.R.S. § 15-112. Subsequently, as a penalty for this violation Huppenthal instructed the Arizona Department of Education to withhold from TUSD 10 percent of its state funding, retroactive from the start of the school year. Meanwhile, the school board's composition had shifted with the death of Judy Burns, a board member who supported MAS. TUSD officials named an independent committee to select Burn's replacement. From over fifty applicants, Alexandre Sugiyma was appointed only a few weeks before a critical TUSD board meeting. His selection was swiftly criticized, because Sugiyma is a lecturer in the same University of Arizona department where TUSD board president and outspoken MAS opponent, Mark Stegeman, is a tenured professor. The newly-constituted board voted 4–1 to suspend the MAS program within days of Huppenthal's ruling. Shortly afterwards, over fifty book titles and other MAS instructional materials were removed from the TUSD classrooms while students were present. These banned books were placed in a repository, and the MAS teachers were re-assigned to other classes. Legal documents about this case are available at www.savethnicstudies.org.

59. Although threats to cuts to funding have historically plagued ethnic studies programs (Rivera and Burrola, 1984; Rochin, [1968] 1973), the tougher math and writing standards adopted by the state of Arizona in the last two years has resulted in only 57 percent of Arizona schools meeting those standards. In 2011, the percent of

Tucson area schools meeting those standards (56 percent) was down from 64 percent in 2010 (Huichochea 2001).

60. Cappellucci et al., 2011.

61. This figure is according to an *Arizona Capitol Times* article available at http://azcapitoltimes.com/news/2011/08/26/huppenthal-to-avoid-witness-stand-in-tusd-hearing/

62. See http://azcapitoltimes.com/news/2011/08/26/huppenthal-to-avoid-witness-stand-in-tusd-hearing/ retrieved 1 September 2011.

63. See also Cacho, 2010.

64. Cacho, 2010, p. 30.

65. Cacho, 2010.

66. Morín, 2005; Santa Ana, 2002, p. 285.

67. Ginwright, Noguera, and Cammarota, 2006.

68. *Arizona Republic*, 2011.

69. Cabrera, 2011.

70. Acuña, 1988; Morín, 2005; Santa Ana, 2002.

71. Cacho, 2010, p. 31.

72. Romano-V., 1969.

73. Tanemura Morelli and Spencer, 2000.

74. Romero and Roberts, 1998.

75. Tanemura Morelli and Spencer, 2000.

76. Freire, 2000. Banking methods refer to traditional top-down teaching approaches that disregard the knowledge that the student brings to the classroom and dismisses the analytic capacity of disempowered students. In this method, the student's head is an empty vessel, the teacher is a funnel, and real knowledge is abstract decontextualized data that teachers "deposit" into the student's mind. Freire's critique is that this method disengages students of the working poor from real learning, so they remain easy targets for further exploitation. For Freire, the student must be actively engaged to critically assess the content of knowledge that teachers offer them. True knowledge provides a powerful set of tools for students to overcome their disenfranchised circumstances.

77. Stanton-Salazar, 2001. Moreover, these new approaches paralleled the human tendency to cooperate and exhibit compassion and caring (Cammarota and Romero, 2009; Romero, A., 2008).

78. Vélez-Ibáñez and Greenberg, 1992.

79. Cacho, 2010.

80. O'Leary, 2006; Stanton-Salazar, 2001; Vélez-Ibáñez and Greenberg, 1992.

81. Cappellucci et al., 2011, 59, emphasis in original.

82. Cappellucci et al., 2011.

83. AIMS is the standardized test in Arizona public high schools that students have to pass in order to graduate. It is administered in three subject areas (reading, math, and writing), and given the first time during the sophomore year. Students have multiple opportunities to pass the test, and final passing rates are based upon the aggregate of all students who have passed the AIMS test after its final offering during their senior year.

84. Department of Accountability and Research. (2011, January 6a). *AIMS achievement comparison for students taking one or more ethnic studies classes: Initial passing rate versus cumulative passing rate by AIMS subject and cohort year.* Tucson, AZ: Tucson Unified School District. For report copies, contact the office of the Director of Accountability and Research, Tucson Unified School District, Education Annex, 442 East 7th Street, Tucson, AZ 85705.

85. Department of Accountability and Research. (2011, January 6a).

86. Department of Accountability and Research. (2011, January 6a).

87. Department of Accountability and Research. (2011, January 6b). *Selected statistics—2010 (four year) graduation cohort.* Tucson, AZ: Tucson Unified School District. For report copies, contact the office of the Director of Accountability and Research, Tucson Unified School District, Education Annex, 442 East 7th Street, Tucson, AZ 85705.

88. Cacho, 2010.

89. Phinney, Jacoby, and Silva, 2007.

90. Phinney, Jacoby, and Silva, 2007.

91. In 1973, after years of litigation and several lower court rulings, the U.S. Supreme Court decided in *Keyes v. School District No. 1 of Denver,* that Mexican Americans were an identifiable minority group within public school systems and protected under the Fourteenth Amendment of the U.S. Constitution. (See Meier and Stewart, 1991, 66–70.)

92. Phinney, Jacoby, and Silva, 2007.

93. García Coll et al., 1996; O'Leary and Romero, 2011; Sellers et al., 2006.

94. Macias, 2006; Romero and Roberts, 1998.

95. Garcia, 2005.

96. Markus and Kityama, 1991.

97. Cappellucci et al., 2011.

98. Appadurai, 2006.

99. Appadurai, 2006, p. 53.

100. West, 2004.

101. Appadurai, 2006.

102. For example, Brown, Carnoy, Currie, Duster, Oppenhiemer, Shultz, & Wellman, 2003.

103. See also Tanemura Morelli and Spencer, 2000.

104. O'Leary and Romero, 2011.

105. Romero and O'Leary, in press.

106. The most frequent type of discipline is a verbal reprimand, which is difficult to document.

107. Meier and Stewart, 1991.

108. Meier and Stewart, 1991.

109. Appadurai, 2006, p. 63.

110. See also Cacho, 2010.

111. Meier and Stewart, 1991.

References

Acuña, R. (1988). *Occupied America: A history of Chicanos.* New York: HarperCollins.

Appadurai, A. (2006). *Fear of small numbers: An essay on the geography of hate.* Durham: Duke University Press.

Arizona Department of Education. (2006). Arizona report card academic year 2005–2006 (For Tucson High Magnet School). Retrieved from http://www.ade.az.gov/srcs/ReportCards/57642007.pdf

Arizona Department of Education. (2011, January 6a). *AIMS achievement comparison for students taking one or more ethnic studies classes: Initial passing rate versus cumulative passing rate by AIMS subject and cohort year.* Tucson, AZ: Tucson Unified School District.

Arizona Department of Education. (2011, January 6b). *Selected statistics—2010 (four year) graduation cohort.* Tucson, AZ: Tucson Unified School District.

Arizona Department of Education. (2011). Accountability and performance measures for schools, No Child Left Behind (NCLB) Annual Yearly Progress (AYP). Retrieved from http://www.ade.az.gov/azlearns/aypdeterminations.asp.

Arizona Legislature (49th Legislature, 1st sess.). (2009). Committee on judiciary senate amendments to S.B. 1069, Retrieved from http://www.azleg.gov/DocumentsForBill.asp?Bill_Number=SB1069&Session_ID=87.

Arizona State Legislature (48th Legislature, 2nd sess.). (2008). Homeland Security Advisory Councils; Membership. Retrieved from http://www.azleg.gov/DocumentsForBill.asp?Bill_Number=1108&Session_Id=86.

Bloemraad, I., & Trost, C. (2008). It's a family affair: Intergenerational mobilization in the Spring 2006 protests. *American Behavioral Scientist, 52*(4), 507–532.

Brown, M. K., Carnoy, M., Currie, E., Duster, T., Oppenheimer, D.B., Shultz, M. M., & Wellman, D. (2003). *Whitewashing race: The myth of a color-blind society.* Berkeley, CA: University of California Press.

Cabrera, N. L. (2011, July 7). Flashpoint over struggle to preserve Mexican-American Studies in Arizona. *Diverse Issues in Higher Education, 28*(11), 37.

Cacho, L. M. (2010). But some of us are wise: Academic illegitimacy and the affective value of ethnic studies. (Viewpoint essay). *The Black Scholar, 40*(4), 28–36.

Cammarota, J., & Romero, A. (2009). The social justice education program: A critically compassionate intellectualism for Chicana/o students. In W. Ayers, T. Quinn, & D. Stovall (Eds.), *Handbook of social justice in education* (pp. 465–476). New York: Routledge.

Cappellucci, D. F., Williams, C., Hernandez, J. J., Nelson, L. P., Casteel, T., Gilzean, G., & Gershom, F. (2011). *Curriculum Audit of the Mexican American Studies Department, Tucson Unified School District.* Miami Lakes, FL: Cambium Learning.

Cohen-Marks, M., Nuño, S. A., & Sanchez, G. R. (2009). Look back in anger? Voter opinions of Mexican Immigrants in the aftermath of the 2006 immigration demonstrations. *Urban Affairs Review, 44*(5), 695–717.

Crawford, A. (2008, October 2). Hispanic panic: GOP Stokes fears of 'illegal' voters. *The Indypendent.* Retrieved 18 February 2012 from www.indypendent.org/2008/10/02/hispanic-panic/

Fix, M., & Zimmermann, W. (2001). All under one roof: Mixed-status families in an era of reform. *International Migration Review, 35*(2), 397–419.

Fraga, L., Garcia, J., Hero, R., Jones-Correa, M., Martinez-Ebers, V., & Segura, G. (2010). *Making it home: Latino lives in America.* Philadelphia, PA: Temple Univesity Press.

Freire, P. (2000). *Pedagogy of the oppressed.* (M. B. Ramos, Trans.). New York: Continuum.

Garcia, C. (2005). *Buscando trabajo*: Social networking among immigrants from Mexico to the United States. *Hispanic Journal of Behavioral Sciences, 27*(2), 3–22.

García Coll, C., Crnic, K., Lamberty, G., Wasik, B. H., Jenkins, R., Vázquez García, H., & McAdoo, H. P. (1996). An integrative model for the study of developmental competencies in minority children. *Child Development 67*(5), 1891–1914.

Ginwright, S., Noguera, P., & Cammarota, J. (Eds.). (2006). *Beyond resistance! Youth activism and community change.* New York: Taylor & Francis.

Goldsmith, P., Romero, M., Goldsmith, R. R., Escobedo, M., & Khoury, L. (2009). Ethno-racial profiling and state violence in a southwest barrio. *Aztlán: A Journal of Chicano Studies, 34*(1), 93–124.

Gómez-Quiñones, J. (1994). *Roots of Chicano politics, 1600–1940.* Albuquerque: University of New Mexico Press.

Gonzalez, K. P. (2001). Inquiry as a process of learning about the Other and the Self. *Qualitative Studies in Education 14*(4), 543–562.

Heyman, J. McC. (1991). *Life and labor on the border.* Tucson: University of Arizona Press.

Horne, T. (2007). An open letter to the citizens of Tucson. Retrieved from http://www.electtomhorne.com/open_letter_01.pdf.

Huicochea, A. (2011, July 27). "Adequate progress" gets harder for schools. *Arizona Daily Star*, A1.

Huntington, S. P. (2004, March/April). The Hispanic challenge. *Foreign Policy.* Available online at http://foreignpolicy.com.

Hurtado, A. (2005). The transformative power of Chicana/o Studies: Social justice and education. *International Journal of Qualitative Studies in Education 18*(2), 185–197.

Inda, J. X. (2006). *Targeting immigrants: Government, technology, and ethics.* Malden MA: Blackwell Publishing.

Kilty, K. M., & Vidal de Haymes, M. (2000). Racism, nativism, and exclusion: Public policy, immigration and the Latino experience in the United States. *Journal of Poverty 4*(1/2), 1–25.

Levitts, J. (2007). The truth about Voter Fraud. Retrieved from http://www.immigrationpolicy.org/index.php?content=fc080724.

Light, I., & von Scheven., E. (2008). Mexican migration networks in the United States, 1980–2000. *International Migration Review, 42*(3): 704–728.

Macias, T. (2006). *Mestizo in America: Generations of Mexican ethnicity in the suburban southwest.* Tucson, AZ: University of Arizona Press.

Markus, H., & Kityama, S. (1991). Culture and The Self: Implications for cognition, emotion, and motivation. *Psychological Review, 98*, 224–253.

Mazón, A., & Weinberg, P. (2005). Prop 200 passes in Arizona making anti-immigrant racism law on the border. *Network News* (pp. 10–12). National Network for Immigrant and Refugee Rights (NNIR).

Meier, K. J., & Stewart, J. (1991). *The politics of Hispanic education: Un paso pa'lante y dos pa'tras.* New York: University of New York Press.

Michelson, M. R. (2001). The effect of national mood on Mexican American political opinion. *Hispanic Journal of Behavioral Sciences, 23*(1), 57–70.

Morín, J. L. (2005). *Latina/o rights and justice in the United States: Perspectives and approaches.* Durham, NC: Carolina Academic Press.

Muñoz, C. (1989). *Youth, identity, power: The Chicano Movement.* London: Verso.

O'Leary, A. O. (2005). In search of El Pueblo Unido: Children's picture books and teaching about community. *The Journal of Border Educational Research, 3*(1), 46–55.

O'Leary, A. O. (2006). Social exchange practices among Mexican-origin women in Nogales, Arizona: Prospects for education acquisition. *Aztlán: A Journal of Chicano Studies, 31*(1), 63–94.

O'Leary, A. O. (2007). Introduction: Movement politics and Chicano Studies. In A. O. O'Leary (Ed.), *Chicano studies: The discipline and the journey,* pp. v–xx. Dubuque, IO: Kendall Hunt Publishing.

O'Leary, A. O. (2009). *Arizona's legislative-imposed injunctions: Implications for immigrant civic and political participation.* Washington, DC: Woodrow Wilson International Center for Scholars. Retrieved 18 February 2012 from www.wilsoncenter. org/sites/default/files/Tuscon%20Eng.pdf

O'Leary, A. O., & Romero, A. J. (2011). Chicana/o students respond to Arizona's anti–ethnic studies bill, SB 1108: Civic engagement, ethnic identity, and well-being. *Aztlán: A Journal of Chicano Studies, 36*(1), 9–36.

O'Leary, A. O., & Sanchez, A. (2011). Anti-immigrant Arizona: Ripple effects and mixed immigration status households under "policies of attrition" considered. *Journal of Borderland Studies, 26*(1), 1–19.

Olsen, L. (2009). The role of advocacy in shaping immigrant education: A California case study. *Teachers College Record, 111*(3), 817–850.

Passel, J. S., & Taylor, P. (2010). *Unauthorized immigrants and their U.S.-born children.* Washington, DC: Pew Hispanic Research.

Pew Research Center. (2011). *The Mexican-American boom: Births overtake immigration.* Washington, DC.

Phinney, J. S., Jacoby, B., & Silva, C. (2007). Positive intergroup attitudes: The role of ethnic identity. *International Journal of Behavioral Development, 30*(5), 478–490.

Pizarro, M. (1998). "Chicana/o Power" epistemology and methodology for social justice and empowerment in Chicana/o communities. *Qualitative Studies in Education, 11*(1), 57–80.

Plascencia, L. (2009). The "undocumented" Mexican migrant question: Re-examining the framing of law and illegalization in the United States. *Urban Anthropology, 38*(2–4), 378–344.

Reuben, J. A. (1998). Reforming the university: Student protests and the demand for a "relevant" curriculum. In G. J. DeGroot (Ed.), *Student protest: The sixties and after,* pp. 153–168. London: Longman.

Rhoads, R. A., & Martínez, J. G. (1988). Chicana/o students as agents of social change: A case study of identity politics in higher education. *Bilingual Review 23*(2), 124–136.

Rivera, J., & Burrola, L. R. (1984). Chicano Studies programs in higher education: Scenarios for further research. *Aztlán: A Journal of Chicano Studies, 15*(2), 277–293.

Rochin, R. I. ([1968] 1973). The short and turbulent life of Chicano studies: A preliminary study of emerging programs and problems. *Social Science Quarterly, 43*(4),
485–894.

Romano-V., O. I. (1969). The historical and intellectual presence of Mexican-Americans. *El Grito, II*(2), 32–43.

Romero, A. (2008). *Towards a critically compassionate intellectualism model of transformative urban education* (Unpublished doctoral dissertation). Tucson: University
of Arizona.

Romero, A. J., & O'Leary, A. O. (forthcoming). "When you know yourself you're
more confident": Resilience and stress of undergraduate students in the face of
"Anti-Ethnic Studies" bills. In J. Cammarota & A. Romero (Eds.), *Raza Studies: The
Public Option for Educational Revolution*.

Romero, A. J., and Roberts, R. E. (1998). Perception of discrimination and ethnocul-
tural variables in a diverse group of adolescents. *Journal of Adolescence, 21*, 641–656.

Romero, M. (2008). The inclusion of citizenship status in intersectionality: What
immigration raids tells us about mixed-status families, the State, and assimilation.
International Journal of the Family, 34(2), 131–152.

Rosen, G. (1973). The development of the Chicano Movement in Los Angeles from
1967 to 1969. *Aztlán 4*(1), 155–181.

Santa Ana, O. (2002). *Brown tide rising: Metaphors of Latinos in contemporary American public discourse.* Austin: University of Texas Press.

Sellers, R. M., Copeland-Linder, N., Martin, P. P., & Lewis, R. L. (2006). Racial
identity matters: The relationship between racial discrimination and psychological
functioning in African American adolescents. *Journal of Research on Adolescence,
16*(2), 187–216.

Sheridan, T. E. (1992). *Los Tucsonenses.* Tucson: University of Arizona Press.

Short, R., & Magaña, L. (2002). Political rhetoric, immigration attitudes, and contemporary prejudice: A Mexican American dilemma. *Journal of Social Psychology,
142*(6), 701–712.

Stanton-Salazar, R. (2001). *Manufacturing hope and despair: The school and kin support networks of U.S.-Mexican youth.* New York: Teachers College Press.

Tanemura Morelli, P. T., & Spencer, M. S. (2000). Use and support of multicultural
and antiracist education: Research-informed interdisciplinary social work practice.
Social Work, 45(2), 166–175.

U.S. Census Bureau. (2006). American community survey. Available at census.gov.

U.S. Census Bureau. (2008). *Utah is fastest-growing state.* Press Release. Accessed
September 17, 2010. Retrieved from http://www.census.gov/newsroom/releases/
archives/population/cb08-187.html.

Vélez-Ibáñez, C. G., & Greenberg, J. B. (1992). Formation and transformation of
funds of knowledge among US.-Mexican households. *Anthropology and Education
Quarterly, 23*, 313–335.

West, C. (2004). *Democracy matters: Winning the fight against imperialism.* New York:
Penguin.

Who's in charge at Tucson Unified? (2011, April 28). Retrieved from http://www.az
central.com/arizonarepublic/opinions/articles/2011/04/28/20110428thur1-28.html.

7

From *Gonzales* to *Flores*

A Return to the "Mexican Room"?

Patricia Gándara

ENGLISH LANGUAGE HEGEMONY has characterized Arizona since its admission to statehood in 1912. In 1910 Arizona voters rejected admission to the union jointly with New Mexico, in large part because New Mexico, whose population was 50 percent Spanish speaking, had dual language policies while Arizona prided itself on being 95 percent "American," and teaching only in English.[1] The state has an equally long history of denying educational rights to Mexican-origin children. While not as pervasive as the segregation of African Americans, separation of Mexican-origin students was widely practiced in the state throughout its history.[2] For example, Jeanne M. Powers describes the period during the mid-1940s:

> While districts argued that segregation was necessary because of students' poor English skills, the segregation of Mexican American students in Arizona's public schools was not an isolated practice but occurred in tandem with other discriminatory practices that restricted the social rights of Mexican Americans.[3]

De la Trinidad (2008) points out that in the post–World War II years, "Communities with significant Spanish-speaking and Native American student populations, particularly mining towns such as Douglas, Ajo, and Clifton, almost always provided separate facilities or classrooms for so-called 'instructional purposes.' . . . In some locations such as Nogales, Tucson, and Williams, separate facilities were provided for 'Negro' pupils while Mexican students were placed in separate classrooms on the grounds that the instruction of these pupils is furthered by placing them with children from similar home environments."[4]

The U.S. Commission on Civil Rights found in its groundbreaking 1972 study of Mexican Americans in the Southwest that the reason for the segregation of Mexican-origin pupils was not for the benefit of these students, as Arizona educational officials often argued. State educational practices, if not always policies, reflected dominant Anglo Arizonans' negative perceptions of Mexican people and culture. The commission cited the following comment in an Arizona newspaper from the 1930s:

> Arizona Mexicans have been segregated from the more fortunate Arizonans, both as strangers belonging to an alien race of conquered Indians, and as persons whose enforced status in the lowest economic levels make them less admirable than other people.[5]

Not a lot has changed. Today it is common to hear similar comments about Mexican immigrants in Arizona. Republican State Senator Karen Johnson was quoted in 2005, saying, "The culture of the United States is being destroyed. The illegals don't want to be a part of American culture. They want to bring their Mexican-Hispanic culture here."[6] Similarly, in an effort to make the case against educating Mexican immigrant students in Arizona schools, in March 2011 another Republican state senator, Lori Klein, read a letter on the senate floor from a substitute teacher who claimed, "Most of the Hispanic students do not want to be educated but rather be gang members [sic] and gangsters. . . . They hate America and are determined to reclaim this area for Mexico."[7]

The letter, which was initially sent to State Senator Russell Pearce, author of multiple anti-immigrant bills, was attributed to a person who was substitute teaching in a suburban Arizona eighth-grade classroom. School personnel refuted the characterization of the students offered by the substitute teacher.[8] Moreover, the teacher in question had been assigned to anger management classes by a court and had restraining orders against him because of his inability to control his anger against his own family. Yet Senator Klein did not hesitate to enter it into the senate record as evidence of the bad behavior of Mexican-origin students.

The segregation of students practiced in Arizona has historically produced much lower academic achievement and much higher dropout rates for the Mexican-origin students,[9] facts that in a chicken-egg argument were used as a basis to continue segregating them. Some Anglo parents and school board members over the century argued that the Mexican children should be separated from the white children because they did not learn as well and did not value education as highly, thus they needed "special attention" in special settings. This often resulted in a "Mexican Room," where they were segregated from their white peers and provided inferior resources and teachers, which lead to an inferior education.[10]

Following on this history of denial of equal educational opportunity, Arizona became one of the first states that a federal court ordered to end segregating its students. In 1951, three years before the *Brown v. Board of Education* decision, U.S. District Court Judge David Ling ruled in a case from the Phoenix area that the "segregation of school children in separate school buildings because of racial or national origin . . . constitutes a denial of the equal protection of the laws guaranteed to petitioners as citizens of the United States."[11] The 1951 *Gonzales* decision and two others from the Southwest, the 1946 *Mendez v. Westminster* California decision and the 1948 *Delgado v. Bastrop* Texas decision, set the stage for *Brown v. Board of Education* in 1954. However, Powers and Patton argue that the 1951 *Gonzales* case was different and significant in that "it was the first case in which a court embraced the social science critique of racism . . . [and] made a clear and unqualified statement that racial segregation in elementary schools was unconstitutional."[12]

Despite the ruling, Arizona continued to segregate Mexican-origin pupils. In 1974 yet another class action suit was filed, this time against the Tucson schools, for segregating Mexican-origin pupils. In *Mendoza v. Tucson School District No. 1*, the district court decided that the school district did not intend to discriminate against the Mexican students, but did find de facto segregation in thirty schools and in 1978 ordered them desegregated. Thus, Arizona has struggled over much of the last century with the segregation of its Mexican-origin pupils in spite of court orders finding such segregation unconstitutional and illegal.

Given this history, it is unfortunate that now in the twenty-first century Arizona again finds itself in the midst of an educational firestorm. It is fueled in part by a twenty-year-old case, *Horne v. Flores*, in which the segregation of Mexican-origin English learners (ELs) in "Mexican Rooms" is again at the center of the debate.[13]

Flores v. Arizona, 1992

The *Flores v. Arizona* case began long before today's notorious anti-immigrant legislation and policies riveted the nation's attention on Arizona. In 1992 Miriam Flores sued the Nogales Unified School District for failing to provide her and other EL students an adequate education. Flores claimed that the district did not provide adequately prepared teachers, adequate instructional materials, or a program supported by sufficient district funds to ensure that she and her fellow EL students were given an equal educational opportunity, as provided in the Equal Educational Opportunity Act (EEOA). The case dragged on for nearly a decade and a half because the state of Arizona refused to obey the federal court's order and explain how its limited funding levels for EL student services bore any rational relationship to the students' actual needs.

To force Arizona to comply, in 2006 the court began fining the state $500,000 a day for failing to respond to its orders. This forced Arizona to appeal and the case ultimately arrived in 2009 at the U.S. Supreme Court. The case then became known as *Horne v. Flores.*

The Legal Rights of Latino Students and English Language Learners

During the second half of the last century, a series of court decisions and federal regulations built a sturdy foundation of educational rights for all children in the United States, but especially for students of color. Beginning with the landmark *Brown v. Board of Education* Supreme Court decision in 1954, black children were guaranteed an equal education in desegregated schools. The Court found that segregated education was inherently unequal and therefore black students had to be provided access to the same schools as white students. It took a decade, however, before the Civil Rights Act codified these rights and provided sanctions that would enforce the law. Title VI of the Civil Rights Act of 1964 would form the basis for outlawing discrimination based on "national origin," which came to be interpreted not just as the foreign born but also those who spoke a language other than English. In 1968, the Congress passed the Elementary and Secondary Education Act, which included Title VII, or the Bilingual Education Act. Though largely symbolic in its initial iteration, it did advance the right of English language learners (ELLs) (at that time known as LEP students, namely, "limited English proficient") to a bilingual education insofar as was possible for local schools. However, to help ensure its passage, the act purposefully did not define "bilingual education" and this would contribute to the controversy around bilingual education in years to come.

In the 1973 Supreme Court case, *Keyes v. Denver School District No. 1,* the right to attend a desegregated school was affirmed for Latino students as well as black students.[14] Within a year of *Keyes,* the rights of immigrant students who did not speak English were extended in significant ways. The Supreme Court, in a unanimous 1974 decision in *Lau v. Nichols,* based on Title VI, found that limited English speaking students must be provided with equal access to the curriculum of the public schools.[15] The Court did not spell out how this was to occur, though the U.S. Department of Education soon followed with regulations that required public schools with a minimum number of pupils who did not speak English to offer bilingual instruction. Although the regulations were controversial and quickly withdrawn, most educators assumed that some kind of bilingual instruction would be necessary to provide access to the curriculum for those students whose English was too weak to study only in English. A month after the *Lau* decision, the Congress passed EEOA, which provided that school districts must "take appropriate action to overcome language barriers that impede equal participation" in instructional programs.[16] "Appropriate action" was not defined until 1981 in the Fifth Circuit case, *Castañeda v. Pickard*,[17] which outlined three criteria for determining if the intent of the EEOA was met: (1) that the intervention be based on sound educational theory; (2) that it be effectively implemented with adequate resources and personnel; and (3) that over time it could be demonstrated to be effective in overcoming language barriers. To date, most challenges to programs for EL students have turned on the first two criteria, perhaps in part because the law did not make clear how much time would need to pass to determine if a program was effective, and in part because effectiveness with EL students tends to be relative. There is no indisputable standard for effectiveness. And while scholars have looked to the Castañeda decision as providing important guidance on appropriateness of programs, there has been little test of the rulings' strength in the courts.

Finally, in 1982, the Supreme Court overturned a Fifth Circuit Court of Appeals decision in *Plyler v. Doe,* with a 5–4 vote, granting all resident children of the United States the right to a free K–12 education, regardless of their legal status.[18] *Plyler* guaranteed the same access to basic schooling for undocumented children as for those who are native born. Fundamentally, the Court found that it did not serve anyone's interest to create a permanent underclass of unschooled individuals, and since the children had no choice in coming to the United States, they should not be punished for an act over which they had no control. Thus, by 1982 rights for immigrant and nonimmigrant Latino students included free public education regardless of legal status in a nonsegregated environment, and access to the core curriculum provided to all other students, with the support of adequately resourced programs designed to overcome any language barriers they may have. Although the term *bilingual education* has been used repeatedly, no firm right to a bilingual education has ever been established, nor has the term been carefully defined in the law.

Proposition 203 and the Four-Hour English Language Development (ELD) Block

In 2000, while the *Flores v. Arizona* case dragged on, Arizona voters passed Proposition 203. Like California's Proposition 227 two years prior, Prop 203 forbade bilingual instruction to ELLs ten years of age or younger under most circumstances. State Representative (and candidate for State Senate) Tom Horne took credit for helping to pass the legislation as he championed the initiative in his role on the House Education Committee. The law established Structured English Immersion (SEI)—a method of instruction that uses English almost exclusively to teach English—as the default language program EL students would receive. Prop 203 set up more impediments than the California law for parents to seek bilingual education or other alternative curricula. With the same specious claims that were used in California, the anti-bilingual education proponents of SEI promised very rapid English acquisition (in one year) and increased EL academic achievement. As is well documented, Arizona's SEI program failed to deliver on any of its claims.[19] As Eugene García, former member of the Arizona English Language Learner Task Force that imposed the current program, and his colleagues noted, "the instructional policies currently in place in Arizona are having a negative effect on the academic achievement and educational experiences of [EL] students."[20]

In 2006, after several years of lackluster results, and with the federal court continuing to pressure the state to demonstrate that it had an effective program for ELs, House Bill 2064 established the Arizona English Language Learner Task Force. The task force was charged with developing a "research-based" EL curriculum that would be provided for a maximum of two years for each EL student. After that, students would be expected to be fully fluent in English. In 2008 the task force implemented statewide a curriculum based on an intuitively attractive but false premise that increased time on task results automatically in a proportional increase in learning. That is, the more time spent teaching something, the greater amount of learning that will take place. However, if the instructional methods are not effective and the students are not actively engaged, learning will not increase, no matter how much time is spent on a task. Further, students cannot maintain attention on a lesson indefinitely. They reach a saturation point beyond which they cannot learn more.[21] The task force believed that if one or two hours of direct instruction in English is good, four hours would be even better, in spite of the lack of educational research to support this contention. An educational consultant of dubious background named Kevin Clark[22] and the task force created four EL courses,[23] which were measured by the state ELL test, Arizona English Language Learner Assessment (AZELLA).

The issue of how best to educate students whose primary language is not English has been the source of considerable debate. However, the debate has more often been fueled by ideology than by actual research findings. To determine which method is most effective, it is imperative to ask, "effective for what?" Most rapid acquisition of English? Best achievement outcomes? Developing skills in more than one language? With respect to acquisition of English, the research concludes that both English-only and bilingual methods tend to yield very similar results. Over time—usually by about fifth grade—students in both programs acquire approximately the same level of skill in English, though English-only methods may result in more rapid acquisition of basic English skills at early grade levels.[24] However, if the goal is superior achievement outcomes, the research shows convincingly that students who are taught to read in their primary language have better long-term reading outcomes.[25] Finally, if the goal is for students to develop capacity in more than one language, bilingual methods are obviously superior. While a few studies have concluded that bilingual instruction is *no more effective* than English-only instruction, no major study has ever concluded that English-only instruction is actually superior to bilingual with respect to achievement outcomes in English,[26] and achievement outcomes in the primary language are rarely ever evaluated.[27] Thus, given that there is no long-term advantage to English-only instruction, either with respect to English acquisition or academic outcomes, and that it prevents ELs from developing their native language skills, which would provide them with the lifetime advantage of being bilingual, it seems that a bilingual education would simply make good sense. Yet an intolerant language ideology— a belief system that supports an English-only mentality toward immigrant students (though not for native English speakers whose parents seek to have their children develop bilingual skills)—holds sway over research. (See Leeman, this volume, for more on language ideologies.)

It is also important to note that there are many models of "bilingual education" and all do not yield the same outcomes. The most common form of bilingual education practiced in the United States is Transitional Bilingual Education (TBE) whose goal is to help students to bridge into English with some support in the native language. Students are typically transitioned into English-only instruction after a period of two or three years. There is no intent with TBE to develop bilingualism or biliteracy, but many studies find that incorporating the primary language in instruction helps students to acquire fundamentals of the core curriculum. Alternatively, in Developmental Bilingual Education, the intent is to create biliterate individuals and so instruction in both English and the native language continues at least through grade school. Carefully designed bilingual classrooms should also integrate EL students with native English speakers as much as possible. Most bilingual classes of whatever kind, however, focus primarily on instructing English learners. Dual Language programs, a third model, have the intent of creating biliterate individuals by mixing both ELLs and native English speakers in the same classroom and teaching in two languages to both groups. These programs have the added advantage that they tend to reduce ethnic and cultural prejudice and enhance intergroup relations by bringing together students from very different backgrounds into equal status instructional settings.[28] That is, both the ELLs and the native English speakers are placed in a situation in which they are learning *from each other.*

In contrast in the Arizona model, students are placed into the four-hour daily ELD program of structured English immersion on the basis of their scores on the AZELLA.[29] The ELD program segregates EL students for *at least* four hours per day in classrooms comprised solely of other students who do not speak English and where teachers are mandated to focus on the teaching of English—and *not* on other academic subjects. There is general agreement in the scholarly literature that "Academic English," the type of English that students need to succeed in academic settings, is only learned when taught in the context of academic subject matter.[30] Simply teaching vocabulary does not teach students how to *think* in and about Academic English. Thus, the research does not support Arizona's practice of completely separating the instruction of English from the instruction of academic content. Moreover, while many researchers note that it is important to teach specific academic language skills to English learners, they also warn that it is critical to provide students with the opportunity to acquire those skills in natural settings,[31] and the most natural setting is with other students who are native English speakers. In sum, the Academic English that English learners need to survive and thrive in school is best learned in language-rich settings, with many opportunities to use academic language in natural settings and in interaction with other speakers of the language—not in segregated classrooms devoted to the teaching of discrete language skills among peers who are equally incapable of modeling strong English usage.

Students in the four-hour program are supposed to remain in these classes until they can test as proficient in English, which the Task Force suggested should normally be one year. However, at the time *Horne v. Flores* went to court, the state of Arizona was keeping no record of how many EL students statewide were annually reclassified as proficient in English to track the effectiveness of its programs.[32] We turn to Karen Lillie and her colleagues, who conducted an ethnographic study in five school districts and eighteen Arizona classrooms. Regarding the four-hour ELD block, Arizona teachers and instructional leaders rejected the Task Force's premise that most students could become fluent in English within one year. Lillie and her colleagues wrote:

> Although the Arizona Department of Education claims that students can exit out of the SEI program in one year, our observations in first through twelfth grade indicated otherwise. After interviewing more than twenty education professionals in all five districts, the response to the question of whether students are passing as proficient in the one-year time frame was a resounding "No." Coaches and teachers noted that it takes students more than a year, and more likely three or four to pass out of the model. . . . [T]he few students that did pass

out after only one year were kindergarteners. [However] many did not pass the AZELLA the following year during their monitor stage and were reclassified and placed back in the four-hour ELD classroom.[33]

Two years in a linguistically-segregated setting with a limited K–12 curriculum condemns many English learners to a potentially unbridgeable achievement gap. However, the pace at which ELD students are able to demonstrate English proficiency has even more immediate consequences for secondary students. Denial of access to the core curriculum (while the student is segregated into the intensive English classes for most of the day) means that most high school EL students are unable to acquire the credits they need to graduate with their peers, much less to be ready for college. For many of these students, the solution to this no-win situation is to drop out. Teachers and principals were acutely aware of this situation:

> [A] principal at the high school level mentioned that ELLs were taking at least up to three years to exit out of the four-hour block. One coordinator commented that only those ELLs who came to the school with a strong schooling background and literacy in their [home language] were able to pass out in under a two-year time frame.[34]

In fact, even one year in a program that withholds instruction in the core academic subjects that are taught to other students can have enormously negative consequences for English learners. It has now been amply demonstrated that most ELLs begin school, at whatever grade level, significantly behind their English-speaking peers,[35] and so from the very beginning there is a gap to be closed. Adding even one year to this gap can make it virtually impossible for these students to catch up with their English-speaking peers, especially when additional instructional time and resources are not provided for these students. This issue was at the center of the 1974 *Lau v. Nichols* Supreme Court decision, when the Court found that LEP students had a right to access to the same curriculum as English-speaking students.

The U.S. Supreme Court Ruling on *Horne v. Flores*

In 2009 the U.S. Supreme Court ruled against Miriam Flores and other EL students. In the case, now called *Horne v. Flores*, the Court ruled that the district court erred in insisting that Arizona had to demonstrate a rational relationship between the funding of programs for ELLs and their effectiveness, citing a hotly contested line of research that suggests money doesn't matter for schooling outcomes. In spite of numerous amicus briefs that cited a large body of research showing a clear relationship between quality of resources and student outcomes, the Court relied heavily on a narrow line of research that argues for a weak relationship between expenditures and academic outcomes.[36] A major problem with the literature on which the Court relied is that it drew conclusions based on economic models that did not distinguish *how* school funds were, or could be, used. This line of reasoning runs counter to common sense. If money does not matter, why indeed, do parents prefer to send their children to well-resourced schools with competent teachers who are paid sufficiently well that they are likely to remain in their positions?[37]

The high court also excused Arizona from not responding to the district court orders on the basis that "a significant change in factual conditions" had likely occurred, and it remanded the case back to the federal district court to "clarify" several issues that could form the basis for concluding that Arizona was in compliance with the federal court order. Among the issues that the Court suggested might be reviewed were whether the state had met its obligation to its EL students by shifting from bilingual education to a Structured English Immersion program, which the Court characterized as "significantly more effective"; as well as if modest increases in funding for education generally had better met the needs of EL students; and if structural and managerial changes that had been made in the Nogales school district (where the lawsuit was first lodged) had appreciably improved the instructional program for its ELLs.

Mounting a Challenge

By the time the remanded *Horne v. Flores* case was heard in federal court in Arizona in the fall of 2010, Horne was in the midst of an election that would promote him from State Superintendent of Public Instruction to State Attorney General, and the case had been joined by the Arizona Legislature. Arizona Governor Jan Brewer had also signed SB 1070, targeting undocumented residents of the state with inspection of documents pertaining to immigration status by any officer of the law who suspected them of being in the country illegally. (For more on SB 1070, see Chin et al., this volume.) This was followed immediately by HB 2281, a bill written by Horne that requires K–12 school districts to dismantle ethnic studies programs that promote "the overthrow of the U.S. government." Districts found to be out of compliance would suffer a 10 percent cut in their budgets. (See O'Leary et al., this volume, for more on HB 2281.)

The state of Arizona spared no expense in hiring a team of lawyers from the state's most prestigious law firms to defend itself in the case rather than going to its in-house state-employed attorneys.[38] By contrast, a very committed and knowledgeable public interest lawyer represented *Flores* with virtually no resources. In addition to being able to access relatively unlimited resources, the Arizona Department of Education (ADE) could also access any district or school information it wanted or needed. However, as State Attorney General, Tom Horne did not hesitate to exercise his power as the state's top attorney to guard the educational agenda he had set in place. Arizona school districts had reason to cooperate with the state and to steer clear of aiding the plaintiffs in the *Flores* case. This was the David versus Goliath political context of the federal court to which *Horne v. Flores* returned in September 2010.

Several key educational rights principles were at stake in this case. The high court had already undermined the EEOA by rejecting the notion that the quality of an educational program can be evaluated in terms of its expenditures. It also weakened the lower federal court's power to order the state to remediate matters of educational inequality. However, more was at stake, namely the very relevance of both *Lau v. Nichols* and *Brown v. Board of Education.* If the federal district court found that the program offered by the state of Arizona for its ELs met the EEOA requirement, that the state "take appropriate action to overcome language barriers that impede equal participation," then any state could choose to segregate its EL students from other English-speaking students up to the entire school day. In effect, districts would be allowed to recreate the infamous "Mexican Rooms." EL students could be denied access to the regular curriculum of math, science, social studies, and so on—until they acquire proficiency in English. And as indicated previously, their segregation could well last years. Districts could also bar secondary students from taking the courses they need to graduate with their peers. This would sanction the idea of "sequential instruction" for ELs: first English, then delayed access to the regular curriculum, opening up yawning gaps in achievement, which schools have seldom, if ever, been able to close, and which appears to undermine the very meaning of *Lau v. Nichols.*

Three months after the U.S. Supreme Court's 2009 *Horne v. Flores* decision, a meeting of nationally regarded scholars and civil rights lawyers was held at the UCLA Civil Rights Project[39] to pose key questions: (1) What information would be needed to make an educationally informed judgment about the effectiveness of Arizona's program of EL instruction? (2) What data already existed to answer these questions? (3) What research should be conducted? Like the attorney for *Flores*, the Project had no funds to conduct the research. Nor would it have much hope of enlisting the ADE to help them gather such data. But the Project had a large network of scholars in the area of English learner education, and understood what was at stake.

Although the Supreme Court decision had suggested four areas that the federal court might consider[40] to determine whether or not the state of Arizona had actually met the requirements of the EEOA, in the UCLA meeting of civil rights researchers and lawyers, including the attorney for Flores, it was decided that four other issues were paramount to understanding the impact of the Arizona program: (1) Could the state justify segregating English learners into "Mexican Rooms" for *at least* four hours per day during which they were not only deprived of interaction with English speakers, but were also denied access to core curriculum? (2) Had the program in place for EL students demonstrated effectiveness either at accelerating English acquisition for these students, or at closing achievement gaps? (3) To what extent had Arizona's policy of screening language minority students to determine their eligibility for language services failed to identify students in need of services? (4) Was the state's English proficiency test, AZELLA, a valid measure of students' language proficiency? In sum, was the way that Arizona was going about educating EL students like Miriam Flores consistent with the "appropriate action to overcome language barriers" that the EEOA required? To answer these questions, it was determined that the following data were required: the content of the program; its effectiveness; the teaching methods utilized; and the testing instruments used both to identify which students belonged in the program and which had ultimately achieved proficiency in English. As this would be fundamentally a *research* endeavor that required highly skilled and ethical researchers, everyone affiliated with the effort understood that results would be reported and published, regardless of what was found.

Twenty-one researchers from the University of Arizona, Arizona State University, Stanford University, and UCLA came forward to conduct the research effort, which became known as the Arizona Educational Equity Project (AEEP).[41] With no more funds than to defray some travel costs,[42] the researchers set about to design and conduct nine separate studies that would attempt to inform the questions that had been outlined in the September 2009 meeting. The nine studies required statewide data collection of teachers, program coordinators, and other school staff, intensive observations in a variety of classrooms in schools and districts, examination of state and district testing data, and reviews of past studies to understand what the latest research had to say about the key issues. And the research would need to be conducted, the data analyzed, and studies written up and reviewed by experts, within a period of about eight months. This was virtually unheard of in the academic world, especially in circumstances in which the researchers had no funds to support the work. But they did it. And twelve independent expert reviewers read and commented on the papers so that other scholars would have confidence in the findings. The AEEP research was made readily available via the Civil Rights Project website[43] and has now been disseminated through two major peer reviewed journals.

The state of Arizona recognized that a well-informed federal court would be less likely to rule in its favor. So, the lawyers for Arizona harassed AEEP researchers, trying in multiple ways to disqualify them as witnesses, and threatening some of them with contempt of court.[44] For example, Tom Horne's attorneys demanded that the AEEP researchers reveal the names of Arizona school district personnel who had participated in the study. The researchers had all sought appropriate Institutional Review Board approval,[45] which included assurances of anonymity. Anonymity is standard scholarly and legal protocol to protect research participants when they take part in politically charged research. Arizona's legal harassment forced some AEEP researchers to withdraw, principally to try to protect the identity of school personnel who had cooperated with their study. In another case, one AEEP researcher's university violated its own procedures when it turned over her data to the court without consulting her and without informing her of her rights. Because the identities of cooperating schools and personnel had already been divulged, the researcher decided that she would appear in court to defend her research.[46] Of course, her reputation was seriously damaged in the eyes of school personnel who had trusted that they would remain anonymous.

Justice from Justice

Meanwhile, both the Office for Civil Rights (OCR) of the U.S. Department of Education, and the U.S. Department of Justice (DOJ) had been monitoring several policies affecting immigrants in Arizona, including the education of ELLs. The DOJ commissioned its own research on the validity of the AZELLA, and reviewed AEEP research findings that had located serious inconsistencies in the AZELLA results.[47] The DOJ also examined AEEP scholarship that demonstrated significant under-identification of EL students using the state's newly instituted (under then-Arizona Superintendent of Public Instruction Tom Horne) single question Home Language Survey: *What is the primary language of the student?* AEEP researchers had demonstrated that students whose first and strongest language was not English could be consistently overlooked by asking only one question of the family. The standard instrument uses at least three questions to try to determine how language is used in the home, with queries about the primary language of the home and the student's first language. In fact, the AEEP scholars had demonstrated that this procedure would likely fail to identify thousands of Arizona EL students who are entitled to services.[48]

Consequently, the DOJ sent two letters to the Arizona Superintendent of Public Instruction. One letter required that Arizona institute an interim plan that would eliminate the AZELLA as the sole instrument to determine eligibility of EL students for services or reclassification to English proficient. In it, the DOJ also required Arizona to adopt an instrument that could be proven valid for these purposes by 2012. The second letter required that Arizona stop using Horn's single question Home Language Survey and re-institute the three question instrument that paralleled the screening process used in most other states. Therefore, the DOJ removed two issues that the AEEP had pursued. Now the trial would focus on whether the state-required SEI program was truly "significantly more effective" than any other available instructional program, and whether the segregated setting in which these students were instructed was educationally defensible.

A Return to the Mexican Room

Arizona's Latino population had been relatively small up until 1980, constituting about 16 percent of the population during the 1970s. On average, in 1980 Latinos attended integrated schools with an average white enrollment of 46 percent.[49] However, over the last three decades, with the growth of the Latino population, segregation has increased sharply. In 2007–2008, the typical Latino student attended a school in which only 27 percent of his peers were white. By that same year, 78 percent of the state's Latino students were in schools with less than half white students. Moreover, 38 percent were in schools that were intensely segregated, where 0–10 percent of the students were white. Additionally, the typical Arizona Latino student attends a school where 50.4 percent of all the children live in poverty. White students attend schools with substantially less poverty (25.6 percent); black students attend schools where 35.5 percent of students are poor. Latino students in Arizona also typically attend schools that have *four times* as many students classified as EL as do the schools attended by the state's white students.[50] Thus, many of today's Latino students in Arizona are triply segregated in their schools: by ethnicity, poverty, and language.

Segregation has extremely detrimental effects on students' learning. Segregated schools for minority students typically have inadequate facilities and materials,[51] less experienced[52] and less qualified teachers,[53] and less successful peers.[54] Moreover, as the concentration of EL students increases in schools, the percentage of fully credentialed teachers qualified to serve them tends to decrease.[55] Taken together, all of these factors tend to produce lower educational achievement for the students who are assigned to these schools.

The dramatic increase in segregation of Arizona's Latino students in the last generation is a serious cause for concern. It is a reason to be especially cautious of exacerbating the situation through policies that create even greater segregation at the school and classroom level. One recent study of student mathematics achievement over the last three decades concluded that although the increase in average education and income of Latino families over this period should have produced significant closing of achievement gaps on a national level, these projected gains were basically canceled out by the damage caused by increased segregation.[56] In a 2010 study scores on the National Assessment of Educational Progress (NAEP) for EL students, Rumberger and Tran concluded that the variable that explained the greatest amount of variance between ELL and non-EL students across different states and urban districts was the degree of segregation they experienced. Thus, they recommended that the most important policy lever that could be enacted by states to increase the achievement of EL students would be to reduce the segregation they experienced in their schooling. Arizona's English Language Learner Task Force, however, recommends the exact opposite: that EL students be segregated for most of their instructional day in a program that denies them access to English-speaking peers and to the content instruction from which English-speaking students benefit.

The Effects of Segregated Schooling for ELLs

Stigmatization

Several studies have shown that ELLs segregated into separate classrooms for English instruction come to feel stigmatized and inferior.[57] In such settings the ELLs become known as "those kids," "LEPers," or "the ELL-ers" by others in the school, and develop a separate identity apart from the other students in the school.[58] Dabach recently interviewed twenty-two teachers of specialized classes for ELLs and showed how their students internalized social stigma in ways that influenced their self-perceptions of intelligence and worth, as well as their motivation in school.[59] Teachers recounted common experiences in which EL students doubted their abilities, talked about their inferiority to other students in the school, and, in cases where they were reclassified as English-proficient, mocked students who remained in ESL classes. One study that surveyed 880 teachers of ELLs in the four-hour ELD block required by Arizona law found that 57 percent of these teachers felt that their ELLs' self-esteem was being damaged by being segregated into these classes, away from their mainstream peers.[60]

Lack of Linguistic Role Models

Another recent study found that the best predictor of an immigrant student gaining a firm mastery of English and doing well in school was if she had a good friend who was a native speaker of English. Without such natural language support, it can be very challenging to learn the language, especially at the level of academic English that is required to do well in school.[61] Lillie and her colleagues in the aforementioned ethnographic study of eighteen Arizona classrooms found:

> When elementary ELs left their classroom for specials such as Art or Music, and in one case for math instruction, they remained grouped throughout the day with the students from their four-hour block classroom. In short, ELs in four-hour model classrooms were spending their entire day with their fellow EL peers. They did not have contact with native English speaking students during academic or fine arts instruction. As teachers noted, this was an aspect of scheduling that meant there was a minimal amount of time in which these students could interact with English proficient peers. Lunch was the one exception where interaction could have been possible. Unfortunately, with the arrangement of the seats forcing classrooms to sit with one another, the segregation of EL students from non-ELs was complete.[62]

The AEEP study that surveyed 880 teachers in eight Arizona districts implementing the four-hour ELD program found that 87 percent of the teachers expressed concern about the EL students being separated from their English-speaking peers and 85 percent agreed with the statement, "separating EL students from English speaking peers can be harmful to their learning."[63]

Many parents also appear to be concerned about the separation of their children from the mainstream. In a separate study of teachers of EL students in Arizona, Hopkins asked seventy-four teachers of English learners in six elementary schools in one large Arizona district how often the parents of their students requested that their children be removed from the four-hour ELD program.[64] Almost half (46 percent) of the teachers noted that parents chose to remove their children from the program either "often" or "sometimes." Only 27 percent said this occurred rarely or never. This is especially significant since it is uncommon for immigrant and non-English-speaking parents to intervene in school decisions. When queried about why parents chose to do this, thirty-five teachers provided specific reasons. Of these teachers, 34 percent offered that parents made this decision because of a lack of good English models and 14 percent made reference to segregation, lack of diversity, or causing students to feel deficient. A typical teacher comment follows:

> They need to have some role models in the classroom. We have not noticed any improvement in the students' language acquisition with the four-hour block. When you teach kindergarten kids, you develop vocabulary all day long. With the four-hour block the big change was that now the EL kids do not have any English role models. . . . [The parents] don't want their children segregated

from the English speakers and they also want other kids who speak English for their child to practice with.[65]

Can Arizona's Segregation of ELL Students Be Justified by Its Outcomes?

To date, the ADE has reported no system-wide evaluation of the effectiveness of its four-hour ELD program, offering instead only anecdotal evidence supplied by district personnel who have collaborated with the state's lawyers. However, one study that involved almost 46,000 students in grades two to twelve in one large district between 2006 to 2010 and that employed very sophisticated methods to control for noninstructional factors concluded that the four-hour ELD program is *not* an effective program. EL students who participated in the four-hour ELD program had the lowest level of academic achievement compared to students in other program options. In fact, the evidence revealed that ELLs who were not in the four-hour program, but instead were in mainstream classrooms with other instructional arrangements (and even those who needed language services but did not receive them), had a better chance of succeeding academically.[66]

The Trial Closes

On January 11, 2011, after twenty-two days of testimony, the federal district court trial ended. No AEEP studies were entered into the record and no expert researchers took the stand. The judge indicated that a decision would be forthcoming within three months; to date, that decision has not been released. The research was referred to frequently, but obliquely, throughout the trial as the Arizona lawyers attempted to refute the findings of studies that criticized the state's policies, without actually identifying the experts. The public interest lawyer for Flores shared privately two days before the trial ended that he would not call any expert witnesses. He believed that he would win the case based on his own cross-examination of the state's witnesses; he considered the state's case to be that weak. Given that he participated in the discussion about the research that needed to be conducted and knew of the massive effort that had been mounted, the research team was extremely disappointed. It was further frustrating when the state's head lawyer argued that the court could not find in favor of Flores because Miriam Flores's attorneys had not entered any statewide evidence, and in fact had withdrawn their witnesses who had statewide evidence.

Researchers can play key roles in civil rights cases, and they certainly helped to shape the arguments in this case, as well as contributing evidence that supported DOJ intervention in Arizona, but they cannot litigate. Ultimately, the role of the researchers will turn on the trust and understanding they have with the litigators. Nonetheless, AEEP stands as the most comprehensive examination of the effects of a state's educational program for ELs ever conducted. Its studies have now been published in various venues where both researchers and lawyers can easily consult them for the next such case that comes along. This historic effort, conducted without funds and in record time by mostly Latino researchers, challenged Arizona's misguided educational policies in ways they had never previously been challenged.

Implications for the Future of EL Education

As we await the district court decision in *Horne v. Flores,* we can only speculate on its future impact on ELs in Arizona and beyond. It will not carry the weight of the Supreme Court decision and so its impact *may* be limited to students in Arizona schools. Nonetheless, the best-case scenario is that thousands of ELs will continue to be subject to an education that almost certainly will not improve their chances of succeeding academically and may well foreclose the possibility of most to achieve at a level commensurate with their more advantaged English-speaking classmates. Unfortunately, individuals who are intent on depriving immigrants and their children of social benefits may well use a decision to advance an anti-immigrant agenda beyond Arizona. They may use a ruling that allows Arizona to continue to segregate its EL students in "Mexican Rooms" and that denies ELs access to the core curriculum to bolster further efforts to pass laws in other states that also seek to minimize the educational opportunities of other EL students. Given the temper of the times and virulent anti-immigrant activity, such a decision could lend support to those who would continue to erode the meaning of *Lau* and further undermine any legal protections for some of the most vulnerable students in our schools. Perhaps by the time this book is published we will know the outcome.

Notes

1. U.S. Commission on Civil Rights, 1972.
2. U.S. Commission on Civil Rights, 1972; Muñoz, 2006.
3. Powers, 2008, p. 473.
4. De la Trinidad, 2008, pp. 72–73.
5. U.S. Commission on Civil Rights 1972, p. 11.
6. Matthews, 2005.

7. http://abcnews.go.com/Politics/illegal-immigration-arizona-teacher-letter-hispanic-students-sparks/story?id=13197243.

8. Wang and Rau, 2011.

9. U.S. Commission on Civil Rights, 1972.

10. Powers, 2008; González, 1990, 1999.

11. *Gonzales v. Sheely*, 96 F. Supp. 1004, 1008.

12. Powers and Patton, 2008, p. 2.

13. This chapter summarizes Gándara and Orfield (2010), among other studies produced at the Civil Rights Project/Proyecto Derechos Civiles at UCLA. This chapter follows the conventions of the field, where English learner (EL) is preferred and is replacing the older term English language learner (ELL). An earlier term, Limited English Proficient (LEP), has fallen out of use, but sometimes appears in legal documents.

14. 413 U.S. 189.

15. 414 U.S. 563 (1974).

16. 20 U.S.C. § 1703[f].

17. 648 F.2d 989 (5th Cir., 1981).

18. 457 U.S. 202 (1982).

19. See Mahoney et al., 2010; García et al., 2010.

20. García et al., 2010, p. 4.

21. See a discussion in Gándara, 1999.

22. A careful search for background information about Kevin Clark reveals very little. He does not maintain a website and has published very little.

23. Conversational English and Academic Vocabulary, English Reading, English Writing, and English Grammar.

24. August and Hakuta, 1997; Genesee et al., 2006.

25. August and Shanahan, 2006.

26. Martinez-Wenzl et al., 2010.

27. Genesee et al., 2006.

28. Genesee and Gándara, 1999.

29. AZELLA classifies ELs as Pre-emergent, Emergent, Basic, or Intermediate. These scores are used for ability grouping and determining the time allocated to the learning of the discrete English skills.

30. August et al., 2010; Bailey, 2006.

31. See Goldenberg and Coleman, 2010.

32. To make matters worse, the Arizona legislature in HB 2064 had previously set a two-year limit per student on funding the SEI program, so programs whose students were not reclassified within two years would be unfunded. This fiscal incentive on school districts to hurry ELLs into mainstream classes may violate the three criterion set out by *Castañeda* defining EEOA, but the Supreme Court did not address this potential civil rights violation in its opinion.

33. In Lillie et al., 2010, the authors continue: "Teachers reported that the amount of time it takes a student to pass out of the program depends on the following factors: prior schooling experience, motivation, and grade level in school" (pp. 25–26).

34. Lillie et al., 2010, p. 40.

35. See, for example, Gándara and Rumberger, 2009.

36. See Hanushek, 1986.

37. See Murnane and Levy, 1996, for a discussion of the missing discourse of how money is used to purchase *quality* education.

38. http://www.douglasdispatch.com/articles/2008/07/11/news/doc4877e922dbc95130306504.txt and http://www.abajournal.com/news/article/ken_starrs_910_hourly_fee_will_be_paid_ariz_spokesman_says/, retrieved 31 May 2010.

39. The Civil Rights Project/Proyecto Derechos Civiles at UCLA is codirected by Gary Orfield and Patricia Gándara, professors at UCLA. Its mission is to create a new generation of research in social science and law, on the critical issues of civil rights and equal opportunity for racial and ethnic groups in the United States. It has commissioned more than 450 studies, published fourteen books, and issued numerous reports from authors at universities and research centers across the country. See http://civilrightsproject.ucla.edu.

40. When the Supreme Court remanded the case to the federal district court, it suggested that four important factual and legal changes might grant Arizona relief from judgment: Congress' enactment of NCLB, structural and management reforms in Nogales, increased state funding for education overall, and the state's adoption of a new ELL instructional methodology (U.S. 557 (2009)). The Supreme Court failed to raise segregation as an issue. The *Flores* lawyers chose to take a different tack and introduce a different set of questions at the federal district court trial. In additional to raising the segregation issue, it focused on two of the three *Castañeda* criteria to determine if the state meets EEOA standards: Was Arizona's SEI program well implemented? And was it effective over time?

41. All studies associated with the Arizona Educational Equity Project are available at: http://civilrightsproject.ucla.edu/research/k-12-education/language-minority-students/arizona-educational-equity-project-abstracts-and-papers

42. Funding was limited to Foundation for Child Development underwriting of local transportation expenses and the cost of flights to the first UCLA meeting.

43. http://civilrightsproject.ucla.edu/research/k-12-education/language-minority-students/arizona-educational-equity-project-overview/?searchterm=arizona

44. http://civilrightsproject.ucla.edu/news/a-threat-to-the-integrity-of-civil-rights-research-in-arizona-and-elsewhere-1.

45. Universities and other research institutions establish IRBs to protect the rights, welfare, and to manage the risk of human participants in research.

46. This incident was the subject of a special presidential panel at the American Educational Research Association conference in New Orleans, April 17, 2011.

47. Namely Florez, 2010, and García et al., 2010.

48. Goldenberg and Rutherford-Quach, 2010.

49. Kasindorf and McMahon, 2001.

50. Dr. Jia Wang of the UCLA Civil Rights Project compiled the 2007–2008 statistics from the Common Core of Education Data of the U.S. National Center for Education Statistics.

51. Phillips and Chin, 2004.

52. Lankford et al., 2002.

53. Clotfelter et al., 2005.

54. Rumberger and Palardy, 2005.
55. IDEA, 2007.
56. Berends and Peñaloza, 2010.
57. Callahan et al., 2009; Dabach, 2010.
58. Olsen, 1997.
59. Dabach, 2010.
60. Rios-Aguilar et al., 2010.
61. Suárez-Orozco, Suárez-Orozco, and Todorova, 2008.
62. Lillie et al., 2010, p. 18.
63. Rios-Aguilar et al., 2010.
64. Hopkins, 2010.
65. Hopkins, 2010.
66. Rios-Aguilar et al., in press.

References

August, D., Goldenberg, C., & Rueda, R. (2010). Restrictive language policies. Are they scientifically based? In P. Gándara & M. Hopkins (Eds.), *Forbidden language. English learners and restrictive language policies,* pp. 139–158. New York: Teachers College Press.

August, D., & Hakuta, K. (1997). *Improving schooling for language minority children: A research agenda.* Washington, DC: National Research Council, Institute of Medicine.

August, D., & Shanahan, T. (Eds.). (2006). *Developing literacy in second language learners. Report of the National Literacy Panel on Language Minority Children and Youth.* Mahwah, NJ: Lawrence Erlbaum.

Bailey, A. (2006). *The language demands of school: Putting Academic English to the test.* New Haven, CT: Yale University Press.

Berends, M., & Peñaloza, R. (2010). Increasing racial isolation and test score gaps in mathematics: A 30-year perspective. *Teachers College Record,* 112, 978–1007.

Callahan, R., Wilkinson, L., Muller, C., & Frisco, M. A. (2009). ESL placement and schools: Effects on immigrant achievement. *Educational Policy,* 23, 355–364.

Clotfelter, C., Ladd, H., & Vigdor, J. (2005). Who teaches whom? Race and the distribution of novice teachers. *Economics of Education Review,* 24, 377–392.

Dabach, D. (2010). *Teachers as a context for immigrant youth. Adaptations in sheltered and mainstream classrooms.* Unpublished doctoral dissertation, University of California, Berkeley.

De la Trinidad, M. (2008). *Collective outrage: Mexican American activism and the quest for educational equality and reform, 1950–1990.* Unpublished doctoral dissertation, University of Arizona.

Florez, I. R. (2010). *Do the AZELLA cut scores meet the standards? A validation review of the Arizona English language learner assessment.* Los Angeles: Civil Rights Project/Proyecto Derechos Civiles; University of California, Los Angeles.

Gándara, P. (Ed.) (1999). *The dimensions of time and the challenge of school reform.* Albany: State University of New York Press.

Gándara, P., & Orfield, G. (2010). *A return to the "Mexican Room": The segregation of Arizona's English learners.* Los Angeles: Civil Rights Project/Proyecto Derechos Civiles; University of California, Los Angeles.

Gándara, P., & Rumberger, R. (2009). Immigration, language, and education: How does language policy structure opportunity? *Teachers College Record,* 111, 750–782.

García, E., Lawton, K., & Diniz de Figueiredo, E. (2010). *The education of English language learners in Arizona: A legacy of persisting achievement gaps in a restrictive language policy climate.* Los Angeles: Civil Rights Project/Proyecto Derechos Civiles; University of California, Los Angeles.

Genesee, F., & Gándara, P. (1999). Bilingual education programs: A cross-national perspective. *Journal of Social Issues,* 55, 655–685.

Genesee, F., Lindholm-Leary, K., Saunders, W., & Christian, D. (2006). *Educating English language learners. A synthesis of research evidence.* New York: Cambridge University Press.

Goldenberg, C., & Coleman, R. (2010). *Promoting academic achievement among English learners: A guide to the research.* Thousand Oaks, CA: Corwin Press.

Goldenberg, C., & Rutherford-Quach, S. (2010). *The Arizona home language survey and the identification of students for ELL services.* Los Angeles: Civil Rights Project/ Proyecto Derechos Civiles; University of California, Los Angeles.

Gonzales v. Sheely, 96 F. Supp. 1004 (D.C. Ariz. 1951).

González, G. G. (1990). *Chicano education in the era of segregation.* Philadelphia: The Balch Institute Press.

González, G. G. (1999). Segregation and the education of Mexican children, 1900–1940. In José Moreno (Ed.), *The elusive quest for equality: 150 Years of Chicano/ Chicana education,* pp. 53–76. Cambridge: Harvard Educational Review.

Hanushek, E. (1986). The economics of schooling: Production and efficiency in public schools. *Journal of Economic Literature,* 24, 1141–1177.

Hopkins, M. (2010). Unpublished data from Sunnyside (AZ) School District.

IDEA. (2007). *Latino educational opportunity report, 2007.* Los Angeles: Institute for Democracy, Education, and Access, University of California, Los Angeles.

Kasindorf, M., & McMahon, P. (2001). Census 2000. Arizona's Hispanic population grew by 88%. *USA Today.* http://www.usatoday.com/news/nation/census/az.htm

Lankford, H., Loeb, S., & Wyckoff, J. (2002). Teacher sorting and the plight of urban schools: A descriptive analysis. *Educational Evaluation and Policy Analysis,* 24, 37–62.

Lillie, K., Markos, A., Estrella, A., Nguyen, T., Peer, K., Pérez, K., Trifiro, A., Arias, M. B., & Wiley, T. G. (2010). *Policy in practice: The implementation of Structured English Immersion in Arizona.* Los Angeles: Civil Rights Project/Proyecto Derechos Civiles; University of California, Los Angeles.

Mahoney, K., MacSwan, J., Haladyna, T., & Garcia, D. (2010). Castañeda's third prong. Evaluating the achievement of Arizona's English learners under restrictive language policy. In P. Gándara & M., Megan (Eds.), *Forbidden language. English learners and restrictive language policies,* pp. 50–64. New York: Teachers College Press.

Martinez-Wenzl, M., Pérez, K., & Gándara, P. (2010). *Is Arizona's approach to educating its ELs superior to other forms of instruction?* Los Angeles: Civil Rights Project/ Proyecto Derechos Civiles; University of California, Los Angeles.

Matthews, M. (2005, August 31). Arizona lashes out at illegal immigration. Stateline. org. http://www.stateline.org/live/ViewPage.action?siteNodeId=136&languageId= 1&contentId=51473.

Mendoza v. Tucson School District No. 1, Ninth Circuit Court of Appeals, 623 F. 2d 1338.

Muñoz, L. (2006). *Desert dreams: Mexican American education in Arizona, 1870–1930.* Unpublished doctoral dissertation. Arizona State University.

Murnane, R., & Levy, F. (1996). Evidence from fifteen schools in Austin, Texas. In Gary Burtless (Ed.), pp. 93–97 *Does money matter? The effect of school resources on student achievement and adult earnings.* Washington, DC: Brookings Institute.

Olsen, L. (1997). *Made in America: Immigrant students in our public schools.* New York: New Press.

Phillips, M., & Chin, T. (2004), School inequality: What do we know? In K. Neckerman (Ed.), *Social inequality,* pp. 467–519. New York: Russell Sage Foundation.

Powers, J. (2008). Forgotten history: Mexican American school segregation in Arizona from 1900–1951. *Equity & Excellence in Education,* 41(4), 467–481.

Powers, J., & Patton, L. (2008, Winter). Between *Mendez* and *Brown: Gonzales v. Sheely* (1951) and the legal campaign against segregation. *Law & Social Inquiry,* 33, 127–171.

Rios-Aguilar, C., González-Canché, M., & Moll, L. (2010). *A study of Arizona's teachers of English language learners.* Los Angeles: Civil Rights Project/Proyecto Derechos Civiles; University of California, Los Angeles.

Rios-Aguilar, C., González-Canché, M., & Sabetghadam, S. (2012). Evaluating the impact of restrictive language policies: The four-hour English language development block. *Language Policy,* pp. 1–34.

Rumberger, R., & Palardy, G. (2005). Does segregation still matter? The impact of and composition on academic achievement in high school. *Teacher's College Record,* 107, 1999–2045.

Rumberger, R., & Tran, L. (2010). State language policies, school language practices, and the English learner achievement gap. In P. Gándara & M. Hopkins (Eds.), *Forbidden language. English learners and restrictive language policies,* pp. 86–101. New York: Teachers College Press.

Suárez-Orozco, M., Suárez-Orozco, C., & Todorova, I. (2008). *Learning a new land: Immigrant students in American society.* Cambridge, MA: Harvard University Press.

U.S. Commission on Civil Rights. (1972). *The excluded student. Educational practices affecting Mexican Americans in the Southwest. Report III.* Washington, DC: Commission on Civil Rights.

Wang, A., & Rau, A. B. (2011). Glendale Elementary School District: Teacher's report wrong. *The Arizona Republic,* March 24, 2011. http://www.azcentral.com/ news/election/azelections/articles/2011/03/24/20110324glendale-district-defends-students.html

8

Illegal Accents

Qualifications, Discrimination, and Distraction in Arizona's Monitoring of Teachers

Jennifer Leeman

IN THE SPRING OF 2010, the *Wall Street Journal* reported that the Arizona Department of Education (ADE) had begun requiring school districts to remove teachers with "heavily accented or ungrammatical" English from classes for English language learners (ELLs).[1] The article described the state policy as requiring removal from Structured English Immersion (SEI) classrooms of those teachers with "heavy accents or other shortcomings in their English," and went on to cite the difficult case of Creighton Elementary School in Phoenix, where the English of two SEI teachers was judged to be inadequate, despite their having completed accent reduction courses. In the context of the firestorm brewing in the state, many observers interpreted the policy as another move against immigrants, or as evidence of a broad anti-Latino racism. Media coverage explicitly linked the removal of teachers with accents with SB 1070—Arizona's 2010 law allowing police to demand documents from anyone suspected of being in the country without authorization (see Chin et al., this volume)—and HB 2281, Arizona's 2010 law banning ethnic studies in secondary schools (see O'Leary et al., this volume). Apparently concerned about the negative publicity, Arizona state education officials denied any anti-Latino or anti-immigrant intent and maintained that they were simply following the federal No Child Left Behind Act (NCLB), which states that teachers of ELLs must be fluent in English. Further, Arizona officials claimed that they had been misquoted, insisted that they had not ordered teacher reassignments, and denied targeting teachers based on their accents.[2] At the time Arizona Superintendent of Public

Instruction Tom Horne told CNN that rather than accents, the policy focused on teachers with "faulty English."[3]

Amidst accusations and denials, precise information about the policy was surprisingly hard to come by. Because the monitoring of SEI teachers was not the result of new legislation (such as SB 1070 and HB 2281), but an apparent change in the interpretation and implementation of existing regulations, the policy was not part of publicly available records. Further, when journalists requested details about just what those policies and regulations were, state officials were not forthcoming. Instead of defining Arizona's policy toward accents, a spokeswoman for the department provided journalists with a copy of the SEI classroom observation protocol, together with the relevant section of NCLB. The protocol has a section labeled "Federal Compliance: Teacher Fluency," which consists of two yes/no evaluations of teachers' language use: "Teacher uses accurate grammar" and "Teacher uses accurate pronunciation," which shows that accent is indeed part of the official evaluation criteria.[4] Further, despite denying the use of accent in the assessment of teachers, state officials repeatedly gave examples of cases of inadequate teachers in which the "problem" was clearly related to accent. For example, in his comments to CNN, Horne illustrated the notion of "faulty English" by citing a teacher who pronounced *comma* as "coma." Officials from the U.S. Department of Justice and the U.S. Department of Education were sufficiently concerned that they launched an investigation into whether Arizona was engaging in illegal discrimination.[5]

Supporters of the ADE policy portray the reassignment or dismissal of teachers with accents as a common-sense move in the best interest of the children. However, as we will see, the no-accent policy is pedagogically flawed and has been widely criticized by experts in the fields of education and language learning. In this chapter, I present the specific criticisms of professional organizations and review research on language variation and accent that support claims that the policy is pedagogically unsound and racially biased. Because Arizona's policy embodies common assumptions about "good" and "bad" language, I include a discussion of these language hierarchies, and of their impact in educational contexts. Next, I discuss the legal status of accent-based discrimination and the implications for Arizona's policy. I conclude the chapter by arguing that the Arizona policy is misguided on three levels: it is pedagogically flawed, it unfairly penalizes Latino teachers, and it contributes to a broader negative portrayal of Latinos in the public sphere. Moreover, the policy and the associated media coverage are part of a larger discourse that distracts from the educational injustices being perpetrated against Latina/o children in Arizona while also reinforcing the stereotypes which undergird public support for more and more repressive measures.

Professional Organizations Speak Out against a Flawed Policy

Whereas Arizona state officials sought to portray the policy as motivated by the desire to provide ELLs with qualified instructors and high-quality instruction, many scholarly and professional associations related to language learning and teaching issued statements condemning the policy. These include: the National Council of Teachers of English (NCTE), Teachers of English to Speakers of Other Languages (TESOL), the American Association of Applied Linguistics (AAAL), and the Linguistic Society of America (LSA). A group of nineteen faculty of the Linguistics Department of the University of Arizona (LDUA) also issued a denunciation. These statements cited empirical research to challenge the assumptions about language learning and teaching inherent in the no-accent policy, arguing that the policy reflected a misguided view of language, language learning, and language teaching, and that the state policy was actually detrimental to schoolchildren. As the LDUA put it, "It is our position, based on decades of scientific investigation into the nature of language, and of language acquisition and learning, that such a policy undermines the effectiveness of teaching and learning of English by non-native speakers and may lead to harmful socioeconomic effects."

The NCTE and TESOL statements focused primarily on issues related to teacher competence and pedagogical practice, while those from AAAL, LSA, and the linguistics faculty argued that the ADE policy targeting teachers with "heavy accents" displayed significantly faulty linguistic knowledge about accent and language acquisition. The education-oriented associations critiqued the overemphasis on language proficiency in general, and on accent in particular, as indicators of teacher competence, arguing that other crucial aspects of teacher qualifications were being neglected in the focus on accents. According to the TESOL statement,

> the distinction between native and nonnative speakers of English presents an oversimplified either/or classification system that is not only misleading, but also ignores the formal education, linguistic expertise, teaching experience and professional preparation of educators in the field of English language teaching.

In addition to sound pedagogical methods, NCTE pointed out the importance of teacher empathy, as well as understanding the students' linguistic and cultural experiences. The organization's position is supported by educational research demonstrating that children learn best when teachers and curricula bridge the gaps between children's home life and school, helping them integrate their familial and community experiences with their academic lives.[6] For these reasons, policies that exclude nonnative English-speaking teachers from SEI classrooms are detrimental to ELL children.

The LDUA and AAAL stressed that there is no such thing as unaccented speech. Rather, everyone has some kind of accent, even native speakers (we will come back to this in the next section). They also argued that Arizona's policy demonstrates a lack of understanding of language and language education, and went on to note that whether or not someone is perceived to have a foreign accent is not a reliable indicator of language proficiency or intelligibility, nor it does correlate with teaching ability. The linguists further argued that children benefit from exposure to a broad range of accents, including foreign accents. For one, both the AAAL and LDUA argued that variability of input has been shown to promote first language acquisition and it stands to reason that varied input, namely a range of foreign as well as native accents, should also promote childhood second language acquisition. In addition, varied linguistic input provides children with comprehension practice and better prepares them for communicating with a broad range of people, which will benefit them in the future. Finally, the professional organizations stressed that attitudes toward accents are closely linked to attitudes toward groups of people associated with those accents. The next section reviews scholarship on language, identity, and language attitudes, by then exploring how policies that target certain kinds of language actually target specific kinds of people.

Language Variation, Identity, and Attitudes toward Accents

Human languages exhibit a great deal of variation. In addition to an astounding degree of variety across languages, all languages also exhibit internal variation in grammar, vocabulary, and pronunciation. Individuals use language differently in different contexts and at different times, and their language use patterns according to social group as well as geographic region. All speakers of a given language speak some dialect or "variety" of that language and everyone has some kind of accent. In the case of English, for example, there are American, British, Jamaican, and New Zealand accents, among many others, and there is no such thing as unaccented English. Just as no language is "better" than another, there are no objective criteria by which to claim that any particular language variety or accent is superior. Chinese is not better (or worse) than Japanese, and a Boston accent is no better (or worse) than a Southern drawl.

While an individual's language variety and accent are shaped by where they are from, who they know, and who they are, this should not be interpreted to mean that identity *determines* how someone speaks. Instead, the relationship between language and identity is a two-way street, and individuals draw from the range of linguistic features in their linguistic repertoires to express different social meanings. For example, people use variation as a resource to highlight various aspects of their identity, or to signal affinity with, or distance from, their interlocutors. Nonetheless, because language varies along social and geographic parameters, it is often possible, without any linguistic training, to identify where someone is from, or with which social groups they identify, just by hearing them say a few words.[7] Further, pronunciation and accent are notoriously impervious to modification; regardless of the degree of second language proficiency ultimately attained, it is extremely rare for someone to completely change their accent or to sound like a native speaker unless they begin learning the language in early childhood. No definitive account has been found for this phenomenon, although possibilities include physical explanations such as brain lateralization and sociopsychological explanations such as the development and solidification of an identity linked to language.[8]

Another aspect of the relationship between language and identity is that particular languages, language varieties, accents, and even the pronunciation of individual sounds can act as symbols or stand-ins for particular groups of people. Once a linguistic feature typical of a specific social group becomes so strongly associated with that group, the feature and the group can serve as indexes of each other. For example, simply using the Boston pronunciation "Pahk the cah" (*park the car*) or saying the Southern "Y'all" (*you all*) evokes specific types of people without mentioning them explicitly. Importantly, these associations do not rely on everyone in the group actually using the linguistic feature in question. For example, in the United States, Spanish is so closely associated with Latino identity that Latinos are seen as "naturally" and inherently Spanish-speaking[9] even though a growing proportion are actually monolingual in English. Because particular ways of speaking are linked with particular group identities, attitudes toward a social group may be expressed in attitudes toward ways of speaking that are associated with that group. Thus, attitudes that purport to be about a specific language, such as French, are rooted in attitudes about people who speak that language.

There are several lines of research empirically demonstrating that language attitudes are inseparable from perceptions of different groups of people. In one series of studies, participants listened to what they believed to be different speech samples and evaluated them on a range of subjective criteria. For example, listeners were asked to judge speakers on their perceived intelligence, trustworthiness, and ambition. Although participants believed they were listening to recordings of different people, in fact they were listening to the same person speaking with different accents, or in different languages. As a whole, these studies have found that listeners' evaluations of various accents correlated highly with their attitudes toward different groups.[10]

Another empirical approach to exploring people's attitudes and stereotypes about language varieties and accents is Dennis Preston's perceptual dialectology research.[11] Rather than having participants evaluate recorded speech samples, Preston asked participants to label dialect areas on a map of the United States, and to rate the English spoken in all fifty states and Washington, D.C., for "correctness" and "pleasantness" on a scale of one to ten. Preston's research demonstrated that people have strong attitudes about the way people in different parts of the country talk—with accent being one of the features commonly used to characterize the speech of different regions—and that these are intertwined with attitudes about the presumed sociocultural characteristics of those areas. Together, the research on language variation and attitudes demonstrates the difficulty of disentangling policies about accent from policies about certain groups of people. In Arizona (as elsewhere), attitudes about Spanish, and about the varieties of English spoken by Latinos, are clearly tied up with attitudes toward the (imagined) speakers of that language and those varieties.

Language Ideologies and "Standard Language"

Within the fields of sociolinguistics and linguistic anthropology, the term *language ideologies* is used to refer to belief systems about language. These beliefs include the perceived relative worth of different languages, language varieties and accents, as well as what constitutes "normal" or "correct" usage, and the relationship of specific languages and linguistic features to various aspects of identity such as race or gender.[12] Scholars stress that language beliefs are not simply a matter of personal opinion. Instead, language ideologies are embodied in societal and institutional discourses and practices, and are tied up with issues of power. Although language ideologies tend to emerge in discussions of language policies and practices, the ideologies are rarely, if ever, just about language. Language ideologies serve as a link between language and broader social structures, and they are intertwined with perceptions of (imagined) speakers as well as ideologies about other social phenomena, such as gender, socioeconomic status, race, and nation.

One common language ideology is the "standard language ideology," which holds that linguistic variation should be suppressed and everyone should speak a uniform "standard language" ("standard English" in the case of the United States). However, given the inherent variability of language, variation can never be completely eliminated and no one actually speaks "standard English." In reality, "standard English" is used to refer to language varieties that are *perceived* to be neutral, correct, and free from regionalisms. Thus, rather than a specific variety that anyone speaks, "standard English" is an idealized abstraction upheld by the standard language ideology.[13]

In addition to valuing uniformity, the standard language ideology establishes linguistic hierarchies by portraying "standard language" as inherently better than other varieties. All language varieties are equal in terms of their expressive ability and their internal coherence and logic. However, societies assign positive social and moral qualities to the idealized standard and those who speak it. In the United States, "standard English" is portrayed as pure and good while other varieties of English are corrupt, lazy, or illogical. Note that beliefs about just which varieties of language are "standard," "correct," and aesthetically more pleasing are not arbitrary: the language varieties considered superior are the ones spoken by powerful elites. In contrast, the language varieties of less powerful groups are portrayed as deviant and defective.[14] This can be seen, for example, in the common portrayal of language varieties associated with African Americans and other racial minorities as "substandard," "impoverished," or "deficient."

The moral hierarchies surrounding "standard" language become so naturalized that they appear to be common sense and objective, and it is easy to overlook the fact that there is nothing intrinsically better about the "standard" variety. Rather than acknowledging that it is the language varieties of the powerful that are depicted as superior, the standard language ideology portrays the preferred ways of speaking as belonging to no one in particular and equally available to everyone. This anonymity and pseudo-universality lend them even greater authority, as if no particular group were being favored.[15] Further, the failure to recognize the link between language and identity on one hand, and between power and "correctness" on the other, permits the undercover use of language as a basis of discrimination.

The standard language ideology is reflected in the Arizona Structured English Immersion (SEI) classroom observation protocol described earlier in this chapter and in particular in the classification of teachers' pronunciation as "accurate" or not. Even among adherents to the standard language ideology there tends to be more acceptance of variation in accent than in other aspects of language such as grammar or spelling. Arizona's policy therefore demonstrates a particularly strong commitment to linguistic hierarchies. Further, by using the term *accurate*, the protocol implies that there is a single agreed-upon standard that can be objectively described, and that everyone has access to. Although the protocol implies that there is a single correct accent, it never defines or describes it.

The linguistic hierarchies and the standard language ideology that support them are not just individual aesthetic preferences or esoteric linguistic evaluations. Instead, common understandings about "good" and "bad" language, and about the speakers of different language varieties, reinforce social hierarchies and contribute to the maintenance of social, political, and economic inequality. The flip side of the elevation of "standard" varieties is that speaking a "nonstandard" variety is often interpreted as a sign of ignorance or laziness. Indeed, a large body of research demonstrates that teachers often make negative evaluations of school children who speak "nonstandard" language or who have accents associated with African Americans or Latinos.[16] Such judgments can be self-fulfilling: children who are so judged become less likely to succeed academically. In turn, this reinforces stereotypes and misconceptions that "nonstandard" language varieties are indicative of illogical or unintelligent thinking, as well as an obstacle to communication. Educational policies and practices that cater exclusively to speakers of prestige varieties or denigrate other language varieties or accents not only reinforce negative attitudes but also create an unequal playing field and put speakers of other varieties and languages at a disadvantage in schools (see Gándara, this volume).

The Standard Language Ideology and Accent-Based Discrimination

In addition to damaging educational consequences for children, the standard language ideology can also lead to language-based discrimination in other contexts. Speaking a language variety considered "nonstandard," or having a stigmatized accent can lead to exclusion from consideration for particular jobs. Many people consider particular ways of speaking are inappropriate for working with customers or speaking in public.[17] Although the notion that one should speak "correctly" may seem like common sense, and that failing to do so is a sign of ignorance or incompetence, in fact it reflects the standard language ideology and can contribute to particular groups of people being excluded from certain jobs.

Although generally not forthcoming about the policy and its consequences, in response to repeated requests from journalists, the Arizona Department of Education did provide a few statistics about the districts and teachers that had been found lacking. In the 2008–2009 school year, seven out of the seventy-three monitored districts were found to have "fluency problems," while 25 out of 1,529 teachers observed were found to have "pronunciation issues." In 2009–2010, nine out of sixty-one districts were identified as having fluency problems, while data on teacher observations were not made available.[18] The department did not provide information about the consequences for those districts or individual teachers, but several newspapers reported anecdotally on teachers being reassigned, or resigning rather than being forced to switch to another grade level. Other teachers participated in accent reduction workshops in the hope of keeping their jobs.

At a time when state and federal budget crises have cut education spending, the potential for layoffs and other staff reductions increase. If accent is part of the assessment of teachers' qualifications, it stands to reason that teachers with accents considered "incorrect" are at greater risk of losing their jobs. Thus, by prioritizing accent, and giving less weight to other qualifications, such as the understanding of students' linguistic and cultural background, pedagogical training, or professional development, the policy not only harms students but also harms particular groups of teachers.

As was noted earlier, although Arizona officials denied targeting any ethnic group, many observers felt the accent policy was part of a broader move against Latinos. This concern was both reflected and reinforced by media coverage of the policy, with most stories explicitly connecting it to HB 2281 and SB 1070. Further, some news reports framed the English fluency "problem" as a relic of bilingual education, which was eliminated in Arizona when voters approved Proposition 203 in 2000. For example, the *Wall Street Journal* article described how in the 1990s Arizona had hired native Spanish speakers, some of them recruited from Latin America to teach in the state's bilingual education programs; after Proposition 203, those teachers switched to teaching in English.[19] Beyond this contextual information, there was some evidence that Latino teachers were being singled out.[20] For one, according to the principal of Creighton Elementary School, when state officials came to her school to conduct classroom observations, they typically visited the classes of teachers with "Spanish surnames."[21] In addition, the examples of problematic accents cited by Horne included "biolet" for *violet* and "tink" for *think,* both of which evoke speakers of Spanish.[22] Therefore, we will now consider the legality of discriminating based on ethnicity or accent.

Accent-Based Discrimination and the Law

Title VII of the Civil Rights Act specifically outlaws workplace discrimination on the basis of race, color, religion, sex, or national origin. The Equal

Employment Opportunity Commission (EEOC), the federal agency charged with enforcing Title VII, includes the following guidance in Section 13 of the Compliance Manual on "National Origin Discrimination" (2002):

> A "national origin group," often referred to as an "ethnic group," is a group of people sharing a common language, culture, ancestry, and/or other similar social characteristics. . . . Title VII prohibits employment discrimination against any national origin group, including larger ethnic groups, such as Hispanics and Arabs, and smaller ethnic groups, such as Kurds or Roma (Gypsies).[23]

While Title VII of the Civil Rights Act prohibits national origin discrimination, as well as discrimination based on "physical, linguistic, and/or cultural characteristics closely associated with a national origin group," an exception is made for cases where "national origin is a bona fide occupational qualification reasonably necessary to the normal operation of that particular business or enterprise." The EEOC compliance manual explains that the assessment of whether accent discrimination is permissible "depends upon the specific duties of the position in question and the extent to which the individual's accent affects his or her ability to perform job duties." Further, "employers should distinguish between a merely discernible foreign accent and one that interferes with communication skills necessary to perform job duties." Importantly, the manual cautions that "linguistic characteristics are closely associated with national origin" and that "employers should ensure that the business reason for reliance on a linguistic characteristic justifies any burdens placed on individuals because of their national origin."[24]

Employers accused of accent-based discrimination often attempt to justify their actions by claiming that if an employee's accent is difficult to understand, this constitutes a legitimate business reason for engaging in linguistic discrimination. However, intelligibility is neither an objective or easily defined construct because individual speakers' language proficiency and accent are not the only factors that determine whether they can be understood. Obviously, the listener also plays an important role in comprehension, and a wide range of linguistic and nonlinguistic factors influence their ability to comprehend someone, including: topic, utterance length and complexity, and listener experience with diverse speakers. Communication requires the participation of both the speaker and the listener, and an inability or unwillingness of the listener to share the communicative burden can lead to a lack of communication breakdown.[25]

In the educational context, college students often complain about the English proficiency and accents of international teaching assistants and instructors. Empirical studies comparing the intelligibility of native and non-native speakers of English reveal that comprehension depends on the listener, as well as the speaker, and that listeners' attitudes are key. In particular, Rubin and his colleagues explored the role of the listeners' preconceptions regarding race in influencing their perception of accent.[26] In these studies, students listened to recorded lectures while also viewing a photograph of a person they were told was the lecturer, and they were asked to rate the lecturer's accent and comprehensibility. All the students heard the same recording, but half of them were shown a photograph of a white person, while the other half were shown a photograph of an Asian person. Students "heard" a foreign accent when viewing the photograph of the Asian instructor but not the white instructor, despite the fact that it was the exact same recording. Even more striking is that students who were shown the photograph of the Asian instructor actually performed worse on a post-lecture comprehension test, demonstrating that listener expectations play an important role in comprehension.

Rubin's quantitative research finding is echoed by Amin's qualitative research with non-white women teaching ESL in Canada.[27] Amin found that for many students, the ideal native speaker of English is a white male, and minority women teachers are often assumed to be non-native speakers. As a result, students delegitimized non-white and female instructors and accorded them less authority. More generally, in the United States, Latinos and Asians are seen not only as racially other but they are also perceived as "perpetual foreigners," regardless of where they were born and raised.[28] Evaluations of whether Arizona's policy constitutes a legitimate job-related justification for removing teachers or a case of national origin discrimination must keep these ideological and racial components of accent perception and comprehension in mind.

Despite the EEOC guidelines, as well as significant research indicating that comprehensibility and accentedness evaluations are influenced by racial stereotypes and preconceptions, the courts often unquestioningly accept arguments about the supposed negative impact of accented speech. In particular, the courts generally have not required an objective assessment of the complainants' speech, the communication requirements of the job, or the impact of accent on the completion of job duties. Instead, judges have relied on employers or their own impressions of the complainant's accent; allowed discriminatory "customer preference" to be taken into account; and simply accepted employers' assertions regarding the purported negative effect of that accent on comprehension.[29] Accent discrimination cases are also striking in that employers often explicitly acknowledge when their decisions are based on language, which stands in sharp contrast to race-based discrimination, which defendants generally deny. Admitting to accent-based discrimination and seeing it as "normal" is consistent with the standard language ideology that views "nonstandard" and non-native varieties as inherently problematic.

Another language ideology at play in the courts' acceptance of accent-based discrimination is the notion that an individual's language and accent are a matter of "choice."[30] Although language learning is a time-consuming endeavor and the overwhelming majority of adult language learners never achieve native-like pronunciation—regardless of the effort they make—public discourse and everyday talk minimize the time required to learn an additional language, fueling the perception that English proficiency can be acquired practically overnight. The view that learning English is easy is apparent in the results of a 2006 Pew Center poll in which a majority of respondents said that recent immigrants don't learn English "within a reasonable amount of time."[31] Because English acquisition and language use are constructed as a choice, the public views language-based discrimination as more benign than discrimination based on seemingly immutable traits, such as race and gender. However, as was discussed previously and has been recognized by the courts, linguistic characteristics (including accent) are also linked to national origin and ethnicity. Thus language has a dual status—both a personal choice and an index of ethnoracial identity—which allows linguistic discrimination to serve as a surrogate for ethnoracial discrimination.[32] Because Latinos are frequently perceived as "Spanish-speakers" regardless of the language they actually speak, the acceptability of language discrimination has particular impact for Latinos.

Explicit portrayal of accent as choice can be found in court rulings of accent discrimination cases. In one case involving a Palestinian teacher, for example, the judge ruled that the teacher's language "was not an immutable characteristic of his national origin but rather was a correctable condition which the plaintiff had chosen not to remedy despite suggestions from his superiors to do so."[33] Similarly, in a case involving a speaker of Hawaiian English, the judge ruled that "there is no race or physiological reason why [the plaintiff] could not have used standard English pronunciations."[34]

Defending Arizona's Policy in the Era of Educational Reform

As was noted earlier, Arizona state education officials responded to journalist requests about the policy by providing journalists with a copy of the NCLB mandate regarding teacher fluency together with the Arizona SEI classroom observation protocol. In their public comments, officials sought to frame the monitoring of accent as an issue of teacher qualifications. For example, then Arizona Superintendent of Public Instruction Tom Horne defended the policy by stating: "This is common sense. If you want to teach math, you need to know math. If you want to teach English, you need to be fluent in English."[35] Along the same lines, Deputy Superintendent of Public Instruction Margaret Garcia Dugan maintained that "our job is to make sure the teachers are highly qualified in fluency of the English language."[36] The discursive strategy of emphasizing teacher qualifications and NCLB allowed officials to deflect accusations of ethnoracial or anti-immigrant bias by tying into popular discourses of educational reform.

In the past few decades, there has been growing public concern regarding the competitiveness of the United States in the global market, as well as anxiety regarding U.S. students' falling standing in international educational rankings. Concurrently, there has been a growing politicization of education: instructional policy that might once have been determined by educational professionals is increasingly subject to political considerations and decided in legislatures and through public referenda. Educational legislation, policy, and the discourse of educational reform emphasize accountability and penalize schools and teachers for low student scores on standardized tests. The current reform movement has also focused on teacher qualifications, such as in discussions of how to attract "quality applicants" to the profession and, increasingly, of how to "weed out" bad teachers. More and more public discussion portrays teachers—as well as other government employees—in a negative light. As a result, framing Arizona's policy as one of removing unqualified teachers seems designed to lend legitimacy and garner public support.

Despite then-Arizona Superintendent of Public Instruction Horne's analogy to math teachers needing to know math, language knowledge is not like other kinds of subject matter. In SEI, English is the subject matter as well as the mode of communication. However, the accent policy judged teachers negatively based on the way they spoke, rather than their content knowledge or teaching ability. For example, it did not inquire whether they could teach students to use English grammar. Although Arizona state officials described their policy as rooted in the NCLB mandate that teachers of ELLs be "fluent" in English, in fact NCLB makes no mention of accent, and leaves it to each state to determine how to assess fluency.[37] Thus, ADE went beyond the federal dictates by specifying pronunciation as one of the two criteria of "fluency."

As was discussed earlier, the EEOC allows accent-based employment decisions "if effective oral communication in English is required to perform job duties." Although the EEOC compliance manual specifically lists teaching as such a job where this might be the case, it cautions that "even for these positions, an employer must still determine whether the particular individual's accent interferes with the ability to perform job duties." Like employers accused of accent-based national origin discrimination in court, Arizona state officials sought to use comprehensibility as a legitimate justification for discrimination. Essentially, they maintained that they were not targeting teachers with accents simply because they had accents, but instead focusing on teachers whose accents interfered with their ability to be good teachers. For example, then State Superintendent Horne emphasized comprehension in his response to a question about the federal investigation by stating: "I'm sure they're going to find everything is fine. Teachers who are teaching English need to be fluent in English, and if kids can understand what they're saying, it's not an issue."[38]

So too, Deputy Associate Superintendent Adela Santa Cruz stated that education officials "look at the best models of English pronunciation. It becomes an issue when pronunciation affects comprehensibility." Further, the SEI classroom observation protocol uses comprehensibility as a measure of accuracy. As was noted earlier, the protocol does not explicitly define or describe "accurate" pronunciation. However, it states: "If the monitor hears a message that is incomprehensible in English from the instructor, this constitutes a 'no' response" and "If the monitor hears words used that are impeding communication, this constitutes a 'no' response." These two statements suggest that comprehensibility serves as a measure of accuracy.

State officials' comments, together with the classroom observation protocol, emphasize the role of comprehension in teacher assessments. However, they do not make clear whose comprehension is key to evaluations nor how comprehensibility is determined. On one hand, Horne seemed to imply that teachers' pronunciation rating is based not on the observer's comprehension, but rather, on the ability of ELL children to comprehend the teacher. While it sounds reasonable to expect children to be able to understand their teachers, it is important to remember that ELLs are precisely those children who do not yet speak English. In other words, the comprehensibility of a teacher's accent is being assessed based on the comprehension of children who may not know English. This is a particularly unusual measure.

In view of the judicial record of accepting ad hoc claims of incomprehensibility as a legitimate justification for accent discrimination, it is not surprising that Horne would claim that accent is only an issue when it affects comprehension. Nonetheless, his assertion is not completely consistent with his own comments. For example, it is extremely unlikely that the examples of "faulty English" that he provided—"biolet," "tink," and "coma"—would actually lead to communication breakdown. Further, Santa Cruz's comment regarding "the best models of English pronunciation" not only reflects a subjective hierarchy of accents, but it also reveals a pedagogical concern that children will imitate their teachers' accents. Johanna Haver, an adviser to Arizona educators, articulated a similar view of language acquisition: "Teachers should speak good grammar [sic] because kids pick up what they hear."[39] These concerns are baseless since research has shown that children acquire the dialect of their peers, not their elders. Together, these comments suggest that the ADE is focusing on accents even when they do not impede communication.

In any case, listener comprehension is an unreliable measure of speaker proficiency, because it is affected not only by the listener's familiarity with the accent in question, but also by the listener's disposition and preconceptions. Further, given the widespread tendency to equate Latino identity with speaking Spanish, together with the perception of Latinos as inherently other and foreign, classroom observers might be prone to "hear" foreign accents in the speech of Spanish-surnamed teachers, even when they are not present. Moreover, teachers who are speakers of Chicano English may be judged to be non-native English speakers who are dominant in Spanish, even if they do not know any Spanish at all, because of the structure of their native English dialect.[40] Because racial and linguistic stereotypes can influence comprehension in addition to perception of accent, using "comprehension," rather than a test of speaking ability or an expert assessment, as a metric for evaluating accent opens the door for inaccurate and prejudicial evaluations.

In addition to harming the children that it purports to protect, Arizona's policy also can discriminate against teachers whose English pronunciation is considered "nonstandard" or "inaccurate," given the lack of clear explanations of the relevance of accent to job performance, the flawed and impressionistic assessment of accent and comprehensibility. As I will discuss in the next section, the policy, as well as the media coverage of the policy, are almost problematic at a third level: their impact on the public representation and perception of Latinos.

Arizona's No-Accent Policy and the Public Representation of Latinos

Since it became part of the United States, Arizona has been the site of significant restrictions on the use of Spanish in schools. This began in the territorial period, and continued through the early twentieth century with the policy of Americanization through English acquisition.[41] The restrictions on Spanish were intensified as the result of the referendum that eliminated bilingual education at the start of the twenty-first century. Arizona's policy of removing teachers who speak with accents represents one more incremental

step in which even the hint of Spanish in a teacher's English has become suspect. Together with the banning of Latino studies, Arizona's accent policy
contributes to a marginalization and discursive erasure of Latino history
and culture within the public schools. This educational policy is inseparable
from a broader anti-immigrant agenda including increased restrictions and
policing of immigrants and Latinos.

Early twentieth century anti-immigrant movements explicitly expressed
concerns about the impact of "undesirable" immigrants on the racial
makeup of the nation. Today, even as the nation's dominant public discourses about immigration construct Mexican immigrants as a threat to
America's racial, cultural, and linguistic identity,[42] contemporary anti-
immigration activists deny that they harbor racist sentiments.[43] Given the
social norms against racism, calls for limiting immigration from Mexico can
garner greater public support when they emphasize issues such as "illegality" or ability and willingness to assimilate, rather than race or ethnicity.[44]
In one empirical study, American participants were asked to judge whether
hypothetical Mexican and English Canadian undocumented immigrants
should be deported. When no other information was provided about the
candidates, American subjects did not express ethnic or racial bias. However, when participants were informed that the immigrants had unpaid
parking tickets, they evaluated Mexicans more negatively than the English
Canadian immigrants.[45] Thus, illegal behavior (i.e., unpaid parking tickets)
served as a nonethnic rationale for discriminating against specific ethnic
groups. Media coverage of immigration reinforces negative stereotypes
about immigrants,[46] and represents all Latin American immigrants as "illegal," regardless of actual immigration status, thus shaping public perceptions of Latina/os more broadly.[47]

Like "illegality," the ADE policy against "inaccurate" accents provides a
nonethnic rationale for discriminating against Latinos. Despite the overwhelming evidence to the contrary, Spanish is portrayed as a threat to
English in the United States, with Spanish-speaking immigrants seen as
unwilling to assimilate linguistically. In contemporary discourse, the term
bilingual has come to mean "Spanish-speaking," and talk of "foreign accents" is more likely to be associated with Latinos than other groups. Thus,
even with the superficially neutral criteria of accuracy and comprehensibility, there is a tacit understanding that Arizona's policy is aimed at Spanish-
speaking immigrants, leading some commentators to ask whether the policy
would also be used to negatively assess other foreign accents. However, like
the study in which unpaid parking tickets served as a rationale for deporting one nationality of immigrants, in Arizona's educational policy, accent

can serve as a proxy for race. Just as the public concern about (unauthorized) immigration focuses almost exclusively on immigration from Mexico, ADE showed little concern regarding Dutch, German, or Swedish accents.[48] Moreover, media coverage that uncritically framed the accent policy as a move against immigrants or Latinos—especially using these two terms almost interchangeably, as some news reports did—may have reinforced the misperception that Latinos are inherently less American than other ethnic groups or that they do not speak English well.

In addition to providing an analogy of the use of accent as an "acceptable" surrogate for ethnicity-based calls to limit immigration, the trope of "illegality" even made its way into some of the media coverage surrounding the monitoring of teachers in Arizona. For example, Fox News opened its report on the policy with the following:

> After passing the nation's toughest state immigration enforcement law, Arizona's school officials are now **cracking down** on teachers with heavy accents. The Arizona department of education is sending evaluators to **audit** teachers and their English speaking skills to make sure districts are **complying with state and federal laws.**[49]

In this excerpt, speaking with an accent is constructed not just as an individual deficiency or a lack of teacher qualifications, but as an *illegal* or malevolent behavior (as noted in boldface) that officials must punish to ensure compliance with the laws.

As we have seen, Arizona's policy is pedagogically flawed and seems likely to have a disproportionately negative impact on Latino teachers, while also contributing to the negative representation of Latinos in public discourse. In addition, the focus on teachers' accents serves as a distraction from a much more serious threat to ELLs: Arizona's broader educational policy. As Gándara (this volume) discusses, eliminating bilingual education, underfunding ELL education, and implementing SEI has had deleterious effects on the linguistic and academic development of Spanish-speaking children. Indeed, Arizona's failure to provide an adequate education for Latino children is the subject of an ongoing lawsuit. Despite Horne's statement that "It's my job to make sure [ELLs are] taught English in the most rigorous, possible way so they can learn English quickly, can compete with their peers, and succeed academically,"[50] the ADE has refused to acknowledge the true obstacles to academic achievement for ELLs. Rather than addressing the documented shortcomings of its educational design, curriculum, and funding mechanisms, the ADE distracted the public with the supposed deficiencies of non-native English-speaking teachers.

Postscript

In the days before this volume went to press, the ADE reached a settlement with the U.S. Departments of Justice and Education, bringing an end to the federal investigation of the policy. Under the agreement, the state agency will no longer target teachers with accents. The agreement does not mean that "fluency" will no longer be required, that teachers with non-native or non-prestige accents will be protected from discrimination, or that state officials acknowledged any problems with the policy. Instead, the agreement transfers responsibility for certifying teacher qualifications from the state to the local districts. School districts that oppose prioritizing accent over other teacher qualifications, such as Tucson and Yuma, will no longer be required to take action against teachers judged to be deficient. However, the agreement does not forbid other districts from implementing discriminatory practices, and state officials were quick to point out that local districts will now be responsible for ensuring that teachers are English-proficient. While it remains to be seen how this new policy will play out, it is clear that some media outlets are again portraying the issue as a conflict between common sense understanding of accents and "bad grammar" as a question of teacher qualifications and language standards. For example, the headline on Fox News Latino read: "Arizona: Teachers Can Have Accents and Use Bad Grammar."

Notes

1. See Jordan, 2010. This chapter follows the nomenclature conventions of the field: EL for English learner or ELL for English language learner.
2. Zehr, 2010.
3. Zehr, 2010.
4. Retrieved on 1 June 2011, from www.ade.az.gov/oelas/.../2009-2010SEIClassroomObservationProtocol.pdf.
5. Bland, 2010; Fehr-Snyder, 2010.
6. Carreira, 2007; Cho and Krashen, 1998; Delgado-Gaitan and Trueba, 1991; Valenzuela, 1999; Walqui, 2000.
7. Baugh, 2003.
8. Moyer, 2004.
9. Leeman, 2004.
10. Edwards, 1989; Gardner, 1988.
11. Preston, 1986, 1989.
12. Kroskrity, 2004; Woolard, 1998.
13. Lippi-Green, 1997; Milroy and Milroy, 1999; Milroy, 2007.
14. Matsuda, 1990/1991.

15. Woolard, 2008.
16. Edwards, 1989.
17. Milroy and Milroy, 1999; Lippi-Green, 1997.
18. Strauss, 2010.
19. Jordan, 2010.
20. Fehr-Snyder, 2010, September 8.
21. Bland, 2010.
22. Jordan, 2010.
23. www.eeoc.gov/policy/docs/national-origin.html
24. www.eeoc.gov/policy/docs/national-origin.html
25. Lippi-Green, 1997.
26. Kang and Rubin, 2009; Rubin, 1992; Rubin and Smith, 1990.
27. Amin, 1999.
28. Chang and Aoki, 1997.
29. Lippi-Green, 1994, 1997; Matsuda, 1990/1991; Smith, 2005.
30. Cameron, 1997.
31. http://people-press.org/files/legacy-pdf/274.pdf
32. Leeman, 2004.
33. *Salem v. La Salle High School* 1983, cited in Valdés, 2001, 155.
34. *Kahakua v. Hallgrem* 1987, cited in Matsuda, 1990/1991, 1345.
35. Fehr-Snyder, 2010.
36. Jordan, 2010.
37. Retrieved on 1 June 2011, from http://www2.ed.gov/policy/elsec/leg/esea02/index.html.
38. Fehr-Snyder, 2010.
39. Jordan, 2010. Haver is featured on the Arizona Tea Party website.
40. Fought, 2003; Santa Ana, 1993.
41. DuBord, 2003.
42. Chavez, 2008; Santa Ana, 2002.
43. Hill, 2008.
44. Short and Magaña, 2002.
45. Short and Magaña, 2002.
46. Santa Ana, 2002.
47. Stewart, Pitts, and Osborne, 2011.
48. Paraphrasing Lippi-Green, 1997.
49. Stegall 2010, my emphasis.
50. Stegall, 2010.

References

Amin, N. (1999). Minority women teachers of ESL: Negotiating white English. Non-native educators in English language teaching. In G. Braine (Ed.), *Non-native educators in English language teaching*, pp. 93–104. Mahway, NJ: Lawrence Erlbaum.

Baugh, J. (2003). Linguistic profiling. In S. Makoni, G. Smitherman, A. F. Ball, & A. K. Spears (Eds.), *Black linguistics: Language, society, and politics in Africa and the Americas*, pp. 155–168. New York: Routledge.

Bland, K. (2010, September 12). Workshop helps foreign-born educators lose accent. *The Arizona Republic.* Retrieved June 1, 2011 at http://www.azcentral.com/arizonarepublic/arizonaliving/articles/2010/09/12/20100912foreign-teachers-accent-english.html.

Cameron, C. D. R. (1997). How the García cousins lost their accents: Understanding the language of Title VII decisions approving English-only rules as the product of racial dualism, Latino invisibility, and legal indeterminacy. *California Law Review, 85*, 1347–1393.

Carreira, M. (2007). Spanish-for-native-speaker matters: Narrowing the Latino achievement gap through Spanish language instruction. *Heritage Language Journal, 5*(1), 147–171.

Chang, R. S., & Aoki, K. (1997). Centering the immigrant in the inter/national imagination. *California Law Review, 85*, 1395.

Chavez, L. R. (2008). *The Latino threat: Constructing immigrants, citizens, and the nation.* Palo Alto, CA: Stanford University Press.

Cho, G., & Krashen, S. (1998). The negative consequences of heritage language loss and why we should care. *Heritage Language Development*, 3–13.

Delgado-Gaitan, C., & H.T. Trueba. (1991). *Crossing cultural borders: Education for immigrant families in America.* London: Falmer Press.

DuBord, E. M. (2003). Language policy and the drawing of social boundaries: Public and private schools in territorial Tucson. *Spanish in Context, 7*(1), 25–45.

Edwards, J. R. (1989). *Language and disadvantage* (2nd ed.). London: Cole & Whurr.

Fehr-Snyder, K. (2010, September 8). Feds probing bias claims against Arizona's non-native English speaking teachers. *The Arizona Republic.* Retrieved June 1, 2011, at www.azcentral.com/community/scottsdale/articles/2010/09/08/20100908 arizona-teachers-federal-government-investigation.html

Fehr-Snyder, K. (2010, September 11). Arizona agency defends English-language teacher scrutiny. *The Arizona Republic.* Retrieved June 1, 2011, at http://www.az central.com/arizonarepublic/local/articles/2010/09/11/20100911arizona-english -language-learner-scrutiny.html.

Fought, C. (2003). *Chicano English in context.* New York: Palgrave Macmillan.

Gardner, R. C. (1988). The socio educational model of second language learning: Assumptions, findings, and issues. *Language Learning, 38*(1), 101–126.

Hill, J. H. (2008). *The everyday language of white racism.* Malden, MA: Wiley-Blackwell.

Jordan, M. (2010, April 30). Arizona grades teachers on fluency. *The Wall Street Journal.*

Kang, O., & Rubin, D. L. (2009). Reverse linguistic stereotyping: Measuring the effect of listener expectations on speech evaluation. *Journal of Language and Social Psychology, 28*(4), 441–456.

Kroskrity, P. (2004). Language ideologies. In A. Duranti (Ed.), *A Companion to linguistic anthropology*, pp. 496–517. Malden MA: Blackwell.

Leeman, J. (2004). Racializing language: A history of linguistic ideologies in the U.S. Census. *Journal of Language and Politics, 3*(3), 507–534.

Lippi-Green, R. (1994). Accent, standard language ideology, and discriminatory pretext in the courts. *Language in Society, 23*(2), 163–198.

Lippi-Green, R. (1997). *English with an accent: Language, ideology and discrimination in the United States.* London: Routledge.

Matsuda, M. J. (1990/1991). Voices of America: Accent, antidiscrimination law, and a jurisprudence for the last reconstruction. *Yale Law Journal, 100,* 1329–1407.

Milroy, J. (2007). The ideology of the standard language. In C. Llamas, L. Mullany, & P. Stockwell (Eds.), *Routledge Companion to Sociolinguistics,* pp. 133–139. London: Routledge.

Milroy, J., & Milroy, L. (1999). *Authority in language* (3rd ed.). London: Routledge.

Moyer, A. (2004). *Age, accent and experience in second language acquisition.* Buffalo, NY: Multilingual Matters.

Preston, D. R. (1989). *Perceptual dialectology: Nonlinguists' views of areal linguistics.* Topics in sociolinguistics series, no. 7. Dordrecht, Holland: Foris Publications.

Rubin, D. L. (1992). Nonlanguage factors affecting undergraduates' judgments of nonnative English-speaking teaching assistants. *Research in Higher Education, 33*(4), 511–531.

Rubin, D. L., & Smith, K. A. (1990). Effects of accent, ethnicity, and lecture topic on undergraduates' perceptions of nonnative English-speaking teaching assistants. *International Journal of Intercultural Relations, 14*(3), 337–353.

Santa Ana, O. (1993). Chicano English and the nature of the Chicano language setting. *Hispanic Journal of Behavioral Sciences, 15*(1), 3–35.

Santa Ana, O. (2002). *Brown tide rising: Metaphors of Latinos in contemporary American public discourse.* Austin: University of Texas Press.

Short, R., & Magaña, L. (2002). Political rhetoric, immigration attitudes, and contemporary prejudice: A Mexican American dilemma. *The Journal of Social Psychology, 142*(6), 701–712.

Smith, G. B. (2005). I want to speak like a native speaker: The case for lowering the plaintiff's burden of proof in Title VII accent discrimination cases. *Ohio State Law Journal, 66,* 231–268.

Stegall, C. (2010, May 22). Arizona seeks to reassign heavily accented teachers. FoxNews .com. Retrieved June 1, 2011 at http://www.foxnews.com/politics/2010/05/22/arizona-seeks-reassign-heavily-accented-teachers.

Stewart, C. O., Pitts, M. J., & Osborne, H. (2011). Mediated intergroup conflict: The discursive construction of "illegal immigrants" in a regional U.S. newspaper. *Journal of Language and Social Psychology, 30*(1), 8–27.

Strauss, V. (2010, May 4). Arizona strikes again: Now it is ethnic studies [Electronic Version]. The Answer Sheet (WashingtonPost.com). Retrieved June 1, 2011 at http://voices.washingtonpost.com/answer-sheet/history/arizona-strikes-again-now-it-i.html.

Strauss, V. (2010, May 27). How Arizona is checking teachers' accents [Electronic Version]. The Answer Sheet (WashingtonPost.com). Retrieved June 1, 2011 at http://

voices.washingtonpost.com/answer-sheet/learning/how-arizona-is-checking -teache.html.

U.S. Equal Opportunity Commission. (2002). *Compliance manual on "National Origin Discrimination." Section 13.* Retrieved June 1, 2011 at http://www.eeoc .gov/policy/docs/national-origin.html.

Valdés, G. (2001). Bilingual individuals and language-based discrimination. In R. D. González & I. Melis (Eds.), *Language ideologies: Critical perspectives on the Official English Movement* (Vol. 2), pp. 140–170. Mahwah, NJ: Lawrence Erlbaum.

Valenzuela, A. (1999). *Subtractive schooling: U.S.-Mexican youth and the politics of caring.* Albany: State University of New York Press.

Walqui, A. (2000). *Access and engagement: Program design and instructional approaches for immigrant students in secondary schools.* Washington, DC: Center for Applied Linguistics.

Woolard, K. A. (1998). Language ideology as a field of inquiry. In B. B. Schiefflin, K. A. Woolard, & P. V. Kroskrity (Eds.), *Language ideologies: Practice and theory,* pp. 3–47. Oxford: Oxford University Press.

Woolard, K. A. (2008). Language and identity choice in Catalonia: The interplay of contrasting ideologies of linguistic authority. In K. Süselbeck, U. Mühlschlegel, & P. Masson (Eds.), *Lengua, nación e identidad: La regulación del plurilingüísmo en España y América Latina* (Vol. 44), pp. 303–324. Madrid: Iberoamericana Editorial.

Zehr, M. A. (2010). Arizona ed. officials weigh in on teachers' fluency issue [Electronic Version]. Learning the Language (Education Week). Retrieved June 1, 2011 at http://blogs.edweek.org/edweek/learning-the-language/2010/05/arizona_ ed_official_weighs_in.html.

9

An Immigration Crisis in a Nation of Immigrants

Why Amending the Fourteenth Amendment Won't Solve Our Problems[1]

Alberto R. Gonzales

All persons born or naturalized in the United States, and subject to the jurisdiction thereof, are citizens of the United States and of the State wherein they reside.[2]

THE CONCERNS OVER ANOTHER TERRORIST ATTACK, a sluggish economic recovery, high unemployment rates, and state and local budget deficits have propelled immigration policy to the forefront of political debate in the United States. America's current approach to immigration is an abject failure, undermining the rule of law and our national security. This has prompted various legislative proposals relating to citizenship, including amending the U.S. Constitution to make clear that children born in the United States to unauthorized immigrants are not entitled to birthright citizenship. The reasons why these various state and federal-level "solutions" are either ineffective in solving our immigration crisis, or likely unconstitutional, are presented in this chapter. Instead, the president and Congress should invest their time and energy to pass comprehensive immigration reform on the federal level.[3]

Present Federal Immigration Policies and Challenges

The recent economic recession brought about staggering job loss nationwide and the highest unemployment rate since the late 1970s and early 1980s.[4] As a result, some Americans, unable to find work or fearful of losing their jobs, believe that unauthorized immigrants[5] will take jobs from

U.S. citizens. In addition, many state and local governments are faced with severe budget deficits, and no longer have the funds to continue providing services to U.S. citizens, due in part to the costs of providing services to the growing unauthorized immigrant population. Many Americans in our post-9/11 society also worry that those who intend to harm our nation will take advantage of our open borders. In response to these fears and realities, citizens across the United States have begun to demand legislative action to solve the nation's immigration crisis.

In recent years, many "solutions" on the local, state, and federal levels have been proposed, but little substantive action has occurred. Among them is the suggestion of a controversial constitutional amendment. In keeping with the Immigration and Nationality Act (INA), common law, and the Constitution, all children born within the United States and subject to its jurisdiction acquire birthright citizenship based solely on the location of their birth. Current law does not consider the citizenship status of a child's parents in determining the citizenship of children born on U.S. soil. Some American citizens and legislators believe that excluding these children from the constitutional guarantee of birthright citizenship would reduce the number of unauthorized immigrants and help solve the current immigration crisis. I disagree.

Like most Americans, I am a descendant of immigrants and a grateful beneficiary of the opportunities available to our nation's citizens. My grandparents emigrated from Mexico in the early twentieth century seeking a better life, and they found it working in the fields and farms of Texas. I am the son of a cotton picker and construction worker who did not go to school beyond the second grade, yet I became the Attorney General of the United States. We live in a country where dreams still come true no matter your last name or skin color. Diversity is one of the great strengths of the United States. The migration of ethnicities, cultures, and ideas has played a vital role in molding America into the great nation that it is today. It is this rich diversity, so entrenched in our national identity, that makes achieving the right immigration policy a most difficult task. We must strive for a policy that promotes our diversity, protects our families, and enhances our foreign policy, national security, and economy.

Our current federal immigration policy has failed to strike this balance. Every sovereign nation has the authority to determine who can be a citizen and who can lawfully be present within its borders. Today, many Americans believe that our federal government has abandoned that responsibility. As this nation's former chief law enforcement officer and a citizen who believes in the rule of law, I cannot condone anyone coming into this country illegally. However, as a father who wants the best for my own children, I understand why parents risk coming to America and being separated from their children for extended periods—especially when there is relatively little chance of prosecution. While immediate action is required to resolve our current immigration crisis, state-level legislation and a constitutional amendment are not effective solutions. Instead, we should pass and enforce comprehensive immigration legislation at the federal level.

Amending the Constitution

The Supremacy Clause of Article VI, Clause 2 of the Constitution declares that the Constitution is the "Supreme Law of the Land."[6] With this supremacy in mind, the framers sought to ensure that the Constitution would only be altered in extraordinary circumstances that could not be addressed effectively through legislation or regulation. They accomplished this by establishing a stringent amendment procedure. According to Article V of the Constitution, a constitutional amendment may be proposed in one of two ways: with approval of two-thirds of both Houses of Congress or upon the application of two-thirds of the states.[7] Once proposed, three-fourths of the states—thirty-eight states—must ratify the amendment for it to go into effect.[8]

Since the Constitution's ratification in 1788, only thirty-three amendments have been proposed.[9] Only twenty-seven of those received the requisite approval from the states.[10] Of those twenty-seven, the first ten, comprising the Bill of Rights, were adopted in 1791.[11] In the 220 years since the Constitution's ratification, it has only been amended seventeen times and Congress has never revised an amendment. Among those seventeen amendments, the Fourteenth Amendment is most critical to the determination of citizenship for immigration purposes and to the current immigration debate.

History and Interpretation of the Fourteenth Amendment

Central to this chapter and to the discussion of amending the Constitution to restrict birthright citizenship is the phrase "subject to the jurisdiction thereof" contained in the Fourteenth Amendment. While unauthorized immigrants may give birth to children within the boundaries of the United States, the children do not automatically obtain birthright citizenship unless they are also "subject to the jurisdiction" of the United States. Much like the term *unreasonable search and seizure* in the Fourth Amendment, the Constitution does not define precisely who is to be considered "subject to the jurisdiction" of the United States. In the absence of a constitutional definition, courts and legislators have been left to interpret the phrase's meaning.

Prior to the Fourteenth Amendment, a constitutional definition of citizenship did not exist.[12] Lacking a precise statutory description, the United States borrowed the concept of *jus soli*—"law of the soil"—from British common law.[13] This doctrine, more commonly referred to as birthright citizenship, provides that any person born within this nation's territory is a citizen of the United States and, therefore, a beneficiary of the protections of the Constitution.[14] It was commonly understood by the courts that the only exceptions to the application of the doctrine of *jus soli* were children born to foreign diplomats, hostile occupying forces, and children born on foreign ships.[15] Until the 1830s, this principle applied to everyone born within the territory, including, in Northern and Southern states alike, free African Americans born in the United States, "even as the judges upheld laws and practices that discriminated against them."[16] With the rise of racial tensions and conflict between the states in the mid-1800s, however, the applicability of this doctrine to freed slaves and their descendents became a topic of hot debate. Were U.S.-born children of African Americans subject to the discriminatory laws or were they entitled to all the benefits of citizenship?

In a divergence from the commonly understood doctrine of birthright citizenship, in 1856 the U.S. Supreme Court handed down its decision in *Dred Scott v. Sanford*.[17] In this case, the Court was faced with the issue of whether a man of African descent who was formerly a slave and whose ancestors entered this country as slaves, upon emancipation was entitled to the rights, privileges, and immunities provided by the Constitution.[18] In this infamous decision, the Court rejected the doctrine of *jus soli* for former slaves and their progeny, regardless of their status as emancipated individuals. The Court further stated that former slaves were neither "citizens" nor "people of the United States."[19] The Court described them as an "inferior class of beings" who did not have the rights and privileges that the Constitution traditionally granted to citizens under the established common law doctrine of birthright citizenship.[20]

This decision placed the protections of the Constitution, otherwise available to other U.S.-born citizens, beyond the reach of African Americans. Congress responded during Reconstruction by passing the Civil Rights Act of 1866 which stated that "all persons born in the United States and not subject to any foreign power, excluding Indians not taxed, are hereby declared to be citizens of the United States."[21] However, an act of Congress cannot override the Constitution, and can be revised or repealed by a subsequent act of Congress. To once and for all "place the right of citizenship based on birth within the jurisdiction of the United States beyond question,"[22] the Fourteenth Amendment was adopted on July 9, 1868. The "Citizenship Clause" of this amendment constitutionalized the common law doctrine of *jus soli* by establishing that "all persons born or naturalized in the United States, and subject to the jurisdiction thereof, are citizens of the United States and of the State wherein they reside."[23] Birthright citizenship was applicable from this point forward to "all persons" born within the United States and "subject to the jurisdiction thereof."

Some commentators argue that the primary issue with regard to birthright citizenship at the time of the Fourteenth Amendment's enactment was the classification of free African Americans, and thus, the phrase "subject to the jurisdiction thereof" does not include unauthorized immigrants.[24] However, the applicability of the Citizenship Clause to children born to immigrant parents was tested in the late 1800s with respect to America's increasingly harsh treatment of persons of Chinese descent. During this period of time, the Chinese became "the first, and most despised, targets of post–Civil War nativism."[25] The United States began implementing discriminatory policies based on the idea that the Chinese were so fundamentally different than Americans that they could never fully assimilate.[26] Some even saw the Chinese as "utterly unfit" and "wholly incompetent to exercise the important privileges of an American citizen."[27] These beliefs led to a large-scale attack on birthright citizenship.[28]

In 1898, the Supreme Court addressed this issue and reaffirmed the Fourteenth Amendment right to birthright citizenship for the children of immigrants in its decision in the *Wong Kim Ark* case.[29] More than one hundred years ago, the Court found that the "common law precedent of birthright citizenship [was] too well-rooted to abandon at that point in the nation's history."[30] It ultimately held that the Citizenship Clause of the Fourteenth Amendment conferred citizenship upon "a child born in the United States of parents of Chinese descent, who at the time of his birth were subjects of the emperor of China, but have permanent domicile and residence in the United States."[31] Based on this permanent domicile and residence, the parents had subjected themselves and their son to the jurisdiction of the United States, thus guaranteeing young Wong Kim Ark citizenship based on the location of his birth. This decision also reinforced the nation's sovereign power to determine what persons should be entitled to citizenship under the Constitution.[32] The Court further reiterated that the nation's jurisdiction "within its own territory is necessarily exclusive and absolute."[33] This set the nineteenth-century foundation for federal authority over immigration.[34]

Some critics argue that, because *Wong Kim Ark* involved a child born in the United States to parents who had established permanent domicile and residence in the United States, the Supreme Court has never spoken on the issue of birthright citizenship for children of unauthorized immigrants. Children born to unauthorized immigrant parents meet the first requirement of birth within the United States. However, to qualify for birthright citizenship under the Fourteenth Amendment, they must also be "subject to the jurisdiction" of the United States. Because the plain language of the Constitution does not provide a definition of who is to be considered "subject to the jurisdiction" of the United States, an analysis of case law is required. The consideration of established precedent reveals three categories of persons deemed not subject to the jurisdiction of the United States: (1) children of members of Indian tribes subject to tribal laws;[35] (2) children born of diplomatic representatives of a foreign state; and (3) children born of alien enemies in hostile occupation.[36] Persons falling within any of these three categories are not considered "subject to the jurisdiction" of the United States, and, therefore, do not automatically become U.S. citizens based on their birth within the United States. Conversely, any person not included in those categories and born on U.S. soil becomes a U.S. citizen as a result of the location of their birth. Because the children of unauthorized immigrants born in America do not fall within any of those three categories, it follows that the Constitution guarantees them birthright citizenship.

The text of another clause within the same section of the Fourteenth Amendment lends further support to the argument that children born here to unauthorized immigrants are to be considered "subject to the jurisdiction" of the United States. The Equal Protection Clause, immediately following the Citizenship Clause, provides that "no state shall . . . deny to any person within its jurisdiction the equal protection of the laws."[37] The close proximity of these similar jurisdictional phrases suggests that they should be interpreted similarly. At least one Supreme Court justice would agree. In *United States v. Wong Kim Ark*, Justice Gray stated:

> It is impossible to construe the words "subject to the jurisdiction thereof," in the opening sentence, as less comprehensive than the words "within its jurisdiction," in the concluding sentence of the same section; or to hold that persons "within the jurisdiction" of one of the states of the Union are not "subject to the jurisdiction of the United States."[38]

While Justice Gray's statement is not binding nor has any precedential weight for the courts, I would argue that it is consistent with established canons of statutory construction. It is a basic principle of these canons that "a statute should be read as a harmonious whole, with its separate parts being interpreted within their broader statutory context in a manner that furthers [the] statutory purpose."[39] Moreover, "a term used more than once in a statute should ordinarily be given the same meaning throughout."[40] Although the Citizenship Clause and Equal Protection Clause use slightly different wording, the term *jurisdiction* appears in each clause. Because these clauses are both contained in the same section of the Fourteenth Amendment, based on the canons of statutory construction, they should be given the same meaning. Accordingly, because the Supreme Court has held that the phrase "within its jurisdiction" applies to unauthorized immigrants,[41] it follows that the phrase "subject to the jurisdiction," located in the sentence immediately preceding the phrase "within its jurisdiction," should apply to unauthorized immigrants as well.

While the Supreme Court has yet to rule on birthright citizenship or the interpretation of "subject to the jurisdiction" in the context of a child born in America to unauthorized immigrants, it appears that if presented with the question, the Court would interpret the Fourteenth Amendment as conveying birthright citizenship, and extend its reasoning in the *Wong Kim Ark* case to include the children of unauthorized immigrants. However, since the federal government has not taken action to alleviate the burdens of a failed federal policy, state and local governments have felt compelled to do so.

Proposed State and Federal Level Solutions

As states are forced to respond to the influx of unauthorized immigrants and the tensions that their presence creates, many have taken matters into their own hands and proposed legislation that they believe would remedy their respective situations. Among the various solutions suggested by state legislators, some of the most recurring themes are the ability to enforce federal immigration laws, tracking money spent directly and indirectly to provide services to persons unlawfully present in the United States, and classification of children born to unauthorized immigrant parents.[42] Federal-level citizenship legislation has taken the form of several bills proposing to reduce the unauthorized immigrant population by clarifying provisions relating to birthright citizenship and debate over the possibility of amending the Constitution.

One of the most controversial state-level attempts to gain control of the illegal immigration problem is Arizona's Senate Bill 1070, discussed elsewhere in this volume.[43] SB 1070 deals primarily with enforcement of federal immigration law and the creation of new criminal laws dealing specifically with immigrants, including trespass by unauthorized immigrants, the stopping and solicitation of workers, and transportation of unauthorized immigrants.[44] Other notable state legislative efforts include: Texas House Bill 113, which would exact a penalty of $10,000 for each day that a county or municipality prohibits or restricts the enforcement of U.S. immigration law,[45] Utah House Bill 116, which would establish a guest-worker program whereby undocumented individuals could obtain permits to work in Utah,[46] and Georgia

House Bill 87 that cracks down on illegal immigration by increasing some enforcement powers and requiring many employers to check the immigration status of new hires.[47] Most recently, Alabama House Bill 56 would require schools to gather statistical data on students' immigration status, businesses to E-verify immigration status of employees, and law enforcement to investigate people's immigration status.[48]

In addition to state-level citizenship legislation, there have been several federal attempts over the last fifteen years to clarify the terminology which grants birthright citizenship to restrict its application to persons with at least one U.S. citizen, national or legal permanent resident parent.[49] One example of a federal-level attempt to clarify citizenship by redefining who is considered "subject to the jurisdiction" of the United States is the Birthright Citizenship Act of 2011, otherwise known as H.R. 140.[50] This bill would amend Section 301 of the INA "to clarify those classes of individuals born in the United States who are nationals and citizens of the United States at birth."[51] While the Fourteenth Amendment sets forth the primary framework, H.R. 140 would essentially redefine the key phrase, "subject to the jurisdiction," to include: "(1) a citizen or national of the United States; (2) an alien lawfully admitted for permanent residence in the United States whose residence is in the United States; or (3) an alien performing active service in the armed forces."[52] This would effectively exclude children born to unauthorized immigrants, commonly referred to as "anchor babies," from the longstanding constitutional guarantee of birthright citizenship. Legislation virtually identical to H.R. 140 was also proposed in 1995, 2007, and 2009.[53]

Perhaps the boldest of these proposals involves amending the U.S. Constitution.[54] While no formal bill has been introduced, some members of Congress believe that a constitutional amendment would help solve the current immigration crisis. In an interview with Fox News, Senator Lindsey Graham proclaimed that he may propose a constitutional amendment that would amend the Fourteenth Amendment to deny birthright citizenship to persons based on the origin of their parents.[55] According to Senator Graham, birthright citizenship is a "mistake." He stated that "people come here to have babies. They come here to drop a child. It's called 'drop and leave.'" They "cross the border, they go the emergency room, have a child, and that child is automatically an American citizen. That should not be the case. That attracts people here for all the wrong reasons."[56] The proponents of H.R. 140 believe that the Citizenship Clause rewards unscrupulous foreigners who break America's laws by giving them an incentive to sneak into the United States to have children here and become attached to this country.[57] According to some, amending the Fourteenth Amendment to exclude children of unlawfully present parents would remove this incentive and reduce the unauthorized immigrant population in the United States.[58]

The current state- and federal-level legislative proposals are only the tip of the iceberg. As long as the federal government avoids taking measures to reform the nation's immigration system, state and federal leaders, immersed in financial chaos, will continue to do what they believe necessary to resolve their particular circumstances and answer their citizens' demands for action. However, as discussed next, amending or attempting to clarify the scope of the Fourteenth Amendment will do little to discourage illegal migration. Many of the state solutions will also be largely ineffective—some likely unconstitutional—in addressing our current immigration crisis.

Redefining Citizenship at the State and Federal Levels Fails to Solve Our Immigration Crisis

While states have proposed intriguing solutions to the immigration crisis, such piecemeal reform to America's intricate immigration system is bad policy and will ultimately prove ineffective. The federal government is better positioned to address these issues on a national level in a coordinated, comprehensive fashion. The issue of illegal immigration lies at a peculiar crossroads between the powers and responsibilities of the federal government's sovereign authority over immigration and state enforcement and police powers. The Supreme Court has held that the "power to regulate immigration is exclusively a federal power."[59] It describes "regulation" as including "a determination of who should or should not be admitted into the country, and the conditions under which a legal entrant may remain."[60] This language preempts many sub-federal actions while permitting state and local governments to take enforcement actions consistent with federal law.[61]

Some examples of state-level citizenship legislation that are likely to be preempted by federal law are proposals that attempt to place children born to unauthorized immigrant parents in a separate class than children born to U.S. citizen parents. For example, Texas House Bill 292 proposes to modify birth certificates so that they contain a field that would record the citizenship status of the infant's parents. Under this bill, birth certificates would not be issued unless one of the infant's parents could prove U.S. citizenship. If the parent could not produce such evidence, a "temporary report of alien birth" would be issued in place of a standard birth certificate. Because this type of legislation appears to recharacterize the citizenship status of children born to citizens of other countries, the courts may ultimately determine that it attempts to "regulate" immigration and is therefore preempted by the federal government. Where these state-level proposals are not preempted, they will create a patchwork network of immigration policy that will ultimately make enforcement of federal and state imposed regulations difficult, if not impossible.

Furthermore, efforts at the federal level to pass a statute to deny birthright citizenship to children born to unauthorized immigrant parents would be contrary to long-standing American common law. A Department of Justice (DOJ) opinion supports this contention. In 1995, Congress considered a bill that proposed to restrict birthright citizenship to exclude children born to unauthorized immigrants.[62] H.R. 1363, more commonly referred to as the Citizenship Reform Act of 1995, proposed to amend Section 301 of INA, "which grants citizenship 'at birth' to all persons 'born in the United States, and subject to the jurisdiction thereof.'"[63] The bill would "deny citizenship at birth to children born in the United States of parents who are not citizens or permanent resident aliens."[64] Analogous with the most recent attempts to define citizenship, this bill inserted provisions that would specify which persons who are to be considered as "subject to the jurisdiction of the United States."[65] Under this bill, two categories of children born on U.S. soil would be deemed "subject to the jurisdiction of the United States" and would therefore acquire birthright citizenship: (1) a child born to wedded parents, at least one of which is a U.S. citizen or a noncitizen national, or a lawfully permanent resident (LPR) who resides in the United States; or (2) children born to an unmarried woman with one of these statuses.[66] The bill attempted to redefine the language of the INA to exclude children born to parents without authorized resident status from automatically acquiring citizenship based on their place of birth.[67] The DOJ deemed H.R. 1363 to be "unconstitutional on its face" and stated that it would "flatly contradict our constitutional history and . . . traditions."[68] The DOJ warned that "it would be a grave mistake to alter the opening sentence of the Fourteenth Amendment without sober reflection on how it came to be a part of our basic constitutional character."[69]

The interplay between the power of the Supreme Court to interpret the Constitution and of Congress to make laws, such as H.R. 140, that are intended to clarify and interpret the Constitution is important to the outcome of the current Fourteenth Amendment debate. As the Supreme Court stated in its decision in the *DeBartolo Corp. v. Florida Gulf Coast Building & Construction Trades Council* case, in much the same way as is the Supreme Court, Congress "is bound by and swears an oath to uphold the Constitution. The courts will therefore not lightly assume that Congress intended to infringe constitutionally protected liberties or usurp power constitutionally forbidden it."[70] This means that if Congress does succeed in passing a law that reinterprets the Citizenship Clause and denies birthright citizenship to children born to unauthorized immigrant parents, the Supreme Court may defer to Congress and sustain the law's constitutionality. However, there are numerous examples where the courts have struck down acts of Congress as unconstitutional because they clearly violate the plain language of the Constitution, or are inconsistent with court precedents interpreting the Constitution.

Finally, amending the Fourteenth Amendment is not the best or most effective way to solve the current immigration crisis and should be considered a last resort, used only when an issue cannot be appropriately addressed through existing avenues. This view is supported by the fact that the framers made the amendment process extremely difficult, requiring an overwhelming consensus among Congress and ratification by a majority of the states. In addition, a constitutional amendment will not address the economic reasons why immigrants continue to come to America. As is evidenced by Senator Graham's statements, many Americans seem to believe that a large portion of immigrants illegally enter America principally with the intent to deliver their children on U.S. soil, so that their children can enjoy all the rights and privileges that the Constitution granted to citizens. However, this incentive at best accounts for a fraction of unauthorized immigrants.[71] The truth is most undocumented workers come here to provide for themselves and their families, in search of a better life, irrespective of the possibilities of U.S. citizenship. To focus momentarily on one sender country, Mexico continues to suffer from widespread economic and political upheaval. As long as debilitating poverty plagues Mexico, its most impoverished citizens will look to America for greater economic opportunities. Excluding the children of unauthorized immigrants from the guarantee of birthright citizenship will not deter many citizens from Mexico and other sending countries from coming to America to provide for their families.

Alternative Solution: Comprehensive Immigration Reform

A hodgepodge approach to reforming America's immigration law will only further complicate an already problematic system. Instead, Congress should pass and enforce comprehensive immigration legislation that secures our borders with the accelerated deployment of additional border agents, supported where appropriate with the National Guard and our military. We should also utilize our newest technology such as motion sensors and unmanned drones instead of building a 3,000-mile fence. I anticipate that opponents of tougher enforcement measures will claim the use of our military constitutes a militarizing of our southern border. Such criticism would be unfounded. Mexico uses its military to patrol its own southern border. The primary mission of our military should be to repel invasions and fight terrorism in countries like Afghanistan; but there is nothing inappropriate in using our military on our southern border solely in a support role to U.S. Customs and Border Protection and other law enforcement agencies.

In addition, our immigration policy should strengthen our national economic policy and promote commerce.[72] By most accounts, unauthorized immigrants contribute to our nation's economy.[73] The positive long-term effects of legal immigration on the American labor market include improved productivity, increased average income for native U.S. citizens and, in a growing economy, an increase in jobs sufficient to ensure that native U.S. citizen employees are not displaced.[74] Therefore, an immigration policy that works with and encourages immigrants to come to America lawfully, particularly skilled immigrants, will contribute to the strength of our economy.[75] Also, there are a number of skilled jobs for which Americans are not available and other low-skill jobs that native-born American citizens just do not want. For example, it is estimated that nearly 60 percent of farm workers in the United States are unauthorized immigrants.[76] Other low-skill fields that employ large numbers of both legal and illegal immigrants include factories, construction, maintenance, and the like.[77] To attract skilled and unskilled workers to fill these positions and sustain our economy, our immigration policy should include a more robust temporary-worker program. To ensure that a temporary worker's presence is only temporary, a portion of that worker's wages could be placed in escrow and released to him when he returns to his home country. Thus, comprehensive immigration reform should include a more robust temporary worker program, without more bureaucracy creating delay and inefficiency, that attracts both high-skilled and low-skilled workers to sustain our economic growth.

While the media often portray illegal immigration through dramatic scenes of people crossing the Rio Grande, digging tunnels, and climbing fences, the truth is that 4 to 5.5 million unauthorized immigrants, nearly half of the entire unauthorized immigrant population, entered the United States lawfully as temporary visitors and subsequently overstayed their visas.[78] Obtaining a nonimmigrant visa for temporary admission to the United States is typically easier and less time intensive than attempting to gain legal permanent resident status. This ease of entry, coupled with the fact that, as of 2006 this nation had "no means of determining whether all the foreign nationals admitted for temporary stays actually leave the country," make the regulation and enforcement of the terms of nonimmigrant visas vital to the success of the U.S. immigration policy.[79] Congress should consider imposing monetary fines and otherwise severely penalize those who overstay their visas. We should also develop a more formal practical process that keeps track of visa overstayers and provides incentives to home countries to help the United States locate and track them.

Instead of rewarding those who break this nation's laws, our immigration policy should reinforce and foster respect for the law through effective enforcement. Effective law enforcement requires the imposition of tougher penalties on employers who hire undocumented workers. Companies that employ unauthorized immigrants save substantial amounts of money on labor and circumvent the process set forth by the INA, which requires the employer to file a visa petition on behalf of the worker and complete the necessary labor certification.[80] Not surprisingly, these workers are vulnerable and sometimes exploited. Moreover, because our current immigration system provides very few visas to those immigrants seeking low-skilled jobs, there is little incentive to attempt to come here legally to work in these areas. More temporary visa categories should be available for needed workers and specialists. Another way to encourage employers to continue to hire without fear of prosecution would be to streamline issuance to temporary workers tamper-proof, picture ID cards by the Department of Homeland Security.[81] Because many foreigners come to the United States seeking employment, this type of policy would provide the United States with documentation of their presence and enable the United States to ensure that those persons remain only temporarily unless they take the appropriate steps to gain a more permanent legal status.

Comprehensive reform must simultaneously secure our borders and also deal with the millions of unauthorized immigrants already present in the United States. I understand that some Americans feel anger over unauthorized immigrants; however, our government is incapable of forcibly removing millions of people at one time. Even if feasible, such action would devastate many industries and would disproportionately affect border states and states with popular ports of entry. Instead, unauthorized immigrants who wish to remain in this country are verifiably employed, pay taxes, and have no criminal record could be allowed to remain in the United States under temporary legal status if they pay a penalty fee as an acknowledgment of violation of the law. A policy that places unauthorized immigrants into a verifiable legal status provides further security for our country in a post-9/11 world. Furthermore, on balance I have no major policy objection with the concept of earned legalization in the future for these individuals if they pay an additional penalty fee, have no criminal record, are verifiably employed, pay taxes, otherwise meet the current standards and requirements of citizenship, and are not given advantage over those who followed the rules in pursuing citizenship.

Some opponents of comprehensive immigration reform claim it is amnesty. I respectfully disagree. "Amnesty" is defined as an act of a government authority by which pardon is granted to a large group of individuals. And "pardon" is defined as the excusing of an offense without exacting a penalty. By definition what I propose does not constitute amnesty.

Comprehensive immigration reform should also include updating the INA,[82] the principle U.S. statute dealing with immigration law.[83] The INA is outdated, confusing, and internally inconsistent. Congress should revise it based upon a coherent set of principles rather than the ad hoc patchwork it has become. The INA should be rewritten so that it can be more easily understood by the average person.

Finally, for federal comprehensive immigration reform to be effective, it must be fully funded at the front and back end of the enforcement process. Because the current policy is in such disrepair, successful comprehensive immigration reform *will* be costly. Permitting the current patchwork system to stay in place, however, will cost much more—it will continue to put our nation's economy and national security at risk. Comprehensive immigration reform was a top agenda item for the Bush administration prior to the 9/11 attacks. For these reasons, I challenge the president and Congress to collaborate to achieve comprehensive immigration reform as one of our nation's top priorities.

Conclusion

Several sources, including the 9/11 Commission, have proposed a set of global immigration agreements that would require collaboration among the governments of various nations to, among other goals, strengthen security for global travel and border crossings.[84] I agree that global cooperation is important in ensuring our national security. However, global cooperation alone is not the solution to our immigration crisis. While increased communication and exchange of information between countries, amplified surveillance and data collection could help to reduce the security risks posed by the current state of immigration,[85] I do not advise agreements with terms that restrict the United States' sovereign ability to decide who is and is not permitted within its territory. In a global economy, it would be wise for the United States to enter into international agreements that benefit its interests. For example, economic conditions in Mexico are undoubtedly a contributing factor pushing Mexicans to the United States. It is in our best interest and helpful to our immigration challenges to assist Mexico.

Through international agreements, the United States can help Mexico build a stronger middle class and implement institutional reform that will bring greater integrity to the Mexican government and help curb the level of violence. The United States should not, however, enter into any international agreement that empowers an international body or another nation to define citizenship in the United States or dictate who can be present within our borders. To forfeit this sovereign power in the name of international unity would be a grave mistake.

However, rejecting international control of our sovereignty does not mean that I accept the status quo. Our nation's immigration crisis has become increasingly more visible and the need for reform has grown increasingly more pressing, provoking states to take more localized actions. Some commentators believe that state actions are motivated in part by the fear that the American identity is changing; a fear that Latinos will be the majority race in the near future. Critics of state action say these efforts are misguided attempts by the current majority to hang on to power. There is undoubtedly some element of fear involved, but that is only half of the story. To the extent there is fear or anxiety, for many people it is fear of change that is uncontrolled and without long-term planning. They worry that our federal leaders are not working toward a migration policy that supports our economic and national security interests.

These state proposed solutions do not address the real economic motivation for unauthorized immigration, are largely ineffective, and only further complicate the current immigration crisis. While some members of Congress believe that statutorily excluding children born to unauthorized immigrant parents from the benefit of birthright citizenship will reduce the illegal immigration population and help to solve this nation's immigration problems, such action is likely unconstitutional and contrary to well-rooted American tradition. To address this nation's immigration crisis, the president and Congress should invest their time and energy to pass comprehensive immigration reform on the federal level.

Notes

1. A similar version of the article featured in this book chapter will appear in *The Minnesota Law Review*, Vol. 96, Issue 6 (2012).

2. Fourteenth Amendment of the U.S. Constitution, section 1.

3. I thank Lindsay Scaief and Arslan Umarov of the Texas Tech University School of Law for their invaluable assistance.

4. See the Bureau of Labor Statistics, Labor Force Statistics from the Current Population Survey: Annual Average Unemployment Rate, Civilian Labor Force 16 Years and Over (2011); Pew Research Center, *Census 2010: 50 Million Latinos Hispanics Account for More Than Half of Nation's Growth in Past Decade* (2011).

5. I recognize that the term used in our immigration laws for unlawfully present noncitizens is *alien*. For purposes of this chapter, I use the term *unauthorized immigrants*.

6. Article 6 of the United States Constitution, clause 2.

7. Article 5 of the United States Constitution.

8. Article 5 of the United States Constitution.

9. See, e.g., Latham, 2005.

10. See, e.g., Latham, 2005.

11. See e.g., *Bute v. Illinois*, 333 U.S. 640, 650 (1948).

12. See e.g., Gunlicks, 1995.

13. Salyer, 2005.

14. Salyer, *supra* note 13, at 52.

15. 19 Op. Off. Legal Counsel 340 (1995).

16. Sayler, *supra* note 13, at 53. See also Ngai, M. Birthright Citizenship and the Alien Citizen, 75 *Fordham Law Review*, 2521, 2528 (2007).

17. Gunlicks, 1995, *supra* note 12, at 554; see *Dred Scott v. Sandford*, 60 U.S. 393 (1857).

18. See *Dred Scott v. Sandford*, 60 U.S. 393 (1857).

19. See *Dred Scott v. Sandford*, 60 U.S. 393 (1857) at 404–405.

20. See *Dred Scott v. Sandford*, 60 U.S. 393 (1857) at 404–405; See Gunlicks, *supra* note 12, at 556–557.

21. Civil Rights Act of 1866, chapter 31, 14 Statute 27 (1886).

22. 19 Op. Off. Legal Counsel 340 (1995).

23. Fourteenth Amendment of the U.S. Constitution, section 1.

24. See, for example, Berger, 1977, who writes: "The authors of the Amendment, far from contemplating a social and political revolution, as defenders of judicial activism maintained, intended only to protect the freedmen from southern Black Codes that threatened to return them to slavery."

25. Salyer, *supra* note 13, at 57.

26. Salyer, *supra* note 13, at 75.

27. Salyer, *supra* note 13, at 59.

28. Salyer, *supra* note 13, at 58.

29. *United States v. Wong Kim Ark*, 169 U.S. 649, 653 (1898).

30. Sayler, *supra* ibid. at 75.

31. *United States v. Wong Kim Ark*, 169 U.S. 649, 653 (1898).

32. Salyer, *supra* note 13, at 75.

33. Salyer, *supra* note 13, at 75.

34. Salyer, *supra* note 13, at 75.

35. Later abrogated by the Indian Citizenship Act of 1924, ch. 233, 43 Stat. 253 (codified as amended at 8 U.S.C. §1401(b) (2000)).

36. See *United States v. Wong Kim Ark*, 169 U.S. 649, 680–682 (1898); *Elk v. Wilkins*, 112 U.S. 94, 99 (1884).

37. Fourteenth Amendment of the U.S. Constitution, section 1.

38. *Wong Kim Ark*, 169 U.S. at 687.

39. Kim, 2008.

40. Kim, 2008.

41. See *Plyler v. Doe*, 457 U.S. 202, 215 (1982).

42. See, for example, HB 292, 82d Legislature, Regular Session (Texas 2011); HB 302, 82d Legislature, Regular Session (Texas 2011); HB 623, 82d Legislature, Regular Session (Texas 2011).

43. See the chapters by González de Bustamante and by Chin et al., this volume. The Court of Appeals for the Ninth Circuit affirmed the federal district court's holding that federal law preempted Ariz. Rev. Stat. Ann. § 11-1051. See *United States v. Arizona*, 641 F.3d 339, 366 (9th Cir. 2011), cert. granted, 2011 WL3556224 (U.S. Dec. 12, 2011) (No. 11-182).

44. The Court of Appeals for the Ninth Circuit affirmed the federal district court's holding that federal law preempted Ariz. Rev. Stat. Ann. § 11-1051. See *United States v. Arizona*, 641 F.3d 339, 366 (9th Cir. 2011), cert. granted, 2011 WL3556224 (U.S. Dec. 12, 2011) (No. 11-182).

45. See HB 113, 82d Legislature, Regular Session (Texas 2011).

46. See HB 116 (Utah 2011).

47. See HB 87 (Georgia 2011).

48. See HB 56 (Alabama 2011).

49. See, for example, Birthright Citizenship Act of 2007, H.R. 1940, 110th Congress (1st Session 2007); Birthright Citizenship Act of 2009, H.R. 1868, 111th Congress (1st Session 2009).

50. See Birthright Citizenship Act of 2011, H.R. 140, 112th Congress (1st Session 2011).

51. Birthright Citizenship Act of 2011, H.R. 140, 112th Congress (1st Session 2011). This language is identical to the stated purpose of the Birthright Citizenship Acts of 2007 and of 2009. See Birthright Citizenship Act of 2009, H.R. 1868, 111th Congress (1st Session 2009); Birthright Citizenship Act of 2007, H.R. 1940, 110th Congress (1st Session 2007).

52. Birthright Citizenship Act of 2011, H.R. 140, 112th Congress (1st Session 2011).

53. See Citizenship Reform Act of 1995, H.R. 1363, 104th Congress (1995); Birthright Citizenship Act of 2007, H.R. 1940, 110th Congress (1st Session 2007); Birthright Citizenship Act of 2009, H.R. 1868, 111th Congress (1st Session 2009).

54. See, for example, Interview by Fox News with Sen. Lindsey Graham (July 29, 2010).

55. See Interview by Fox News with Sen. Lindsey Graham (July 29, 2010).

56. Interview by Fox News with Sen. Lindsey Graham (July 29, 2010).

57. See Interview by Fox News with Sen. Lindsey Graham (July 29, 2010).

58. See Interview by Fox News with Sen. Lindsey Graham (July 29, 2010).

59. *DaCanas v. Bica*, 424 U.S. 351, 354 (1976).

60. *DaCanas v. Bica*, 424 U.S. at 355.

61. See *DaCanas v. Bica*, 424 U.S. at 354–355.

62. See, for example, Citizenship Reform Act of 1995, H.R. 1363, 104th Congress (1995), which proposed to deny birthright citizenship to persons born within the jurisdiction of the United States.

63. Citizenship Reform Act of 1995, H.R. 1363, 104th Congress (1995); 19 Op. Off. Legal Counsel 340 (1995).

64. Citizenship Reform Act of 1995, H.R. 1363, 104th Congress (1995).

65. Citizenship Reform Act of 1995, H.R. 1363, 104th Congress (1995).

66. Citizenship Reform Act of 1995, H.R. 1363, 104th Congress (1995).

67. See Citizenship Reform Act of 1995, H.R. 1363, 104th Congress (1995). Note that the language this bill attempted to redefine just happens to mirror that of the Citizenship Clause of the Fourteenth Amendment.

68. 19 Op. Off. Legal Counsel 340 (1995).

69. 19 Op. Off. Legal Counsel 340 (1995).

70. *DeBartolo Corporation v. Florida Gulf Coast Building and Construction Trades Council*, 485 U.S. 568, 575 (1988).

71. See *DeBartolo Corporation v. Florida Gulf Coast Building and Construction Trades Council*, 485 U.S. 568, 575 (1988).

72. See Chávez and Hoewe, this volume.

73. For a fiscal analysis of the contributions and costs of immigrants to Arizona, see Gans, in this volume.

74. Peri, 2010.

75. See Federal Reserve Bank of Dallas, *From Brawn to Brains: How Immigration Works for America* (2010).

76. Preston, 2010.

77. See, for example, Preston, 2010; Gordon H. Hanson, Migration Policy Institute, *The Economics and Policy of Illegal Immigration in the United States*, 1 (2009).

78. See Pew Hispanic Center, Fact Sheet: Modes of Entry for the Unauthorized Immigrant Population 1-5 (2006), http://pewhispanic.org/files/factsheets/19.pdf.

79. Pew Hispanic Center, *Fact Sheet: Modes of Entry for the Unauthorized Immigrant Population*, at 2.

80. See INA §212(a)(5).

81. See Ries, 2010.

82. Also known as the McCarran-Walter Act, the INA was enacted into law on June 27, 1952, Pub. L. 82-414, 66 Stat. 163 (June 27, 1952), and has been amended many times since then.

83. Prior to 1952, other statutes combined to govern U.S. immigration law.

84. See National Commission on Terrorist Attacks upon the U.S., 9/11 Report, Ch. 12.4, available at http://www.9-11commission.gov/report/911Report_Ch12.htm (last accessed June 16, 2011).

85. See National Commission on Terrorist Attacks upon the U.S., 9/11 Report, Ch. 12.4, available at http://www.9-11commission.gov/report/911Report_Ch12.htm (last accessed June 16, 2011).

References

19 Op. Off. Legal Counsel 340 (1995).

75 Fordham L. Rev. 2521, 2528 (2007).

82-414, 66 Stat. 163 (June 27, 1952).

Berger, R. (1977). Government by judiciary: The transformation of the Fourteenth Amendment, xv (2d ed.) *12 Valparaiso University Law Review, 3.*

Birthright Citizenship Act of 2007, H.R. 1940, 110th Congress (1st Session 2007)

Birthright Citizenship Act of 2009, H.R. 1868, 111th Congress (1st Session 2009).

Birthright Citizenship Act of 2011, H.R. 140, 112th Congress (1st Session 2011).

Bureau of Labor Statistics. (2011). Labor force statistics from the current population survey: Annual average unemployment rate, civilian labor force 16 years and over.

Bute v. Illinois, 333 U.S. 640, 650 (1948).

Citizenship Reform Act of 1995, H.R. 1363, 104th Congress (1995).

Civil Rights Act of 1866. ch. 31, 14 Stat. 27 (1886).

DaCanas v. Bica, 424 U.S. 351, 354 (1976).

DeBartolo Corporation v. Florida. Gulf Coast Building & Construction Trades Council, 485 U.S. 568, 575 (1988).

Dred Scott v. Sandford, 60 U.S. 393 (1857).

Elk v. Wilkins, 112 U.S. 94, 99 (1884).

Federal Reserve Bank of Dallas (2010). *From brawn to brains: How immigration works for America.* Available http://dallasfed.org/fed/annual/2010/ar10b.pdf.

Fox News. (2010). Interview with Senator Lindsey Graham, July 29.

Gunlicks, M. (1995). Citizenship as a weapon in controlling the flow of undocumented aliens: Evaluation of proposed denials of citizenship to children of undocumented aliens born in the United States, *63 George Washington Law Review, 51, 557.*

Hanson, G. (2009). *The economics and policy of illegal immigration in the United States 1.* Migration Policy Institute.

HB 56 (Alabama 2011).

HB 87 (Georgia 2011).

HB 113, 82d Leg. Reg. Session (Texas 2011).

HB 116 (Utah 2011).

HB 292, 82d Leg., Reg. Session (Texas 2011).

INA §212(a)(5) June 27, 1952, Pub. L.

Indian Citizenship Act of 1924, chapter 233, 43 Statute 253 (codified as amended at 8 U.S.C. §1401(b) (2000)).

Kim, Y. (2008). *CRS Report for Congress. Statutory interpretation: General principles and recent trends 1.* Washington, DC. Congressional Research Service. Available at http://www.fas.org/sgp/crs/misc/97-589.pdf (last accessed June 16, 2011).

Latham, M. (2005). The historical amendability of the American Constitution: Speculations on an empirical problematic. *55 American University Law Review 145–156.*

National Commission on Terrorist Attacks upon the U.S., 9/11 Report, Ch. 12.4, available at http://www.9-11commission.gov/report/911Report_Ch12.htm (last accessed June 16, 2011).

Ngai, M. (2007). Birthright citizenship and the alien citizen, *75 Fordham Law Review, 2521, 2528.*

Peri, G. (2010). *The impact of immigrants in recession and economic expansion 5.* Migration Policy Institute.

Pew Hispanic Center. (2006). *Fact Sheet: Modes of entry for the unauthorized immigrant population 1-5,* http://pewhispanic.org/files/factsheets/19.pdf.

Pew Research Center. (2011). *Census 2010: 50 million Latinos Hispanics account for more than half of nation's growth in past decade.*

Plyler v. Doe, 457 U.S. 202, 215 (1982).

Preston, J. (2010, July 9). Illegal workers swept from jobs in "silent raids." *The New York Times*. http://www.nytimes.com/2010/07/10/us/10enforce.html.

Ries, L. (2010). B-Verify: Transforming E-Verify into a biometric employment verification system, *3 Albany Government Law Review 271, 296*.

Salyer, L. (2005). The contest over birthright citizenship. In David A. Martin & Peter H. Schuck (Eds.), *Immigration stories* (pp. 51–86). New York: Foundation Press.

United States Constitution, Amendment 14, section 1.

United States Constitution, Article VI, clause 2.

United States Constitution, Article V.

United States v. Wong Kim Ark, 169 U.S. 649, 653 (1898).

Part III

MASS MEDIA ROLES

10

National Perspectives on State Turmoil

Characteristics of Elite U.S. Newspaper Coverage of Arizona SB 1070

Manuel Chavez and Jennifer Hoewe

DESPITE THE GENERALLY ACCEPTED NOTION that the United States is a country of immigrants, the process of immigration always has been a source of social and political conflict. In the 1840s, as numerous Irish families and individuals arrived on the East Coast, they were harassed, intimated, and abused—some New York politicians proposed restrictions to their acceptance into the United States (Jensen, 2002). Likewise, Germans were repeatedly beleaguered and prohibited from using their traditions, language, and cultural norms (Kazal, 2004). Italians, at the end of the 1880s and beginning of the 1890s, were tagged as prone to crime, heavy users of alcohol, and uninterested in assimilating (Luconi, 1999). As such, each of these ethnic groups were blamed by previous immigrant generations for the problems that the country experienced at the time. At the present time, it seems Mexicans, and other Latin American immigrants, are receiving the cold shoulder of U.S. citizens and enduring the harassment of U.S. politicians, who have been successful in implementing new laws to restrict and control them. This phenomenon is particularly evident in Arizona.

The current negative political atmosphere toward Mexican immigrants evolved slowly and steadily since the last major reform—the Immigration Reform and Control Act of 1986 was signed by President Ronald Reagan. For the last twenty-five years, some U.S. political forces have resisted large-scale reforms. Few attempts to pass any significant legislation have obtained the president's signature, such as the Illegal Immigration and Immigrant Responsibility Act of 1996. Meanwhile, some bipartisan attempts failed in the Senate, including the Secure America and Orderly Immigration Act of 2005 proposed by Senators Ted Kennedy and John McCain.

Other efforts by independent and bipartisan commissions, including prominent politicians, have been pushed back or simply ignored, as was the case of a Council on Foreign Relations report on U.S. immigration policy presented by Republican Governor Jeb Bush and Democrat Thomas F. McLarty III (2009). The report outlined a comprehensive agenda to regulate and control the current conditions of immigration, particularly undocumented immigration. The report recognized the different actors, conditions, and forces of immigration, making special note of employers' roles, the importance of effective and sensitive law enforcement, and the processes to regularize illegal immigrants already in the country. Despite the constructive perspective of the report, it emphasized the Task Force's belief that reform efforts should require the "asserted" implementation of the rule of law (p. 64), which gave little guidance for handling modern immigration problems.

Bush and McLarty's report (2009) also recognized the roles and pressures on *local jurisdictions* with additional burdens to their public services. Yet, there was no evidence that these pressures were critical burdens to local entities to the point of necessary action independent of the federal government. In Arizona, however, politicians increased their rhetoric about the burden illegal immigrants put on state finances, pushing action to the state level. Among other arguments, the use and "abuse" of public services among immigrants and their families was central in the public opinion debate leading to the passage of Arizona Senate Bill 1070.

Despite these ideas, the American public appeared not fully informed of such studies, which fostered an environment of polarizing rhetoric among politicians and interest groups. Eventually, enough public and political support was gained to pass Arizona Senate Bill 1070. Arizona SB 1070, formally titled "The Support Our Law Enforcement and Safe Neighborhoods Act," was signed into law by Arizona Governor Janice Brewer on April 23, 2010. The law requires resident aliens to register with the U.S. government and then carry their registration documents with them at all times. Failure to do so would result in a misdemeanor and likely would end in deportation. The law gives police officers the right to ask for these documents upon "reasonable suspicion." After it was signed into law, its constitutionality was challenged, largely due to possible civil rights violations. Several lawsuits then were filed, including one by the U.S. Department of Justice on July 6, 2010, resulting in a preliminary injunction that halted the law from taking full effect (see Chin et al., this volume). The U.S. Supreme Court was scheduled to hear oral arguments in *Arizona v. the United States* in April 2012.

To begin comprehending the apparent public support for measures to control immigration, academics should examine how Arizona SB 1070 was covered by the news media, including what information was provided to news consumers as well as what was missing from elite newspaper reports on the topic. Since elite U.S. news media set the tone both nationally and internationally in terms of the importance of issues, elite U.S. newspapers (i.e., those with the highest circulations) are the focus of this study. They set the agenda for other national news outlets as well as regional and local news outlets (Dearing & Rogers, 1996, p. 12). Thus, continued study of them proves necessary for media scholarship.

In particular, the recent passage of Arizona SB 1070 captured the news media spotlight in early 2010 and drew the attention of media scholars. The day after the bill was signed into law, the *New York Times* used its front page to run a story with the headline, "Arizona enacts stringent law on immigration." The *Washington Post* followed suit by dedicating a portion of its front page to a story headlined "Ariz. Governor signs tough immigration bill; Obama calls it 'misguided.'" *USA Today*, however, did not cover the story. Based on these varied responses, it becomes important to uncover how the elite U.S. press perceived the importance of and reported on Arizona SB 1070.

The purpose of this chapter is to analyze U.S. news media coverage of Arizona SB 1070 before and after the bill was signed into law. This chapter will explain the role of the news media in the United States and its implications in the formation of public opinion and provide a synthesis of prior academic research on news media coverage of immigration. Then, it will analyze the frames used by three major U.S. newspapers when covering Arizona SB 1070 before and after it was signed into law. Since a bill with such national impact should have been brought into the national spotlight prior to being signed into law, elite news media ought to have made the public aware of it before its wave of influence was felt across the nation and even internationally. As such, this study will examine the dates of publication to determine if attention was brought to Arizona SB 1070 prior to it being enacted into law. Lastly, the implications of this news coverage will be discussed and future research will be suggested.

Implications of News Media Frames

A critical analysis of how the news media presented Arizona SB 1070 is necessary to determine how public opinion could be influenced by these news stories. In particular, this study seeks to examine which frames were used in the coverage of Arizona SB 1070. Framing, in its most frequently conceptualized definition (Weaver, 2007), is the process of selecting portions of a perceived reality and making them more visible in a communication text in such a way that elicits a problem definition, causal attribution, moral evaluation, or solution (Entman, 1993, p. 52). More specifically, reporters construct frames when writing headlines, leads, questions, and the like, to give a story structure. De Vreese (2004) found that frames within news stories shape public opinion; they help individuals compartmentalize their thoughts upon which they can categorize other information and make judgments. In other words, frames go beyond the agenda-setting function of the press (i.e., telling readers what to think about) by telling readers how to think about a certain issue or event; in this case Arizona SB 1070. Ultimately, frames influence the public's perception of an event or series of events, roughly translated as public opinion.

The news media's ability to affect individual beliefs and attitudes as connected to a greater change in public opinion has implications for future immigration-related policies. The subsequent effect is a change in public policy. For example, the U.S. democratic system of government allows for a shift in public opinion to influence voting results. Voting results affect legislators and legislation. Furthermore, the news media affect politicians' opinions much in the way that they affect news consumers' opinions (Domke, Watts, Shah, & Fan, 1999). The magnitude of public opinion change has obvious national and international consequences in terms of future immigration policies.

Therefore, we consider frames generated in the coverage of Arizona SB 1070. Our study classifies frames as structural elements often used by reporters.

Immigration in U.S. Minds and U.S. News Media

Scholarly research that examines news coverage of Mexican immigration is still in its fledgling stages (e.g., see Cambridge, 2005; Chavez, 2001; Chavez, 2008; Santa Ana, 2002; Santa Ana, Lopez, & Munguia, 2010). While some research has focused on descriptions and analyses of the immigration experience, the most recent and overarching study of the news coverage of Mexican immigration was published in 2010. Chavez, Whiteford, and Hoewe (2010) examined four elite newspapers' coverage of Mexican immigration. The authors analyzed the content of 160 news stories published in the *New York Times*, *Washington Post*, *USA Today*, and *Wall Street Journal*. They found the topic most frequently addressed in news stories about Mexican immigration was crime. They also found most of these news stories were aimed toward influencing public opinion, which is important to note because a shift in public opinion has been shown to have the ability to influence public policy. Chavez, Whiteford, and Hoewe's findings serve as a good starting point for the study at hand in terms of the connection between the news media, Mexican immigration, and public opinion.

Prior to that study, Fernandez and Pedroza (1982) examined news coverage of Mexican immigrants in the United States by analyzing stories published in the *New York Times, Los Angeles Times, Washington Post,* and *Arizona Daily Star.* Their six-year period of analysis found stories with unbalanced and sometimes faulty or inaccurate reporting. The authors concluded that this coverage could affect the public's beliefs about Mexican immigrants.

The findings presented in this chapter coupled with poll results have implications toward the structuring of public opinion in both the theoretical and real terms. An Associated Press/Gfk poll conducted between May 7, 2010, and May 12, 2010, asked 1,002 people in the United States about their opinions on illegal immigration (Gfk, 2010). When asked if they thought being in the United States without proper documentation should be a serious or minor offense, 60 percent believed it should be a serious offense. Sixty-nine percent also thought illegal immigration was an extremely serious problem in the United States. Moreover, in another survey question, the largest percentage of respondents (42 percent) favored Arizona SB 1070. These findings indicate initial support of Arizona SB 1070 and the tenets for which it stands, which are important components to consider when assessing the total implications of the bill and law and the associated news coverage.

As such, this chapter is important in determining whether the trends found in prior research reappear in news coverage of Arizona SB 1070, as it relates directly to immigration (primarily Mexican immigration). Its findings will help in the assessment of the news media's objective presentation of the controversial, if not polarizing, issues of immigration and immigration policy.

Research Questions

It is important to identify the length and placement of each news story about Arizona SB 1070 in these elite newspapers because it will help determine the importance placed upon each story by the publication. For example, news stories located in the "A" sections of newspapers are considered to be of some importance, particularly if they are on the front page of this section.

RQ1: How long were the news stories published by elite U.S. newspapers about Arizona SB 1070, and where were they placed within the newspaper?

The public should be made aware of important political issues prior to feeling their actual impact. Serving the proverbial watchdog function, newspapers (and other forms of news media) should have alerted the public to the implications of the bill before its being signed into law on April 23, 2010. This knowledge would have allowed the public to alert their respective lawmakers of how to best represent their constituencies.

RQ2: How many news stories were published by elite U.S. newspapers about Arizona SB 1070 before and after it was signed into law?

Identifying the frames used by these newspapers will help uncover how the implications and passage of Arizona SB 1070 were presented to the public.

RQ3: What frames were used by elite U.S. newspapers in their coverage of Arizona SB 1070?

Methodology

Content analysis was used to analyze the news media's coverage of Arizona SB 1070 in the four months surrounding the bill's being signed into law. This study decidedly selected elite U.S. newspapers in which to examine coverage because they report on national and international issues and garner international readership. Although SB 1070 was a state bill, its passage had national implications. Furthermore, elite U.S. newspapers have the ability to influence public opinion and public policy (Gans, 2003; McCombs, 2005; Schudson, 2002). The newspapers under examination here include the *New York Times, Washington Post,* and *USA Today.* According to BurrellesLuce (2010), a company that tracks figures for the most circulated newspapers, they are within the top five in terms of circulation for U.S. newspapers: *USA Today*—1,826,622 daily; *New York Times*—951,063 daily; and *Washington Post*—578,482 daily.

The period of this study ranges from February 23, 2010, two months before Arizona SB 1070 was signed into law, until June 23, 2010, two months after Arizona SB 1070 was signed into law. This study includes a census of all news stories published from Monday to Sunday and includes stories published both in print editions and on websites (excluding duplicate stories). Only news stories were needed for this analysis, so opinion pieces were removed from the search results. Also, only news stories about Arizona SB 1070 were analyzed; stories about another topic that merely mentioned the bill were extracted from the search results. Stories were located using LexisNexis through keyword searches of all combinations of "Arizona" in the headline or lead and "immigration law" or "Support Our Law Enforcement and Safe Neighborhoods Act" or "1070" in the body.

The first research question was addressed by coding each news story for the following variables: name of newspaper, headline of story, length of story, and placement of story within the newspaper (provided by LexisNexis). The second research question was addressed by coding each story for its date of publication (provided by LexisNexis).

The third research question was addressed by identifying the frames used to construct each news story. Frames were identified during the coding process then used consistently to analyze each story. A total of six frames were used to categorize each news story, and each story could have more than one frame. The six frames included crime, economics, elections, legislation, public protest, and public support.

The first frame, *crime*, was used in such a way as to emphasize the criminal aspect of illegal immigration, the drug war, and border violence as well as other matters of law enforcement. For example, the *New York Times* published a story on June 20, 2010, called "In border violence, perception is greater than crime statistics" that detailed the perceptions and implications of illegal immigration as a criminal activity. *Economics*, the second frame, focused on economic issues, which in most cases included businesses' boycotts of Arizona due to the law's passage. For example, the *New York Times* published a story on June 20, 2010, with the headline: "Embargoing Arizona proves not to be so easy," which was about the attempts of California businesses, business organizations, and lawmakers to boycott all things Arizona. (This story also included the *public protest* frame.) Third, stories using the *elections* frame revolved around political candidates' attempts to be elected to office. For example, the *New York Times* published a story on May 22, 2010, called "Arizona law reveals split within G.O.P." that examined the complicated position of many politicians nationwide in whether or not to support Arizona SB 1070 for fear of losing votes in the upcoming election. The *legislation* frame incorporated strong emphases on the legal matters involved in the bill's passage and the subsequent appeals and lawsuits. For example, the *Washington Post* published a story on April 29, 2010, called "Justice weighs suing Arizona to block immigration law; Obama says legislation threatens to undermine 'notions of fairness.'" This story was about the steps involved in suing the state of Arizona for passing SB 1070 as well as President Barack Obama's objection to the law. The fifth frame was *public protest*. Stories employing this frame focused on public protests and their involvement and impact on the passage of and subsequent reactions to the bill. For example, a story published in the *Washington Post* on May 7, 2010, called "Suns speak out instead of playing it safe" explained the Phoenix, Arizona, NBA team's decision to wear jerseys that read "Los Suns" instead of the usual "Suns" in protest of Arizona SB 1070. Conversely, the sixth and final frame was *public support*. Stories that utilized this frame were structured to highlight public support of Arizona SB 1070. For example, the *New York Times* published a story on May 30, 2010, called "The two sides intersect in immigration debate," which was about the public's response to the bill's passage. (This story also included the *public protest* frame.)

Results

A total of sixty-six news stories about Arizona SB 1070 were published in the *New York Times, Washington Post,* and *USA Today* between February 23, 2010, and June 23, 2010. Of those stories, all but two (97.0 percent) were between one and 1,500 words in length, and fifty-seven (86.4 percent) were published in the "A" sections of the newspapers. The *New York Times* published the majority of the stories (53.0 percent), whereas the *Washington Post* and *USA Today* published twenty-one stories (31.8 percent) and ten stories (15.2 percent), respectively.

The vast majority of news stories published in these three newspapers were composed after the bill was signed into law on April 23, 2010. Sixty-two of the sixty-six stories (93.9 percent) were published after this date. No stories were published on April 23, 2010. All of the stories published before April 23, 2010, were published in the *New York Times.*

Of the frames identified, the most utilized was that which represented public protest. The public protest frame was found in thirty-eight stories (57.6

TABLE 10.1
Number and Percentage of Article Word Count and Placement

	New York Times	Washington Post	USA Today	Total
Story Count	35	21	10	66
Article Word Count				
1–500	9 (25.7%)*	6 (28.6%)	9 (90.0%)	24 (36.4%)
501–1,000	10 (28.6%)	9 (42.9%)	1 (10.0%)	20 (30.3%)
1,001–1,500	15 (42.9%)	5 (23.8%)	0 (0.0%)	20 (30.3%)
1,501–2,000	1 (2.9%)	1 (4.8%)	0 (0.0%)	2 (3.0%)
Article Placement				
"A" section	32 (91.4%)	17 (81.0%)	8 (80.0%)	57 (86.4%)
other	3 (8.6%)	4 (19.0%)	2 (20.0%)	9 (13.6%)

*Percentages calculated based on the respective newspaper.

TABLE 10.2
SB 1070 Articles Appearing before and after April 23,* by Number and Percentage

	New York Times	Washington Post	USA Today	Total
Before	4 (11.4%)†	0 (0%)	0 (0%)	4 (6.1%)
After	31 (88.6%)	21 (100%)	10 (100%)	62 (93.9%)

*Date that Governor Brewer signed SB 1070.
†Percentages calculated based on the respective newspaper.

percent). The second most used frame was legislation. Thirty-five stories (53.0 percent) used this frame. The next most used frames were crime and public support, each of which represented 16.7 percent of the stories. The economics frame was identified in eight stories (12.1 percent), and the elections frame was found in four stories (6.1 percent).

The individual newspapers followed a similar pattern to that of the whole. The *New York Times'* most used frame was public protest (60.0 percent), which was followed by the legislation frame (45.7 percent). The *Washington Post* used the public protest frame most frequently (61.9 percent), and the legislation frame followed (57.1 percent). *USA Today*, however, used the legislation frame most frequently (70.0 percent). It used the public protest and crime frames an equal number of times (40.0 percent each). Also noteworthy, it used the crime frame significantly more than the other publications (*New York Times*—3 percent; *Washington Post*—19.0 percent).

How Elite U.S. Newspapers Informed the Public about Arizona SB 1070

All three newspapers kept most stories at less than 1,500 words (typical news story length is between 500 and 1,500 words) and published the majority in the first sections of their print editions. Usually the first sections attract more

TABLE 10.3
Number and Percentage of Frames*

	New York Times	Washington Post	USA Today	Total
Crime	3 (8.6%)†	4 (19.0%)	4 (40.0%)	11 (16.7%)
Economics	5 (14.3%)	2 (9.5%)	1 (10.0%)	8 (12.1%)
Elections	3 (8.6%)	1 (4.8%)	0 (0.0%)	4 (6.1%)
Legislation	16 (45.7%)	12 (57.1%)	7 (70.0%)	35 (53.0%)
Public Protest	21 (60.0%)	13 (61.9%)	4 (40.0%)	38 (57.6%)
Public Support	5 (14.3%)	4 (19.0%)	2 (20.0%)	11 (16.7%)

*Stories may have more than one frame; percentages may not total 100 percent.
†Percentages calculated based on the respective newspaper.

attention than news published on secondary sections. Within these "A" sections, the *New York Times* and *Washington Post* each published three stories about Arizona SB 1070 on their front pages, whereas *USA Today* printed two such stories. Among all sixty-six stories published, only two were wire stories, which indicates each newspaper's willingness to devote one or more of its own reporters to cover Arizona SB 1070. This action signifies the importance placed upon this issue by each newspaper.

On the other hand, these newspapers did not place importance on Arizona SB 1070 prior to when it was signed into law on April 23, 2010. The vast majority of stories were published after this date, illustrating that this law was not on the news radar prior to its enactment. The *Washington Post* and *USA Today*, in particular, neglected to alert the public as to the possible implications of Arizona SB 1070 before it became law. The *New York Times*, however, printed four stories about Arizona SB 1070 prior to April 23, 2010, which may have been because the *Times* has a bureau in Phoenix. Three of these stories detailed the possible implications of the bill if it were signed into law. The remaining story discussed the criminal aspect of illegal immigration and how the bill's mandates would be handled by police officers as well as the conflicting opinions of police officers about the bill. Both the *New York Times* and the *Washington Post* published a story on April 24, 2010, about the new law, but *USA Today* did not report on it until April 27, 2010.

As previously noted, the news media ought to serve its watchdog function by making the public aware of important political issues prior to their enactment as law. This knowledge gives individuals the opportunity to contact lawmakers regarding their support of or opposition toward the issue, and lawmakers ought to hear from their constituencies to decide how to best represent them. *USA Today* and the *Washington Post*, in particular, did not serve the public well in this regard. *USA Today* completely ignored the bill until three days after it was signed into law, and the *Washington Post* did not alert the public until the day the bill was signed into law. Because most of these national papers did not report on SB 1070 until after the bill was signed into law, citizens outside of the state likely remained uninformed about the issue and therefore were less likely to take part in the public debate about the bill.

The stories about Arizona SB 1070 in these three newspapers used similar frames. The most used frame in all sixty-six stories was the frame that focused on public protest. Nearly 60 percent of all the stories about Arizona SB 1070 published in these three publications included the public protest frame. In fact, thirteen stories used only the public protest frame, nine of which were published in the *New York Times*. Conversely, only about 17 percent of stories included the public support frame, and none of the stories used only the public support frame. In fact, the public protest frame was included in ten of the eleven stories that used the public support frame. More simply put, the public protest frame was used most frequently and also frequently was used without the presence of another frame. In contrast, the public support frame was not as frequently used and almost always was found in a story that included the public protest frame.

These results are consistent with the tendency of news media to gravitate toward controversial events (e.g., protests) but also may indicate each publication's bias against Arizona SB 1070. These three newspapers chose to emphasize the public's distaste toward Arizona SB 1070, while public opinion polls painted a contradicting picture. Such a bias has implications in the extended shaping of public opinion. As previously noted, if the public is consistently presented with a particular frame, it may adopt this frame as a way to categorize and judge future information. It then is possible that newspapers may have an impact in the long-term public opinion of Arizona SB 1070.

Moreover, these newspapers' coverage of Arizona SB 1070 did not reflect the actual public sentiment toward it at the time. A CBS News poll published on July 13, 2010, found 57 percent of the 966 adult Americans surveyed thought Arizona SB 1070 was an appropriate measure for dealing with illegal immigration. A much smaller 23 percent of respondents thought the law went too far. Rather than reporting on the reality of the public's reaction to Arizona SB 1070, the *New York Times, Washington Post,* and *USA Today* chose to emphasize the minority portion of the public that objected to the law. Simply put, these newspapers presented a distorted image of the public's reaction to the law within their news coverage of Arizona SB 1070.

Elite U.S. newspapers reporting opposition to SB 1070 is a finding consistent with that of Chavez, Whiteford, and Hoewe (2010). Both studies found that some elite newspapers focus on the daily lives and families of undocumented immigrants. That is, Chavez, Whiteford, and Hoewe (2010) found the *New York Times'* "framing of its stories tended to be more compassionate about the difficulties Mexican immigrants confront in moving to the United States" (p. 121). The study at hand found that the *New York Times* used the public protest frame in 60 percent of the stories it published about Arizona SB 1070. Both examples illustrate the tendency of the *New York Times* to sympathize with illegal immigrants by publishing stories framed compassionately toward illegal immigrants and stories framed negatively toward legislation working against illegal immigrants.

This finding may be consistent with the notion that the *New York Times* operates under a liberal agenda (as was shown in Groseclose & Milyo, 2005). It also may be indicative of a future change in public opinion toward immigration. For example, Hoewe and Zeldes (forthcoming) found news coverage of the overturning of anti-miscegenation laws in 1967 to be sympathetic toward interracial couples wanting to marry. The general sentiment at the time, however, was not in favor of such unions. Since then, public opinion (and the law) has become much more favorable toward interracial marriage. In fact, a 2007 Gallup Poll found 77 percent of Americans "approve of marriages between blacks and whites" (Carroll, 2007). This example may be indicative of a change to come in the public's perception of (and possibly the law regarding) Mexican immigrants and immigration reform in the United States. That is, if following a similar path, public opinion toward Mexican immigration may grow more sympathetic and even accepting in the coming years.

The Future of Research on News Coverage of Immigration

This chapter sought to uncover the patterns in news coverage of Arizona SB 1070 in the *New York Times, Washington Post,* and *USA Today.* It took great interest in the timing of the news stories published about Arizona SB 1070 as well as the frames used to construct the stories. The results indicate several notable consistencies among the three publications.

Our study attempts to shed light on elite U.S. news media coverage of this controversial immigration policy legislation. Given that the law has national implications, further research should be conducted to improve our findings. We found evidence of elite newspaper bias against Arizona SB 1070, yet further research should be conducted to clarify our results. Also, this study demonstrated neglect in coverage of an important bill, nationally and internationally, prior to it being signed into law. This finding ought to prompt some introspection among journalists and news organizations in hopes of providing the public with more information on a national level about controversial legislation prior to it becoming law.

Furthermore, this chapter should prompt continued scholarly research about news coverage of immigration, particularly Mexican immigration. The news coverage of Arizona SB 1070 following the period of this study should be analyzed. In addition, news coverage of Arizona SB 1070 ought to be examined across elite television and radio news media both during the time of this study as well as the time period after this study. Also, it should be examined in both periods within local and regional news sources, including newspapers and television and radio stations. All of these analyses will contribute to a growing line of research regarding news coverage of immigration and help journalists understand the implications of the timing of their stories as well as frames they use when reporting on the topic.

References

BurrellesLuce. (2010). *Top media outlets: Newspapers, blogs consumer magazines and social networks.* Retrieved from http://www.burrellesluce.com/system/files/BL_2010_Top_Media_List_Updated_May202010.pdf.

Bush, J., & McLarty, T. F., III. (2009). *U.S. Immigration Policy.* Washington, DC: Council on Foreign Relations Press.

Cambridge, V. C. (2005). *Immigration, diversity, and broadcasting in the United States, 1990–2001.* Athens: The Ohio University Press.

Carroll, J. (2007, April). *Most Americans approve of interracial marriages.* Retrieved from http://www.gallup.com/poll/28417/most-americans-approve-interracial-marriages.aspx.

Chavez, L. R. (2001). *Covering immigration: Popular images and the politics of a nation.* Berkeley: University of California Press.

Chavez, L. R. (2008). *The Latino threat: Constructing immigrants, citizens and the nation.* Palo Alto, CA: Stanford University Press.

Chavez, M., Whiteford, S., & Hoewe, J. (2010). Reporting on immigration: A content analysis of major U.S. newspapers' coverage of Mexican immigration. *Norteamérica, 5*(2), 111–125.

Condon, S. (2010, July 13). Poll: Support for Arizona immigration law hits 57 percent. Retrieved 23 February 2012 from www.cbsnews.com/8301-503544_162-20010460-503544.html

Cotte, Elizabeth. (March 2011). Interview with authors.

Dearing, J. W., & Rogers, E. M. (1996). *Agenda setting.* Thousand Oaks, CA: Sage.

de Vreese, C. H. (2004). The effects of frames in political television news on issue interpretation and frame salience. *Journalism and Mass Communication Quarterly, 81*(1), 36–52.

Domke, D., Watts, M. D., Shah, D. V., & Fan, D. P. (1999). The politics of conservative elites and the "liberal media" argument. *Journal of Communication, 49*(4), 35–38.

Entman, R. M. (1993). Framing: Toward clarification of a fractured paradigm. *Journal of Communication, 43*(4), 51–58.

Fernandez, C., & Pedroza, L. (1982). The border patrol and the news media coverage of undocumented Mexican immigration during the 1970s: A quantitative content analysis in the sociology of knowledge. *California Sociologist, 5*(2), 1–26.

Gans, H. J. (2003). *Democracy and the news.* Oxford: Oxford University Press.

Gfk Roper Public Affairs & Media. (2010, May). *The AP-Univision poll.* Retrieved from http://www.ap-gfkpoll.com/pdf/APUnivision%20Poll%20May%202010%20Hispanic%20Topline_1st%20release.pdf.

Groseclose, T., & Milyo, J. (2005). A measure of media bias. *Quarterly Journal of Economics, 4,* 1191–1238.

Hoewe, J., & Zeldes, G. A. (forthcoming). Overturning anti-miscegenation laws: News media coverage of the Lovings' legal case against the State of Virginia. *Journal of Black Studies.*

Jensen, R. (2002). "No Irish need apply": A myth of victimization. *Journal of Social History, 36*(2), 405–429.

Kazal, R. A. (2004). The interwar origins of the white ethnic: Race, residence, and German Philadelphia, 1917–1939. *Journal of American Ethnic History, 23*(4), 78–131.

Luconi, S. (1999). Mafia-related prejudice and the rise of Italian Americans in the United States. *Patterns of Prejudice, 33*(1), 43–58.

McCombs, M. (2005). Agenda setting function of the press. In G. Overholser & K. Hall Jamieson (Eds.), *The press* (pp. 156–168). Oxford: Oxford University Press.

New York, NY: Central Broadcasting Service. Retrieved from http://www.cbsnews.com/8301-503544_162-20010460-503544.html.

Santa Ana, O. (2002). *Brown tide rising: Metaphors of Latinos in contemporary American public discourse.* Austin: University of Texas Press.

Santa Ana, O., Lopez, L., & Munguia, E. (2010). Framing peace as violence: Television news depictions of the 2007 police attack on immigrant rights marchers in Los Angeles. *Aztlán: A Journal of Chicano Studies, 35*(1), 69–101.

Schudson, M. (2002). The news media as political institutions. *Annual Review of Political Science, 5,* 249–269.

Weaver, D. H. (2007). Thoughts on agenda setting, framing, and priming. *Journal of Communication, 57,* 147.

11

Not Business as Usual

Spanish-Language Television Coverage of Arizona's Immigration Law, April–May 2010

Mercedes Vigón, Lilliam Martínez-Bustos,
and Celeste González de Bustamante

Introduction

> Margarita loves singing, as well as Patricia; Brian is playing with his video
> games; Jesus likes to be on the computer; Luis enjoys going to the park. . . .

THIS IS HOW CARMEN, an undocumented immigrant mother, introduced her younger children to Telemundo audiences in a report about the "divided families" aired on *Arizona: Hora Cero* (Arizona: Zero Hour), an hour-long special produced by Telemundo in July 2010, *Separación de familias* (Divided Families).

Carmen, who preferred not to reveal her real name, also described the day U.S. authorities went to her home, handcuffed her husband, and took him away on charges of identity fraud. He was later deported for being in the country without proper authorization. Carmen also explained how this separation impacted her family. In one of the program's most poignant moments, she introduced her eldest son, twenty-year-old Emanuel, who is helping to support his family. He is a U.S. Marine who had just returned from a tour of duty in Afghanistan. The reporter also interviewed Carmen's second child, eighteen-year-old Luis, who wants to follow in his brother's footsteps and join the Marines. Luis submitted his application to the Marines, but he was not allowed to join because, as the only sibling without legal immigration status, his application was rejected.

With this report, Telemundo illuminated the realities of many "mixed-status" families; in this case a father expelled from the country for working without legal documents, at the same time his eldest son served in the Afghanistan war. Through reports like these, Telemundo and Univision countered the arguments of those who called for the expulsion of undocumented immigrants to prevent them from "taking advantage of the system" without making contributions to the country. Further, Carmen's story provides an example of how Univision and Telemundo, the two largest Spanish-language networks in the United States, included the voices of the Hispanic community during the passage of Arizona's contentious immigration law. In contrast to general market English-language media, Telemundo and Univision stories followed very closely the evolution of the legislative measure known as Senate Bill (SB) 1070, aired local, national, and international reactions, and documented the Hispanic community in-depth and with nuance. (See Chavez & Hoewe, this volume, about English language news coverage of SB 1070.)

On April 23, 2010, Arizona Governor Janice Brewer signed SB 1070 into law. The law, officially titled "The Support Our Law Enforcement and Safe Neighborhoods Act," makes being an unauthorized immigrant a state crime and requires legal immigrants to carry identification documents to prove their legal status. Since the law was signed, several lawsuits have been filed to challenge the law, and numerous states have attempted to pass similar legislation. (See Chin et al., this volume, for a legal analysis of SB 1070.)

Supporters of SB 1070 claimed that state legislation was necessary because the federal government "failed to secure the U.S.-Mexico border." In some cases, English-language media appeared to favor SB 1070. Some outlets conflated the issues of immigration and violence without any evidence to prove that a correlation existed between the two:

> The illegal immigration problem is perhaps more prevalent now than ever before—with increased drug cartel violence south of the border, which shows up often in the valley in the form of drop houses for drugs and human cargo.[1]

News coverage on Univision and Telemundo, the two main U.S. Spanish-language networks, whose programming targets Hispanic audiences, provided a counterbalance to coverage that uncritically connected undocumented immigration with the drug war. Governor Brewer, conservative members of the Arizona Legislature, members of Congress, and other supporters of SB 1070 argued on English-language media that the measure would protect the state's citizens. In contrast, Univision and Telemundo presented distinct perspectives by including the voices of immigrants, activists, and undocumented workers. The analysis presented in this essay shows that Spanish-language TV news focused on mobilizations and marches against the measure, activists, immigrants contributing to the economy, undocumented immigrants without connections to drug smuggling, and data and experts that refuted stereotype images that linked undocumented immigrants to violence.

Telemundo and Univision stories tried to inform, raise awareness, influence, or change. This essay will demonstrate that the ultimate goal of Telemundo's and Univision's coverage about Arizona's immigration law was to influence and facilitate change. It was clear that for Univision and Telemundo executives, producers, reporters, and anchors covering SB 1070 it was not business as usual.

Additionally, we will show there was a fine line between Spanish-language networks' roles as public servants and social advocates. Some local news outlets claimed Univision's and Telemundo's coverage was unbalanced. After Telemundo televised a newscast on location in downtown Phoenix for several days in May at the site of ongoing immigrant rights' protests, Fox Phoenix criticized the Spanish-language networks for "backing" the protests.[2]

Spanish-language network executives did not appear to shy away from criticism. In February 2010, now former executive vice president of Telemundo Network News Ramón Escobar had just begun his new position as EVP, and SB 1070 became the first major story under his direction. Escobar said that it was crucial to inform his audience about what was happening minute by minute. Escobar added that the Hispanic news media needed to be as vigilant as blacks were during the civil rights movement of the 1960s.[3]

Our chapter has four main sections. First, we outline the importance of Spanish-language media in the context of the immigration debate. Second, we describe the methodology used in the analysis. Third, we present qualitative and quantitative findings from interviews with network news executives and journalists, and a content analysis. Fourth, we conclude with an explanation of the successes of Spanish-language television news coverage about SB 1070, as well as point to some of its shortcomings.

The Importance of Spanish-Language Media in the Context of the Immigration Debate

In their comparison of Spanish-language TV news and general market television news,[4] Alexandre and Rehbinder identified trends in news that led to the production of different Hispanic "portraits":

> The two universes were most different when covering immigration. In the Hispanic world, immigrants play an important role in news stories and the community at large—they work and raise families, and their views are solicited. On English TV news, immigrants don't even have walk-on parts. Less than half of

one percent of all stories in the Anglo media was about immigration. By contrast, almost a tenth of Spanish-language stories related to immigration issues (9 percent).[5]

Moreover, for years scholars have recognized media influence as one of the key factors in shaping political behavior. As Fowler and Ridout explain, these studies showed that the media have power to set agendas, while other studies prove that news media can increase citizen knowledge.[6] Santa Ana went even further when he stated that "mass media are the single most influential source of public influence, public dispute, discussion, and dialogue, to wit, discourse."[7]

When analyzing the general market coverage of Latinos, scholars have noted that it had not developed much. Studies provide ample evidence that general market media consistently overlooks issues relevant to Hispanics and provides meager coverage that matters to minorities, repeating the same themes (such as undocumented immigrants and the possible influence of the Hispanic vote) over and over again. Further, a year-long content analysis on the news product of six major-market television news stations showed that minorities, especially Hispanics and African Americans, have the most number of appearances in sports and crime stories. Ironically, this occurred in a year that the crime rates nationwide were in decline.[8]

Indeed, scholars who study how the news media create a public discourse of fear have conceptualized a "problem frame" used by the media to promote widespread messages stressing fear and danger.[9] Analyzing this news framing has allowed scholars to identify a message of fear in general media which intertwines with race and ethnicity: "The poor, dispossessed, and most recently franchised segments of society are disproportionately associated with the largest fear application—crime."[10]

Finally, scholars have emphasized the significance of Spanish-language media, especially Univision and Telemundo, and the need for further research giving better understanding of the impact of these media outlets.[11] Further, scholars recognize television as "the most important information medium for Hispanics."[12]

Given the role that Spanish-language media play in the daily lives of Latinos, and the deficiencies in English-language media regarding coverage of this population,[13] our research asks three questions: How did Spanish-language television news networks report on SB 1070, an issue key to Latino communities across the country? We do this by asking, what "frames" were most often used to tell the story of SB 1070? And, third, what is the extent to which Spanish-language television news influenced the public sphere by providing a counter narrative to most general market media?

Benedict Anderson's frequently referenced cultural theoretical framework about "imagined communities" is particularly useful in explaining how

Spanish-language media provide opportunities that help its audiences shape their own Hispanic identities.[14]

Cultural, political, and economic access to the public sphere is central for disciplining citizenship and constructing imagined communities. The ethnic news media in relation to the general market media play an important role in determining the socially constructed borders of the imagined community, a conceptualization of community that recognizes both its elasticity and limitations.[15] Therefore, the coverage by Univision and Telemundo of Arizona's immigration law should be understood and analyzed not only as a reaction, but as an alternative to negative depictions in general market media. In this regard, our study tests Molina Guzmán's hypothesis about whether Univision's and Telemundo's coverage of the Arizona immigration law influenced "dialogue in the public sphere by engaging in an oppositional relationship with general-market media reports on issues of immigration and providing alternative narratives for the public in their local communities."[16] At the same time, there is some evidence that immigrants used the news information and public services provided by Spanish-language media to start their own process of becoming part of U.S. society.[17] We argue that Telemundo's and Univision's news coverage of SB 1070 provided an opportunity that aided Hispanics in shaping their own identities.

Similar to Molina Gúzman and Riggins, we are interested in "exploring how ethnic news outlets produce competing meanings."[18] Specifically, we want to know what "meanings" Telemundo and Univision aired and how the networks' reporters approached their stories to make them pertinent to their audiences. Further, it is by looking at the intersections among politicians, media, and the public that this study intends to build upon Entman's cascade model that posits the relationship between political elites, the media, and the public as a cascade that flows in multiple directions.[19]

Methodology

This research is a qualitative analysis of Univision and Telemundo networks' coverage of the passage and public response to SB 1070 in April 2010; complemented by quantitative research of 121 news reports from Univision's national newscast at 6:30 p.m. during the months of April and May 2010. The data for the content analysis was obtained using Univision and Telemundo archives. For the quantitative section of the study, we use "framing" to identify the focus of Telemundo and Univision news reports. Media scholars have used this methodology extensively and in a variety of ways. Our methodology is deductive and thematic, in that we selected predetermined frames (e.g., "conflict" and "economic") from previous studies about politics and news coverage to find out how Spanish-language television networks portrayed SB 1070 to its audiences. In short, framing:

> [D]eals with all aspects of communication, from how journalists organize news articles around central axes to create coherent contexts, to how audiences unpack those frames to comprehend and reproduce the issues. They present information in such a way that audiences readily may infer meanings and "what the story is about."[20]

The analysis included: (1) stories that focused on SB 1070, and the impact that the debate on the law was having in the Hispanic communities and future projections; and (2) stories that provided reactions to or demanded reactions from Hispanics, nonprofit organizations, legislators, government officials, and international neighbors.

To get a more precise idea of the networks' objectives and weight of the news coverage during this period, we interviewed Telemundo and Univision executives, producers, and reporters involved with the April–June 2010 news coverage. We interviewed Ramón Escobar, former Telemundo EVP of news, four times and had several follow-up phone interviews and e-mail messages. We also interviewed Escobar's assistant producer Marianth Villarroel and communicated with her by phone and e-mail. Finally, we spent several hours interviewing Gabriela Vélez, producer from Telemundo's news magazine *Al Rojo Vivo*.

Daniel Coronel, Univision vice president of network news, had just stepped into this position (January 21, 2011) when we began our research, so he selected Johanna Usma, a producer for news anchors Jorge Ramos and María Elena Salinas, to work with us.[21]

Ramón Escobar, Telemundo EVP of news, requested that his producers compile a summary of the 2010 coverage on the Arizona law and reactions. Telemundo archives were not as detailed as those obtained through Univision. Telemundo producers reviewed rundowns (summaries of daily national newscasts), selected the stories, and retrieved scripts for each story. Producers identified eight stories for the months of April and May. Telemundo aired many more, but only eight were archived. Because they did not provide a representative sample of Telemundo's coverage of the subject, these eight news items were discarded from the quantitative content analysis and used only to provide context.

Univision has a more robust archival system, making it easier to identify news reports by reviewing the daily rundowns. The scripts for most of Univision packages (stories generated by and voiced by reporters) were not archived, so the network provided the "airchecks" or newscast recordings of the daily newscasts: a total of 121 stories were collected from the Univision airchecks. The methodology of this essay is also inspired by the work of Rosenstiel and his coauthors and Vigón.[22] Although Rosenstiel and his coauthors worked on local newscasts, some of the parameters from their "Quality Grading Criteria" can be applied to a content analysis of Spanish-language national newscasts. These are:

1. Community Relevance: designates the effort of the news organization to present stories relevant to any of their audiences. As Carmen's revealed, Telemundo and Univision coverage tried to make the issue of undocumented immigration relevant for nonimmigrants and naturalized immigrants.
2. Authoritativeness: designates the credibility of each story by the inclusion of relevant and expert sources.
3. Balanced Viewpoints: designates the number of viewpoints provided in a story.
4. Balanced Sourcing: designates the number of sources provided in a story.

Specific attention was paid to the length and the dominant frame of each news report. For example, from a total of 121 stories collected for the content analysis, eighty-two (72 percent) were long-format reports (two to two-and-one-half minutes in length). Typically, Spanish-language newscasts include stories that vary in length from twenty seconds to four-and-one-half minutes; the longer the report the more likely reporters are to include a diversity of perspectives and sources, as well as in-depth analysis.

Using the predetermined frames used in Semetko and Valkenburg[23] we identified five news frames that would most likely be applicable to this study: conflict, human interest, attribution of responsibility, morality, and "economic consequences." Preliminary analysis demonstrated that "conflict" was the most dominant frame for stories, followed by six stories that fit into the "economic consequences" frame. No stories included "human interest," "attribution of responsibility," or "morality" as dominant frames. We then analyzed how many stories could be also seen as "reactions" to the passage of the Arizona legislative measure. There was a correlation between "conflict" stories and "reaction" stories, as we found that most of the conflict stories were also categorized as reactions.

Qualitative Findings: "Immigration: A National Debate"

Univision and Telemundo producers and executives considered the coverage of Arizona's SB 1070 to be one of the most important and "critical issues affecting the Hispanic community nationwide."[24] As a result, Spanish-language network executives and producers did not approach the subject as routine breaking news, but as a major ongoing story. They sought to report and explain the proposed bill and its passage to their audiences in the context of the nation's larger debate over undocumented immigration.

In Univision's case, the importance of its coverage is best illustrated by a primetime program "Immigration: A National Debate," a town hall meeting which aired on May 14, 2010. In the program, the network aired comments from numerous sides of the debate and put forth questions to elected government officials and Hispanic candidates running for public office about SB 1070 and its future. As one media analyst pointed out:

> For a sense of whether this is significant, just try to remember the last time the country's English-language networks turned over an hour of prime time for a public affairs debate that did not involve presidential candidates.[25]

Indeed, during our interviews about coverage we identified a "sense of duty" among the Spanish-language network journalists; a need to raise awareness about the significance of this event which some compared to the civil rights movement of the 1960s. Univision news producer Elizabeth Cotte exemplified this line of thought when reflecting on the successes of the network's coverage:

> We explained to our audiences that what was happening was due to the lack of action on the part of the federal government. We reminded them that the U.S. did not become such an "anti-immigrant nation" until September 11, 2001. We also let them know that a democratic system should not treat them so bad; explained which parts of the Arizona law were presumed to be unconstitutional, and which others violated their human basic rights.[26]

Both networks chose to report on certain aspects of the issue that allowed viewers to: (1) recognize the already mentioned federal legislative vacuum; (2) listen as well as contextualize the complaints of supporters of SB 1070, such as some ranchers who claimed they were living on the border in fear of the human or drug traffickers; (3) discern specific problems from the rest of the undocumented immigrants working in the country; (4) highlight undocumented immigrants' struggles and abuses; (5) provide information that could help immigrants, their descendants, and nonimmigrant Hispanics better understand their rights and opportunities in the United States, as well as learn how they could play an active role in shaping the national immigration debate; and (6) help viewers understand the potential consequences of the Arizona law and how it could impact all Hispanics— undocumented or not.

Public Service versus Advocacy Role

The qualitative analysis revealed that Univision and Telemundo took very seriously their public service mission to provide information to help undocumented residents understand that they were not alone, that they had legal rights and the support of advocacy groups and many members of Latino immigrant communities. The networks accomplished this by reporting on local, national, and international reactions to the law. Almost 75 percent, or ninety-nine of all the stories aired on Univision, included reactions to the measure, with additional information about possible implications and ways that Latinos could play a role in shaping the debate. One example was the predominance of coverage by Univision and Telemundo of pro-immigrant rights rallies in Arizona during the time before and after SB 1070 was signed into law. For example, on April 20, 2011, Univision opened its newscast with two stories dedicated to the topic. One story showed a group of students who organized protests against the law, and another showed how hundreds of community leaders had collected 85,000 petitions in support of a veto of the law. Video for the lead story included a group in an act of civil disobedience, with shots of activists chained to the front of the capitol building in Phoenix. After the signing of the bill, reporters followed very closely groups of Hispanic activists in other parts of the state and country involved in similar civil disobedience actions, their gains and setbacks, and always made sure to present moderate comments from Hispanic civic leaders who called for peaceful and respectful mobilization. The networks included video of rallies organized in other parts of Phoenix and Tucson, Arizona, as well as rallies in other cities such as Los Angeles and Chicago that have some of the country's largest populations of Hispanic residents. Network reporters also followed events in other cities and states where people expressed concerns about the consequences and possible repercussions of the law. Both networks also aired stories about legislative initiatives similar to SB 1070 in other states, and the unsuccessful congressional effort to advance national immigration reforms.

The networks also covered the pro-immigrant rights rallies that are traditionally held on May 1. Because of the passage of the Arizona law, in 2010 the rallies became a venue for demanding that the federal government, and especially Hispanic legislators, oppose implementation of the law, avoid the introduction of similar legislation in other states, and push for a broader discussion of federal immigration reform. For example, on May 1, 2010, the Univision national news team broadcasting from Los Angeles dedicated the entire newscast to the rallies in the context of the Arizona law. The first story included a long report (one minute forty-seven seconds) that explained the need for immigration reform and another minute of conversation between the reporter and the anchor, during which both further explained the issue.

Both Univision and Telemundo broke with their regular news programming and scheduled all their news shows to cover these Arizona events on April 23 and May 1. During the first five days of May, Univision mobilized its main anchors, sending Jorge Ramos to Arizona, Edna Schmidt to Los Angeles, María Elena Salinas to the White House, and Enrique Teutelo to Miami. Telemundo also presented nationwide news coverage with live reports from coast to coast. English-language media, including cable news channels like CNN and Fox News, featured the rallies in their newscasts, but did not provide "wall-to-wall coverage."[27]

Finally, in their daily stories, reporters from both Univision and Telemundo confronted those who supported the Arizona law and those who would have preferred not to take a stand on the issue, including elected officials and candidates running for congressional office. When confronting supporters of the legislative measure, reporters let them first state their reasoning and then asked them specific questions. But most of the time, in their reports they included experts, representatives of civil rights and Hispanic advocacy groups, and the stories of "ordinary people" and families who dismantled the arguments of the SB 1070 supporters. The earlier story of Carmen and her family exemplifies how the networks faced the association of undocumented immigrants with the conflict frame of insecurity and fear. These "ordinary people stories" helped to counteract the negative discourse that depicts Hispanics as individuals who refuse to become active members of U.S. society. Among other examples of such stories were those that highlighted successful immigrants and those showcasing the contributions of Hispanic workers.[28]

Both Univision and Telemundo used a great deal of newsroom resources to cover the ongoing story. The two networks sent national reporters to Arizona from April to July 2010. On several occasions, both networks provided continuous live coverage in each of their news programs and news magazines from morning to night, including April 23 when Arizona Governor Brewer signed the bill into law, and on May 1 during pro-immigrant rights rallies. Univision had three national reporters on the scene, and a camera recording the events near the Arizona capitol twenty-four hours a day.[29] Producers and executives for both networks say that their coverage of SB 1070 continued throughout the following twelve months. As Telemundo's Escobar explained:

> From the time the law passed the House, until it was heard in the court and implemented, Telemundo almost continuously had a reporter, at times several reporters, and many times an anchor presence in Phoenix. After the law reached the U.S. Ninth Circuit Court of Appeals, Telemundo continued coverage by deploying a reporter to cover all the proceedings. Many special reports were filed

from the viewpoint of protesters, activists, legislators, law enforcement and experts. Key persons interviewed included: Governor Jan Brewer, legislator Russell Pearce (sponsor of the law), Sheriff Joe Arpaio, [members from the conservative group], Border sheriffs such as Pinal County's Paul Babeu, activists ranging from grass-roots individuals such as Salvador Reza to well-known leaders such as Dolores Huerta and artists such as Shakira and Jenni Rivera. [. . .] After the case went to the Ninth Circuit Court of Appeals, Telemundo remained vigilant covering every step of the courts review up until the moment, April 11, [2011] when they handed down their decision.[30]

Alina Falcón, Univision president, stated:

The possible implementation of Law SB 1070 in Arizona and its implications for the ongoing national debate on immigration reform is an issue of vital importance to the Hispanic community. [. . .] We have been, and continue to deliver on our commitment to provide the timeliest information on issues that directly impact Hispanics in this country.[31]

Quantitative Analysis: Framing the Arizona Law

The conflict frame emerged as the dominant frame in most of Univision's national coverage, representing 93 percent or 117 stories out of a total of 121. The remaining stories (four) presented an economic impact frame. (Although they were not included in this part of the analysis, the eight stories provided by Telemundo also had a dominant frame of conflict.) The most common conflict was between supporters and opponents of SB 1070. And although Univision (and Telemundo) did not ignore Hispanics and others who favored the legislative measure, such as state, federal legislators, or government officials, these viewpoints were characterized as voices of dissent. Indeed, reporters made a conscientious effort to insert in each long-format story at least one of these voices of dissent, for the sake of "balance." As we already mentioned, almost 75 percent or ninety-nine of all the stories aired on Univision included reactions to the law SB 1070. As the reporters explained why some Hispanics felt excluded, they also acknowledged that not all Hispanics think alike. For example, in the lead story on May 27, 2010, which showcased different reactions to the passage of the law and efforts to combat its implementation, Univision reporter Luis Megid explained that for supporters of SB 1070 "the implementation of the law was extremely important." Immediately after, Megid introduced a sound bite of a Hispanic woman from the conservative group American Citizens United, who stated: "We know that the laws need to be enforced so we don't end up in the same situation as Mexico. Look how Mexico is now: lawless!"

Nevertheless, although Univision stories showed clear points of view that supported SB 1070, these perspectives more often than not appeared to be more of a courtesy than a serious attempt to broaden the understanding of these views. They were inserted in the stories in the appropriate context; nonetheless, they were presented as a minority view. This contradicted the polls of the time, which showed that a majority of Americans supported SB 1070. It was clear that the focus of this coverage was not to confront individual statements, but to present a counter narrative to general market media's historical tendency to use a fear frame when referring to Hispanics.

Story Formats

Univision's coverage of the Arizona law and resulting reactions included a large number of long-format stories, with 75 percent (ninety-nine) of all stories more than two minutes in length. Moreover, shorter-format stories frequently focused on international reactions, surveys, or very specific reactions such as those from heads of state. For example, on May 21, 2010, when Mexican President Felipe Calderón Hinajosa expressed deep concern about the Arizona law to President Barack Obama, Univision did not air any corresponding video. Because of their length, shorter stories provide limited content-analysis value according to the Quality Grading Criteria.[32] These reports generally present only one source and one opinion, ranking very low in providing balanced sourcing or balanced viewpoints. The longer-format reports allowed reporters to present more in-depth explanations of the issues and include experts and members of Hispanic communities.

A peculiarity of Telemundo and Univision coverage was the length of the longer stories. They were twice as long as their counterparts in English-language networks, in which stories are mostly shorter than one minute. One of the reasons is that the Spanish language is "wordier" than English: it is estimated that on average, Spanish sentences are approximately 20 percent longer than English sentences.[33]

In fact, the shortest story filed by reporters in the first ten days of May was one minute forty-seven seconds, and the longest was two minutes twenty seconds in length. Each newscast had at least two stories longer than two minutes. This contradicts the efforts made by the Spanish-language network management during the 1990s, a period when reporters were pushed to file shorter stories (within a limit of one minute and forty-five seconds),[34] paralleling the pattern already established by their counterparts at English-language stations when covering Latinos.[35] This is one of the few aspects where Spanish-language news practice seems to have taken a different direction than the English language news, as shown by this research and other recent studies.[36]

Sources

An examination of sources included on Univision revealed that forty-seven stories (almost 40 percent) of the stories had more than four interviewees, twenty-one reports (17 percent) had three sources, and nine reports (7 percent) had two; and the rest, forty-four stories (36 percent) had one. In theory, the more sources a report includes, the greater the chance of diversity and balance. This was not the case in all the reports aired on Univision. For example, one April 27 story from a reporter based in Mexico City detailed the reactions to the passage of SB 1070 from the Mexican government and authorities. The report had a total of ten sources, including at least six on-camera interviews, with one point of view that supported the new law. Another sound bite was from President Felipe Calderón who condemned the new law and said, "It would open the doors to discrimination and abuse." Another source was from the Mexican Ministry of Foreign Relations that advised Mexican citizens not to travel to Arizona. And yet another source, this time the national leader of the PAN (National Action Party) called for "an international tourism boycott of Arizona" and demanded that all Mexicans avoid the state.

Balanced Viewpoints: "Our" Perspective versus the "Others"

Analyzing the number of sources in a story is of little value without explaining the perspectives that were included. Among the Univision stories, 38 percent (forty-five stories) provided multiple points of view. In some stories, the reporter interviewed several immigrants and immigrants-rights advocates who participated in protests, which were juxtaposed against interviews with Arizona's governor and other views that ranged from negative portrayals to cautiousness and misunderstandings about immigration and Hispanics.

Nevertheless, 26 percent (thirty-one) of the Univision stories had mostly one point of view. This categorization refers to the stories that might have briefly acknowledged other points of view, only to later bury it alongside information and sources that contrasted it. For example, one April 27 report focusing on Arizona boycotts included nine interviewees, with only one sound bite questioning the activity. That particular story explained the reasons for the boycott and the way in which local governments across the country such as Los Angeles and San Francisco were planning to prevent their employees and agencies from spending money in Arizona. The minority response came from a Hispanic from the Arizona Chamber of Commerce, who explained that the last thing small businesses needed at that moment was a widespread boycott. When asked about these findings, network producers countered that there was not a conscious effort to bury or ignore other perspectives; it was the type of coverage that helped create these asymmetries.

Thirty-eight percent (forty-five) of the Univision stories had only one point of view. One story filed by a Univision reporter in Guatemala included interviews with government officials who deplored the bill, along with deported Guatemalan immigrants who claimed they were mistreated while they lived as undocumented workers in Arizona. Other short stories originated mostly from wire services, when correspondents or reporters were not available, such as the reactions among members of the international community with brief comments about SB 1070, from Mexican President Felipe Calderón, Mexican legislators, Colombian singer Shakira, and even Prince William of Great Britain. Some stories with only one point of view included coverage of supporters of the law—such as former Alaska Governor Sarah Palin—but they were the exception. More often than not, short stories mentioned breaking news that reporters apparently did not have time to develop.

Authoritativeness: Choices, Voices, and Principal Actors

We have discussed the sources and the points of view Univision used during the SB 1070 coverage. Now, we turn to evaluating the credibility of each story, analyzing the inclusion of relevant and expert sources. As mentioned earlier, we use the Quality Grading Criteria, which grades the stories depending on the number and relevance of experts and sources.

Fifty-five percent (sixty-seven stories) featured on-camera interviews with experts or other sources. This category included television interviews with representatives of immigrant rights groups, advocacy groups, and civil rights groups, including the National Council of La Raza, American Civil Liberties Union (ACLU), Mexican American Legal Defense Fund (MALDEF), and legal experts. Members of the Arizona legislature and members of the U.S. Congress also fit into this category. Nine percent, or eleven stories, had information from experts or attribution to sources without showing their interviews on camera, and the rest, 36 percent (forty-four stories) featured nonexperts or nonmajor actors in the story, such as "persons on the street" interviews. In general market media, a 36 percent rate of nonexperts sources is considered negative: they are mostly random opinions from people on the street with minimum statistical value. Yet with respect to Spanish-language TV coverage of SB 1070, we argue that was important to include immigrants, rally participants, and "everyday" Hispanics because they were the on-the-ground experts regarding how the law was impacting Latino immigrant communities.

Therefore, when examining the types of sources alongside the points of view, 60 percent of the reports received the highest marks in three areas: "balanced sources," requiring three or more sources; "balanced viewpoints," presenting a mix of opinions; and "authoritativeness," expert, credentialed sources or on-camera interviews.

In stories that fit the economic impact frame, all reports included at least one expert such as an analyst, government official, legislator, business owner, or business employee. One report that contained the economic impact frame noted that many Arizona undocumented immigrants were afraid to leave their homes, and some decided to move out of state once the bill became law. This story included interviews with Hispanic business owners and service employees who spoke about businesses that were experiencing a decline in revenue as a result of the exodus of Latinos from Arizona. One worker complained that a once-bustling restaurant was now nearly empty.

Some reports featured officials who represented Hispanic constituencies, and who were asked to respond to economic and social losses related to SB 1070. For the most part, however, the economic reports featured Hispanics who were negatively impacted by this legislative measure.

Our source analysis with respect to economic impact frame reports revealed that these stories began by presenting community concerns, followed by confrontation of officials or a call to action. In other words, the thrust of these stories was not only to explain how Hispanics were being affected by the economic fallout, but also to lobby for immigration reform. According to the Quality Grading Criteria, these reports received the highest marks regarding Community Relevance.[37] As we have already mentioned, Univision focused more than 40 percent of its stories on giving voice to different views, mainly from Hispanics, who confronted the general market media's fear frame. This can be verified by analyzing the principal actors in Univision's coverage. Members of the Hispanic activists and advocacy groups represented the most common actors, appearing in 30 percent (thirty-six) of all news reports; along with immigrant voices, that were represented as principal actors in 11 percent (thirteen) of the news stories.

Another aspect of Univision coverage was trying to influence the debate by demanding responses from the U.S. authorities and officials. In this area, news reports that featured federal government officials and legislators comprised 24 percent (twenty-nine stories) of the coverage.

Arizona government officials and legislators, along with law enforcement and immigration authorities, played a much smaller role in Univision's coverage, compared to members of the category of Hispanic activists and advocacy groups. Eight stories (7 percent) featured state public officials or legislators, in general favoring the immigration law,[38] and five (4 percent) included immigration or police officers as the principal actors in the report.

Again, state public officials as well as immigration and law enforcement members often represented supporters of the Arizona law, the "others"[39] for

Univision. In this case, "others" included mostly Anglo individuals who favored SB 1070. They appeared many other times as sources in the stories, but hardly ever as principal actors. Principal actors were the centerpiece of the news report, and the most relevant source.

Interestingly, in 83 percent (ninety-nine) of the stories, principal actors criticized "others." Principal actors were for the most part immigrant advocates, and immigrants who protested the passage of SB 1070. In the rest of the coverage, 18 percent (twenty-two) of the stories, principal actors did not criticize "others." The majority of these reports (almost 60 percent or thirteen) were stories with federal government officials and legislators as principal actors. They explained their political positions on immigration and provided tentative alternatives, such as unsuccessful attempts to pass immigration reform on the federal level. Many of these elected officials were navigating the treacherous waters of the 2010 midterm election.

The findings presented here (Table 11.1) illuminate a sharp contrast between the way Spanish-language networks and general market national networks cover Latinos.[40] The Network Brownout reports show that more than one-third of the English-language network stories which referred to Hispanics analyzed had no sources[41] and lacked diversity viewpoints.[42] These reports along with newer studies also demonstrate that less than one in a hundred stories on general market national network news programs feature Latinos.[43]

Conclusion: When the "Others" Begin to "Other"

Telemundo and Univision considered the 2010 Arizona immigration law a significant story to cover and air on their national network news broadcasts.

TABLE 11.1
Principal Actors in News Stories

	Number of Stories	Percentage of Stories
Latino advocacy activists and groups	36	30%
Anglo advocacy activists and groups	10	8%
Federal officials and legislators	29	24%
Arizona officials and legislators	8	7%
Immigrants	13	11%
Police and immigration officers	5	4%
Experts	11	9%
Others	7	6%
Person on the Street	2	1%
Total	**121**	100%

In particular, the networks focused on explaining what the story meant to Hispanics, personally and politically, and providing information showing that all Hispanics, whether authorized to be in the country or not, could have a voice, have their rights respected, and play a potential role in shaping the national immigration debate. Therefore, networks framed the story as part of a national year-long debate over immigration reform, and not a fleeting "breaking news" report. Univision and Telemundo delivered empowering messages and, as every producer and executive interviewed for this research agreed, their coverage intended to fulfill a public service duty. Still, as former Telemundo EVP of News Ramón Escobar acknowledged other networks such as Fox TV denounced their coverage as advocacy journalism, accusing the networks of failing to air balanced coverage.

During April and May 2010, the networks, through their extensive coverage, explained the potential consequences of SB 1070 to their viewers. The reports covered reactions in Arizona, as well as in communities across the United States. Using Rosenstiel and his coauthors' Quality Grading Criteria, we demonstrated that Univision and Telemundo invested a great deal of time and resources to report stories that reflected a high degree of Community Relevance. The sources included in news reports were authoritative, as in the case of experts such as government officials, immigrant-rights advocates, and legal experts with profound knowledge of the issues. Other voices represented in news reports were people with first-hand knowledge of immigration conflicts, including immigrants themselves who shared information about the impact of the law on their daily lives. This represents the main differences regarding immigration coverage between the general market media and Spanish-language television.

It is clear that the networks gave voice to members of nonprofit organizations, activists, and Hispanic groups, as well as those who supported the law. But both points of views did not get the same attention. Negative views (coming from Hispanics or from Anglos) toward immigration reform and Hispanics in general, were represented in the majority of the stories, especially in longer format stories. To frame stories as a conflict, there have to be at least two sides; and Telemundo and Univision accomplished it by emphasizing the most outrageous views that demonized one side such as Maricopa County Sheriff Joe Arpaio. Yet sources that expressed negative views about Hispanics generally never emerged as principal actors of the story. The point of view they represented was ostracized as "the other," a minority view, and inundated by information aimed to contradict it. As Said theorized, the construction of "others" implies creating a mirror of what is inferior or alien— ironically something that Hispanic activists have accused English-language media of doing. Our case study has revealed that one of the messages created in Hispanic network coverage about immigration seems to be "you are either with us, or against us," along with the creation of an "other." Through this "othering," and because most of Univision's coverage employed a conflict frame, despite the network's one-hour primetime debate that invited a wide variety of immigration opinions, Spanish-language networks might have missed an opportunity to serve as a vehicle for deepening understanding about the issue as well as helping to bridge differences.

At the same time, Univision and Telemundo successfully built a counter frame to the frequent negative portrayals of immigrants and Hispanics in most English-language media. By engaging the Hispanic constituencies and pressing federal legislators, Spanish-language networks increased the potential to influence their audiences.[44] By demonstrating solidarity of immigrant rights groups and their civic rights actions, the networks contributed to form the identity of its public. In summary, Univision and Telemundo created alternative messages to general market media through representations of Hispanic individuals as victims but also activists and leaders. As a result, the networks illuminated different levels of political participation.

Ironically, in so doing, Spanish-language networks adopted some of the same general market media practices they attempted to counter. They helped in construct a group of "others"; the first step toward the creation of a stereotype.[45] Telemundo and Univision stories also contributed to a discourse of fear by choosing to frequently include the most outrageous and polemic anti-immigrants examples, such as the statements of Maricopa County Sheriff Joe Arpaio.

As the law winds its way through the courts, the story of SB 1070 appears far from over. For Univision, the law exemplifies the focal point of the national debate over immigration. For media scholars, Spanish-language news coverage of the law brought to the fore the struggle of ethnic media against exclusion, as well as pointed out an opportunity that alternative media provide to redefine a group on the group's own terms. Giving voice to the voiceless, and covering a wide variety of issues related to one of the most controversial immigration laws in recent history, Univision and Telemundo engaged in some of the best and the worst journalism practices. The future will tell if they will attempt to create better understanding among communities or if they fall into the same tropes as general market media, by constructing and perpetuating stereotypes of "others."

Notes

1. MyFoxPhoenixNews.com, April 23, 2011.
2. MyFoxPhoenix, June 23, 2011.

3. Ramón Escobar sent this information in an e-mail message on April 20, 2011, after holding several meetings with his reporters and producers about their Arizona immigration coverage.

4. For the purpose of this research, we consider "general market" media to be media that do not cater specifically to minorities, ethnicity, or particular cultures.

5. Alexandre and Rehbinder, 2002.

6. Carpini et al., 1994; Chaffee and Frank, 1996; Fowler et al., 2009.

7. Santa Ana, 2002, p. 56.

8. Pease et al., 2001.

9. Altheide, 1997.

10. Altheide and Michalowski, 1999, p. 499.

11. Albarrán, 2009; Gibens, 2009; Vigón, 2010.

12. Fowler et al., 2010; de la Garza et al., 2003.

13. Chávez, 2010; Santa Ana, 2002.

14. Anderson, 1991.

15. Molina Gúzman, 2006, p. 292.

16. Molina Gúzman, 2006, p. 292.

17. Pantoja et al., 2008, p. 503; Félix et al., 2008, p. 632.

18. Molina Gúzman, 2006, p. 283; Riggins, 1992.

19. Entman, 2004.

20. Pinto and Prado, 2010, pp. 6–7.

21. We met in person four times, spoke often on the telephone, and exchanged frequent e-mails. We also had a two-hour interview with Elizabeth Ann Cotte, a senior news producer at Univision for the past thirteen years, and someone who was involved in the Arizona SB 1070 coverage from day one.

22. Rosenstiel et al., 2007; Vigón, 2010.

23. Semetko and Valkenburg, 2000.

24. *Business Wire*, July 22, 2010.

25. Stelter, 2010.

26. Cotte, interview.

27. Stelter, 2010.

28. Univision, May 1, 2010.

29. Cotte, interview.

30. Ramón Escobar sent this information in an e-mail message on April 20, 2011, after holding several meetings with his reporters and producers about their Arizona immigration coverage.

31. *Business Wire*, July 22, 2010.

32. Rosensteil et al., 2007.

33. Villa, 2006.

34. We both witnessed these efforts from 1994 to 1999 during our work as line and executive producers for Telenoticias, a twenty-four-hour Spanish-language news station partly owned by Telemundo. During this period, Telenoticias produced Telemundo's daily national newscasts.

35. Montalvo and Torres, 2006; Subervi-Vélez et al., 2004, 2005.

36. Vigón, 2010; Moran, 2006.

37. "Community relevance" is defined by an effort to present emergency or national information relevant for their audiences and "significance" with a focus on issues, ideas, or policy (Rosenstiel et al., 2007).

38. The exception was Phil Gordon, the mayor of Phoenix, who opposed the law.

39. In *Orientalism*, Edward Said defined *other* as "a mirror image of what is inferior and alien."

40. Montalvo and Torres, 2006; Subervi-Vélez et al., 2004, 2005.

41. Subervi-Vélez et al., 2004.

42. Montalvo and Torres, 2006.

43. Santa Ana, at press 2012.

44. Entman, 2004, p. 17.

45. Hilton and Von Hippel, 1996.

References

Albarrán, A. B. (2009). Assessing the state of Spanish language media: A summary and future directions. In A. B. Albarran (Ed.), *The handbook of Spanish language media* (pp. 294–299). New York: Routledge.

Alexandre, L., & Rehbinder, H. (2002). Separate but equal: Comparing local news in English and Spanish. *Project for Excellence in Journalism*. Retrieved on February 17, 2009, from http://www.journalism.org/node/230.

Altheide, D. L. (1997). The news media, the problem frame, and the production of fear. *The Sociological Quarterly, 38*(4), 647–668.

Altheide, D. L., & Michalowski, R. S. (1999). Fear in the news: A discourse of control. *The Sociological Quarterly 40*(3), 475–503.

Anderson, B. (1991). *Imagined communities: Reflections on the origin and spread of nationalism* (Revised and extended edition). London: Verso.

Carpini, M. X., Keeter, S., & Kennamer, J. D. (1994). Effects of the news media environment on citizen knowledge of state politics and government. *Journalism Quarterly 71*(2), 443–456.

Center of Immigration Studies [an organization in Washington that advocates for enforcement and lower levels of immigration]. *Trends in immigrant and native employment*. Retrieved on February 20, 2009, from http://www.cis.org/articles/2009/back509.pdf.

Chaffee, S., & Frank, S. (1996). How Americans get political information: Print versus broadcast news. *The ANNALS of American Academy of Political and Social Science, 546*(1), 48–58.

De la Garza, R. O., & Yetim, M. (2003). The impact of ethnicity and socialization on definitions of democracy: The case of Mexican Americans and Mexican. *Mexican Studies, 19*(1), 81–104.

Entman, R. (2004). *Projections of power: Framing news, public opinion and U.S. foreign policy.* Chicago: University of Chicago Press.

Félix, A., González, C., & Ramírez, R. (2008). Political protest, ethnic media and Latino naturalization. *American Behavioral Scientist, 52*(4), 618–634.

Fowler, E. F., Hale, M., & Olsen, T. (2009). A matter of language or culture: Coverage of the 2004 U.S. elections on Spanish- and English-language television. *Mass Communication and Society, 12*(1), 26–51.

Fowler, E. F., Hale, M., & Olsen, T. (2009). Spanish- and English-language local television coverage of politics and the tendency to cater to Latino audiences. *The International Journal of Press/Politics, 14*(2), 232–255.

Fowler, E. F., & Ridout, T. N. (2010). Advertising trends in 2010. *The Forum, 8*(4), Article 4, 1–16.

Gibens, G. (2009). Univision and Telemundo: Spanish language television leaders in the United States. In A. B. Albarran (Ed.), *The handbook of Spanish language media* (pp. 237–244). New York: Routledge.

Has illegal immigration improved since SB 1070 become law? (April 23, 2011). [Television broadcast]. New York: Fox News. Retrieved from http://www.myfoxphoenix .com/dpp/news/immigration/has-illegal-immigration-improved-since-sb-1070-became-law-04232011.

Hilton, J., & Von Hippel, W. (1996). Stereotypes. *Annual Review of Psychology 47,* 237–271.

The meaning of this weekend's immigration marches. (2010, May 3). *Newsweek Blog: The Gaggle.* Retrieved on April 23, 2011 from http://www.newsweek.com/blogs/the -gaggle/2010/05/03/the-meaning-of-this-weekend-s-immigration-marches.html.

Molina Gúzman, I. (2006). Competing discourses of community: Ideological tensions between local general-market and Latino news media. *Journalism 7*(3), 281–297.

Montalvo, D., & Torres, J. (2006, October). *Network brownout report 2006: The portrayal of Latinos and Latino issues on network television news, 2005.* Washington, DC: National Association of Hispanic Journalists. Retrieved on November 20, 2009, from http://www.nahj.org/resources/2006Brownout.pdf.

Moran, K. C. (2006). Is changing the language enough? The Spanish-language alternative in the USA. *Journalism, 7*(3), 389–405.

Oboler, S. (1995). *Ethnic labels, Latino lives: Identity and the politics of (re)presentation in the United States.* Minneapolis: University of Minnesota Press.

Oliver, M. B. (2003). Race and crime in the media: Research from a media effects tradition. In A. Valdivia (Ed.), *A companion to media studies* (pp. 421–436). London: Blackwell.

Pantoja, A. D., Magaña, L., & Menjívar C. (2008). The spring marches of 2006: Latinos, immigration, and political mobilization in the 21st century. *Behavioral Scientist 52,* 499–506.

Pease, E. C., Smith, E., & Subervi, F. (2001, October 10). *The news and race models of excellence project: Overview connecting newsroom attitudes toward ethnicity and news content.* Poynter. Retrieved November 2009 from http://www.poynter.org/content/ content_view.asp?id=5045.

Pew Project for Excellence in Journalism. (2009). *2009 annual report on American journalism.* Retrieved on October 16, 2009, from http://www.stateofthemedia.org/2009/narrative_yearinthenews_ethnic.php.

Pew Project for Excellence in Journalism. (2010). *2010 annual report on American journalism.* Retrieved on June 1, 2011, from http://stateofthemedia.org/2010/ethnic-summary-essay/hispanic/.

Pinto, J., & Prado P. (2010). Environmental conflict and new media in South America: The social construction of international environmental disputes, presented on the Latin American Studies Association (LASA) XXIX International Congress, 1–37.

Project for Excellence in Journalism. (2004). *2004 annual report—Spanish-language media.* Retrieved on February 11, 2009 from http://www.journalism.org/node/594.

Riggins, S. H. (1992). The promise and limits of ethnic minority media. In S. H. Riggins (Ed.), *Ethnic minority media: An international perspective* (pp. 276–288). Newbury Park, CA: Sage.

Rosenstiel, R., Just, T. B., Pertilla, A., Dean, W., & Chinni, D. (Eds.) (2007). *We interrupt this newscast: How to improve local news and win rating, too.* New York: Cambridge University Press.

Said, E. W. (1978). *Orientalism.* New York: Vintage.

Santa Ana, O. (2002). *Brown tide rising: Metaphors of Latinos in contemporary American public discourse.* Austin: University of Texas Press.

Santa Ana, O. (at press, 2012). *Juan in a hundred: Representations of Latinos on the Network News.* Austin: University of Texas Press.

Semetko, H. A., & Valkenburg, P. M. (2000). Framing European politics: A content analysis of press and television news. *Journal of Communication, 50*(2), 93–109.

Separación de familias [Divided Families]. (25 July 2010). [Television broadcast]. *Noticiero Telemundo.* Retrieved from http://msnlatino.telemundo.com/informacion_y_noticias/Noticiero_Telemundo/video_player?uuid=7a34cf1f-df59-405a-820c-5da4514d7907.

Stelter, B. (2010, May 13). Univision to hold prime time debate on immigration. *The Media Decoder Blog.* Retrieved on April 28, 2010 from http://mediadecoder.blogs.nytimes.com/2010/05/13/univision-to-hold-prime-time-debate-on-immigration.

Subervi-Vélez, F., Torres, J., & Montalvo, D. (2004, December). *Network brownout Report 2004: The portrayal of Latinos & Latino issues on network television news, 2003. Quantitative & qualitative analysis of the coverage.* Washington, DC: National Association of Hispanic Journalists. Retrieved on November 14, 2009 from http://www.nahj.org/resources/NetworkBrownout2004.pdf.

Subervi-Vélez, F., Torres, J., & Montalvo, D. (2005, June). *Network brownout report 2005: The portrayal of Latinos & Latino issues on network television news, 2004 with a retrospect to 1995. Quantitative & qualitative analysis of the coverage.* Washington, DC: National Association of Hispanic Journalists. Retrieved on November 14, 2009 from http://www.nahj.org/nahjnews/Brownout%20Report%202005.pdf.

Telemundo backs Arizona protest. (2011, April 23). [Television broadcast]. New York: Fox News. Retrieved on June 23, 2011 from http://www.myfoxphoenix.com/dpp/news/local/phoenix/telemundo_arizona_protest_05242010.

Univision provides unparalleled coverage of Arizona's controversial SB 1070 immigration law. (22 July 2010). *Business Wire.* Retrieved on March 20, 2011 from http://www.businesswire.com/news/home/20100722006083/en/Univision-Unparalleled-Coverage-Arizona's-Controversial-SB1070-Immigratio.

U.S. Census Bureau. (2008, May 1). *U.S. Hispanic population surpasses 45 million now 15 percent of total.* Retrieved on February 10, 2009 from http://www.census.gov/Press-Release/www/releases/archives/population/011910.html.

Vigón, M. (2010). Covering the news for Spanish speaking USA, May 2008. *Journal of Spanish Language Media 3,* 24–40. Retrieved from http://www.spanishmedia.unt.edu/english/downloads/journal/Vol.3.pdf.

Villa, J. (2008). How to target Spanish researchers. [Tweet]. Retrieved on June 29, 2011 from http://searchengineland.com/how-to-target-hispanic-searchers-14785.

12

Between Heroes and Victims

Mexican Newspaper Narrative Framing of Migration

Manuel Alejandro Guerrero and Maria Eugenia Campo

M EXICO HAS A TRADITION OF MIGRATION. According to the *World Migration Report 2010,*[1] Mexico is on track to become the country with the greatest number of migrants, and they mainly live in the United States.[2] The *Migration and Remittances Factbook 2011* stated that 11.9 million Mexican citizens lived abroad, ahead of India (11.4 million), Russia (11.1 million), and China (8.3 million).[3]

Migration is a complex phenomenon involving many factors. In the Mexican public sphere, however, migration is not reflected with much complexity. Mexican national media mostly covers the multifaceted processes of migration superficially. Besides local media along the northern border of the country, National newspapers seldom cover immigration as a topic and the coverage is usually poor. In this chapter, we analyze the narrative frames through which the issues of migration are represented by national newspapers. We contend that a recurrent pair of images in the national print media represents migrants both as heroes and victims, a narrative frame that has been dominant in the discourse of government and nongovernment organizations (NGOs) alike. We first analyze the coverage of migration issues in the Mexican national press for one year, 2010, to discuss the general features of the migration/migrant narrative frames. We then present national news media coverage of two particular 2010 events, the passage of Arizona Senate Bill 1070, and the murder of seventy-two Central and South American migrants in the state of Tamaulipas as they traveled to the U.S. border. We first demonstrate that Mexican national newspapers employ the shallow and circumstantial "victims/heroes" frames to cover the issue. Second, we argue that these narrative frames do not offer the Mexican public access to wider discussions of internal migration patterns, immigration to and through Mexico, or policy implications of these demographic and economic migration processes.

Introduction

In April 2007 Mexican President Felipe Calderón spoke in Washington about Mexican migration to the United States. That evening the president said, paraphrasing Churchill, that the members of the U.S. Congress should recognize the rights of Mexican migrants since "through blood, sweat and tears they have already conquered a place in their own right in the American economy and society." He further expressed his "admiration for those countrymen, who filled with courage, valor, audacity and decision, risked their lives in their journey to the U.S."[4] The way President Calderón refers to Mexican migrants in the United States reflects the two frames through which politicians and public authorities have for at least the last fifteen years characterized migrants, as *victims* and as *heroes.*[5] The Mexican national media framing blatantly mirror these frames and rarely contest them.

We first summarize general framing theory to explain how we operationalize our definition. In the second part we analyze the coverage of migration issues in Mexican national newspapers during 2010 to show how two frames organize, define, and explain those issues. In the third part, we contrast the national newspaper coverage of two news events: the passage of Arizona's SB 1070. Here again, the coverage is framed through the (previously mentioned) paired images of Mexican migrants. However, national newspapers frame the murder of seventy-two Central and South American migrants differently. These framings have important implications for Mexican public debate and public policy regarding migration and human rights.

On Frames and Methodology

Though the term *frame* has been widely used in social science research in the last forty years, its definition, scope, and research methods remain unsettled. In communication studies, frames and framing have been used in different ways (Goffman 1974). (For other types of framing analysis, see Vigón, Martínez-Bustos, & González de Bustamante and Chavez & Hoewe, both in this volume.) Gamson and Modigliani define frames as "a central organizing idea or story line that provides meaning to an unfolding strip of events.

... The frame suggests what the controversy is about, the essence of the issue."[6] In his seminal article on framing, Entman says that "to frame is to select some aspects of a perceived reality and make them more salient in a communicating text, in such a way as to promote a particular problem definition, causal interpretation, moral evaluation and/or treatment recommendation for the item described."[7] Similarly for Reese, "frames are organizing principles that are socially shared and persistent over time, that work symbolically to meaningfully structure the social world."[8] Scheufele identifies four framing processes: *frame building*, the construction of the message by the media or other speakers; *frame setting*, the influence of media and communication frames on frames in thought; *individual effects*, the impact of frames in thoughts on individuals, attitudes, or behavior; and *journalists as audiences*, the possible effect of citizens' actions on the original framing building process.[9]

We may say, following D'Angelo, that framing seems more a research program than a single paradigm, since framing research uses a variety of methods and perspectives.[10] The work in this chapter, according to Scheufele's classification noted previously, enters into the *frame building* category, since we concentrate on specific media content discerning the fundamental elements of narratives of news stories, rather than the possible effects on the individuals and their subsequent attitudes or behavior. Narrative frames, then, *define problems*—determine what a causal agent is doing with what costs and benefits, usually measured in terms of common cultural values; *diagnose causes*— identify the forces creating the problem; *make moral judgments*—evaluate causal agents and their effects; and *suggest remedies*—offer and justify treatments for the problems and predict their likely effects.[11]

Our framing research combines quantitative and qualitative analyses of a comprehensive set of articles that appeared in three Mexican national newspapers in 2010. Our goal is to reveal the narrative frames used to characterize Mexican migration and migrants. We quantitatively examined the following variables: number of articles; their placement; kind of sources; and variety/ number of sources. Qualitatively, we analyze the texts of each article to establish how the main problem is defined; its causes; whether and what kind of a moral judgment is expressed; and, if solutions are suggested for the problem.

News Coverage and Framing of Mexican Migration in the National Printed Press

Mexican studies of the migration of Mexicans to the United States was initiated in the 1930s by the anthropologist Manuel Gamio.[12] Since then migration has been discussed widely from sociological, economic, labor studies, political, and international relations perspectives. Jorge Durand classifies all these Mexican studies as either demographic sociology (focused on the theoretical construction of migration) or historical anthropology (focuses on regional differences).[13] According to Patricia Espinosa, director of the Migration Studies Program at the Universidad Iberoamericana, communication studies have discussed Mexican migration in terms of the production of television programming, media consumption, and media produced by and for migrants. However, she notes that almost no studies have addressed media framing of migration.[14]

In this chapter we analyze news items related to Mexican migration issues that appeared in the national printed press during the year 2010. We selected three leading newspapers: *El Universal*, *Reforma*, and *La Jornada*. Our corpus comprises all the news items of these newspapers that were printed in 2010, between January 1 and December 31. All were printed in Mexico City and distributed in the largest cities in the country.[15] We do not include the regional or local printed press because few are available electronically. Moreover, a large number of local and regional newspapers reproduce or otherwise base their own migration articles on the national newspapers and national radio news broadcasts.

The first stage for ordering the information is based upon analysis of the "formal structure of the article text,"[16] which in part refers to the location of the news item in the newspaper, but we keep track of other variables such as the number of news items per newspaper and the type, diversity, and number of sources. The idea is then to start from the most visible aspects of the coverage through a simple quantitative description. A more qualitative approach is then developed for analyzing, coding, and arranging the information, which will be explained next.

We begin with the total number (n=2,007) of news stories on migration and migratory issues printed in the three newspapers, excluding items referring to SB 1070 and to the murder of seventy-two migrants, because we will analyze them as separate case studies. Looking at the total number of articles that appeared in the three prominent Mexican newspapers, *Reforma* had the largest number of news items on migration (n=1,020), almost double that of *La Jornada* (n=529) and *El Universal* (n=459). One possible reason for its extensive coverage may be that *Reforma* is a sister newspaper of *El Norte*, a very important daily published in the city of Monterrey, which has great interest in topics related to the U.S.-Mexico border.

Figure 12.1 shows the total number of migration articles published in 2010. The coverage peaked in April, when Arizona Senate Bill 1070 passed; in August when seventy-two Central and South American migrants were murdered; in November when the Global Forum on Migration took place in

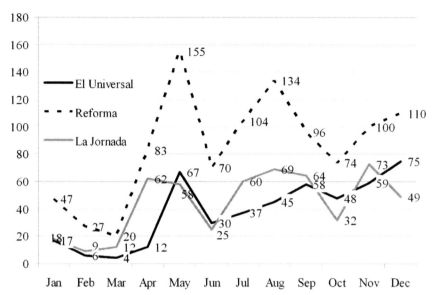

FIGURE 12.1
Number of news stories printed by three Mexican national newspapers per month in 2010.

Puerto Vallarta; and in December when the U.S. Congress failed to pass the DREAM Act. Otherwise consistent and increasing coverage of migration issues can be noted in the three newspapers.

Table 12.1 shows the story placement of news articles on migrants and migration in the newspapers. Front page placement differed among the three newspapers: for *El Universal*, 8 percent of the news items appeared on its front page, while for *Reforma* 10.8 percent appeared there, and *La Jornada* devoted the greatest coverage to its front page with 15.9 percent. In general, the majority of the news on migrants and migration appears in the national news sections: *El Universal*, 33.6 percent, *Reforma* and *La Jornada*, 50.4 percent each. However, while half of the migration news items in *La Jornada* and *Reforma* appeared in this section, only one-third of *El Universal*'s migration news items appeared there. A notable aspect is that *El Universal* devoted far more space to opinion pieces about migration (10.2 percent) compared to 1.1 percent of *Reforma* and 1.8 percent of *La Jornada*. Different placement proportions among the three national newspapers indicate differing judgments of newsworthiness about the migration issue.

Table 12.2 deals with news sources. Here, excluding editorials and opinion columns, Table 12.2 shows that the newspapers employ few sources on this topic: *El Universal*, 1.67 sources per news item; *Reforma*, 1.16 sources per

TABLE 12.1
Migration News by Section for Three Mexican National Newspapers

	El Universal	Reforma	La Jornada
Front Page	37	110	84*
National	154	515	267
States/front page	6	15	—
States	69	28	46
World/front page	10	143	—
World	67	70	19
Mexico City/front page	2	6	0
Mexico City	17	14	16
Opinion	47	12	10
Business/Economy	3	20	13
Entertainment	30	1	2
Editorials	7	—	0
Sports	6	14	0
Culture	3	11	0
Society	0	58	71†
Justice	0	3	—

*Since *La Jornada* uses a tabloid format, it is coded both as first and back pages.
†The social issue section in *La Jornada* is called "Society & Justice."

TABLE 12.2
Type and Number of Sources for Migration News Stories in 2010

Type	El Universal	Reforma	La Jornada
Mexican federal government officials	181	273	164
Mexican politicians	47	61	73
Mexican police	83	157	94
NGOs	104	189	131
Academics and experts	12	35	21
Migrants	75	98	82
Migrants' relatives	17	31	21
Newspaper investigative reports	12	17	9
No source cited	22	32	15
U.S. government officials	40	134	48
Non-NGO international (news) agencies	16	32	24
Church	25	57	42
Other	42	62	33
Totals	676	1178	757
	(1.67)	(1.16)	(1.46)

news item, and *La Jornada,* 1.46 sources per news item. These figures reveal relatively limited investigative journalistic practices in Mexico on this topic.

More importantly, the news-making process is quite dependent on one source: Mexican federal officials. Table 12.2 illustrates the similar patterns across the newspapers: first, Mexican federal officials (*El Universal* 26.7 percent, *Reforma* 23.1 percent, and *La Jornada* 21.6 percent); second, NGOs (*El Universal* 15.3 percent, *Reforma* 16 percent, and *La Jornada* 17.3 percent); and third, Mexican police (*El Universal* 12.2 percent, *Reforma* 13.3 percent, and *La Jornada* 12.4 percent). The similarities of sources can be attributed to Mexican journalistic practice when covering this issue, such as attending the same press conferences and reprinting and/or discussing the same nonmedia, governmental, and scholarly reports, instead of committing resources to fund costly independent investigative reports. Only with the fourth information source does the pattern begin to differ: for *Reforma* it comes from U.S. government officials (11.3 percent), while for the other two dailies the fourth source includes the migrants themselves (11 percent for *El Universal,* and 10.8 percent for *La Jornada*).

Finally in this section we want to point out some interesting aspects of newspaper vocabulary use. List 12.1 shows the words that appeared more than one thousand times in the 2,007 texts of Mexican national newspaper stories about migrants and migration.

LIST 12.1
Words appearing more than one thousand times in 2010 news coverage about migrants and migration in three mainstream Mexican newspapers

Human rights (usually, "violations of") (1,623)
Rights (usually, "lack of") (1,332)
Undocumented (*indocumentado,* used as a noun to refer to individuals) (1,296)
Death/murder/killing (1,202)
Aggression (1,176)
Accident (1,161)
Unsafe (i.e., the conditions immigrants face both in their journey and in the United States) (1,128)
Illegal/legal (1,109)
Deportation/deported (1,098)
Difficulties (i.e., the conditions immigrants face) (1,056)
Abuse/abusing/abused (1,055)
Denounce (1,036)

Agent (both Border Patrol and Mexican National Immigration Institute) (1,021)
Protection (and "lack of" it) (1,014)
Migra (colloquial Mexican Spanish for the Border Patrol) (1,012)
Survive/survival (1,007)
Tráfico, traficantes, traficar, and *pollero* (i.e., human smuggling, while excluding drug smuggling. *Pollo* "chicken" is colloquial Mexican Spanish for "unauthorized migrant" and *pollero* "chicken farmer" is colloquial for "migrant smuggler") (1,004)

Mexican national newspaper stories about migration are composed of certain frequently used words that depict the on-the-ground circumstances of the migrants. The way national media discourse depicts and frames migration depends on the language that the sources use to define and discuss this complex issue. The most frequently used words describe the specific material conditions of migrants, not the fundamental causes or other *structural explanations* of migration. The news does not reflect analysis of or debate on this topic. Instead they offer descriptions. Of course, we cannot make general conclusions solely on the use of high frequency words, but these descriptors are used to convey the everyday vulnerability of Mexican migrants who, lacking adequate legal protections, are left to face adversity on their own. We expand on this observation in the following section when we ask: What was the general narrative of these migration news stories into which these words were inserted?

The Frames: Victims and Heroes

To answer this question, we analyzed the content of each migration news item during the year 2010 for the three newspapers. One must be careful here not to confound narrative frames with news item content. Recall that we follow Entman's definition of frames as salient aspects of a communicating text that promote a particular way to define, interpret, assess, and treat a specific situation. We will focus on those aspects of the news items that support these four frame functions.

Before we enter the discussion on migrants and migration framings, something must be said in relation to the content found in the news. Table 12.2 revealed that very few sources were attributed in the news items, making them appear to be strongly dependent on the primary source. The four main sources for the news stories offer some insight: Mexican federal government officials, NGOs, police officials, and migrants themselves account for more than 60 percent of the newspaper sources. The primary source, Mexican federal government officials, was rarely contested by or contrasted with other sources, and certainly contributed to the particular frame used to write the news item. The lack of source diversity allows us to say, in general, that the typical migration news item source is a Mexican federal government official who frames the news story narrative in terms of the precarious conditions of the migrants during their journey, the accidents they have, and the abuses they are subjected to both during their journey to the United States and while they are there. The official discourse also asserts that the federal government is at the frontline of the defense of migrants. In contrast, in news reports that attributed information to an NGO source, the migration topics were the same, but NGOs tended to denounce corrupt Mexican authorities. When Mexican police officials became the main source, the news stories focused on the victimization of migrants, usually by organized crime, including the infamous *polleros*, "chicken ranchers," as the human traffickers are called. Migrants are called *pollos*, "chickens," in colloquial Mexican Spanish. Finally, news stories based on the narration of migrants or their relatives tended to be human interest stories that detailed the difficulties and abuse migrants faced. These stories usually emphasized migrants' personal plight, like missing their families who remained in Mexico, descriptions of their mostly physical work and the austere conditions in which they live to send back most of the money they earn, their solitude, their experiences with the *Migra*, descriptions of their personal journey to the United States, and, for those who have established themselves in the United States, the difficulties to reunite their relatives in the United States. In brief, these represented portraits of individuals dealing with adversities in their search for a better life.[17]

The framing of migrant and migration news stories can be discerned by answering the following questions: How is the narrative conflict characterized in the news stories, what appears to be the nature of the conflict, and how is the problem described? Who or what appears to be responsible for the situation? Do the news writers make any moral judgments? How do the news stories evaluate the actions committed by the causal agents, as well as their possible effects? Finally, does the news content suggest any solution to the problem? What strategies are suggested and who must carry them off?

We analyzed all the news items (n=2,007) on migrants and migration appearing in 2010 in the three newspapers and established separate codes for the ways the stories defined problems, interpreted causes, assessed the situations, and suggested solutions. These questions served as code-building guides. We analyzed the news texts focusing on the news item language and their intrinsic connections to wider social processes.[18] Words do not simply describe particular facts of news stories, but also construct their wider interpretative contexts. Words do not simply describe particular of news stories, but also construct their wider interpretative contexts. We first identified the range of arguments contained in the news articles. We then extracted the arguments from each of the news items, and then classified them according to the previously mentioned four framing functions. We then arranged those arguments in terms of their thematic structure, that is, the logic of the narrative parts. This enabled us to develop the incipient narrative framing categories with their properties and an incipient coding paradigm (or logic diagram). And finally, we inferred the logical relations among the arguments to present a set of themes that condense and reflect the frames. List 12.2 presents the themes that frame the Mexican national newspaper stories on migrants and migration.

LIST 12.2
Newspaper framing of migrants and migration according to Entman's four functions of framing

1. Definition of problem
   a. A context of illegality surrounds most Mexican migration to the United States
   b. The migrants face adversity on their journey to the United States
   c. The migrants deal with daily difficulties in the United States
2. Causes
   a. Migrants are constantly subject to abuse from corrupt Mexican authorities and U.S. ICE agents
   b. Migrants risk their lives to journey to the United States
   c. Migrants' human and civil rights are not respected in the United States
3. Moral judgment
   a. Migrants seek a better life in the United States
   b. U.S. authorities permit inhumane treatment of migrants (border patrol tolerate anti-immigrant hate-groups such as "vigilantes" and "Minutemen")
4. Suggested remedies
   a. The United States must recognize migrant (often unspecified) rights
   b. (An unspecified) "fair" migratory agreement between Mexico and the United States is needed

List 12.2 reveals the frames of the stories on migrants and migration. The arguments generate a set of victimization terms in which individuals seeking "a better life" face adversities of all kinds. The Mexican national newspaper image of the migrant is simultaneously a victim who faces powerful adversities, and a hero nonetheless for striking out at the United States and beating the odds.[19] Each newspaper employs the same frames. Two key aspects of this standard framing are that Mexican migrants are victims of a system that marginalizes them, and that the fight for migrant rights is centered in the United States. Note that Mexican national newspapers favor the coverage of circumstantial events and of specific conditions of migration, and within this authorized framing any discussion of the *structural causes* of migration is difficult to develop.

Applying the Framing Model: Two Cases

In this section we analyze two specific news events as Mexican newspaper case studies to assess if the general migrant frame (as mentioned) is valid. Here again we will use news items drawn from the same three newspapers. Our first case study is the news coverage of Arizona's Senate Bill 1070.

Case 1: Arizona Senate Bill 1070

On April 23, 2010, Arizona Governor Janice Brewer signed into law the Support Our Law Enforcement and Safe Neighborhoods Act, known as the Arizona Senate Bill 1070 (or simply SB 1070), which penalizes migrants who enter the United States without documentation (the unauthorized entrance into the United States), and all those who hire, transport, and employ undocumented migrants. The law was scheduled to go into effect on July 29, 2010, but several organizations, including the U.S. Department of Justice, filed legal challenges over its constitutionality and compliance with U.S. civil rights regulations, asking for a judicial injunction against its enforcement. The Mexican federal government officially condemned the law that, according to President Calderón, "criminalizes migration and migrants."[20] One week after the governor's signature, the Arizona Legislature passed House Bill 2162, which amended the SB 1070 provisions that most agreed would discriminate and violate human rights.[21] The day before the law was to take effect, Federal Judge Susan Bolton issued a preliminary injunction that blocked the law's controversial provisions. The state of Arizona appealed the injunction. A U.S. Supreme Court ruling is pending in 2012. (For more on SB 1070, see Chin et al., this volume.)

In Mexico, SB 1070 was widely covered. A total of 776 news items about SB 1070 were published in the three newspapers. *Reforma* again published the most news items on the issue, with a total of 440 items, more than double the number of items of each of the other two newspapers, *La Jornada* (n=180) and *El Universal* (n=156).

Figure 12.2 presents the total number of news items by month per daily during 2010. The two peaks correspond to the April passage of the bill, and

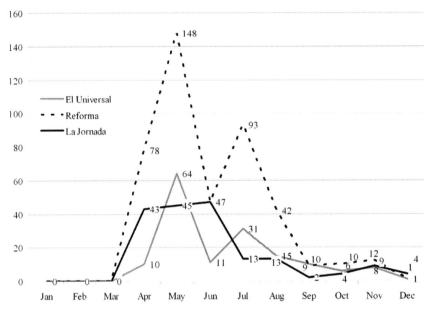

FIGURE 12.2
Total number of news items per month by daily on Arizona Senate Bill 1070.

in late July a large number of articles on the various mass demonstrations against it as well as denunciations, including NGOs, the Catholic Church, and migrant rights organizations, as well as incidents of immigrant abuse apparently committed by U.S. authorities in Arizona in the name of the new law. By the second week of August, the coverage fell dramatically, once Justice Bolton suspended the most notorious aspects of the new law. After that, the discussion of SB 1070 in the Mexican national newspapers slowly faded.

Table 12.3 reaffirms that few sources informed the new items about SB 1070: *El Universal*, 1 source per news item; *Reforma*, 1.45 sources per news item, and *La Jornada*, 1.41 sources per news item. Again these data reveal the limited investigative practices in Mexican journalism. In this instance, Mexican national newspapers depended on international news agencies for information. Interestingly, of the Mexican newspaper articles based on news agency information, 75 percent included a reporter byline. For *Reforma* and *El Universal* international press agencies were its first source, and for *La Jornada*, its second one. Of the total 776 news reports on SB 1070, 298 were written using information from international press agencies, but only nine stories reprinted with no changes. So, even in cases when using international press agency information, the Mexican news writers did not rely solely on that one source. In general, the second most cited source was a U.S. government official (271 news items), but in different percentages: 30.2 percent for

TABLE 12.3
Type and Number of Sources for SB 1070 News Stories

Sources	El Universal	Reforma	La Jornada
Mexican government officials at all levels	32	136	61
Mexican politicians	13	21	13
Mexican police	3	3	2
NGOs	14	27	23
Academics and experts	5	4	7
Migrants	6	19	11
Newspaper investigative reports	8	1	7
No source cited	5	13	9
U.S. government officials	26	194	51
Non-NGO international (press) agencies	35	201	53
Church	3	6	6
Other	6	16	12
Total	156	641	255
	(1.006)	(1.45)	(1.41)

Reforma, 16.5 percent for *El Universal*, and 20 percent for *La Jornada*. For the latter two newspapers it was actually their third source, behind a Mexican federal government official source. The most cited U.S. government sources were Arizona and federal officials. However, representatives and other political figures (U.S. governors willing to implement similar laws in other states) were also cited. In general, the third source was, again, a Mexican federal government official—for *La Jornada* it was its first source—but in this news event the authorities were more diverse than in the general treatment of the migration, since local Mexican and state authorities (especially those from the state of Sonora) were frequently cited. The fourth kind of source used by all three newspapers were NGOs; the fifth were Mexican politicians.

Regarding word frequencies, we rank ordered the most repeated words that appeared at least 386 times in news articles on SB 1070 at frequencies equivalent to List 12.1.

LIST 12.3
Words appearing more than 386 times in the
2010 news coverage of SB 1070 in all three newspapers

Arizona (the state or its officials) (912)
Government (821)
Discrimination/discriminatory (701)
Rights (668)
Undocumented (*indocumentados*) (656)
Deportation/deported (614)

Prosecution/prosecute (593)
Racist/racism/race (576)
Illegal/legal (502)
Migra (439)
Abuse/abused (412)
Protest/protesting/protestors (398)

Six boldfaced words noted in List 12.3 also appear in List 12.1. These most frequently used words carry particularly negative connotations and denotations regarding Mexican migrants in relation to the passage of SB 1070. The word *racism* (and its variants) appears here, and it relates in the texts to three situations: how some groups characterize SB 1070; the attitudes of some Americans in Arizona and the United States who support SB 1070; and the anti-Mexican sentiment felt mostly along the U.S.-Mexican border. Now, how are these words and other frequently appearing words used, in which narratives, and what are the frames they help to convey?

As in the year-long data set, we codified the 776 news items in terms of how they defined problems, interpreted causes, assessed situations, and suggested specific solutions. Again, information was arranged into thematic structures of the arguments of the news.

LIST 12.4
Mexican national newspaper framings of SB 1070

1. Definition of problem
   a. Deterioration of already precarious conditions of Mexican migrants in Arizona
2. Causes
   a. Arizona SB 1070 signed into law
3. Moral judgment
   a. SB 1070 violates civil and human rights
4. Suggested remedies
   a. The SB 1070 must be abolished
   b. Similar bills in the United States must be opposed
   c. A migratory agreement between Mexico and the United States is more urgent

List 12.4 presents the framing of SB 1070 by Mexican national newspapers. Where List 12.2 framed Mexican migrants' already precarious plight, in List 12.4 the *problem* is a deterioration of these conditions caused by the passage of the SB 1070. The moral judgment is that SB 1070 criminalizes migrants in violation of their civil and human rights. The suggested solutions either advocate that SB 1070 and similar bills must be opposed and abolished, or more widely, that a migration agreement must be reached between Mexico and the United States. This specific framing retains the two central aspects from the general migration framing, that Mexican migrants are victims of a system that marginalizes and subjects them to abuse, and that the latest cause is the passing of SB 1070. It focuses the attention on the U.S. side of the migratory equation, and on the actions of Americans who favor or who oppose SB 1070. Moreover, the third feature of the general framing is expanded: Mexican authorities are portrayed as constant critics of migrant abuse and of SB 1070, as well as the steadfast moral companions of the migrants. Once again, structural causes of migration are not easily discussed within the framing of this case study; the framing limits news depictions to circumstantial events that were detonated by passage of SB 1070.

Case 2: The Murder of Seventy-two Central and South American Migrants

On August 24, 2010, in the middle of a road in the northern Mexican state of Tamaulipas, a wounded man struggled toward a Mexican Marine post. The man, an unauthorized Ecuadorian migrant, said he had barely escaped alive from a nearby ranch where members of the infamous "Zetas" drug cartel shot to death many migrants who, along with him, were on their way to the United States. On the ranch, the Mexican Marines discovered seventy-two bodies of people who were identified as migrants from El Salvador, Guatemala, Ecuador, and Brazil. The event made the national newspapers, primetime television, and radio newscasts and sparked an unprecedented debate in Mexico about the increasing peril of migrants as they cross Mexico on their way to the United States. This debate had been absent in the Mexican mainstream news reports in spite of a steady stream of reports and studies about the worsening Mexican violence against migrants. For instance, the National Human Rights Commission (NHRC) had only recently reported on the extremely dangerous circumstances of migrants crossing Mexico, on increased organized crime-related kidnappings of migrants without a corresponding increase response by Mexican authorities in charge of their safety.[22] The NHRC reported 9,758 documented migrant kidnappings during the final six months of 2008 alone.[23] The Ecuadorian survivor's ghastly story of the murder of seventy-two migrants became a regular topic in the Mexican news during the last months of 2010, with a total of 310 news items published in the three newspapers. Again, given its sister paper's proximity to the U.S.-Mexico border, *Reforma* published the largest number of news on the issue, with a total of 133 items, while *La Jornada* published 88 and *El Universal* 89 news items.

Figure 12.3 presents the monthly appearance of news items from August to December 2010. *Reforma* covered the murder with fifty-one news items in

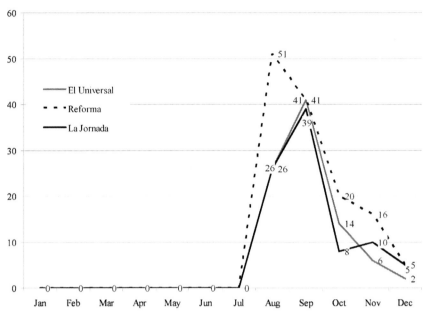

FIGURE 12.3
Total number of news items per month on the murder of 72 Latin American migrants in Mexico.

August, while both *La Jornada* and *El Universal* published twenty-six news reports that month. In September, however, the coverage became more balanced: *Reforma* and *El Universal* published forty-one reports each and *La Jornada* thirty-nine news items. In September, the Mexican national newspapers printed official statements released by the respective governments of the murdered migrants and commented on them. Also, during that month more detailed reports were published on the increase in Zeta kidnappings of migrants in northeastern Mexico, and the United Nations' call for justice. The newspapers reported that certain Mexican authorities reemphasized their ongoing fight against organized crime. Additionally, the newspapers gave accounts of police investigations and a high-level Secretariat of *Gobernación* declaration that accused some officials of the Mexican Institute for Migration of colluding with organized crime.[24] The newspapers reported on NGOs' studies on the rights and abuses of migrants as they crossed Mexico, on accounts of the sad return of kidnap victims' bodies to their home countries, and on the criticisms that politicians, experts, and NGOs meted out to Mexican authorities. Curiously, in October and November the number of news stories declined abruptly. By December only twelve news items appeared, reporting on NGO studies or op-eds addressing the overall grim circumstances of migrants traveling in Mexico.

Table 12.4 presents interesting figures on the news sources. For *El Universal* and *Reforma*, the first source was Mexican federal government officials (eighteen and twenty-nine news items respectively), while for *La Jornada* that source was its second source (twenty-seven), behind the police (twenty-three news items). For *Reforma*, the second source of its news was the international news agencies, while for *El Universal*, the second largest number of news items was composed of opinion columns that did not cite any sources. In these cases, the news based on international agencies reported the predictable reactions of the Ecuadorian, Salvadoran, and Guatemalan governments calling for the swift arrest and prosecution of violent traffickers and kidnappers. International agencies were additionally used to report on how other Latin American media discussed the murder.

The news items without sources were mostly opinion columns about the poor treatment Latin American migrants face while crossing Mexico and the failure of Mexican authorities to respond to proliferating kidnapping gangs. The third most cited source for *Reforma* was the Mexican police (twenty-three news items), for *El Universal* Mexican politicians (eighteen), and for *La Jornada* the international press agencies (twenty). News stories based upon police reports detailed the ongoing investigation of the case, the murder of one federal attorney who was had been investigating the case, and the capture and prosecution of individuals linked to the murder. Mexican opposition party politicians decried how ineffective the federal government was at tracking down those responsible for the crime, and its inability to guarantee people minimal personal safety.

TABLE 12.4
Type and Number of Sources for News Stories on Tamaulipas Murders

Source	El Universal	Reforma	La Jornada
Mexican government officials	18	29	23
Mexican politicians	15	9	14
Mexican police	13	23	27
NGOs	10	22	18
Academics and experts	3	7	1
Migrants	9	8	3
Migrants' relatives	1	—	—
Newspaper investigative reports	3	6	3
No source cited	16	23	4
U.S. government officials	1	1	3
International (press) agencies	12	16	20
Church	2	5	3
Other	5	5	3
Total	108	154	122
	(1.21)	(1.23)	(1.38)

Again, regarding the frequency of the words, this time we decided to consider only those words that appeared more than 154 times, since the total of 310 news stories appeared on the murder of the seventy-two migrants. List 12.5 shows these words.

LIST 12.5

Words appearing more than 154 times in reports in
three newspapers about the 2010 murder of seventy-two migrants

Migrants (399)
Death/murder/killing (343)
Narcos (drug traffickers) (325)
Human right (236)
Abuse/abused (231)
Massacre (212)
Illegal/legal (204)
Survivor/survive (192)
Aggression (171)
Claim (159)
Zetas (156)

The news stories about the mass murder used some of the same frequently used words as in List 12.1. These words again have negative connotations and denotations, but construct a somewhat different frame of victimization that is specifically attributed to organized crime and the corruption of some Mexican authorities. Second, the two framings are either on the circumstances of the murder and organized crime, or are a larger framing of corruption of some Mexican authorities. This will become clearer when we consider the narrative framing constructed to describe and explain the killing. Again we analyzed the 310 news items on the basis of the four functions of framing. List 12.6 presents the themes of the arguments that were inferred, that is, the framing of the news.

LIST 12.6

Newspaper framing of the murder of seventy-two
Central and South American migrants

1. Definition of problem
   a. Organized crime kidnaps (and in this case, murders) migrants in transit through Mexico

2. Causes
   a. For the Mexican government, NGOs, experts, politicians:
      - Organized crime—especially Zetas—controls important migrant transit routes
   b. For NGOs, experts, politicians:
      - Mexican authorities are unable/unwilling to protect Latin American migrants
      - Mexican authorities sometimes collude with organized crime
3. Moral judgment
   a. For the Mexican government, NGOs, some experts and politicians:
      - It is outrageous that organized crime kidnaps and kills migrants crossing Mexico
   b. For NGOs, experts, politicians:
      - It is unacceptable that Mexican authorities are inefficient at protecting migrants from organized crime, and immoral that some Mexican authorities participate in human trafficking
4. Suggested remedies
   a. For the Mexican government:
      - By intensifying the war against organized crime, criminals will be captured and prosecuted to face justice
   b. For foreign governments:
      - Criminals must be brought to justice
   c. For NGOs, experts, politicians:
      - Mexican authorities must provide migrants with better protection against organized crime

The narrative framing conveys images of victimization, linked specifically to organized crime and to abuse of some corrupt Mexican officials. In turn, in spite of these general images of victimization, there are actually two ways of framing the causes, moral judgments, and solutions: the kidnappings by organized crime rings. For the Mexican government, the cause is Zeta control of the migration routes, while for NGOs and other actors, the causes are Mexican authorities who are unwilling to control or are colluding with organized crime. As for moral judgments, the Mexican government condemns the kidnapping of migrants, while other actors additionally condemn the inefficacy of Mexican authorities to protect migrants' basic rights. Finally, as the suggested remedies, the Mexican government proposes the prosecution of all those responsible for kidnapping migrants (within the wider fight against crime in general), while others call not only for justice, but for proper protection of basic rights.

Analysis and Discussion

This is the first empirical study of narrative framing of migrants and migration in Mexico's national newspapers. Though more research is required, we believe that this chapter is a good starting point. We identified the Mexican national newspapers overall framing of migrants/migration, which emphasizes the precarious migration to the United States and the difficulties migrants face once there. Mexican newspaper frames stress that migrants are victims of a system that marginalizes them, notwithstanding they are portrayed as individuals who overcome adversities as they rightfully search for a better life. However, the Mexican national press still employs certain words that show a certain lack of knowledge of the actual debates that migrants are having in the United States. Striking examples are words such as "legal/illegal."[25]

The moral judgments presented by the newspapers hold that migrants are entitled to a better life and that they condemn the transgressions of their rights, especially when they are arrested in the United States without documentation and treated as criminals. Regarding remedies, the news framing focuses mostly on the U.S. side of the migratory equation, calling for respect of migrants' rights and a comprehensive binational migratory agreement.

In this framing, Mexican federal authorities appear as resolute denouncers of abuses, as unfaltering promoters of legal actions against the bill, and as the constant moral companion of the migrants. This framing favors a circumstantial reporting, not deeper analyses of structural causes of migration. The news reports draw on very few sources, making news coverage highly dependent on a single source, which generally remained uncontested or non-contrasted. To summarize, Mexican federal government officials are the most cited news source in almost all stories and are the frame-setters of national newspapers on migrants and migration reporting.

In the case of coverage about SB 1070, Mexican national newspapers used the general migration/migrant framing. Coverage of SB 1070 shared more than half of the most frequently used words with the general framing, using these words in very similar ways to portray and narrate the Arizona events in ways not unlike other migration reporting. In sum, SB 1070 was reported as a state government action that exacerbated the danger that Mexican migrants face in Arizona.

Mexican national newspaper coverage of the murder of seventy-two Central and South American migrants was framed through images of victimization, but in spite of using almost half of the same most frequent words of the general migration/migrant frame, there was a difference. The Mexican national newspapers portrayed their victimization in terms of the specific actions of organized crime and corrupt or complicit Mexican authorities.

Moreover, while federal Mexican authorities characterized such crimes as part of a wider discourse of fight against organized crime, other actors (NGOs, opposition politicians, and experts) framed the cause of the murder in terms of the inefficacy and corruption of some Mexican officials who are unable to protect migrants, and who sometimes collude with organized crime.

Thus framing of the murder of the seventy-two migrants differs because this event occurred in Mexico (not in the United States) involving Central and South American migrants (not Mexicans) in which Mexican authorities play a confounding role of either colluding with criminals or being an inept police force (not the steadfast moral partners of the migrants). The sudden drop off of national news stories on the murders in October and November remains unaccounted for. We offer a tentative hypothesis: Mexican federal authorities are the main frame-setter for Mexican national newspapers on migration issues. We must leave this speculation to further research and debate.

Notes

1. International Organization for Migration, 2010.
2. According to the International Organization for Migration. See the executive summary of its *World Migration Report 2010—The Future of Migration: Building Capacities for Change*, released in December 2010.
3. World Bank, 2010.
4. Herrera Beltrán, 2007.
5. Durand, 2004.
6. Gamson and Modigliani, 1987, p. 143; Gamson, 1992.
7. Entman, 1993, p. 52, original italics removed; Entman, 2004.
8. Reese, 2001, p. 11.
9. Scheufele 1999, 2000.
10. D'Angelo, 2002.
11. Entman, 1993, p. 52.
12. Alanís Enciso, 2003.
13. Moran Quiroz, 1995.
14. Interview with Dr. Patricia Espinosa de los Ríos at the Universidad Iberoamericana in Mexico City, 24 May 2011.
15. Independent auditors certify Mexican newspaper print runs. In 2010 *Reforma* printed 146,309 copies a day; *La Jornada* printed 107,666 copies a day; and *El Universal* printed 56,138 copies during weekdays and 117,863 in weekends. See http://pnmi.segob.gob.mx/.
16. Deacon, Pickering, Golding, and Murdock, 1999.
17. Two examples: Sandra Hernández Del Río entered Arizona with a tourist visa. She stayed and invested in a small *lonchería* (fast-food stand). Police accused her of participating in human trafficking. After those charges were dropped, the police remitted her

to immigration officers who, according to her, beat her. She was deported in an irregular manner; only two of her three sons were allowed to accompany her (Llanos Samaniego, 2010). Anastasio Hernández Rojas, an undocumented Mexican, lived quietly for twenty-one years in California. He was detained during a traffic incident. According to witnesses, Border Patrol agents beat him to death (Martínez, 2010).

18. The text analysis was proposed by the Glasgow Media Group (Philo, 1999; Philo and Berry, 2004).

19. To be clear, although the media frame does not represent merely settling down as heroic; overcoming the circumstances to settle down in the United States is depicted in quite positive terms.

20. "México condena ley contra inmigrantes," on *El Universal*, 25 April 2010.

21. Reuters, "Tregua a migrantes. Frenan la Ley Arizona," in *La Jornada*, 29 July 2010.

22. *Informe Especial sobre los Casos de Secuestro en contra de Migrantes*, 2009 (Special Report on Cases of Kidnapping of Migrants).

23. *Informe Especial sobre los Casos de Secuestro en contra de Migrantes*, 2009, p. 9.

24. Georgina Saldierna published the following: (3 September 2010) "Se revisa el trabajo de Cecilia Romero, afirma Blake Mora," *La Jornada*; (4 September 2010) "Ofrece SEGOB vigilancia federal," *Reforma*; and (4 September 2010) "Emprenderán estrategia para dar protección a migrantes," *La Jornada*.

25. See Santa Ana, 2002, Santa Ana et al., 2007.

References

Alanís Enciso, F. S. (2003). Manuel Gamio: El inicio de las investigaciones sobre la inmigración mexicana a Estados Unidos. In *Historia Mexicana, 52*(4) (Abril–Junio), México, COLMEX. Accessed 23 May 2011 from: http://codex.colmex.mx:8991/exlibris/aleph/a18_1/apache_media/BPRKMNG6CXRR6CJESE5MPNED6L46B7.pdf.

Comisión Nacional de los Derechos Humanos. (2009). *Informe especial sobre los casos de secuestro en contra de migrantes*. Accessed on 23 May 2011 from: http://www.cndh.org.mx/INFORMES/Especiales/infEspSecMigra.pdf.

D'Angelo, P. (2002). News framing as a multiparadigmatic research program: A response to Entman. *Journal of Communication, 52*, 870–888.

Deacon, D., Pickering, M., Golding, P., & Murdock, G. (1999). *Researching communications: A practical guide to methods in media and cultural analysis*. London: Arnold/Oxford University Press.

Durand, J. (2004). From traitors to heroes: 100 years of migration policy. *Migration Information Source*. Accessed on 22 March 2011 from: http://www.migrationinformation.org/feature/display.cfm?ID=203.

El Universal. (2010, April 25). México condena ley contra inmigrantes. Accessed 23 May 2011 from: http://www.eluniversal.com.mx/notas/675458.html.

Entman, R. (1993). Framing: Toward clarification of a fractured paradigm. *Journal of Communication, 43*(4), 51–58.

Entman, R. (2004). *Projections of power: Framing news, public opinion and U.S. foreign policy*. Chicago: University of Chicago Press.

Gamson, W. (1992). *Talking politics.* New York: Cambridge University Press.

Gamson, W., & Modigliani, A. (1987). The changing culture of affirmative action. *Research in Political Sociology, 3,* 137–177.

Goffman, E. (1974). *Frame analysis.* New York: Free Press.

Herrera Beltrán, C. (2007, April 28). Calderón: La migración, "fenómeno natural"; insta al Capitolio a lograr reforma en el tema. *La Jornada.* Accessed 23 May 2011 from: http://www.jornada.unam.mx/2007/04/28/index.php?section=politica&article =007n1pol.

International Organization for Migration. (2010). *Executive summary: World migration report 2010—The future of migration: Building capacities for change,* IOM. Accessed on 2 March 2011 from: http://www.iom.int/jahia/jsp/index.jsp.

La Jornada. (2010, July 29), by Reuters. Accessed 23 May 2011 from: http://www .jornada.unam.mx/2010/07/29/politica/002n1pol.

Llanos Samaniego, R. (2010, July 19). Entré con papeles a EU, invertí en un negocio y me deportaron por la *ley Arizona, La Jornada.* Accessed 19 July 2011 from: http:// www.jornada.unam.mx/2010/07/19/capital/033n1cap.

McCombs, M. (1997). New frontiers in agenda setting: Agendas of attributes and frames. *Mass Communication Review, 24*(1–2), 32–52.

Morán Quiroz, L. R. (1995). Reseña de 'Tendencias de estudios migratorios' de Jorge Durand. *Espiral,* septiembre–diciembre, pp. 199–205. Retrieved on 19 July 2011 from http://redalyc.uaemex.mx/src/inicio/ArtPdfRed.jsp?iCve=13820411#

National Human Rights Commission. (2009). *Informe especial sobre los casos de secuestro en contra de migrantes.* México DF: CNDH.

Philo, G. (Ed.) (1999). *Message received. Glasgow Media Group research, 1993–1998,* London: Longman.

Philo, G., & Berry, M. (2004). *Bad news from Israel.* London: Pluto.

Reese, S. (2001). Framing public life: A bridging model for media research. In S. Reese, O. Gandy, & A. Grant (Eds.), *Framing public life: Perspectives on media and our understanding of the social world* (pp. 7–31). Mahwah, NJ: Lawrence Erlbaum.

Reforma. (2010, September 4). Ofrece SEGOB vigilancia federal. Accessed 23 May 2011 from: http://www.reforma.com/edicionimpresa/paginas/20100904/pdfs/ rNAC20100904-002.pdf.

Saldierna, G. (2010, September 3). Se revisa el trabajo de Cecilia Romero, afirma Blake Mora. *La Jornada.* Accessed on 23 May 2011 from: http://www.jornada.unam .mx/2010/09/03/politica/015n3pol.

Santa Ana, O. (2002). *Brown tide rising: Metaphoric representations of Latinos in contemporary public discourse.* Austin: University of Texas Press.

Santa Ana, O., with Treviño, S. L., Bailey, M., Bodossian, K., & de Necochea, A. (2007). A May to remember: Adversarial images of immigrants in U.S. newspapers during the 2006 policy debate. *Du Bois Review: Social Science Research on Race, 4*(1), 207–232.

Scheufele, D. (1999). Framing as a theory of media effects. *Journal of Communication, 49*(1), 103–122.

World Bank. (2010). *Migration and remittances Factbook 2011.* Accessed on 23 March 2011 from: http://siteresources.worldbank.org/INTLAC/Resources/Factbook2011- Ebook.pdf.

Part IV
PROSPECTS

13

Immigration in the Age of Global Vertigo

Marcelo M. Suárez-Orozco and Carola Suárez-Orozco

IMMIGRATION IS CONSTITUTIVE of the American experience. It is the foundational narrative of the nation's birth, it is a dynamic shaping of the here and now, and above all, it is a social force that will define our shared destiny. Immigration as history-and-destiny is a rare feature—a soft exceptionalism that the United States shares with only a handful of other nations such as Canada, Australia, New Zealand, and Argentina. Yet immigration always generates push back. In the current era, when immigration is closely bound with globalization, these twin forces activate feelings of vertigo—the dizziness that comes with a sense of losing control. While on the surface the debate over immigration may be framed by legitimate questions (Should the United States cut or increase the number of immigrants it accepts in times of severe economic crisis? What are the best ways of protecting U.S. borders in a time of war and global terrorism? Should family ties still determine who gets in or should brainpower, skills, and education be the keys to open the gate?), below the surface lurks a dark iceberg of nativism waiting to sink the next ship of new arrivals.

Taking the long view, immigration's inherent duality proves enduring: we celebrate it looking backward, but fear it in the here and now. One hundred years ago, there was panic as unprecedented numbers of poor peasants from Eastern Europe (many of them Jews), from Ireland, and from the Mediterranean (most of them Catholics) came out of ships and began settling in the Lower East Side of Manhattan. Their religions, their languages, their feared atavistic criminal impulses, *alas,* their very essence, coalesced around the archetype of the immigrant as "other": incommensurable and beyond any hope of blending in or melting down no matter how much heat the melting pot could generate.

Today we can look back fondly and marvel at the epic journey by which Emma Lazarus' "wretched refuse"[1] became the backbone of the American middle class. The feared Jews and Catholics of yesteryear became among the most successful of America's white ethnics. Retrospective distortions and altered history aside, there is much to admire. Irony of all ironies: Catholics and Jews now form the entire roster of the U.S. Supreme Court, without a single WASP as a sitting Justice, inviting the handy refrain "only-in-America." But the teary-eyed retrospective focus is not easy to sustain in troubled times. When we turn to the here and now, the blinding light of sun-drenched Arizona comes into sharp focus. In Arizona, the immigrant "other" of yesteryear returns. How did sunny Arizona come to embody the dark side of immigration?

The combustive cocktail igniting the Arizona firestorm mixes three noxious chemicals that when kept apart may be harmless but when combined prove explosive. First, Arizona has endured a severe shock to its economy. Arizona's real estate—a sector of the economy that had both stimulated and benefited from mass immigrant labor during the boom years—crashed with the collapse of Lehman Brothers and the start of the Great Recession. According to the Case-Shiller Index home prices in the greater Phoenix area declined by 55.9 percent from 2006 to 2011.[2] Second, Arizona's demographic asymmetry between older, whiter, wealthier, native citizens, and a rapidly growing younger, darker, poorer, immigrant population is second to none in the United States. Long a retirement magnet, aging white baby boomers have grown dramatically in Arizona (and elsewhere in the Sun Belt). Arizona now has the steepest "generation gap" in the nation between its adult population (65 percent white) and its child population (58 percent nonwhite). According to William Frey, "These gaps could signal emerging cultural and political divisions across generations."[3] Third, Arizona has experienced rapid growth in its unauthorized immigrant population. The Tucson sector of the U.S. Border Patrol more than doubled the apprehensions of unauthorized immigrants—from approximately 300,000 apprehensions in 1998 to over 600,000 by 2005.[4]

Any two of these combinations can be easily tolerated. The rate of immigration can accelerate and the numbers of unauthorized immigrants can get to be quite high, but in a time of economic growth and prosperity immigration is rarely a top concern. What is unacceptable is the combination of all three variables at once.

There is nothing unique about Arizona. In a sense we are all Arizonans. Before Arizona there was California (remember Proposition 187?) and after it there were Alabama[5] and Georgia[6]—states that seem to be competing for establishing the most anti-immigrant climate in the nation. The Arizona firestorm captures an American *habitus*: the perennial "backdoor" mechanism that eases, *sotto voce,* cheap labor when needed and discards it when deemed no longer useful. The backdoor *habitus,* a term we borrow from Pierre Bourdieu,[7] is the dark shadow to immigration's mythic Golden Door. America's bad habit, the fix that unauthorized immigration has always provided, makes "illegal" immigrants doubly useful: needed labor in times of plenty and disposed of in times of want, easy scapegoats in the era of global vertigo. If we did not have "illegal" immigrants we would need to invent them.

Unauthorized immigrants are like all other immigrants—neither saints nor devils. Taking the long view, the anomaly of mass unauthorized immigration, with its precise starting date—November 9, 1989 (the day the Berlin Wall fell), and an end date of September 15, 2008 (the day Lehman Brothers filed for bankruptcy and the beginning of the Great Recession), may turn out to be but a fleeting moment in the unfolding story of American immigration. From 1990 to 2011, the generation of the heady days of the End of History and the Washington Consensus,[8] well over one million immigrants entered the United States every year for twenty years. Worldwide immigration went from 155 million in 1990 to 214 million—in 2010.

Golden Door, Backdoor, Trapdoor

The United States has always had a Golden Door and a backdoor immigration system.[9] The front door system is narrated as the mythic passage through the golden gate where orderly immigrants waited their turn to eagerly join the American family. While never legitimate, the backdoor worked to the satisfaction of its two primary constituents—businesses and unauthorized workers—until very recently. Seasonal workers would cross the southern border to do the jobs American workers shunned. They would typically save their earnings and routinely go back to their countries. If not immediately needed, they would be deported *en masse.* "During the Depression, as many as a million Mexicans, and even Mexican-Americans, were ousted, along with their American-born children, to spare relief costs or discourage efforts to unionize. They were welcome again during World War II and cast as heroic 'braceros.'"[10] By 1954 the "heroic" immigrants *alas* became redundant again and the Immigration and Naturalization service put into effect "Operation Wetback," rounding up and deporting approximately one million people to Mexico. Between cycles of mass deportations and the self-deportations of undocumented workers, the United States never quite experienced what it has today: a mass of permanently settled "illegal immigrants."

The seeds of mass unauthorized immigration are to be found in an unlikely place: the baby boom generation. They would become members of the largest middle class generation in American history. The more educated baby boomers would abandon varied and vital sectors of the economy to focus their skills in new, better paid jobs, and more pleasant working conditions. A growing army of immigrant workers—with and without papers, would fill this vacuum.

If the baby boomers gave birth to mass unauthorized immigration, a new culture of deregulation—finding its apotheosis in Ronald Reagan, saw it come to maturity. Unions were decimated or terribly weakened. Businesses flourished in the new climate of deregulation. They began grooming an ever more flexible workforce that could be summoned and dismissed with agility to favor the ebbs and flows of the business cycle. Immigrants—archetypical flexible workers—uncomplainingly worked long hours, under difficult circumstances, with no job security.

International trade likewise became the focus of deregulation. The North American Free Trade Agreement (NAFTA) was built on the promise that deregulating trade between the United States, Mexico, and Canada would be a win-win. As barriers fell, new jobs would be created, American companies would have access to the vast Mexican market, and Mexico would be able to create much-needed jobs ushering growth and stability. In reality, while the Mexican economy grew, NAFTA proved uneven—stimulating growth in certain sectors but also proving disastrous for large numbers of newly vulnerable Mexican workers especially in the rural south. The incentives for migration north became even more irresistible than before.

By the 1990s the American economy was booming. Millions of new immigrant workers, with and without papers, were lured to fill the need in construction and real estate services, agriculture, and food production. At a time of economic expansion and job growth, few worried about the long-term consequences of mass unauthorized migration. On the last year of the roaring 1990s the United States experienced something it had never seen before: well over 1.5 million border crossers were apprehended entering the country without papers.

The era of deregulation sealed a bad faith arrangement: employers had access to a rich supply of immigrant workers with little in terms of work site controls. Employment enforcement became the poor cousin of booming immigration control machinery. While growing resources flooded the southern border, little was directed to monitor job site violations. And in the unlikelihood of an inspection, employers could claim to be in compliance with simply a cursory inspection of "papers" without being held accountable for their legitimacy.

While businesses had a *carte blanche*, the episodic concerns on border controls gained new momentum. In the early 1990s, then-Governor Pete Wilson grabbed national headlines by loudly proclaiming that unauthorized immigrants were "invading" the state of California. A new border control strategy took hold. Following Texas' lead California started "Operation Gatekeeper." A large concentration of resources and personnel in the heavily trafficked areas were put into effect and sections of the border were nearly hermetically sealed. There were unanticipated consequences—slowing the flow in the San Diego area meant that more remote areas in Arizona experienced a corresponding increase in unauthorized flows. And, though the crossings became more dangerous and expensive, the availability of good jobs continued to pull immigrants into the American workplace.

By the end of the century, the freely swinging back gate that once let people in and then let them out again was becoming a one-way trapdoor. No one who had gone through the ever-more remote dangerous and expensive crossing would voluntarily face the trip back through again.

In the aftermath of 9/11, the southern border came to be regarded as a significant security threat to the homeland. Unauthorized immigration would now be conjoined with the threat of terror leaking. The southern sector became a tangible embodiment of a new amorphous and ever-present risk of a terrorist attack that could originate from anywhere in the world. Massive resources were deployed at the southern border. But the effectiveness of sealing the border remained underwhelming as unauthorized crossing continued at a crisp pace after the terrorist attacks of 9/11. The global tremors that shocked the world the day Lehman Brothers collapsed did more to slow unauthorized immigration than the architecture of the U.S. government aggressively deployed at the southern sector.

Crimigration Nation

The brutal killings of three college friends and the attempted murder of another young man in a schoolyard in New Jersey shocked the nation in August 2007. Six MS-13 gang members, known as Maras or Mara Salvatruchas, carried out the execution style attack. One of the murderers was an unauthorized immigrant from Peru who had two previous arrests for sexually assaulting a young child and for a bar brawl—both offenses that should have led to deportation.[11]

Almost exactly three years later, in August 2010 in Virginia, a Bolivian unauthorized immigrant, twice before arrested for driving while intoxicated, and awaiting a deportation ruling after having been released on his own recognizance, crossed over a median and crashed into a car carrying three nuns; one died as a result.[12]

These cases came to embody everyone's worst fears. According to the executive director of the Federation for American Immigration Reform, "illegal immigrants are more prone to illegal activity than the rest of the population."[13] Former Tennessee Senator Fred Thomson (of *Law & Order* fame), running on the 2008 Republican Presidential primaries, minced no words, "Twelve million illegal immigrants later, we are now living in a nation that is beset with people who are suicidal maniacs and want to kill countless men, women, and children."[14] Closer to the border, Arizona's Governor Janice Brewer made a link between "illegal immigration" and organized crime: "I believe today, under the circumstances that we're facing, that the majority of the illegal trespassers that are coming into the state of Arizona are under the direction and control of organized drug cartels and they are bringing drugs in."[15] In nearby Texas, fellow Republican Governor Rick Perry announced there is "great terror on our southern border."[16] Many citizens came to believe that immigrants, and unauthorized immigrants in particular, contributed to the crime problem.

Unauthorized immigrants by definition break one law—upon their unauthorized entry into the United States. But does breaking this law at the border make them more prone to be lawbreakers in general?

The barbaric drug-related violence destabilizing Mexico—especially the Northern region—ups the ante. What used to be alluring border towns inviting weekend escapes for bored teenagers in search of adventure and avid shoppers looking for bargains have become the frontline of a savage war over terrain to control America's insatiable demand for illegal narcotics.

Will the escalating violence on the Mexican side of the border spill over into the United States? According to FBI data, the top four big cities in America "with the lowest rates of violent crime are all in border-states: San Diego, Phoenix, El Paso, and Austin."[17] While the root of the problem is on the U.S. side of the border—guns and the demand for narcotics, the worst of the violence remains on the Mexican side—claiming approximately 40,000 Mexican lives. Drug running, human trafficking, and smuggling along the U.S. border are part of globalized criminal networks, but we cautiously distinguish foreign-born criminals involved in transnational criminal enterprises from immigrants in the traditional sense of the word.[18] Cartel lords and their foot soldiers of the booming drug and arms trade between Latin America, Canada, the Caribbean, and the United States have no interest in settling in the United States—indeed they do everything to avoid coming under U.S. jurisprudence. To confuse transnational drug and arms runners, smugglers, and terrorists with immigrants is both a statistical fiction and unhelpful. It adds kerosene to a raging firestorm.

Research on undocumented immigration has long demonstrated that the majority of unauthorized immigrants are workers, seeking opportunities even if it is in the most unforgiving, dirty, dangerous, and demanding jobs the American economy has to offer—in agriculture, construction, and service industries.[19] Yet international criminals are collapsed with immigrants in the crime statistics (such as incarceration rates), inflating and inflaming the image of immigrants' contribution to crime and disorder.

What is the nexus, if any, between immigration and crime?

Disinterested scholars have found that among immigrants "the rate of all crime has been less than among natives."[20] U.S. border towns with high concentrations of immigrants tell an interesting story: Latinos, two-thirds of whom are immigrants or the children of immigrants, have lower homicide rates than whites or blacks.[21] In the iconic city of immigration, New York, criminologist Andrew Karmen found that the despite the fact that immigrants tend to be disproportionally young, male, and poor, thus statistically at greater risk of engaging in criminal activities, the opposite is true. Karmen concludes that immigrants in New York are "a surprisingly law-abiding" population.[22]

In a series of systematic studies, the chair of the sociology department at Harvard, Robert Sampson, considered the relationship between immigration and crime, concluding that immigration—including unauthorized immigration—is linked with *lower* crime rates even in the most disadvantaged urban neighborhoods. Nationally, he points out, "Increasing immigration tracks with the broad *reduction* in crime the United States has witnessed since the 1990s."[23] While such correlations may not be entirely conclusive, Sampson also demonstrated through a series of detailed neighborhood-level studies in Chicago that the higher the concentration of immigrants and the more the linguistic diversity in a neighborhood, the lower the homicide rates. Sampson's data suggest that immigrants are less prone to violence than native-born Americans from a variety of backgrounds:

> Notably, we found a significantly lower rate of violence among Mexican-Americans compared to Blacks and Whites. A major reason is that more than a quarter of those of Mexican descent were born abroad and more than half lived in neighborhoods where the majority was also Mexican. In particular, first-generation immigrants (those born outside the United States) were 45 percent less likely to commit violence than third-generation Americans, adjusting for individual, family, and neighborhood background. Second-generation immigrants were 22 percent less likely to commit violence than the third generation.[24]

Unauthorized immigration tends to engender its own forms of deviancy. An in-depth study in the border area of San Diego County found that unauthorized immigration was linked to: "public order misdemeanors, such as urinating in public, and non-violent 'survival crimes' such as theft of bedding, food, and cash."[25] The most recent data from the Department of Homeland Security paint a similar picture of low-level offenses. In 2009, under the Secure Communities immigration enforcement program to catch and deport criminal aliens, vastly expanded under President Obama, data "show that a vast majority, 79 percent of people deported under Secure Communities had no criminal record or had been picked up for low-level offenses, like traffic violations and juvenile mischief."[26]

There is another nexus between unauthorized immigration and crime: undocumented immigrants often become the targets of crimes.[27] Yet they are less likely to report crimes committed and less likely to cooperate with authorities in the pursuit of justice. In Maricopa County, Arizona, Sheriff Joe Arpaio has sown terror among immigrant families with his extreme policing strategy. Crime has been declining throughout Arizona;[28] the rate of crime is down 12 percent—currently lower than it has been since 1976.[29] Instead of employing modern techniques of community policing (as do many of the surrounding counties who have demonstrated *plummeting crimes rates* ranging from 14 to 31 percent) Maricopa County has experienced an *increased* rate in crime of a staggering 58 percent.[30] There, criminals see a green light to prey on unauthorized immigrants, sensing their crimes will go unreported.[31]

What the research on immigration and crime reveals is entirely consistent with a pragmatic understanding of human migration. The lure of work and better wages is powerful. Immigrants, especially unauthorized immigrants, feel both lucky and optimistic about their opportunities. Above all they want to stay clear of the law and of drawing any unwanted attention to their presence. They stay under the radar, do their work, save their money, and many nurture quietly the hope of one day returning home with a nest egg. This motivational framework neutralizes all of the well-established factors that would make them more prone to commit crimes—concentrated poverty in socially disorganized neighborhoods, single male status, and relative youth. Immigrant motivation, work ethic, and optimism trump all.

But, of course, there are exceptions—the bad apples we previously described in the horrible cases. They come to embody every citizen's worst fear, make for great media hype, political grandstanding, and are the perfect vehicle to mobilize Arizona-like xenophobic sentiment.

How Immigrants Become "Other": Unauthorized Immigration

No human being can be "illegal." While there are illegal actions—running a red light or crossing an international border without the required authorization, one action should not come to define a persons' existence. The terms *illegal, criminal,* and *alien,* often uttered in the same breath, conjure up unsavory associations.[32] Unsettling and distancing ways to label people, they have contributed to the creation of our very own caste of untouchables.

In many cases, "illegal status," or what we prefer to term unauthorized status, may be not be voluntary. We prefer this term to *undocumented immigrant* as many have documents or could have documents but often find themselves in a limbo state pending a formal legal outcome.

In the mid-1990s, Sonia Martinez, mother of four children, all under the age of ten, became a young widow when her husband was stricken with cancer. With a limited education and no means to support her family on a rancho in rural southern Mexico, she reluctantly left her children behind in the care of her mother and crossed the border without papers. The week after arriving Sonia took up a job as a live-in housekeeper and nanny in the Southwest. Every month she faithfully sent money home to her family. She called them every week. Each time she called, they had less and less to say to her. Lovingly, she selected presents for each of her children over the course of the year. By Christmas she would make the pilgrimage back to her rancho to see her children and, Santa-like, shower them with American gifts. But the sweet visits home were always too short and she would soon have to face the dangerous and expensive crossing back to California, relying on the help of treacherous *coyotes* (smugglers) she hired each time. After September 11, as border controls tightened, she no longer dared to make the trek back and forth. She has stayed behind the trapdoor on this side of the border and has not seen her children since then.[33]

Sonia found herself a young widow and in a post–NAFTA Mexican economy with promised jobs that simply never materialized and in an unforgiving economy for poorly educated, unskilled, rural workers. Plentiful jobs in the Southwest economy in the mid-1990s, relatively comfortable working conditions as a live-in housekeeper and nanny in a middle class neighborhood, and an extremely advantageous wage differential proved irresistible. Although not raising her children came at a high emotional cost, the ability to support them was its own reward.

In 1998, Hurricane Mitch devastated Honduras, leaving little in the way of work opportunities. Like many others, Gustavo Jimenez made his way north, dangerously riding atop trains through Central America and Mexico and then crossed with a hired *coyote* into Texas. He worked a series of odd jobs but found it difficult to find steady work. Then, yet another hurricane changed his fate. When Katrina devastated New Orleans in 2005, ample work opportunities opened—dirty work in horrific conditions were hard to fill over the long haul of the cleanup and reconstruction. Mr. Jimenez quickly found work:

"Who, but us migrants would do these hard jobs without ever taking a break? We worked day and night in jobs Americans would never do, so that the Gulf could be rebuilt." But he found that he would be treated with disdain. It left him mystified. On one hand, "I know that by coming here illegally I am breaking the law," but he added, "I did not come to steal from anyone. I put my all in the jobs I take. And I don't see any of the Americans wanting to do this work."[34] Gustavo's story is both old and new. Unauthorized immigrants have always been called upon to do the jobs on the dark side of the American economy. The post-Katrina cleanup is a fitting example. Adding insult to injury, these workers are the target of disdain and disparagement. The stigma of the work gets attached to them—as if those doing dirty, demanding, and dangerous jobs themselves by mimesis become dirty, despised, and dispensable.

Hervé Fonkou Takoulo is a college-educated professional with a knack for stock trading in his spare time. Mr. Takoulo arrived in the United States in 1998 on a valid visa from the troubled African nation of Cameroon. He took to New York like a duck to water. He graduated with an engineering degree from the State University of New York and married a U.S. citizen hailing from California. She was the vice president of a Manhattan media advertising company. The biracial professional couple was ecstatic when President Obama spoke of his dual African and American roots. Takoulo's wife, Caroline Jamieson, "recalled that she cried when Mr. Obama said during a 2008 campaign speech, 'With a mother from Kansas and a father from Kenya'—I said, 'Oh, Hervé, even the alliteration is right—with a mother from California and a father from Cameroon, our child could do the same!'" She cried again but for a very different reason when the letter she wrote to President Obama resulted in her husband's arrest. The letter to the president "explained that Ms. Jamieson, 42, had filed a petition seeking a green card for her husband on the basis of their 2005 marriage. But before they met, Mr. Takoulo, who first arrived in the country on a temporary business visa, had applied for political asylum and had been denied it by an immigration judge in Baltimore, who ordered him deported." Surely, this president with his extensive personal experience in Africa would understand that Cameroon had a horrendous record of human rights abuses. Instead of the hoped for presidential reprieve, the asylum seeking Obamista was met by two immigration agents, "in front of the couple's East Village apartment building. He says one agent asked him, 'Did you write a letter to President Obama?' When he acknowledged that his wife had, he was handcuffed and sent to an immigration jail in New Jersey for deportation."[35]

When she was four, Marieli's father was assassinated in front of his wife and children. Left as a widow responsible for her family, Marieli's mother reluctantly left Guatemala for the United States, as she put it, "in order to be able to feed my family." Once in California, she applied for asylum status and waited patiently for her papers to be processed. The unforgiving bureaucratic labyrinth took six years and a small fortune to complete. Only then could she begin the process of applying to reunite with her children. In the meantime, the grandmother, who had been raising the children in her absence, died. With no one to care for them and after having patiently waited for years, Marieli's mother made the drastic choice of having her children make the crossing without papers. Finally, at age eleven, after having spent more than half her childhood away from her mother, Marieli arrived in northern California after being smuggled into the country by *coyotes*. Recognizing she "owed everything" to her mother but at the same time angry she had been left behind for so long, the reunification with the mother she barely knew was a rocky and bittersweet one. Marieli is now an unauthorized immigrant waiting in limbo.

The Reagan-inspired U.S. wars of proxy in El Salvador, Guatemala, and Nicaragua of the 1980s resulted in systematic killings—largely of noncombatant civilians, massive displacements of people, and the beginning of an international exodus of biblical proportions not only to the United States but also to neighboring Latin American countries. The U.S. invasion of Iraq has made Iraqis top the list of formally admitted refugees in the United States in 2009. While those escaping our foreign policy debacles often make it through the legal maze, thousands of others fall through every year.

The cases reveal how war and conflict drive human migration. But the heart also plays an unanticipated but powerful role. Work, war, and love are behind almost every migrant journey—authorized or unauthorized.

Many come here fully aware that they will be breaking a law by crossing without the proper documents, but in other cases accidents, misunderstandings, and an unforgiving bureaucracy can turn good faith errors into labyrinths without exit.

During his tour of duty in Iraq, Lt. Kenneth Tenebro "harbored a fear he did not share with anyone in the military. Lieutenant Tenebro worried that his wife, Wilma, back home in New York with their infant daughter, would be deported. Wilma, who like her husband was born in the Philippines, is an illegal immigrant. . . . That was our fear all the time." When he called home, "She often cried about it. . . . Like, hey, what's going to happen? Where will I leave our daughter?" The Tenebro's story, like many others, began as a love story and an overstayed visa. They met several years ago while Wilma was on vacation in New York at the end of a job as a housekeeper on a cruise ship. Love kept her from returning to the Philippines, and ultimately she overstayed her visa. Today, the lieutenant and the wife face an unhappy choice: "Wilma is snagged on a statute, notorious among immigration lawyers, that makes it virtually impossible for her to become a legal resident without first leaving the United States and staying away for 10 years." Lt. Tenebro is not alone—thousands of U.S. soldiers facing dangerous tours of duty have the additional burden of worrying that loved ones close to them will be deported.[36]

Combined, these testimonies embody the varieties of unauthorized journeys into the United States. Synergetic "push" and "pull" factors coalesce, luring immigrants away from familiar but relatively scarce surroundings to an alluring unknown. Immigrant optimism springs eternal. While some fly in with documents and visas and simply overstay, more immigrants come undetected through the southern border. Often they hire dangerous *coyotes* (typically from Mexico or Central America) or *snakeheads* (working from as far away as China, India, or Russia). Immigrants pay a very high price for these unauthorized journeys. While the crossing from Mexico to the United States can run approximately $3,000, the costs of longer passages are substantially higher, running up to an exorbitant $30,000 per journey. Those who arrive under the long shadow of transnational smuggling syndicates often face a period of protracted indentured servitude, as they must pay back exorbitant crossing fees. Whether the journey begins in Fujian, China, or Puebla, Mexico, tough border controls have made the crossing more dangerous than ever before—on average more than a person a day dies at the southern border attempting to cross.

The Children of Unauthorized Immigrants

Unauthorized immigrants are neither from Mars nor Venus. The majority have roots in American society. While some are married to U.S. citizens, others partner with migrants already here. Nearly half of unauthorized immigrants live in households with a partner and children. The vast majority of these children—79 percent—are U.S. citizens by birth.[37] The number of U.S.-born children in mixed-status families has expanded rapidly from 2.7 million in 2003 to 4 million in 2008.[38] Adding the 1.1 million unauthorized children living in the United States (like Marieli) means that there are 5.1 million children currently living in "mixed-status" homes.[39]

Nowhere is the story of the unauthorized immigration more dystopic than for the children who grow up in the shadows of the law. On an unbearable steamy afternoon on July 2010, Carola Suárez-Orozco found herself in a somber Congressional chamber testifying on behalf of the American Psychological Association in front of an ad hoc committee of the United States House of Representatives headed by Arizona's Congressman Raúl Grijalva (D-Tucson). At her side were two children—precocious, overly serious. A congressional photographer afterward whispered to Carola that in over twenty years on the job he had never seen such young children testify before the U.S. Congress.

> Eleven-year-old Mathew Parea was poised and collected as he spoke in the august chamber. At a tender age, he had already been active in social justice causes for several years including a four-day fast honoring the patron saint of migrant workers, César Chávez. Mathew spoke on behalf of thousands of children of migrant families. His steady voice was riveting: "I am here to tell you about my fears growing up in Arizona. Children want to be with their parents because we know that our parents love us. The laws in Arizona are just unjust and make me fear for my family. I am always worried when my family leaves the house that something might happen to them. I think about it when my dad goes to work that he might not come back or when I go to school that there might not be someone to pick me up when I get out."[40]

> Heidi Portugal, physically appeared younger than twelve, yet she carried herself in an unsettling serious manner. Her story embodies the immigrant dream turned nightmare: "At only 10 years of age I had a sad awakening the day of February 11th. When I woke up, I found out that my mother had been arrested. . . . My biggest preoccupation was my two little brothers and sister. What was going to happen to them? And what about my little brother that my mother was breast feeding?" She went onto explain how as the eldest sister, she took on the responsibility of caring for her younger siblings, how her mother was deported, and how she has never seen her mother again. She went on, "Before, I would admire all uniformed people that protect our country . . . [but they] took away the most precious thing that children can have, our mother. With one hit, they took away my smile and my happiness."[41]

Mathew and Heidi are part of an estimated one hundred thousand citizen[42] children whose parents have been deported. They face an impossible choice no child should have to make—staying in the United States with relatives or going with their parents to a country they do not know. These youngsters are a caste of orphans of the state, citizen children who day in and day out lose "the right to have rights"[43]—for them the protections of the Fourteenth Amendment are an elusive mirage. Children whose parents are detained and or deported by Immigration and Customs Enforcement exhibit multiple behavioral changes in the aftermath of parental detention, including anxiety, frequent crying, changes in eating and sleeping patterns, withdrawal, and anger. Such behavioral changes were documented for both short-term after the arrest as well as in the long-term at a nine-month follow-up.[44]

They also experience dramatic increases in housing instability and food insecurity—both important dimensions of basic developmental well-being.

Such insecurities, while heightened for children whose parents are detained, is ongoing for children growing up in mixed-status households. These insecurities exist even though unauthorized immigrants have very high levels of employment; among men, fully 94 percent are active in the labor force (a rate substantially higher than for U.S.-born citizens—83 percent and legal immigrants—85 percent). At the same time, more than 30 percent of children growing up in unauthorized households live below the poverty line. Harvard psychologist Hiro Yoshikawa, in his detailed study of infants and their families, documents the range of penalties American-born preschool children of unauthorized parents face. First, the children's housing and economic situation was often quite fragile. Second, unauthorized parents were less likely to take advantage of a range of benefits to which their citizen children are entitled (like Temporary Assistance to Needy Families, Head Start, the Women, Infants and Children Nutritional Program, Medicaid, and others). Lastly, they had less access to extended social networks that can provide information, babysit, or lend money in a crisis.[45]

While the majority of children of unauthorized immigrants are citizen children (4 million), there are some 1.1 million children who just like Marieli who have no papers. Many arrive when they are very young, others in their teen years. These children grow up in America, attending American schools, making American friends, learning English, and developing an emerging American identity. Every year approximately 65,000 young people graduate from high schools without the requisite papers to either go on to college or to legally enter the work force.

Unauthorized immigrants live in a parallel universe. Their lives are shaped by forces and habits that are unimaginable to many American citizens. Work and fear are the two constants. They lead to routines, where the fear of apprehension and deportation is an ever-present shadow in their lives. Dropping off a child to school, a casual trip to the supermarket, a train or bus ride, expose them to the threat of apprehension, deportation, and the pain of being separated from their loved ones.

Mass unauthorized immigration has become a social phenomenon with deep structural roots in American institutions. The responsibility must be shared beyond the immigrants themselves to the businesses that thrive on their labor, the middle class families who rely on them for housekeeping, babysitting, landscaping, and other amenities, consumers who have come to expect their affordable produce and rapid delivery services, and all citizens who have consciously or unconsciously enabled a dysfunctional system to flourish. Above all the political class shares the bulk of the responsibility by oscillating between denial, grandstanding, and hysterical scapegoating. They have brought us demagogic, unworkable, and self-defeating policy proposals.

Broken Lines

Outcry over our broken immigration system is focused on the borderline. Frustrated and fearful, Americans ask, "Why won't these illegals get in line like everybody else?" On the surface that is a perfectly reasonable question.

The reality, however, is that there is no orderly line to join. The terrorist attacks of September 11 threw sand in an already rusty machinery of legal immigration. In countless U.S. consulates and embassies the world over and in U.S. Citizenship and Immigration Services offices all over the country, millions wait in interminable queues. New security considerations brought an already inefficient system to a near standstill.

There are nearly 3.5 million immediate family members of U.S. citizens and permanent lawful immigrants waiting overseas for their visas.[46] In U.S. consulates in Mexico alone, approximately a quarter of a million spouses and minor children of U.S. citizens and permanent lawful residents wait to legally join their immediate relatives north of the border. In the Philippines, approximately 70,000 spouses and minor children are in the same situation. The average wait in line for these countries is from four to six years for spouses and under-age children. If you are a U.S. citizen and your sister is in the Philippines you will have to wait twenty years before she can join you. If you are a U.S. citizen and would like to sponsor your unmarried adult child in Mexico, you will wait sixteen years and spend considerable resources.

The visa allocation system for work permits is no more functional.[47] The annual quota for work visas is 140,000 per year; as this includes spouses and children, the actual number of workers is much lower. There is no systematic queue for low-skilled workers. There are a million people waiting in Mexico alone in any given year.[48] As Roxanna Bacon, the chief counsel for the United States Citizenship and Immigration Services in Washington, D.C., succinctly stated, "Our housing industry, our service industry, our gardening, landscape industry, you name it—it's been dependent for decades on Mexican labor. None of these people qualify for an employment-based visa. So when the hate mongers say, 'Why can't they wait in line? Can't they get a visa?'—there aren't any visas to get! There is no line to wait in! And that's why everyone who knows this area of law says without comprehensive immigration reform you really aren't going to solve any of these pop-up issues."[49]

Reasonable voices have been driven off stage, while demagogic venting, grandstanding, and obfuscation saturate the airwaves, the print media, the Internet, and town halls throughout the nation. Rather than offering new solutions, an amalgamation of cultural xenophobes and economic nativists has joined together to fuel the fire. Xenophobes see mass immigration, especially from Latin America, as a growing menace to the pristine tapestry of American culture that would be stained by new arrivals from the "Brown" continent. Economic nativists wring their hands: immigration presents unfair competition for ever-scarcer jobs as well as putting downward pressure on wages. For them, immigration has come to embody the globalization in all its pathologies. Immigrants are tangible representations of enormous and amorphous problems—the globalization of terror, the outsourcing of jobs, and the discomfort of being surrounded by strangers (dis)figuring the social sphere with exotic languages, cultural habits, and uncanny ways. Somberly, we must point out the obvious: this combustible cocktail has all the same ingredients that ignited the massacre in Norway on July 2011 by a xenophobe obsessed with the immigrant threat and multiculturalism.[50]

The Threshold of Belonging and Shared Fate

Americans by a large majority (72 percent) believe that the federal government is not doing enough to prevent unauthorized immigration.[51] Although they are split on building more fences on the border with Mexico (50 percent support while 50 percent oppose), they agree by large margins that we should be doing more to find employers who hire unauthorized immigrants (64 percent) and put in more border patrol agents (81 percent).[52] Americans are unsettled with continued unauthorized immigration.

Monetary and personnel allocations for border enforcement have grown enormously over the last three consecutive administrations. Between 1990 and now, the United States increased its border patrol from a force of 3,733 to 20,000.[53] The combined expenditure in 2009 for the U.S. Customs and Border Protection and U.S. Immigration and Customs Enforcement was a staggering $14.9 billion.[54]

For the first time in a generation, there is now a significant reduction in the flows of unauthorized immigrants into the United States. The new numbers tell a dramatic story. While in the year 2000 there were approximately 1.7 million border-crossing apprehensions, by 2010 the number of apprehensions had dropped to 463,000.[55] Immigration scholars, Douglas Massey among them, estimate that the net traffic of unauthorized immigrants from Mexico "has gone to zero and it is probably a little bit negative."[56] Concurrently, under the Obama administration the United States began deporting the largest numbers of unauthorized immigrants in decades.[57] What has led to the dramatic reduction in unauthorized entries and the overall decline in the total numbers of immigrants without papers is a combination of the deep economic crisis, the enhanced border control program, and the intensification of deportations under President Obama as well as changing economic, demographic, and social conditions in the sending countries—Mexico above all.

Taking control of the border and keeping unauthorized immigrants out does nothing to fix the snarled queue of would-be legal migrants patiently waiting their turn, nor the bigger issue of what to do with the ten to eleven million unauthorized immigrants already here.

For the political class, unauthorized immigration makes for perfect theater. This is the theater that would have us "clarify" the Fourteenth Amendment, to strip citizenship from the four million U.S.-citizen children born to unauthorized immigrants. Never mind that it would thus overnight add another four million "illegals" to an already astronomical number. Equally theatrical and unhelpful were the claims by Senator Lindsey Graham, which spread like wildfire through the airwaves, about "anchor babies." "People come here to have babies. They come here to drop a child. It's called 'drop and leave.'" Drop and leave? This accusation flies in the face of evidence: more than 80 percent of unauthorized immigrant women had been living in the United States one or more years before giving birth. Never mind that the animal husbandry-sounding "dropping a baby" does nothing to give legal status to the mother.

Everyone knows that the United States has neither the infrastructure nor the financial capacity to deport en masse ten or eleven million unauthorized migrants (and in the process split up millions of families), yet these scenarios are entertained. The American people are by and large not buying the Arizona-like antics. In 2010, a CNN opinion research poll found that overwhelming (81 percent) people support the idea of "creating a program that would allow illegal immigrants already living in the United States for a number of years to stay here and apply to legally remain in this country permanently if they had a job and paid taxes."[58]

How do we get beyond Arizona? Below we offer a set of consistent principles, based on a realistic understanding of how global migration works in the twenty-first century, and a humane sensibility to get beyond past wrongs and find common ground.[59] Three decades of basic research in this area lead us to conclude that unauthorized immigrants who invest and risk so much to make the journey to the United States would readily sign on for such action.

Ours is a two-phase project. The first phase would begin with the creation of a registry where unauthorized immigrants who have been here for three years and/or have close family ties with U.S. citizens would sign an affidavit acknowledging their unauthorized entry into the United States. Second, they would undergo a background security check in which they would have the opportunity to demonstrate evidence of a crime-free record and supply proof of a work history as well as payment of taxes. Third, they would furnish proof of good moral character and standing in the community in the form of three affidavits from community leaders such as a supervisor, a teacher, or a religious leader.

In the second phase, those who qualify would pay a $6,500 fine that would serve both as a penalty for breaking the law upon entry and as a processing fee to cover the program's costs ($6,500 is approximately half what it costs the average U.S. employer today in fees to process and recruit a new immigrant worker from overseas).[60] Those who cannot afford the fine would have the option of completing in-kind community volunteer work. Lastly, they would need to enroll and complete a course of study of English as well as basic U.S. history and U.S. government. Only then would they would earn the right to permanent lawful residency status.

This program rests on the logic of citizenship as cultural practice rooted in family and community relations. Unauthorized immigrants would have to pass what we call a "belonging threshold." It would benefit those who have roots as revealed in family relationships, a work history, community participation—paying taxes, staying clear of the law, exhibiting good moral character and engaging in the community by learning the language, learning U.S. history, and about U.S. government. Such individuals would have de facto passed the "belonging threshold" and their regularization would take them out of the shadows.

The current *legal* immigration system works as a bloated nineteenth-century bureaucracy in a twenty-first century world. The ensnarled, frustrating, broken queues create enormous incentives for people to cut in line. The system for bringing motivated low-skilled workers together with employers who want to hire them needs to be brought out of the feudal era and into the twenty-first century. While some propose new boutique approaches to guest worker programs, we disagree. Liberal democracies have proven to be notoriously inefficient at making such programs work. Two generations of research on guest worker programs show that in the final analysis, nothing is more permanent than guest workers. That is the experience in disparate places from Germany to California. We need in place a twenty-first-century agile mechanism that would "be allowed to fluctuate from year to year in response to macro-economic conditions."[61] We do not believe that an arbitrary quota should be set, as the number of migrants needed would fluctuate according to need from year to year. Those admitted would be able to transfer their permits from one employer to another—portability is important to project worker rights. We strongly agree with the Brookings Institution's recommendation for "a program of non-renewable provisional visas valid for a fixed term of five years, at the expiration of which individuals would have the option of either returning to their country of origin or applying for permanent status."[62] This system should have the necessary provisions and protections enabling workers to switch employers, making their permits portable, and ensuring other basic worker protections.

We are also realists. If recent experience is a good predictor, these recommendations for a systemic overhaul may, lamentably, not be accomplished immediately—at least not without a protracted political battle that the Obama administration seems increasingly unable and unwilling to fight.

What then can be done immediately? It is hard to argue against plucking the lowest—and sweetest—of the hanging fruit. Regularizing the status of over a million youth and emerging adults who have continuously lived in the United States through childhood, earned a high school diploma or a GED, and have gone on to college or military service is good policy and the right thing to do. The bipartisan Development, Relief, and Education for Alien Minors Act (DREAM Act) "would provide approximately 360,000 unauthorized high school graduates with a legal means to work and attend college, and could provide incentives for another 715,000 youngsters between ages 5 and 17 to finish high school and pursue secondary education."[63] Even in an immigration world where little makes sense, frustrating and blocking the pathways of these youth is particularly nonsensical. These children after all cannot be held responsible for breaking the law at the border (how did Cory break the law when she was brought here at age three?), have benefited from a taxpayer-subsidized education, have played by the rules, and have graduated from high school, making them fully functional members of the American family. These youth have passed the "belonging threshold" with flying colors. Yet, they can neither work nor can they take advantage of the full range of educational opportunities available beyond high school. It's bad for them and bad for us.

Taking the long view, even without any further migration, the United States will experience the greatest demographic transformation in a century. The citizen children of immigrants now constitute the fastest growing sector of the child population. *Alas* it is too late for Arizona to clumsily rush to close the barn door. The future is galloping ahead and its deep imprints have immigration written all over.

Notes

1. From the poem "The New Colossus" by Emma Lazarus (1849–1887).
2. See Streitfeld, 2011.
3. Frey, 2011, p. 9. Also see http://www.brookings.edu/~/media/Files/rc/papers/2011/0628_census_frey/0628_census_aging_frey.pdf
4. More unauthorized crossings in Arizona's unforgiving desert led to more deaths at the border: "Further, the increase in deaths occurring within the Tucson

Sector accounted for the majority of the increase in deaths along the southwest border. For example, our analysis of the NCHS data indicates that the increase in deaths in the Tucson Sector from 1990 to 2003 accounted for more than 78 percent of the total increase in border-crossing deaths along the entire southwest border" (Government Accounting Office, 2006, p. 17). See www.gao.gov/new.items/d06770 .pdf, accessed July 31, 2011.

5. See Preston, 2011.

6. Altschuler, 2011.

7. Bourdieu, 1990.

8. Francis Fukuyama, in 1993 the deputy director of the State Department's Policy Planning Staff, argued that the swift replacement of seemingly durable authoritarian regimes with liberal governments signaled the end of the global twentieth century ideological war, and capitalism won. "A true global culture has emerged, centering around technologically driven economic growth and the capitalist social relations necessary to produce and sustain it." History, which Fukuyama defined as the clash of political ideologies, ended. While Fukuyama's views conveniently meshed with George W. Bush administration's international ambitions, history and competing grand narratives continue apace (see Fukuyama 1993). As for the Washington Consensus, this is the dominant orientation of the last thirty years toward market-friendly international economic policies that was touted by mainstream economists, journalists, and global institutions like the International Monetary Fund and World Bank. The 2008 global financial collapse brought greater attention to long-standing criticisms of this vision, since its hallmark policies are said to have contributed to the global financial meltdown.

9. Zolberg, 2008.

10. Bernstein, 2006.

11. Fahim, 2008.

12. Dinan, 2010.

13. Beirich, 2007.

14. Sampson, 2008.

15. Goodsell, 2010.

16. See Rice, 2011.

17. Huffington Post.com (2010). U.S.-Mexico border safety: Area is one of the safest parts of America. June 3.

18. In 2009, the leading crimes committed by aliens removed from the homeland were traffic offences and, redundantly, immigration violations (over 31 percent), another third were drug offenses. See *Immigration Enforcement Actions, 2009.* Department of Homeland Security, www.dhs.gov/files/statistics/immigration.shtm.

19. Bean and Lowell, 2007.

20. Suárez-Orozco and Suárez-Orozco, 2001, p. 49.

21. See Lee, Martinez, and Stowell, 2008. Also see Lee and Martinez, forthcoming.

22. Karmen, 2000, p. 215.

23. Sampson, 2008, p. 29.

24. Sampson, 2008, p. 29.

25. Wolf, 1988, p. 23.

26. Immigration bait and switch. *New York Times Editorial.* August 18, 2010, p. A22.

27. Wolf, 1988.

28. Federal Bureau of Investigations (2010). Table 4: Crime in the United States: Preliminary uniform crime report. Washington, DC; Department of Justice. Retrieved from www.fbi.gov/ucr/prelimsem2009/table_4al- ca.html

29. San Diego Immigrant Rights Consortium (2010). America's voice education fund (2010). The notorious record of Maricopa County, AZ's Sheriff Joe Arpaio. July 19. Retrieved from immigrantsandiego.org/?p=917.

30. San Diego Immigrant Rights Consortium (2010).

31. Archibold, 2010.

32. Santa Ana, 2002.

33. Note that we have used a pseudonym; this case is from IS @ NYU data—see http://steinhardt.nyu.edu/scmsAdmin/media/users/ef58/metrocenter/Online_Sup plemental_Notes.pdf.

34. Gustavo's quotes are to be found in Orner, 2008.

35. Bernstein, 2010.

36. Preston, 2010.

37. Passel and Taylor, 2010.

38. Passel and Taylor, 2010.

39. Passel and Taylor, 2010.

40. See Testimony of Carola Suárez-Orozco before the United States House of Representatives, www.apa.org/about/gr/issues/cyf/immigration-enforcement.aspx.

41. See Testimony of Carola Suárez-Orozco before the United States House of Representatives, www.apa.org/about/gr/issues/cyf/immigration-enforcement.aspx.

42. See Testimony of Carola Suárez-Orozco before the United States House of Representatives, www.apa.org/about/gr/issues/cyf/immigration-enforcement.aspx

43. Arendt, 1966.

44. Chaudry et al., 2010.

45. Yoshikawa, 2011.

46. Anderson, 2010.

47. Anderson, 2009a.

48. U.S. State Department (2009). *Annual report on immigrant visa applicants in the family sponsored and employment based preferences registered at the National Visa Center as of November 1. Annual Report on Immigrant Visas.* Washington, DC: U.S. States Department.

49. Bacon, 2010, as quoted to A. Deveare-Smith.

50. See http://www.huffingtonpost.com/marcelo-m-suarezorozco-and-carola -suarezorozco/we-are-all-norwegians-now_b_911072.html. Retrieved July 29, 2011.

51. CNN opinion Research Corporation Poll, 2010, *Immigration.* August 6–10. Retrieved from www.pollingreport.com/immigration.htm.

52. CNN opinion Research Corporation Poll, 2010.

53. Anderson, 2010.

54. See Apprehensions by the U.S. Border Patrol Fact Sheet. Department of Homeland Security, 2011. Retrieved July 29, 2011, from http://www.dhs.gov/xlibrary/assets/statistics/publications/ois-apprehensions-fs-2005-2010.pdf.

55. See Apprehensions by the U.S. Border Patrol Fact Sheet. Department of Homeland Security, 2011. Retrieved July 29, 2011, from http://www.dhs.gov/xlibrary/assets/statistics/publications/ois-apprehensions-fs-2005-2010.pdf.

56. See www.nytimes.com/interactive/2011/07/06/world/americas/immigration.html.

57. According to the Department of Homeland Security in 2009, "393,000 foreign nationals were removed from the United States—the seventh consecutive record high. The leading countries of origin of those removed were Mexico (72 percent), Guatemala (7 percent), and Honduras (7 percent)." See *Immigration Enforcement Actions, 2009*. Department of Homeland Security. Retrieved July 31, 2011 from www.dhs.gov/files/statistics/immigration.shtm.

58. CNN opinion Research Corporation Poll, 2010. *Immigration*. August 6–10. Retrieved July 31, 2011, from www.pollingreport.com/immigration.htm.

59. Hanson, 2009.

60. See also Anderson, 2009b; Galston, Pickus, and Skerry, 2009.

61. National Foundation for American Policy, 2010. Employment-Based Green Card Projects point to Decade long Waits. See http://www.nfap.com/pdf/091117pb.pdf.

62. Hanson, 2009, p. 13.

63. Galston, Pickus, and Skerry, 2009.

64. Gonzalez, 2009, p. 4.

References

Altschuler, D. (2011, June 24). Georgia and Alabama anti-immigration laws. http://www.americasquarterly.org/node/2611.

Anderson, S. (2009a). *Employment-based green card projections point to decade-long waits*. Arlington, VA: National Foundation for American Policy. Retrieved from www.nfap.com/.

Anderson, S. (2009b). *New research recommends combining work permits and bilateral agreements to reduce illegal immigration, enhance security and save lives at the border*. Arlington, VA: National Foundation for American Policy. Retrieved from www.nfap.com/.

Anderson, S. (2010). *Family immigration: The long wait to immigrate*. Arlington, VA: National Foundation for American Policy. Retrieved from www.nfap.com/.

Anderson, S. (2010, May 20). Four steps to fix immigration. *Forbes*. Retrieved from www.forbes.com/2010/05/19/immigration-reform-policy-opinions-contributors-stuart-anderson.html.

Archibold, R. C. (2010, June 19). On border violence, truth pales compared to ideas. *New York Times*. Retrieved from www.nytimes.com/2010/06/20/us/20crime.html.

Arendt, H. (1966). *The origins of totalitarianism*. New York: Harcourt.

Bacon, R. (2010, May 22). One Border, Many Sides. *The New York Times.* Retrieved on 22 February 2012 from www.nytimes.com/2010/05/23/opinion/23deavere -smith.html?scp=8&sq=Deveare-Smith&st=cse&pagewanted=1

Bean, F. D., & Lowell, B. D. (2007). Unauthorized immigration. In *The new Americans: A guide to immigration since 1965.* M. Waters & R. Ueda (Eds.) (pp. 70–82). Cambridge, MA: Harvard University Press.

Beirich, H. (2007). Getting immigration facts straight. *Intelligence Report.* No. 126. Southern Poverty Law Center.

Bernstein, N. (2006, May 22). 100 years in the back door, out the front. *New York Times.* Retrieved on July 31, 2011 from www.nytimes.com/learning/teachers/ featured_articles/20060522monday.html?scp=10&sq=Ari%20Zolberg&st=cse.

Bernstein, N. (2010, June 18). Plea to Obama led to an immigrant's arrest. *New York Times.*

Bourdieu, P. (1990). *The logic of practice.* Stanford, CA: Stanford University Press.

Chaudry, A., Pedroza, J., Castañeda, R. M., Santos, R., & Scott, M. M. (2010). *Facing our future: Children in the aftermath of immigration enforcement.* Washington, D.C.: Urban Institute.

Dinan, S. (2010, August 2). Illegal immigrant killed nun released by Feds. *The Washington Post.* www.washingtontimes.com/news/2010/aug/2/illegal-immigrant-killed-nun-released-by-feds/?clear_cache_true.

Fahim, K. (2008, May 13). Newark triple murder suspect gets 8 years in assault. *New York Times.* www.nytimes.com/2008/05/13/nyregion/13brawl.html.

Frey, W. H. (2011). *America's diverse future: Initial glimpses at the U.S. child population from the 2010 census.* State of metropolitan America series, no. 29. Washington, DC: The Brookings Institution.

Fukuyama, F. (1993). *The end of history and the last man.* New York: HarperPerennial.

Galston, W., Pickus, N., & Skerry, P. (2009). *Breaking the immigration stalemate: From deep disagreements to constructive proposals.* A report from the Brookings-Duke Immigration Policy Roundtable, p. 14. Retrieved on July 31, 2011 from brookings. edu/...immigration.../1006_immigration_roundtable.pdf.

Gonzalez, R. (2009). *Young lives on hold: The college dream of undocumented students.* Washington, DC: The College Board, p. 4.

Goodsell, G. (2010, June 28). Arizona governor calls illegal immigrants mules. *Catholic Online.* Retrieved from www.catholic.org/national/national_story.php?id=37145.

Hanson, G. H. (2009). The economics and policy of illegal immigration in the United States. Washington, DC: Migration Policy Institute, pp. 12–13. Retrieved on July 31, 2011 from www.migrationpolicy.org/pubs/Hanson-Dec09.pdf.

Karmen, A. (2000). *New York murder mystery.* New York: New York University Press, p. 215.

Lee, M. T., & Martinez, R. (forthcoming). Immigration reduces crime: A review of the emerging scholarly consensus. In W. F. MacDonald (Ed.), *Immigration, crime and justice in the sociology of crime, law, and deviance.*

Lee, M. T., Martinez, R., & Stowell, J. (2008, Summer). Immigration and homicide: A spatial analytic test of the social disorganization theory. *Journal of Social and Ecological Boundaries, 3*(2), 9–31.

Orner, P. (Ed.). (2008). *Underground America: Narratives of undocumented lives.* San Francisco, CA: McSweeney's.

Passel, J. S., & Taylor, P. (2010). Unauthorized immigrants and their U.S.-born children. Washington, DC: Pew Research Center. Retrieved from pewhispanic.org/reports/report.php?ReportID=125.

Preston, J. (2010, May 8). Worried about deploying with family in limbo. *New York Times.*

Preston, J. (2011, June 3). Alabama, a harsh bill for residents here illegally. *New York Times.* Retrieved from http://www.nytimes.com/2011/06/04/us/04immig.html?_r=2&scp=1&sq=immigration%20in%20Alabama&st=cse.

Rice, A. (2011, July 31). Life on the line. *The New York Times.* Retrieved from http://www.nytimes.com/2011/07/31/magazine/life-on-the-line-between-el-paso-and-juarez.html?ref=magazine&pagewanted=all.

Sampson, R. J. (2008). Rethinking crime and immigration. *Contexts, 7*(1), 28–33.

Santa Ana, O. (2002). *Brown tide rising: Metaphoric representations of Latinos in contemporary public discourse.* Austin: University of Texas Press.

Streitfeld, D. (2011, May 31). Bottom may be near for slide in housing. *New York Times.* Retrieved from www.nytimes.com/interactive/2011/05/31/business/economy/case-shiller-index.html?ref=business#city/PHX.

Suárez-Orozco, C., & Suárez-Orozco, M. (2001). *Children of immigration.* Cambridge, MA: Harvard University Press.

U.S. Government Accountability Office. (2006). Illegal immigration. *Border-crossing deaths have doubled since 1995; Border Patrol's efforts to prevent deaths have not been fully evaluated.* Report GAO-06-770. Washington, DC: Government Printing Office.

Wolf, D. (1988). *Undocumented aliens and crime: The case of San Diego County.* La Jolla, CA: La Jolla Center for U.S. Mexican Studies.

Yoshikawa, H. (2011). *Immigrants raising citizens: Undocumented parents and their young children.* New York: Russell Sage Foundation.

Zolberg, A. (2008). *A nation by design: Immigration policy in the fashioning of America.* Cambridge, MA: Harvard University Press.

14

Can America Learn to Think Globally?

We Don't at Our Own Risk

Otto Santa Ana and Celeste González de Bustamante

Today it is relatively costless to attack immigrants in general and Hispanics in particular because, in their quest for integration and acceptance, this population has been loathe to support ethnic confrontations. However, this scenario can change if, seeing themselves repeatedly portrayed as culturally inferior and as a threat to the nation, these groups see no option but to coalesce into a militantly political block. The recent history of immigration to America is strewn with policies and campaigns that have backfired. One can only hope that the rise of migrant and Hispanic political militancy where none existed before does not become the latest episode of this unenviable saga.

—Alejandro Portes[1]

IN 2011, TO OPEN HER INDEPENDENCE DAY PROGRAM, the ABC host of *This Week with Christiane Amanpour*, voiced over black and white film images of early twentieth century immigrants on steam ships and the Statue of Liberty:

Give me your tired, your poor, your huddled masses, yearning to breathe free. These are words that most Americans and many immigrants know by heart; lines inscribed on the Statue of Liberty that greeted new immigrants at the dawn of the last century. And now the conversation has changed, and so has this melting pot nation. Today's newcomers are not being welcomed with open arms.

Amanpour's opening statement included two common faults that contribute to Americans' limited ability to think about immigration.

The first fault is "historical amnesia." As numerous chapters in this volume have stressed, despite the words written on the Statue of Liberty, this nation has never really welcomed immigrants with open arms. Policies designed to attract a cheap labor pool and for welcoming immigrants are two different things. While the dominant narrative proclaims ours "a nation of immigrants," it bears pointing to the two sides of the immigration coin.[2] When the nation's economy is growing, U.S. commerce promotes the virtues of America and its "American Dream" of the unbounded opportunity for the hardest worker. Workers from other countries are recruited for the lowest paid and least desirable work.[3] They come, do the work, dream the Dream, and honor their end of the bargain. In the past they came in extraordinary numbers. For example, from 1880 to 1920 the United States accepted 24 million immigrants when its own population numbered much less than 100 million.[4] Nowadays, they are far fewer; an estimated 12 million unauthorized immigrants live among over 300 million Americans.

However, when the economic cycle wanes, then the very same immigrant is considered a menace. Evidence for this attitude abounds in American history. For example, between 1929 and 1935 authorities mobilized the U.S. military to force the repatriation of 500,000 Mexican immigrants and their U.S.-born children.[5] Likewise the recession of 1953 led to the infamous Operation Wetback of the following year. And the post–Cold War recession of the early 1990s set the stage for California's infamous Proposition 187.

The other problem with Amanpour's opening statement is that it presumes our country remains a "nation of immigrants." More accurately, we are the descendants of immigrants; their numbers are comparatively low compared to earlier times. We rely on this ineffectual nationalist discourse to help us deal with our diversity.[6] In contrast, today's predominant discourse of the public sphere makes the immigrant out to be a fearsome specter when in fact the immigrant day laborer or service worker is the most defenseless person.[7] Further, the so-called American Dream, the effort to pull themselves up "by their bootstraps" to make a better life is not exceptional to the United States. It's a human desire to improve one's condition in the midst of adversity. Insofar as we accept this myth, we will be unable to see anything else, especially solutions beyond our national boundaries.

The reasons for our collective historical ignorance are beyond the scope of this chapter, but journalism, which claims to offer an authoritative daily accounting of America's unfolding reality and is an important source of the nation's understanding of the nation and the world, has no excuse. These days the news media too often amplify the imagery of anti-immigrant demagogues; meanwhile news executives demonstrate no concerted strategy to moderate such anti-democratic discourse. They conveniently argue that they are only giving the public what it wants; read: what sells. So the public sphere, of which the news media is its most important institution, foments ignorance and fear.

During the twentieth century, the American century of military, economic, and cultural dominance, our citizenry was indifferent to escalating globalization because we were its greatest beneficiaries. In the twenty-first century, our nation cannot afford the luxury of self-deception. One of nation's major problems, immigration, cannot be effectively addressed when the electorate does not understand that global economic, political, and social forces cannot be contained at the nation's border. Raising higher walls will not stop the desperate.

In 2010 Arizona's leadership acted defensively, as if a nostalgic way of life could be resurrected if only immigrants were eliminated. The authors of SB 1070 wanted to rid Arizona of immigrants, particularly Latino immigrants. But this approach will ultimately be unsuccessful. As noted by *Arizona Firestorm* contributors Chin et al. (chapter 5), SB 1070 only exacerbates social tensions and does not strike at the roots of immigration—only at the most vulnerable individuals. SB 1070 also injures the state. Gans decisively demonstrated (chapter 4) that Arizona in fact gains economically from its immigrant workers, a thesis that has been repeatedly stated by any number of staunchly conservative Arizona economic and business groups. Yet despite well-developed economic arguments that show immigrants contribute rather than harm from the economy, if this volume has demonstrated anything, readers should now understand that xenophobic political interests in Arizona in 2010 supplanted the state's financial and social interests. Only in spring 2011, after the state had lost over $200 million as a result of a national boycott, and only after Governor Janice Brewer's position in office had been secured, did lawmakers vote down a dangerous omnibus bill that would have resulted in even greater exclusion of the state's Latinos and immigrants.[8]

So what are we to make of this? As many Latino and other opponents of these wall-raising efforts have stated, Arizona's chauvinistic legislative leaders have sought to maintain the slipping Anglo hegemony on the backs of immigrants. To press their case for greater border defensiveness, they characterize their foe as the "illegal" immigrant. This criminalizing discourse, as Chin et al., Gonzales (chapter 9), and Leeman (chapter 8) describe, oversimplifies the multidimensional realities of global immigration.[9] Further, such rhetoric does nothing to allay the desperation; it only frightens a demoralized older white electorate.

This is not statesmanship; it is demagoguery. It is also shortsighted. Leeman, Gándara (chapter 7), and Ochoa O'Leary et al. (chapter 6) demonstrate that Arizona's top educators have limited, not expanded, the educational options of its immigrant and Latino youth. These actions divest the state's future work force of its full productive capacity. In a short generation, then, relatively undereducated Mexican Arizonans will vie for work in an increasingly competitive global marketplace. This does not bode well for Arizona. But as González de Bustamante noted (chapters 2 and 3), Arizona's history is studded with measures that favored Anglos at the expense of other Arizonans and the state as a whole. Still to date, neither the state nor the nation has moved beyond law enforcement strategies to address the situation.

Where were the news media during the firestorm? Perhaps it was not by intent, but they were fanning the flames. *Arizona Firestorm* authors Chavez and Hoewe (chapter 10) and Vigón et al. (chapter 11) demonstrate that while the news media offer abundant reporting on the conflicts, they offered little edifying coverage on the fundamentals of immigration. As Guerrero and Campo note (chapter 12), Mexico's news media are no better.[10] As a result of shortsighted reporting, news consumers, these nations' electorates, are left uninformed and vulnerable to Russell Pearce-like obsessiveness and Tom Horne-like cynical exploitations. In this light, it may not be surprising that in 2011, Georgia and Alabama have followed Arizona's lead with even more stringent immigration laws that are also likely to have adverse statewide economic impacts,[11] and which have especially restrictive educational provisions on children who will become the next generation of Georgians and Alabamans. Insofar as the media do not promote reason and reflection across the country, they sow anxiety and harvest fear. Consider the current 2012 presidential election cycle: How often have the candidates referred to global processes or international collaboration? Journalists should reconsider their very active role in the spread of fear over immigrants, and the polarized tenor of political discourse in our country.

The news media is a powerful vehicle for public discourse that divides or unifies the country. In the case of Arizona 2010, the media contributed to discord. Similarly scholars speak of the responses to globalization as demarcation and integration,[12] and to this we turn.

What would better local and regional responses to immigration look like? A great deal of skepticism exists over transnational accords about immigration. Indeed, former U.S. Attorney General Alberto Gonzales advised against agreements that restricted "the United States' sovereign ability to decide who is and is not permitted within its territory." So what are the concerns?[13] One argument is that transnational pacts reduce the sovereignty of the nation-state when laws are established by world federations. Other nagging doubts are fears that immigration accords will force the United States to hand over a portion of its wealth to its poorer neighbor, or that such accords are always failures.[14] The first is ludicrous, and the second makes no sense when multinational trade pacts are negotiated regularly across the globe.

However, Attorney General Gonzales did not slam the door on transnational cooperation on immigration policy. He wrote: "It would be wise for the United States to enter into international agreements that benefit its interests," specifically working with Mexico to reduce its push out factors by helping better Mexican economic conditions. Guerrero and Campo also noted that the Mexican national newspapers frequently expressed interest in a binational immigration pact. Still, such an accord on Mexican undocumented immigration has not been a viable political initiative since the Twin Towers fell.[15] But a decade has passed, Bin Laden is dead, and bilateral conversations are overdue.[16] In 2012, Mexico is also in the midst of an election year; perhaps this might be a prime opportunity for the two nations to begin to talk transnationally and not unilaterally as the United States is prone to do.

Historically speaking, the United States and Mexico have entered agreements to deal with labor and trade, most notably through the 1942 Mexican Farm Labor Supply Program, informally known as the Bracero Program, and the NAFTA, the 1994 accord that set up a trilateral trade bloc of Canada, Mexico, and the United States. Although neither accord dealt directly with immigration, proponents of such measures argued that they would reduce undocumented migration. They did not. The reality was both accords served as "pull factors" resulting in an increase in nonauthorized immigration to the United States. The Bracero Program, which ran off and on until 1964, was fraught with problems. U.S. employers, who were responsible for paying laborers a fair wage and providing adequate housing arrangements often abused workers and forced workers to live in substandard housing.[17] Mexican officials also failed to honor their commitments to its citizens.[18]

In 1994 NAFTA lifted trade barriers for U.S. investment in Mexico and allowed goods to move more freely between these countries. But as the accord was developed, Mexico and the United States chose to avoid the immigration issue "out of fear that it would derail the whole project."[19] Economic issues overshadowed the labor side of free trade, at a time when border security tightened and anti-immigrant sentiments increased. Ironically, as the two countries became more economically interdependent, the United States worked to keep cheap labor out. These two accords exemplify what Kitty Calavita calls a "paired opposition," the idea that, for example, the politics of the economy do not fall in line with the demands of the economy.[20]

So, what will happen if there are talks? As in all transnational political moves, several factors are involved.[21] First, the processes driving immigration are global, but its effects will always be felt at the local level. And any effort to change the rules of the game, so to speak lowering or raising parts of the border fence, will politicize these issues. Moreover, the political reaction and mobilization (activism and lobbying) to bilateral negotiations on immigration will be viewed at the national and local level in terms of winners and losers. Thus the economic and cultural sectors with the most at stake will be most energized. While not a perfect comparison, NAFTA taught us some key lessons about international accords. The first is that the likely winners will be transnational business, entrepreneurs, and more skilled work forces; the losers would likely be traditionally protected sectors, less skilled workers, and those most favoring the cultural status quo, since resistance is, at best, a rearguard action.

NAFTA's unintended consequences are also lessons for future immigration policy negotiations.[22] It increased immigration to the United States when Mexico opened its markets to corn sold by U.S. government-subsidized agribusiness. Mexican subsistence farmers could not compete, lost the ability to provide for their families, and millions were forced to migrate. These painful lessons, however, should not keep Americans from negotiating with Mexicans. We cannot address most of our nation's major problems, such as terrorism, immigration, and climate change, without our international friends and neighbors. Nor can we address these issues and others, such as our declining world competitiveness, from a false position that the American hegemony remains intact and permanent.

In short, transnational agreements should pivot on the human dimension of trade equation, rather than on the economic dimension. The abuses of past guest worker programs must be addressed with strong safeguards that compel both governments and moneyed interests to treat workers on both sides of the border as people—rather than labor pools. Such a bilateral migration agreement should contain "mechanisms that provide serious incentives for enforcement of workers' rights," such as "automatic monetary sanctions for breaches of rules in international agreements," which will "significantly strengthen the rights and obligations created by the agreement."[23] NAFTA should be renegotiated, which was what President Vicente Fox intended prior to the 9/11 attacks. Since the U.S. economy will continue to require low-cost labor, then adjustments must be made so that workers are able to move more freely, safely, and out of the shadows. Then local receiving communities in the United States will be somewhat sheltered from unplanned migration of workers.

What can we do in the meanwhile? As the editors of a volume on the shortcomings of state-level policy responses to and media coverage of immigration frictions, we should offer some recommendations to ameliorate these social tensions, since immigration cannot be eliminated, only indirectly managed by legislation, and the news media are doing a poor job explaining the new fundamentals of our smaller planet. We begin with the local receiving communities.

These communities are most affected by immigration, yet little consideration has been given to constructive actions that they can undertake. However, Michael Jones-Correa recently published a report for the Center for American Progress in which he compares two American towns, and their different responses to uninvited newcomers.[24]

One homogeneous small town in Nebraska faced for the first time unauthorized immigrants who were drawn to a meatpacking factory. Public concern led to a referendum that directed the town to severely penalize landlords who rent to the immigrants and to require all employers to use E-verify to confirm the status of potential employees. The new statute cost $1,000,000 a year to implement, forcing the town of 26,000 to raise taxes to pay for it. But the newcomers did not leave, so the two communities now live side by side but not together. Meanwhile tensions have increased across the town. Four council members, the mayor, and the city administrator resigned within a year that the statute was enacted.[25]

Another predominantly white American town of 50,000 in Maine that also had never dealt with immigrants initially reacted to African newcomers with hostility. But town leaders chose to work to integrate the people of this strikingly different culture with ESL classes and job training. The natives sought help to assure that the newcomers' children would not fall behind and so all the children would learn more quickly to get along. Classes for long-time residents were also held to ally fears and to dispel myths. These efforts cost money and patience, but ten years later there is one community. The newcomers are not assimilated. Differences remain, but both mutual respect and the city's tax base have grown. As the current mayor boasted: "Our immigrant entrepreneurs are bringing new life and energy to the downtown . . . a dozen immigrant-owned businesses occupy formerly vacant storefronts."[26]

There are alternatives to endlessly raising walls against economic refugees. Jones-Correa recommends that locals in the recipient community recall the Golden Rule, and actively work against fear and ignorance. His report lays out steps to proactively receive newcomers into the community, including four key strategies drawn from the experiences of people who have been "keenly engaged with immigrant integration." Above all, native community leaders who themselves are deeply embedded in local networks must make the first move. They should reach out to newcomers with optimism and passion for their communities. This is paramount, but it need not be the mayor or other city official. Clergy have stepped up at times; but one can imagine that even a young person or small group of respected individuals can take the first step, if they are personally woven into the social fabric of the receiving community, are enthusiastic about reaching out a welcoming hand, and are willing to publicly reject demagoguery and hatred. What follows are efforts to create opportunities for direct contact between newcomers and long-time residents to chase away mutual doubts and to initiate a sense of a shared future. This will lead to calls for more resources, which in turn requires steps to build partnerships between state and local governments and newcomers. A final critical objective is to reframe the issues about immigrants, to contest misconceptions, and to reject bigotry.[27] These local strategies do not require federal or state government policy changes. The report goes on to say nonetheless that the federal government will play a central role in immigrant integration for "funding adult literacy, educating children, providing information on naturalization, and easing refugees into the job market" to integrate immigrants into American society. State and local governments with their agencies or programs are frontline agents for immigrant integration, as are private foundations for material and human resources. Finally, nongovernmental organizations (NGOs) and community organizers who are the advocates for newcomers have a role. They should recognize that it is in everyone's best interest to reach out (beyond their base) to build support among long-time residents. This proactive citizen's agenda recognizes that our nation is stronger when its diverse communities work together, rather than against one another.

In this volume we have thrown many darts at the news media, but we have offered little explanation for their shortcomings, mainly because that is beyond the central theme of this book. Nevertheless some concluding thoughts on this issue are warranted. First, every journalist, whether she works for herself producing a homespun citizen's blog or is one of the nation's top-paid anchors, functions within what journalism scholars call "a hierarchy of influences."[28] There are five levels of influence that contribute to what gets published or not, and how that information is constructed: individual, news media routines, organizational, extra-media level (government and external pressures), and the ideological. Some of the pressures that work against the possibilities for quality journalism include: a 24/7 news cycle that impedes putting news into multiple contexts (particularly a global context); high levels of media ownership concentration; economic interests of media companies; entrenched ways of producing certain types of stories; and reporters' biases. This explanation does not absolve media producers, but it does provide some reasons for the persistence of superficial and subpar journalism.

The main culprit that drives these pressures is the economic imperative of big media. While big media have always been interested in turning a profit, editorial content has eroded to an unprecedented extent in the face of increasing economic pressure. For example, the parent company of ABC is now Walt Disney, a corporation whose primary goal has been to entertain, not to inform. Of course, picking on ABC alone is not fair. In general, the overarching goal of corporate media is profit oriented rather than civic oriented.

While Spanish-language media in the United States are not immune to the capitalistic logic of news media production, Vigón et al. (chapter 11) point out that when it came to immigration, in 2010 Univision and Telemundo chose to embrace their "duty" to educate as well as inform. Some critics would say the networks crossed the line by taking on an advocacy role. Nevertheless, general English-language media might do well to follow Spanish-language media's lead and better serve the public by giving them not just what they *want* (eye-catching and conflict-oriented stories), but what they *need* to be an electorate that is knowledgeable regarding global processes. Of course, this is subjective, but most would argue that the status quo is untenable, and the American public needs its media to go beyond the superficial regarding not just immigration, but all important topics. In this era of political and ethnic division, big and small media alike need to abandon old patterns of "manufacturing hysteria" and "manufacturing consent" and produce news with a higher level of social commitment.[29]

Despite the seemingly overwhelming pressures on journalists, members of the news media can and sometimes do effect positive change. In 2011, the Society of Professional Journalists (SPJ) passed a resolution calling upon newsrooms across the country to refrain from using the pejorative term *illegal alien.* Organizations such as the SPJ and the National Association of Hispanic Journalists should continue to pressure journalists to live up to their responsibilities to educate as well as inform.

Citizens can and should do their part to create more quality news programming and publications by demanding more from members of the news media and corporate media. In some cases, citizen journalists (those journalists not formally trained) through blogs and social media have compelled traditional media to adhere to standards of excellence and to seek innovative and inclusive ways of producing quality news. Readers, viewers, and listeners can do more for themselves and their neighbors by looking beyond only those media that reaffirm their own worldviews and attitudes. If we are to have an informed and engaged citizenry that works to strengthen democracy, news consumers must learn to understand diverging viewpoints, need to get their information from numerous sources, and consult a variety of media platforms, such as television news, online news organizations, magazines, and even that old stodgy product known as the newspaper.

Finally, the scholarly community of communication and journalism studies bears some responsibility to change the news media landscape. When it
comes to significant issues such as immigration, there must be greater collaboration and activity between the academic community and practitioners.
Scholars often only present their research to other scholars, and consequently
too often their work does not move beyond the proverbial "ivory tower."
However, some institutions have begun to bridge this gap. In 2010, Lucila
Vargas, a professor in the University of North Carolina School of Journalism
and Mass Communication, created "Latijam," short for Latino Journalism
and Media at Carolina. The multiplatform project connects researchers,
Spanish-language media professionals, and college as well as high school students. Latijam is one of the positive ways in which the academic community
and community-at-large have responded to one of the fastest growing Latino
populations in the country.[30] In spring 2011, at the University of Arizona,
professors Celeste González de Bustamante and Maggy Zanger brought
together faculty from nine universities and a community college along the
U.S.-Mexico border to establish a binational organization called the Border
Journalism Network (BJN)/*La red de periodismo de la frontera*. Funded in part
by the Dart Center for Journalism and Trauma and the Gannett Foundation,
the BJN seeks to improve news coverage along the border, and provide training and teaching materials for scholars, professionals, and students on both
sides of the border.[31]

The idea of the nation defines the modern era. Political, academic, and
business sectors all play a role in how the peoples of various nations conceptualize themselves. However, since Benedict Anderson first made his compelling
argument, we recognize that the news media play a decisive role in creating,
from strangers, an "imagined community" of sentiment and orientation as
well as national affiliation.[32] The interaction of people through news media
created a common emotional identity. Today's mass media saturation of everyday life would have been unimaginable a century ago, as has the media's
capacity to create common identities, or to reinforce differences.

As the editors of this volume, we have sought to expand readers' perspective beyond immigration as a national problem, so to engage a wider public
sphere and to consider the major factors—beyond the nation—that propel
worldwide demographic change. Media correspondents, scholars, and informed citizens should speak of *global migration* patterns, not simply immigration into the United States. Adjusting our citizenry's focus will allow
them to consider the full range of strategies—national and international—to
address immigration effectively and humanely. Otherwise, Alejandro Portes's
warning will continue to hang over our heads: long-term defamation of entire
groups of people can lead to civil unrest.

Notes

1. Quoted in Coates and Siavelis, 2009, p. xi.
2. See Benjamin, 2000.
3. In 1917 the United States initiated guest labor programs, and again in 1942 with the Bracero Program.
4. Brownstein and Simon, 1993.
5. Balderrama and Rodríguez, 2006; Hoffman, 1974, p. 126.
6. Benjamin, 2000.
7. Said, 1994.
8. See Fernández, 2011. The Center for American Progress estimated that the state of Arizona could end up losing up to $253 million in economic output as a result of tourism and convention boycotts.
9. See also Santa Ana, 2002; Santa Ana et al., 2007.
10. One troubling observation about Mexican news media is the common practice of journalists who refer to undocumented people as *ilegales* (illegals). In contrast, the National Association of Hispanic Journalists has campaigned to get U.S. journalists to refrain from using the term *illegal* as a noun. See http://www.nahj.org/nahjnews/articles/2006/March/immigrationcoverage.shtml. Also see Santa Ana, 2006.
11. Rivoli, 2011; Georgia's agricultural industry, 2011.
12. Kriesi et al., 2005.
13. Altinay, 2010.
14. Altinay, 2010, p. 2.
15. Ten years ago George W. Bush and Mexican President Vicente Fox were on track to sign such an accord. After September 11, 2001, the United States has focused its energies on homeland security, and bilateral negotiations on immigration policy have not resumed. However, two-nation agreements between Mexico and the United States are regularly made. Most recently we can point to an accord on transnational trucking, a stalled element of the 1994 trilateral North American Free Trade Agreement. The mixed merits of NAFTA do not preclude new talks between Mexico and the United States on immigration.
16. Likewise, the global recession has reduced demand, lowering the pull of immigration, and Douglas Massey reports that Mexico is developing greater capacity to provide work for its population, including rising educational levels and a reduction in the Mexican birth rate. See Cave, 2011.
17. Galarza, 1964.
18. The Mexican government withheld 10 percent of the wages of the 2.5 million braceros in a collective savings fund for workers, but less than 2 percent ever collected it. The lost funds would have grown in the ensuing years to $150 million. After a decade of court wrangling, the government agreed to pay approximately $3,500 to ex-braceros or their survivors in lieu of reimbursement, if they could provide appropriate documentation (Schiller, 2001; Rodriguez, 2008; Knaub, 2011).
19. Bickerton, 2001, p. 895.
20. Calavita, 1994, p. 145.
21. Kriesi et al., 2005, p. 922.

22. See Public Citizen's webpage: http://www.citizen.org/Page.aspx?pid=53.1

23. Bickerton, 2001, p. 918.

24. Jones-Correa, 2011.

25. Associated Press, 2011.

26. Jones-Correa, 2011, pp. 6–7.

27. Jones-Correa, 2011, pp. 2–3.

28. Shoemaker and Reese, 1996.

29. Felman, 2011; Herman and Chomsky, 1988.

30. To view the bilingual content on Latino Journalism and Media at Carolina, see http://latijam.jomc.unc.edu/latijam/.

31. Celeste González de Bustamante was recently elected Head of the Border Journalism Network/*La red de periodismo de la frontera*. For more information, see: www.borderjnetwork.com or through Twitter:@BorderJ_Network and Facebook: Border Journalism Network.

32. Anderson, [1983] 1991.

References

Altinay, H. (2010). The case for global civics. Global working paper #35. Washington, DC: Brookings Institution. Retrieved on 1 August 2010 from www.brookings.edu/papers/2010/03_global_civics_altinay.aspx.

Anderson, B. [1983] 1991. *Imagined communities: Reflections on the origin and spread of nationalism* (Revised and extended edition). London: Verso.

Associated Press. (2011, 17 September). Fremont, Neb., official steps down—latest in rash of resignations since immigration law. Retrieved on 22 September 2011 from http://www.therepublic.com/view/story/33bc4e19273940e085f7f6da9bcafc75/NE--Fremont-Resignation/.

Balderrama, F. E., & Rodríguez, R. (2006). *Decade of betrayal: Mexican repatriation in the 1930s.* Albuquerque: University of New Mexico Press.

Benjamin, T. (2000). *La Revolución: Mexico's great revolution as memory, myth, and history.* Austin: University of Texas Press.

Bickerton, M. A. (2001). Prospects for a bilateral immigration agreement with Mexico: Lessons from the Bracero Program. *Texas Law Review 79*, 895–919.

Brownstein, R. and Simon, R. (1993, 14 November). Hospitality Turns to Hostility. California has a Long History of Welcoming Newcomers for Their Cheap Labor—Until Times Turn Rough. *Los Angeles Times*, A-1.

Calavita, K. (1994). U.S. immigration policy: Contradictions and projections for the future. *Indiana Journal of Global Legal Studies, 2*(1), 143–152.

Cave, D. (2011, July 6). Better lives for Mexicans cut allure of going north. *The New York Times.* Retrieved on 6 July 2011 from www.nytimes.com/interactive/2011/07/06/world/americas/immigration.html?emc=eta1.

Coates, D., & Siavelis, P. (Eds.) (2009). *Getting immigration right: What every American needs to know.* Washington, DC: Potomac Books.

Felman, J. (2011). *Manufacturing hysteria: A history of scapegoating, surveillance and secrecy in modern America.* New York: Pantheon Books.

Fernández, V. (2011, January 26). How much do anti-immigration bills really cost? *New America Media.* Retrieved on 28 January 2011 from http://newamericamedia .org/2011/01/how-much-do-anti-immigration-bills-cost.php.

Galarza, E. (1964). *Merchants of labor.* Santa Barbara, CA: McNally and Loftin.

Georgia's agricultural industry lost tens of millions of dollars last harvest and many farmers say they will plant less in the upcoming season due to a labor shortage triggered by a strict immigration law, two new studies show (2011, October 7). *Latin American Herald Tribune.* Retrieved from http://www.laht.com/article.asp?ArticleId =430515&CategoryId=12395.

Herman, E. S., & Chomsky, N. (1988). *Manufacturing consent: The political economy of the mass media.* New York: Pantheon Books.

Hoffman, A. (1974). *Unwanted Mexican Americans in the Great Depression: Repatriation pressures, 1929–1939.* Tucson: University of Arizona Press.

Jones-Correa, M. (2011). *All immigration is local: Receiving communities and their role in successful immigrant integration.* Washington, DC: Center for American Progress.

Knaub, M. (2011, October 6). Consulate still seeking handful of ex-braceros. *Yuma Sun News.* Retrieved from http://www.yumasun.com/articles/consulate-73534 -jose-mexican.html#ixzz1b0GZfOif.

Kriesi, H., Grande, E., Lachat, R., Dolezal, M., Bornschier, S., & Frey, T. (2005). Globalization and the transformation of the national political space: Six European countries compared. *European Journal of Political Research 45,* 921–956.

Maynard Institute. (2011, September 28). SPJ urges end to "illegal alien," "illegal immigrant." Retrieved on 29 September 2011 from http://mije.org/richardprince/ unity-backer-has-second-thoughts#SPJ.

Rivoli, D. (2011, October 7). Alabama immigration law: Worker-strapped farm groups doubt prisoner remedy. *International Business Times.* Retrieved from http:// www.ibtimes.com/articles/227258/20111007/alabama-immigration-law-georgia -inmates.htm.

Rodriguez, J. (2008, October 18). Lawsuit settlement enables ex-braceros to file claim. Retrieved from www.recordnet.com/apps/pbcs.dll/article?AID=/20081019/A_ NEWS/810190315.

Said, E. W. (1994). *Orientalism.* New York: Vintage Books.

Santa Ana, O. (2002). *Brown tide rising: Metaphoric representations of Latinos in contemporary public discourse.* Austin: University of Texas Press.

Santa Ana, O. (2006). Journalists aren't vigilantes, so why do they talk like them? *Hispanic Link Weekly Report, 24*(20).

Santa Ana, O., with Treviño, S. L., Bailey, M., Bodossian, K., & de Necochea, A. (2007). A May to remember: Adversarial images of immigrants in U.S. newspapers during the 2006 policy debate. *Du Bois Review: Social Science Research on Race, 4*(1) 207–232.

Schiller, D. (2001, April 8). Laboring over Braceros. The program's history is studied in light of Sen. Gramm's interest in a modern guest-worker plan. *San Antonio*

News Express. Retrieved from http://nl.newsbank.com/nl-search/we/Archives?p_product=SAEC&p_theme=saec&p_action=search&p_maxdocs=200&p_topdoc=1&p_text_direct-0=0EB97298D6362557&p_field_direct-0=document_id&p_perpage=10&p_sort=YMD_date:D&s_trackval=GooglePM.

Shoemaker, P. J., & Reese, S. D. (1996). *Mediating the message: Theories of influences on mass media content.* (2nd ed.). White Plains, NY: Longman.

Index

About the Contributors

Nolan L. Cabrera is an assistant professor in the Center for the Study of Higher Education at the University of Arizona. His scholarship focuses on whiteness formation, Latina/o students, and racism in higher education. Dr. Cabrera's articles have appeared in *The Review of Higher Education, Journal of Latinos and Education, The Journal of Higher Education, Research in Higher Education, Phi Delta Kappan,* and the *Hispanic Journal of Behavioral Sciences.* He is also coauthor of the monograph, *Advancing in Higher Education: A Portrait of Latino College Students Entering Four Year Institutions, 1975–2006.*

Maria Eugenia Campo is a graduate researcher at the Universidad Iberoamericana. Her research interests include the sociology of the news and news framing in Venezuela.

Manuel Chavez is the director of graduate studies and professor at the School of Journalism at Michigan State University. He works on issues related to North American governmental cooperation, border issues, news media, international relations, border security, and impacts on the press. He studies international news coverage and models of access to information, accountability, and transparency related to the news media. He has published numerous scholarly articles and books, is the past-president of the Association for Borderlands Studies, and is currently the chair of the International Communication Division of the Association for Education of Journalism and Mass Communication. He is co-coordinator of graduate studies of the Chicano/Latino Studies Program at MSU.

Gabriel J. (Jack) Chin is professor of law at the University of California, Davis, School of Law, where he teaches and writes about criminal law and procedure, immigration, and race and law. He previously served as the Chester H. Smith Professor of Law at the University of Arizona Rogers College of Law. For much of 2010 and 2011, he has been researching, writing, and speaking about Arizona's SB 1070 and other state efforts to regulate immigration.

Patricia Gándara is professor and co-director of the Civil Rights Project at UCLA. Her research focuses on educational equity and access for low income and ethnic minority students, language policy, and the education of Mexican-origin youth. Her most recent books are *The Latino Education Crisis: The Consequences of Failed Social Policy* (with Frances Contreras), Harvard University Press, 2009; and *Forbidden Language, English Learners and Restrictive Language Policies* (edited with Megan Hopkins), Teachers College Press, 2010.

Judith Gans directs the Immigration Policy Program at the Udall Center for Studies in Public Policy, and teaches Political Economy of U.S. Immigration Policy in the economics department, both at the University of Arizona. Her expertise encompasses the role of immigrants in the nation's economy, and the macroeconomic and demographic forces driving global migration. She is editor on the upcoming *SAGE Debates on Immigration* (Sage, 2012) a reference volume that uses a point/counterpoint format to explore the prominent aspects of the U.S. immigration debates.

Alberto R. Gonzales is the Doyle Rogers Distinguished Professor of Law at Belmont University College of Law and of Counsel to the law firm of Waller Lansden Dortch & Davis in Nashville, Tennessee. He was appointed the eightieth Attorney General of the United States in 2005 by President George W. Bush, and he served in the Bush administration from 2001 to 2005 as White House counsel. While Bush was governor of Texas, Gonzales served as his general counsel, and subsequently served as Secretary of State of Texas and then on the Texas Supreme Court. Most recently, Gonzales was a visiting professor at Texas Tech University.

Celeste González de Bustamante is assistant professor in the School of Journalism at the University of Arizona and an affiliated faculty member at the Center for Latin American Studies. González de Bustamante received her Ph.D. in history at the University of Arizona. Her book (in press), *"Muy Buenas Noches": Mexico, Television and the Cold War* is being published by the University of Nebraska Press. Her research interests include the history of news media in Mexico, Brazil, and the U.S.-Mexico borderlands. She has been an academic fellow at the Dart Center for Journalism and Trauma at

Columbia University, and research fellow at the Udall Center for Studies in Public Policy, and is a founding member of the binational academic and professional organization, Border Journalism Network/*La red de periodismo de la frontera.* For fifteen years prior to entering the academy, González de Bustamante reported and produced commercial and public television news, covering politics and the U.S.-Mexico border.

Juan González is co-host of the nationally syndicated television and radio show *Democracy Now!* and a columnist for the *New York Daily News.* González is a two-time winner of the George Polk Journalism Award for commentary, former president of the National Association of Hispanic Journalists, and author of several books, including *Harvest of Empire: A History of Latinos in America* (2nd edition, 2011), and (with Joseph Torres) *News for All the People: The Epic Story of Race and the American Media* (2011).

Manuel Alejandro Guerrero is currently the dean of the Department of Communication and director of "Ibero 90.9 FM Radio" at the Universidad Iberoamericana, in Mexico City. He is also a member of the National System of Researchers, and academic coordinator of the Professional Electoral Service at the Federal Electoral Institute in Mexico. He holds a Ph.D. in political and social science from the European University Institute in Florence, Italy, and an M.Phil. in Latin American studies from the University of Cambridge.

Carissa Byrne Hessick is a professor of law at Arizona State University's Sandra Day O'Connor College of Law. Before joining the faculty at Arizona State, Professor Hessick served as a Climenko Fellow at Harvard Law School. She is a graduate of Columbia University and Yale Law School. Her previous publications on Arizona's SB 1070 have been referenced by a number of major news outlets, including the *Wall Street Journal* and *The Economist.*

Jennifer Hoewe is University Graduate Fellow within the College of Communications at Pennsylvania State University. Her research interests include media effects, specifically the news media's ability to develop and perpetuate stereotypes through the uses of framing, cueing, and priming. She completed her master's degree in journalism at Michigan State University and was named Outstanding Graduate Student.

Anna Ochoa O'Leary is assistant professor of practice in Mexican American studies and codirector of the Binational Migration Institute at the University of Arizona. For her research on repatriated and deported migrant women on the U.S.-Mexico border she was awarded the 2006 Garcia-Robles Fulbright fellowship. She has authored numerous articles on issues of immigrant women and on Latino/a education, as well as a textbook: *Chicano Studies, The Discipline and the Journey* (Kendall-Hunt, 2007). She is now editing a two-volume encyclopedia, *Undocumented Immigrants in the United States Today: An Encyclopedia of Their Experience* (ABC-CLIO, forthcoming 2013).

Jennifer Leeman is associate professor of Spanish at George Mason University and research sociolinguist at the U.S. Census Bureau. Her research interests include ideologies and discourses of language, race, ethnicity, and nation; Spanish in the United States; and critical pedagogy and heritage language education. Her recent journal publications include "Identity and Activism in Heritage Language education," in *Modern Language Journal* (with L. Rabin and E. Román-Mendoza) and "Commodified Language in Chinatown: A Contextualized Approach to Linguistic Landscape" in the *Journal of Sociolinguistics* (with G. Modan) and "The Sociopolitics of Heritage Language Education," in Rivera-Mills and Villa's anthology, *Spanish of the U.S. Southwest: A Language in Transition.*

Lilliam Martínez-Bustos is assistant professor in the School of Journalism and Mass Communication at Florida International University. Before joining FIU, she spent more than two decades as a broadcast journalist in English-language and Spanish-language television. She worked as a producer in the Washington bureaus of the NBC-Telemundo and Univision networks. She also worked at Boston affiliates of PBS, CBS, and ABC. She earned a B.A. from the University of Puerto Rico and a M.S. at the University of Southern California, where she was a fellow at the Center for International Journalism.

Marc L. Miller is Vice Dean and Ralph W. Bilby Professor, University of Arizona Rogers College of Law.

Michelle Rascón is a graduate of Tucson Unified School District's Ethnic Studies Program. She went on to receive her degree in anthropology and Mexican American studies from the University of Arizona, where she conducted research on substance abuse prevention with adolescents in South Tucson. The Coalición de Derechos Humanos honored another strand of her research, on the migrant deaths along the border, with a Corazon de Justicia award. She is pursuing a M.S. in justice studies at Arizona State University with the intent to study how immigration policy affects adolescent youth.

Andrea J. Romero is associate professor of family studies and human development and also Mexican American studies at the University of Arizona. With training in applied social psychology, she focuses on healthy development of minority adolescents, how adolescents navigate cultural, family, neighborhood, and political contexts. She has published several articles on bicultural context of stress and coping of adolescents. Recently, she co-authored an article on the political and emotional responses of Chicana/o students to SB 1108 in the journal *Aztlán*.

Otto Santa Ana, born, raised and educated in Arizona, is associate professor in Chicana and Chicano studies at UCLA. One strand of his scholarship focuses on how mass media reproduce societal inequity. The American Political Science Association recognized his first book, *Brown Tide Rising: Metaphoric Representations of Latinos in Contemporary Public Discourse* (University of Texas Press) as the 2002 Book of the Year on ethnic and racial political ideology. His book (in press), *Juan in a Hundred* (University of Texas Press, 2012) builds on this work. It is a comprehensive study of the visual semiotics of U.S. television news about Latinos.

Carola Suárez-Orozco is professor of applied psychology and codirector of Immigration Studies at NYU. She publishes widely on an array of topics related to immigrant children, youth, and their families, including educational achievement, immigrant family separations, the role of familial unauthorized status on developmental outcomes, the "social mirror" in identity formation, the function of mentors in facilitating youth development, and gendered experiences of immigrant youth. Her books include: *Learning a New Land: Immigrant Children in American Society; Children of Immigration; Transformations: Migration, Family Life, and Achievement Motivation among Latino Adolescents;* and *The New Immigration: An Interdisciplinary Reader.* She currently serves as the chair of the American Psychological Association Task Force on Immigration.

Marcelo Suárez-Orozco is Courtney Sale Ross University Professor of Globalization and Education at NYU. He works on conceptual and empirical problems in the areas of cultural psychology and psychological anthropology with a focus on the study of mass migration, globalization, and education. He is the author of 150 scholarly papers, award-winning books, and edited volumes published by some of the leading scholarly outlets in the world, and such journals as *Harvard Educational Review, Harvard Business Review, Harvard International Review, Harvard Policy Review, Ethos, International Migration, Anthropology and Education Quarterly, Revue Française de Pédagogie,* and *The Journal of the American Academy of Arts and Sciences.*

Mercedes Vigón, associate professor and associate director of the International Media Center in the School of Journalism and Mass Communication at

Florida International University, is a native of Spain. She trained journalists in Mexico, Nicaragua, and Paraguay and also worked as a television news director for Net Financial News. She was an executive producer and international writer for CBS Telenoticias, and a journalist with UPI. She is fluent in Spanish, French, and English.